Global Poverty

Global Poverty

A Theological Guide

Justin Thacker

scm press

Published in 2017 by SCM Press
Editorial office
3rd Floor, Invicta House,
108–114 Golden Lane,
London EC1Y 0TG, UK

H
Y
M
N
S
Ancient
&Modern

SCM Press is an imprint of Hymns Ancient & Modern Ltd (a registered charity)
13A Hellesdon Park Road, Norwich,
Norfolk NR6 5DR, UK
www.scmpress.co.uk

British Library Cataloguing in Publication data

A catalogue record for this book is available
from the British Library

978 0 334 05515 0

Typeset by Manila Typesetting Company
Printed and bound by CPI Group (UK) Ltd

Contents

Acknowledgements

This book is dedicated to the staff and students of Cliff College, Derbyshire, UK. Portions of the text, especially Part 4, were initially delivered as lectures on my public theology undergraduate course and global justice masters course. I want to thank the students for their input and engagement and for providing me with an opportunity to test out the material prior to publication. I should also thank those students who wrote dissertations in related areas for stimulating my own thinking and pointing me in the direction of blogs and other sources of which I was unaware. Particular thanks go to Tim Taylor and Esther Lindop in this regard. I am also especially grateful to Jack Key for producing the subject index for the book.

Thanks also to Marijke Hoek, Carol Kingston-Smith, Ben Pugh, Ruth Valerio and in particular Jonathan Warner for providing helpful comments on earlier drafts of this work. This published work represents my views, not theirs, and any remaining inaccuracies are my responsibility alone.

I want to thank my family – my wife Cathi and children, Grace, Joel and Alicia – for their undying support during many months of work. I could not have done this without your love.

Finally, in this book I engage with, and to some extent critique, the theologies of some Christian development agencies. Nothing in this book should be taken to suggest that those agencies are not worthy of financial support for the work that they do. My critical comments, such as they are, are levelled at some of their theological musings, not at their practical work itself. In light of this, all royalties from this book will be donated and divided equally between the work of Christian Aid, International Justice Mission and Tearfund – three organizations who undertake exemplary work on behalf of the global poor.

Introduction

They say that you should not judge a book by its cover, but I wonder what you saw in the cover of this book. Perhaps you didn't look closely and initially thought it was just a pair of hands playing with paint; perhaps you saw a posture of prayer as if the hands were reaching out to God, asking for help for our stricken world; perhaps you imagined the hands belonged to God and this was a picture in which he held the world in his palms; or maybe you saw someone begging, pleading with those of us who are wealthy to help in their distress. My intention behind the cover was none of these. Instead, the reason I chose this image is because it spoke to me of the way in which each one of us holds the world, and in particular the world's poor, in *our* hands.

It is a truism that the world we live in is far more connected globally than has ever been the case. Financial transactions in London can reverberate around the world in less than a millisecond, and our consumer and environmental decisions can have literally global impact. I wonder if I asked you to examine every piece of clothing you were wearing right now if you knew its country of origin. You might want to put this book and your cup of coffee down in order to do just this. Look at the labels and see whose labour you are wearing. I have just done the same and found myself wearing clothes from Bangladesh, China, Guatemala and India. As I look at these clothes and the stitched seams, I wonder about the fingers and hands that laboured so that I could be dressed. What were the conditions in which they worked? When was the last time they got a rest, or were fed, or drank water? Were they paid a decent salary for the clothes I now wear on my back? If I asked you about the smartphone in your pocket, would you be aware that the cobalt in its battery might have come from child labour in the Democratic Republic of the Congo?[1] And is the coffee you are drinking fairly traded? Is the light by which you read this book powered from a renewable source? All of this is not to induce guilt, but rather to emphasize the global impact of the decisions that we take.

Indeed, the Amnesty International report that highlights the issue of cobalt mining illustrates the complexity of the challenges we face. Cobalt is used in all kinds of rechargeable batteries, including those used in electric vehicles. For environmental reasons, I drive such a hybrid car myself, but it never occurred to me that the cobalt used in its battery might have come from child labour in the DRC. On the one hand, then, I want to contribute to the reduction of global emissions and therefore the deaths of millions of children in Africa by driving my hybrid (see Chapter 5), but at the same time my well-meaning intentions might well have contributed to the death or at least hardship of other African children. The situation seems so unbelievably complex that too often we give up trying.

And that is the problem?

In his book, *Economics of Good and Evil*, Tomas Sedlacek provides an analogy of a group of people who find themselves in a completely dark room, unsure how to get out. Into this problematic comes a strong, loud voice: 'I know where the door is. Hurry after me, follow my voice.'[2] Of course, in that situation, most people will follow the voice, but what if the voice is evil or simply mistaken and in fact leads the people into a wall or even worse into a hole? Instead, the safer but more time-consuming option is for the people to get down on their hands and knees and slowly but steadily make their way round the room until they find the way out. I tell this story because sometimes our approach to global poverty is like the people in that room: we want the quick, easy fix, especially if it's coming from someone shouting loudly enough:

'Just tell me which charity to support, and how much to give.'

'All of their problems are caused by corruption – we should stop giving them money till they sort their own houses out.'

'It's all the fault of the WTO, bring on the revolution!'

'Capitalism is the only solution that's been shown to work. They need investment, not aid.'

But often – for the right solution to emerge – what is required is for us to take the slow, painful path. And this is the approach I am taking in this book. Global poverty is complex. It has multiple causes in the present, compounded by multiple antecedents in the past, and if we include the inevitable impact of climate change then multiple sequelae in the future. As well as its multiple causes, how poverty affects individuals varies tremendously from context to context. All of this means that if we are trying to find our way to a solution to poverty, there is no easy path to follow. The voices who shout the loudest – whether they be neoliberal capitalists or development charities – may not necessarily be those that will lead us to the most appropriate exit. We need to do the slow, patient and complex work of thinking about poverty in the round. And that is why I have adopted the approach I have to this book.

In essence, the book is a systematic theology of global poverty. At first sight, that might seem somewhat unusual, but let me explain why I have taken this approach. As John Webster indicates, the form of systematic theology is that it is both comprehensive and coherent.[3] Such comprehensiveness does not lie in an attempt to be exhaustive – either in historical, biblical or theological terms. Such a task would be impossible. Rather, the comprehensiveness of systematic theology resides in its attempt to address a particular topic in the round or as a whole picture. The rationale for such an approach is that God is one and in his revelation of himself reveals himself in his simplicity as both coherent and unified. This is not to deny for a moment that there exist tensions, if not outright contradictions, in the biblical canon, but rather to point to the unified nature of God who has revealed himself in the canon of Scripture. Therefore, in examining global poverty from the perspective of Creation, Fall, Israel, Redemption and Consummation, I am not remotely suggesting that I have provided an exhaustive theological account of poverty, nor am I suggesting that my account of poverty is comprehensive in the sense that all other contributions are mere details within a schema that I have provided. And neither is this work an attempt at a biblical survey of the topic.[4] Rather, I have adopted this approach because it provides us with what could be called a symphonic account of theology. I have outlined multiple perspectives on the theology of global poverty, perspectives viewed through the lenses of Creation, Fall, Israel, Redemption and Consummation. I have chosen these particular perspectives because they are in line with traditional divisions of theological material and because through their particular foci they together provide a certain completeness, though not exhaustiveness, in their perspectives. They are, if you like, a political map of the world where not every town or district is listed, but at least every country is outlined. Of course, such a map is not a full schema of the world, for it is merely a political map, rather than a geological one or a health one or a population one. Nevertheless, as a political map, it is comprehensive if not exhaustive. Inevitably, therefore, in order to provide such an outline I cannot go into the detail that my topic might otherwise justify. There are also some major theological topics that I have either addressed somewhat briefly (atonement) or not at all (incarnation).[5] This is not to suggest that such topics are not relevant to global poverty, but simply that space does not allow for what would be an exhaustive survey if every relevant aspect of theology was discussed adequately. While in this book I do provide an overall argument, my main purpose is to chart the territory under discussion. As such, this book is more of a survey than a monograph. Nevertheless, sometimes standing back and surveying the whole terrain is precisely what enables us to get a clearer picture, and it is in that regard that I do advance a particular argument within the book. That is what I am attempting in this theological guide. I trust it will provide one particular rounded picture of how this topic might be understood.

At the same time, a systematic approach has the explicit virtue of internal coherence. I do not share Lyotard's belief that incoherence is the price worth paying to say something interesting. Rather, if we believe that the one God has revealed himself to us then we can expect that systematic reflection on that revelation will be amenable to some degree of internal congruity. A systematic approach to theological reflection emphasizes this aspect and so seeks to draw out the ways in which a particular doctrine of redemption intersects with one's account of sin, the fall and Israel, or how a particular eschatological perspective links to creation and redemption. Of course, the great danger in such a process is that one forces different perspectives into an artificial alignment that does damage to the contextual truth that one is trying to articulate. This of course is the justifiable and particular concern of constructive theology. Nevertheless, as I have already said, my approach in this book is not so much to provide an exhaustive account of the theology of poverty but rather one particular systematic theology. It would be perfectly possible for other systematic theologies of poverty to be written, including ones that I would largely (possibly completely) agree with. Indeed, an earlier subtitle for this book was 'A systematic theology of global poverty'. The indefinite article there is very important for it speaks to the fact that this book is not the only possible way to think systematically and theologically about poverty; it is just one. The point I am making, however, is that I have deliberately schematized the theology in the way that I have because I want deliberately to draw out the connections between different core components of theology as they speak to the question of poverty.

Finally, this is a work of systematic theology in that it seeks not only to be comprehensive (without being exhaustive), internally coherent (without being forced) but also externally coherent. Throughout the book I have deliberately interacted in some depth with the secular development and economic literature in order to ensure that this is a work of public and apologetic relevance. As Moltmann has said:

> Its subject alone makes Christian theology a *theologia publica*, a public theology. It gets involved in the public affairs of society. It thinks about what is of general concern in the light of hope in Christ for the kingdom of God. It becomes political in the name of the poor and the marginalized in a given society. Remembrance of the crucified Christ makes it critical towards political religions and idolatries. It thinks critically about the religious and moral values of the societies in which it exists, and presents its reflections as a reasoned position.[6]

In terms of the public apologetic content of the book, I have two primary aims. The first is to argue *on theological grounds* that the international economic order, and in particular global expressions of capitalism, are neither all good, nor all bad. Ultimately, some version of capitalism is the solution to global poverty. However, this doesn't mean that the *current* global approach to capitalism could not be made more just. Significant adjustments are required to global capitalism to make it more pro-poor and pro-just, but these refinements do not constitute a call to overthrow the current structures but rather a plea for a reformed capitalism.

Second, I also want to suggest *on theological grounds* that aid is not the long-term solution that the poor require and that in reality too much aid fosters a range of anti-poor sequelae. Nevertheless, until we have a more equitable global society some forms of aid are both necessary and of value, and therefore it should not be withdrawn entirely but rather viewed as an essential but temporary measure.

Of course, a number of secular authors have also argued along these lines. However, the Christian and theological literature has tended not to do so.[7] The vast majority of the theological literature exploring poverty either concludes that an unjust political order is the problem and aid or revolution is the solution, or concludes that poverty is due to laziness and corruption and unfettered capitalism is the solution. I reject all of these responses as inadequate and too simplistic.

In this way, this book either has something that will annoy everyone or, read another way, something that will please everyone. To the political left, at least the left that believes revolution is the answer, I suggest that they have failed to take seriously the problem of sin, that simply reversing the despots does nothing to ultimately solve the challenge of poverty. To the moderates, especially the moderate liberals who believe in the power of aid, I challenge this as too

4

utopian, and question whether they have an adequate doctrine of redemption. And to those on the right who consider unfettered growth capitalism to be the answer, I suggest that they are blind to the structural sin that surrounds us and that they are denying both the nature of God and the creation mandate which he has given to us.

The structure of the book is then as follows. After this introduction, in Part 1: Creation, I discuss the inherent dignity that is bestowed upon us by being created in the image of God, and following Moltmann argue for a greater corporate sense of that image. In the process, I discuss the nature of poverty as relational and multidimensional, as well as the de-dignifying effect of certain forms of aid.

In Part 2: Fall, I draw attention to the nature of sin as 'culpable shalom breaking', and then show how almost all of us fail to recognize the depth and breadth of sin in our lives. This is particularly the case as we consider our complicity in the problem of structural injustice and in the thorny question of international debt. I make the argument that, in reality, it is we in the West who owe the poorer parts of the world, and as such not only should much international debt be wiped out, but we should seriously consider how we can make reparations for the injustices we have committed and continue to pursue.

Part 3: Israel begins by outlining the purpose of God in establishing the nation of Israel, namely that it would be *a holistic blessing to all nations*. It then goes on a journey through the Exodus, the Jubilee principles, the law and the prophets, in each case demonstrating how God was either reiterating his purpose for the nation or calling them to account for their failure to live by that purpose.

Part 4: Redemption explores individual versus corporate accounts of salvation and ends up outlining a Christus victor model of atonement. This is then discussed in light of a range of both secular and Christian theories of development. Along the way, most of the secular theories are criticized either for being too individualistic or too blind to the problem of sin. The Christian theories – liberation theology, Pentecostal theology and Catholic social teaching – often suffer from the same challenges, partly due to their weddedness to the secular paradigms, and the section concludes by contrasting two particular theologies of development as articulated by two major Christian development charities: Christian Aid and Tearfund.

The final Part 5: Consummation section begins by discussing the nature of the hope which awaits us, and then investigates the problem of aid utopianism. In particular, Jesus' statement that 'the poor will always be with you' is shown not to be a counsel of despair but rather a call to action. The section concludes by demonstrating the contemporary ethical relevance of a number of Jesus' eschatological parables.

In conclusion, I draw attention to the problem of inequality and ask in light of all the material we have surveyed, 'What then is our goal?' Is it economic growth, equality of outcome or opportunity, or something else? My answer draws on a range of material, but ends up returning to the corporate understanding of the *imago Dei* that was discussed in Part 1 and challenges us to appreciate that those of us in the West who think we have 'arrived' are in need of liberation just as much as those who are poor. The epilogue draws on a Tearfund report to set out a series of practical recommendations that might guide our actions in the present.

My own experience of global poverty involved four months as a medical student, and a year as a paediatric doctor, in Papua New Guinea and Kenya respectively. I also worked for just over two years in international development running healthcare projects globally, but especially in East and West Africa. While my field experience has definitely informed the theology that you will find in this book, I think I have probably been more influenced by the global theologians I encountered during my years on the World Evangelical Alliance Theological Commission and the Lausanne Theology Working Group. These theologians, many of whom were from low-income countries, as well as others I have since met or read, have persuaded me that the dominant paradigms of aid or capitalism need to be challenged. On a daily basis, they see not just the poverty I write about but also how many of the attempts of the West to address that poverty, despite stemming from right motives, end up doing damage to communities and create more problems than they solve. As far as possible, I have tried to reflect their voices in this work, which is why you will find numerous references to theologians from low-income countries. I believe they are a group that are still not being heard sufficiently.

I conclude this Introduction with a quotation from Lesslie Newbigin, who also spent much of his life working among the global poor. The approach he outlines here is essentially that which I am proposing in this book, and indeed 'Patient Revolutionaries' was the original title for this book. It certainly sums up the approach that I believe we need to take:

> We are not conservatives who regard the structures as part of the unalterable order of creation, as part of the world of what we call 'hard facts' beyond the range of the gospel, and who therefore suppose that the gospel is only relevant to the issues of person and private life. Nor are we anarchists who seek to destroy the structures. We are rather patient revolutionaries who know that the whole creation, with all its given structures, is groaning in the travail of a new birth, and that we share this groaning and travail, thus struggling and wrestling, but do so in hope because we have already received, in the Spirit, the firstfruit of the new world (Rom. 8.19–25).[8]

Notes

1 'This is what we die for': Human Rights Abuses in the Democratic Republic of the Congo Power the Global Trade in Cobalt, 2016, Amnesty International, available at: www.amnesty.org/en/documents/afr62/3183/2016/en/ (accessed 10 August 2016).

2 T. Sedlacek, 2011, Economics of Good and Evil, Oxford: Oxford University Press, p. 322.

3 J. Webster, 2007, 'Introduction: Systematic Theology', in K. Tanner, J. Webster and I. Torrance (eds), *The Oxford Handbook of Systematic Theology*, Oxford: Oxford University Press.

4 For examples of these, see C. Wright, 2006, *The Mission of God: Unlocking the Bible's Grand Narrative*, Nottingham: InterVarsity Press; D. Hughes, 2008, *Power and Poverty: Divine and Human Rule in a World of Need*, Downers Grove, IL: InterVarsity Press; J. Donahue, 2004, *Seek Justice that You May Live*, Mahwah, NJ: Paulist Press; A. Barrera, 2013, *Biblical Economic Ethics*, Lanham, MD: Lexington Books.

5 The interested reader should see Samuel Wells' recent book for an exploration of incarnation in relation to poverty. S. Wells, 2015, *A Nazareth Manifesto*, Chichester: John Wiley & Sons.

6 J. Moltmann, 1999, *God for a Secular Society: The Public Relevance of Theology*, London: SCM Press, p. 1.

7 Exceptions to this would include C. Elliot, 1987, *Comfortable Compassion*, London: Hodder & Stoughton; P. Vallely, 1990, *Bad Samaritans*, London: Hodder & Stoughton; and to some extent C. Moe-Lobeda, 2013, *Resisting Structural Evil*, Minneapolis, MN: Fortress Press.

8 L. Newbigin, *The Gospel in a Pluralist Society*, London: SPCK, p. 209.

PART I

Creation

I

The image of God and the dignity of humanity

Being created in the image and likeness of God means that the human person cannot become a slave to any economic or political system; the human person cannot become a means to an end; and the human person is not expendable and should not become objectified or a mere thing to be abused, neglected, exploited or exposed to any structure of sin which threatens or diminishes the dignity of the person.[1]

In his recent work on creation, David Fergusson makes the point that the Bible talks about God as creator in numerous passages outside of Genesis 1–3. As such, 'Creation is about the nature of God, our own identity as creatures of the earth, and the future of the world as it is re-created.'[2] It is not just about how the universe began. This is important because we often treat the doctrine of creation as merely the prelude to the main story of sin and redemption. It is as if creation is nothing more than the backdrop, the scenic architecture in which the narrative of salvation can take place. This is a mistake. And it is a particular mistake when we come to consider the place of humanity in God's purposes. For one of the most significant aspects of the doctrine of creation is the inherent dignity that is conferred upon humanity through God's creative acts.

Whenever I am talking to those who dismiss as mere fiction the Genesis accounts of creation, I often draw attention to the alternative ancient Near Eastern (ANE) myths about the origins of humanity. For while the Genesis account may or may not have got its chronology scientifically precise, it does at least present a vision of humanity as that which is to be celebrated. In contrast, many of the other ancient Near Eastern cosmogonies characterize humanity as merely the detritus of the gods. Beginning then with the Enuma Elish, a Babylonian cosmogony, the purpose of the narrative is not to describe creation as such but rather to glorify the god Marduk. Indeed, creation itself is seen as the bloody remnant of a titanic battle between Marduk and Tiamat.[3] In this context, humanity is portrayed as being in slavery to the gods:

Let me put blood together, and make bones too.
Let me set up primeval man: Man shall be his name.
Let me create a primeval man.
The work of the gods shall be imposed (on him), and so they shall be at leisure.[4]

A similar point is made in the Epic of Atrahasis, an Akkadian epic from the same era, where humanity is given to 'bear the yoke' and 'assume the drudgery of the god'. Gordon Wenham describes how in these cosmogonies humanity is merely an 'afterthought' of the gods' creative action, where the main activity is in demonstrating their power and dominion.[5]

In this context – and the Genesis accounts were almost certainly written in this context – the picture of humanity presented in the opening chapters of the Bible is remarkably different. In the first place, humanity is presented not as an afterthought or by-product of creation but as its purpose. The whole structure of Genesis 1 is designed not so much as a literal chronology but rather as a theological polemic in which, at least according to one author, humanity is presented as the 'pinnacle of creation'.[6]

This does not mean that the sole purpose of non-human creation is to serve humanity. As the wisdom literature makes abundantly clear, all of creation exists to bring glory to God (Ps. 19.1; 50.6; 97.6). Nevertheless, part of the way in which non-human creation brings glory to God is precisely by means of enabling humanity to flourish – as it in turn flourishes alongside humanity.[7] It is precisely this point that some evangelical climate change sceptics seem to miss. To consider non-human creation as existing only for our benefit is on a par with reducing sex to the benefit of just one partner. Instead, it is in the mutual flourishing of both human and non-human creation that God is glorified as our God-given purposes are realized. So God's purpose in the created order is for both humanity and the rest of the created world to flourish, not one at the expense of the other, but both in tune with their specific divinely mandated telos.

At the same time, however, it is important to acknowledge that, theologically speaking, we are not the same as the rest of creation. This is not to deny evolution, with which I am happy to concur, nor is it to provide a justification for exploitative domination of non-human creation. However, it is to argue that cognitively, socially, morally, emotionally and most importantly spiritually we are distinct. Notwithstanding the fact that animals do have rights of some form which we need to uphold and protect, very few people really think that the lion which kills the gazelle is guilty of murder. And they think this not just in the legal sense – which is obviously the case – but also morally. It might well be that in the age to come the 'lion will lie down with the lamb', but that does not mean our present-day carnivores have committed a moral failing in failing to anticipate that full eschatological reality. This distinction between humanity and the rest of creation is signalled not just by our place in the creation narrative as its culmination on day six, but also because it is only to humans that the divine image is conveyed. 'So God created humankind in his image, in the image of God he created them; male and female he created them' (Gen. 1.27).[8]

This is a task that is given only to humanity. While the non-human created order certainly gives praise to God, it does not image God in its role and purpose. The greatest lie of evolutionism (note that I am not referring to evolution) is the belief that we are, in the words of the Bloodhound Gang, 'nothin' but mammals'. Nelson puts it well:

Humans have much in common with the rest of creation, but they cannot succumb to being *only* an animal. It is natural, for example, for male white-tail deer to try to inseminate as many females as they are able. It is natural for male bighorn sheep to beat their male rivals to the point of death . . . Yet Christianity would rightly call such behaviours 'sins' when done by humans. While there is and ought to be continuity between the human being and the rest of creation, the overlap of behaviour between humans and nonhuman creatures cannot be total.[9]

It is for this reason that we should not treat one another as if we were merely animals. Having said that we are created in God's image, and that this confers not just dignity but also distinction upon humanity, we still need to explore further what this image of God (*imago Dei*) actually means, for its precise definition remains a topic of debate.

Jewish exegetes have tended to downplay the obvious connection with God, choosing instead to understand the *imago Dei* either as humanity created *sui generis*, or as created in the image of the angels (based on the context of Gen. 1.27). In contrast, Christian theologians have had far less difficulty in outlining a correlation between God and the nature of humanity. The question has been what kind of correlation.

While initially the patristic debates often focused on whether a distinction should be drawn between 'the image of God' as that which we bear after the fall, and the 'likeness of God', which we bore pre-fall and which will be restored at the consummation, in more recent times a consensus has emerged that no sharp distinction should be drawn between the two Hebrew phrases. Instead the focus has been on the nature of the *imago,* and here a wide range of options has been considered. In the fourth century, Augustine argued that it referred to the human capacity for rationality, in particular via our spirit. In contrast, Athanasius, writing a little earlier, thought that it referred to our ability to relate to God.

In surveying the historical literature, Middleton suggests that we can distinguish between a majority metaphysical, substantialistic interpretation and a minority relational view. The former looks for some analogy between the being of God and humanity, whether that analogy resides in rationality, immortality, freedom or personhood. As we have seen, Augustine would stand squarely in this tradition. By way of contrast, the minority tradition has argued for a much more dynamic understanding of the concept. Middleton suggests that this began with Luther,[10] but according to Anatolios we see this idea present in Athanasius in the fourth century. He writes:

> The statement that humanity was created according to the Image is simultaneously anthropological and christological: to be created according to the Image is to be granted a participation in the one who is the true and full Image of the Father.[11]

According to Middleton, however, both of these approaches have failed to take sufficiently seriously both the Hebraic and ANE context for the Genesis account. When such contextual factors are explored what becomes particularly clear is what he terms the 'royal function' of the *imago Dei*.[12]

> On this reading the imago Dei designates the royal office or calling of human beings as God's representatives and agents in the world, granted authorized power to share in God's rule or administration of the earth's resources and creatures.[13]

The background context that leads to this conclusion is not just the semantic range of *tselem,* the Hebrew word for image, but more importantly the ANE use of the phrase 'image of God'. This phrase was almost exclusively applied to kings and pharaohs in their function as representative of (a) god on earth. While of course such a reading could lend weight to an exploitative anthropology of the kind that Lynn White has chastised,[14] Middleton argues for a socio-political reading of Genesis 1 that actually represents a reversal of power relations. His point is that if we accept a sixth-century BC canonical dating for Genesis (irrespective of its pre-canonical form) then the political context for its readers was one of subjugation under Babylonian exile. Given this situation, the text serves to remind readers of their priestly and kingly duty to represent YHWH on earth. 'Thus, far from constituting an oppressive text, Genesis 1 was intended to subvert an oppressive social system and to empower despairing exiles to stand tall again with dignity as God's representatives in the world.'[15]

In a relatively rare excursion into the theology of international development, Rowan Williams, the former Archbishop of Canterbury, points out that when the poor become subjects rather than custodians of creation they are reversing the creation mandate[16] to steward the creation that has been given to us.

> To be human is to be *consciously* involved in giving meaning to the world you inhabit; and so a situation in which you have no power to exercise that creativity, where you are expected to be passive in relation to what lies around you, is a situation in which the image of God is obscured . . . To be stuck in a reactive relation to the material world, incapable of getting beyond subsistence, survival, is a tragedy in the light of what humanity could be. To recover the image of God must mean recovering an intelligent and creative way of relating to and working with the environment – not by being set free from dependence on the environment but by being able to shape it and direct it in certain ways so as both to express and to increase the creative liberty of human persons in harmony with the flourishing of all creation.[17]

It would seem then that a parallel can be drawn between the injustice, exploitation and indignity that would have been felt by Israelite exiles in Babylon and the poverty experienced by many in low-income countries (LICs) today.[18] And just as the concept of *imago Dei* restored dignity to the Babylonian exiles, so it can do the same for our brothers and sisters across the globe. Whether one is a Dalit woman, a street child in Brazil, an HIV-infected prostitute in Kinshasa, one still bears the image of God just as any king, president or priest. In his survey of the *imago Dei* terminology, J. Richard Middleton concludes:

What ties together this whole trajectory from Genesis 1 to the New Testament is the consistent biblical insight that humanity from the beginning – and now the church as the redeemed humanity – is both gifted by God with a royal status and dignity and called by God actively to represent his kingdom in the entire range of human life, that is, in the very way we rule and subdue the earth.[19]

In this way, we note the so-called 'democratizing' aspect of the *imago Dei*. One of the most remarkable features of the Genesis account is not that humans were created in the image of God. We have already noted that this was the norm for kings and pharaohs. What was remarkable, however, was the way in which the whole of humanity is presented in this way – both men and women. A number of implications would seem to follow from this reality. The first is simply that in creating men and women, God was not creating mere vassals or, even worse, as the other ANE myths indicated, slaves. If God's purpose had been to find himself a representative on earth, then the expected practice of designating kings alone as image-bearers would have sufficed. The fact that we all bear the image suggests instead that the focus of this reality is not God as such, but human beings. It is our intrinsic worth and dignity that is the focus of this teaching, not our instrumental worth as representatives of God.

In addition, as image-bearers, each and every one of us has a purpose. At first sight it may seem that I am returning to the instrumentality that I have just denied. But I am not, for my point is not so much that each of us has a role as such, as if, for instance, our image-bearing function could be completed by each one of us undertaking precisely the same set of tasks, as if we existed in some cosmic call centre. Rather my point is that as a collective, we all have a purpose, contributing both individually and corporately as God's representatives on earth. The parallel here is of course Paul's teaching on the body in 1 Corinthians 12. The body functions fully precisely because each part plays its part, and it seems to me that the same concept is operative here in the doctrine of the *imago Dei*.

This concept leads us on to perhaps the most startling conclusion that can be drawn from the *imago Dei* language: the idea that the image does not reside as such in an individual but in the whole of humanity as a corporate entity. This idea has been particularly developed by Jürgen Moltmann. For Moltmann, it is not just the individual who represents God, but rather humanity as community. His argument to this effect proceeds in this way. In Hebraic literature there was no clear separation between body and soul. Given this, our representative function as the image of God must rest in the whole of who we are as persons – it cannot rest merely in our soul, or mind, or body, and so on. Yet human beings are created not as sexless entities, but as *men* and *women*. Therefore, a full representation of the image of God requires *both* men and women, and if it requires both men and women then the full *imago Dei* necessarily requires a corporate, social and communal entity. Hence, the *imago Dei* refers to the whole human community as it exists in relation both to God and to one another. At times, he points to the family as the prime example of this:

The image of the family is a favourite one for the unity of the triunity: three Persons – one family. This analogy is not just arbitrary. What it means is that people are made in the image of God. But the divine image is not the individual; it is person with person: Adam and Eve . . . are . . . an earthly image and parable of the Trinity . . . Whatever we may think about the first human family as Trinitarian analogy, it does point to the fact that the image of God must not merely be sought in human individuality; we must look for it with equal earnestness in human sociality.[20]

At other times, it is found in a more general sense of human community. Rejecting the individualistic view of the image of God, he writes: 'But if we instead interpret the whole human being as *imago*, we then have to understand the fundamental human community as *imago* as well.'[21] And so:

This community already corresponds to God, because in this community God finds his own correspondence. It represents God on earth, and God 'appears' on earth in his male-female image. Likeness to God cannot be lived in isolation. It can be lived only in human community. This means that from the very outset human beings are social beings . . . Consequently, they can only relate to themselves if, and to the extent in which, other people relate to them. The isolated individual and the solitary subject are deficient modes of being human, because they fall short of the likeness to God.[22]

The only possible reason why God created all of us in his image is precisely because God is faithfully represented only when all of as a collective image him to the world. It is then not just that each of us has a purpose, but that each of us has a specific purpose in imaging God to the world, and as we do that together God is glorified.

The significance of all of this for the topic before us is simply: *the inherent dignity that belongs to each one of us by virtue of our creation in God's image is obscured in the context of poverty.* As I have shown, the doctrine of creation repeatedly teaches us that we have an inherent worth that is conferred upon us by the creator God. But in a context of poverty, such dignity is often perceived and experienced as absent. In the first place, it is often experienced in a range of acute material deprivations.

In 1999, the World Bank published the first in its *Voices of the Poor* reports. It was based on interviews with 60,000 people classed as materially poor, and among other aspects it collected and analysed their understanding of what it means to be poor. Unsurprisingly, poverty was often defined in terms of a lack of material goods and personal well-being. Comments such as the following were typical:

It's the cost of living, low salaries, and lack of jobs. And it's also not having medicine, food and clothes. (Brazil 1995)

When I leave for school in the mornings I don't have any breakfast. At noon there is no lunch, in the evening I get a little supper, and that is not enough.

So when I see another child eating, I watch him, and if he doesn't give me something I think I'm going to die of hunger. (Gabon 1997)

Don't ask me what poverty is because you have met it outside my house. Look at the house and count the number of holes. Look at my utensils and the clothes that I am wearing. Look at everything and write what you see. What you see is poverty. (Kenya 1997)[23]

As we have indicated, such material lack is not how things are meant to me. It is not how things are meant to be because our role, our purpose as representatives of the King, as bearers of the divine image, is to ensure our own collective flourishing in concert with the created order. Genesis 1 and 2 reminds us that before the fall the Adamic mandate was to:

'Be fruitful and multiply, and fill the earth and subdue it; and have dominion over the fish of the sea and over the birds of the air and over every living thing that moves upon the earth.' God said, 'See, I have given you every plant yielding seed that is upon the face of all the earth, and every tree with seed in its fruit; you shall have them for food.' (Gen. 1.28–29)

The Lord God took the man and put him in the garden of Eden to till it and keep it. (Gen. 2.15)

Given this, when 800 mothers die each day in pregnancy or childbirth, or when in Angola almost 2 in 10 children fail to reach their fifth birthday, they are not being fruitful and multiplying. When lack of food contributes to almost half of all childhood deaths, or even when a single person goes to bed hungry, they are not subduing the earth, they are not exercising the rule that God envisaged. Of course words such as 'subdue' and 'rule' have been used to justify all kinds of exploitative practices in relation to our planet. However, that is not what is meant here. Rather, they are intended to indicate that as we steward the rest of creation appropriately then this will lead to a state of mutual flourishing in which the planet and humanity fulfil their God-given purposes, indeed their calling. As such, any failure to flourish is not just a humanitarian tragedy, but is the thwarting of God's purposes for the whole of creation. No wonder Paul can write in Romans 8 of creation's longing for liberation both of itself and of its children. For non-human creation finds its telos not in dominion over humanity but in mutual flourishing. It was Alfred Lord Tennyson who put this in poetic form in writing of those:

Who trusted God was love indeed
And love Creation's final law
Tho' Nature, red in tooth and claw
With ravine, shriek'd against his creed.

When Tennyson wrote this in 1850, the context was the apparent conflict between science and Christianity, but what is so often missed in that debate is that the real conflict is not between those two different ways of understanding the world, but rather the conflict between the way things are meant to be and the way things are. In this sense, poverty should be conceived of primarily as a teleological antithesis, and it is in that apparent loss of a God-given status that a felt loss of dignity subsists. The person in poverty not only has the daily struggle for food, clothing, shelter and good health, but they know that this is not how things are meant to be.

Now, if this were the state of everyone, then while life would be hard, and while we would be acutely conscious of our inability to fulfil our God-given mandate, we would at least recognize that we are all in the same predicament. However, that is not the present state of affairs. For, the poor suffer a double loss of dignity. Not only is their daily struggle for survival laboured, but this is compounded by the knowledge that others on this planet do not struggle in the same way. The divine image was conveyed on each and every one of us not because God was being fair but because, as I have already indicated, God's purposes are fulfilled only as we all together as one body flourish, fill and steward creation.

This point seems to be missed by both secular philosophers (which is entirely understandable) and some evangelical theologians (which is not). John Rawls famously suggested that in order to construct a fair society we should imagine ourselves behind a veil of ignorance. The question he poses is how we would construct society if we did not know in advance what position in society we would subsequently obtain. Whatever it is we come up with is what constitutes the fair society.[24] My purpose here is not to quibble with Rawls, and a number of critiques have been offered both from other secular philosophers and from a theological perspective.[25] My point is simply that I am not advocating a more equitable society based on some notion of justice or fairness. I am, at this stage at least, proposing it for teleological reasons, that this is not how God created the world to be. For, God's purposes were that all of humanity would exist in mutual flourishing and in this way image him to the world. As such, whenever any part of humanity is not flourishing, subduing the rest of creation and so on, then this is counter to God's purposes and so wrong irrespective of any notion of 'fairness'.

Given his presuppositions and the fact that he was not writing a theological treatise, Rawls can be excused for not acknowledging this point. Wayne Grudem and Barry Asmus cannot. Both write explicitly from a Christian perspective and suggest that they are providing a biblical and theological account of poverty. On this issue of equality they first dismiss the idea by quoting Milton Friedman and then suggest that our reticence about inequality may simply be the result of envy. They do acknowledge that the biblical mandate should encourage some sense of 'equality of opportunity', but they then set up a straw man when they write:

Individuals have differing skill sets, levels of willingness to work hard, intelligence, desires, preferences and even luck (or rather from a Christian point of view, divine providence). Because of this, complete economic equality is impossible to create, and efforts to do so are destructive and cause havoc.[26]

I am not aware of anyone who argues for 'complete economic equality'. Rather, what many advocate is that while high-income countries (HICs) waste over 600,000 tonnes of food every day, 6,000 children should not die each day of hunger-related causes, that while Americans spend $21 million per day on cosmetic products, more than 1.3 billion people should not have to survive on less than $1.25 per day. This is not complete economic equality. It is simply to say that the divine mandate is that every one of us should flourish in whatever ways that might mean given our various attributes and contexts. The problem, which Grudem and Asmus fail to acknowledge, is that far too many in our present world are not flourishing in those terms, and for that to be a reality while so many of us do at least flourish economically represents a gross violation of God's intended purposes.

As I have suggested, God could have done things otherwise. He could have made us all the same. He could have selected out individual rulers to bear his image, but that is not what happened. He chose us all to be the image-bearers because each one of us has a part to play in the grand ecclesiological orchestra that is humanity. Therefore, whenever any part cannot fulfil its function, which in practice means when any part does not flourish and subdue non-human creation, then collectively we are failing.

In addition, though, to such material deprivations, it is often the case that poor people themselves define their poverty in terms of the psychological impacts of being poor. Indeed, for many poor people, it is not the material deprivation that they find most difficult, it is rather these psychological impacts. So, Michael Taylor summarizes his survey of many such voices by writing:

> It has to do with the inner feelings of poor people and their states of mind. Apart from the obvious stress and anxiety associated with the constant battle to survive, there are many references to the low self-esteem of the poor, their loss of dignity, their humiliation, their feelings of inadequacy and even their sense of shame. Some come to doubt 'the inherent value of their humanity'.[27]

In a similar way, the Voices of the Poor series drew attention to this facet when they wrote:

> Poverty has important psychological dimensions such as powerlessness, voicelessness, dependency, shame, and humiliation. The maintenance of cultural identity and social norms of solidarity helps poor people to continue to believe in their own humanity despite inhuman conditions.[28]

Numerous examples could be given of this, but here is just a selection from that report:

> Poverty is pain; it feels like a disease. It attacks a person not only materially but also morally. It eats away one's dignity and drives one into total despair. (Moldova 1971)[29]

19

Being well means not to worry about your children, to know that they have settled down; to have a house and livestock and not to wake up at night when the dog starts barking; to know that you can sell your output; to sit and chat with friends and neighbors. That's what a man wants. (Bulgaria)[30]

Poverty is lack of freedom, enslaved by crushing daily burden, by depression and fear of what the future will bring. (Georgia 1997)[31]

In their book, *When Helping Hurts*, Steve Corbett and Brian Fikkert draw attention to the contrast in understanding between how materially rich people view poverty and how the materially poor themselves talk of their own predicament:

Poor people typically talk in terms of shame, inferiority, powerlessness, humiliation, fear, hopelessness, depression, social isolation, and voicelessness. North American audiences tend to emphasize a lack of material things . . . This mismatch between many outsiders' perceptions of poverty and the perceptions of poor people themselves can have devastating consequences for poverty alleviation efforts.[32]

The reason all of this matters is because many well-intentioned efforts at poverty alleviation focus exclusively on material aspects of poverty but in the process compound the feelings of inferiority that are a corollary of material poverty. In this way, what we give with one hand we may take away with another. This represents the problem of paternalism and is the subject of our next chapter.

Notes

1 S. Ilo, 2014, *The Church and Development in Africa*, Eugene, OR: Pickwick Publications, p. 14.

2 D. Fergusson, 2014, *Creation*, Grand Rapids, MI: Eerdmans, p. 2.

3 J. R. Middleton, 1994, 'The Liberating Image? Interpreting the Imago Dei in Context', *Christian Scholar's Review* 24:1, p. 17.

4 S. Dailey, 2008, *Myths from Mesopotamia*, rev. edn, Oxford: Oxford University Press, p. 261.

5 G. Wenham, 1987, *Genesis 1–15*, Dallas, TX: Thomas Nelson, p. xlix.

6 G. Hasel, 1974, 'The Polemic Nature of the Genesis Cosmology', *Evangelical Quarterly* 46, April–June, p. 90. Fergusson suggests that God's rest on the seventh day represents the 'climax of the story' rather than the creation of humanity. Fergusson, *Creation*, p. 2. God's rest clearly represents the culmination of the narrative, but that does not necessarily translate into a value judgement of importance. Moreover, the absence of the 'rest' motif from the Genesis 2 account of creation and a concomitant focus on the creation of humanity does indeed suggest that Hasel is correct to describe humanity as the 'pinnacle' of creation.

7 The language of flourishing will be used throughout this book, but should not be confused with the eudaemonism of Aristotelian origin. While Christian versions of eudaemonism, such as Thomistic versions, do incorporate relational aspects,

I find eudaemonism to be unhelpfully individualistic with its focus on the personal well-being or happiness of the individual, and tending to treat relationships as an add-on, albeit a necessary one, to that individual. As will become clear, by human flourishing I mean something that is more thoroughly relational and corporate than traditional eudaemonism.

8 Unless otherwise stated, all Scripture quotations are taken from the New Revised Standard Version (Anglicized).

9 D. Nelson, 2011, *Sin: A Guide for the Perplexed*, London: T & T Clark, p. 117. This is not to deny the biblical warrant for the idea that in some sense animals have souls or spirits (Eccles. 3.21), it is merely making the point that they are not created in the image of God and as such we are distinct.

10 J. R. Middleton, 2005, *The Liberating Image: The Imago Dei in Genesis 1*, Grand Rapids, MI: Brazos Press, p. 20.

11 K. Anatolios, 2011, *Retrieving Nicaea: The Development and Meaning of Trinitarian Doctrine*, Grand Rapids, MI: Baker, p. 107.

12 Middleton, *Liberating Image*, p. 29.

13 Middleton, *Liberating Image*, p. 27.

14 L. White, 1967, 'The Historical Roots of Our Ecological Crisis', *Science* 155, 10 March, pp. 1203–07.

15 Middleton, 'The Liberating Image?', pp. 21–2.

16 This is frequently referred to as the 'cultural mandate'. However, I think it is theologically and biblically more appropriate to refer to it as the 'creation mandate'.

17 R. Williams, 2009, 'A Theology of Development', p. 5. Available at http://clients.squareeye.net/uploads/anglican/documents/theologyofdevelopment.pdf (accessed 8 July 2015).

18 There remains an ongoing debate as to the best term to refer to those countries in which many people live on less than $1.25 a day. Terms such as 'developing', 'less developed', 'underdeveloped', 'third world' or even 'two-thirds world' are all prejudicial. 'Poor' is too simplistic as poverty has multiple dimensions. The 'majority world' and 'Global South' have many attractions, but the former is insufficiently intuitive and the latter is geographically inaccurate – consider Australasia! Hence, for want of a better phrase I will be using the World Bank phrases of low-income countries (LICs) and high-income countries (HICs) throughout this book. Occasionally, I will also use the phrase 'the West', but this is when I specifically mean Europe and North America, and will usually be in relation to our colonial exploitation of LICs.

19 Middleton, 'The Liberating Image?', p. 24.

20 J. Moltmann, 1993, *The Trinity and the Kingdom*, Minneapolis, MN: Fortress Press, p. 199.

21 J. Moltmann, 1985, *God in Creation*, London: SCM Press, p. 241.

22 Moltmann, *God in Creation*, p. 223.

23 D. Narayan *et al.*, 1999, *Voices of the Poor Volume 1: Can Anyone Hear Us?* Washington, DC: World Bank, pp. 26, 29.

24 J. Rawls, 1999, *A Theory of Justice*, Cambridge, MA: Harvard University Press.

25 From a secular point of view, see R. Nozick, 1974, *Anarchy, State and Utopia*, New York: Basic Books, and from a theological perspective, C. Villa-Vincencio, 1992, *A Theology of Reconstruction: Nation Building and Human Rights*, Cambridge: Cambridge University Press.

26 W. Grudem and B. Asmus, 2013, *The Poverty of Nations: A Sustainable Solution*, Wheaton, IL: Crossway Books, pp. 50, 210–11. See also Bradley and Lindsley, who make the same point when they write, 'In fact, the people I know who are most obsessed with money are not the wealthy but those who have to struggle to get by. Envy of the rich is another sin the Scripture warns against.' A. Bradley and A. Lindsley (eds), 2014, *For The Least of These: A Biblical Answer to Poverty*, Grand Rapids, MI: Zondervan, p. 18.

27 M. Taylor, 2003, *Christianity, Poverty and Wealth*, London: SPCK, p. 4.

28 D. Narayan *et al.*, 2000, *Voices of the Poor Volume 2: Crying Out for Change*, Washington, DC: World Bank, p. 7.

29 Narayan, *Can Anyone*, p. 6.

30 Narayan, *Crying Out*, p. 37.

31 Narayan, *Can Anyone*, p. 31.

32 S. Corbett and B. Fikkert, 2009, *When Helping Hurts*, Chicago, IL: Moody Publishers, p. 51.

2

The problem of paternalism

In their book, Corbett and Fikkert describe five different forms of paternalism that can compound the feelings of inferiority that are experienced by the poor.[1] The first of these is 'resource paternalism' – the idea that we have what they need, and they are dependent on what we have in order to meet their needs. The core philosophical idea behind paternalism is that it is acceptable, indeed good, to limit someone else's autonomy by interfering or seeking to influence the manner in which they express that autonomy. In respect of resources, such behaviour would be evident when you give a man a fish despite the fact that he already has a fishing rod and a well-stocked river. Such a proverbial example might seem unrealistic, but the same thing happens when development projects dump excess food aid in a particular region or country and in the process collapse local markets, destroying the agricultural community. In a recent report, Oxfam gave the following examples where practices of this type have occurred:

> In 2002/2003 food aid donors over-reacted to a projected 600,000 metric tonne food deficit in Malawi, causing a severe decline in cereal prices and hurting local producers.
> In 2000, Guyanese rice exports to Jamaica were displaced by US food aid which suddenly doubled following a bumper crop in the USA.[2]

Such practices, however, can also occur at a much more personal level when well-meaning visitors or even aid workers offer material resources that are simply not required. There is sometimes an attitude in the West that Africans, for instance, are so poor we should give them whatever we do not want, but, as Stan Chu Ilo has said:

> Is it not shocking that in many cases machineries, automobiles, electronic products, cellular phones, and generic drugs which are no longer deemed safe outside of Africa are sent or sold to Africans? The poor must not continue to be the garbage dump for the rich; nor should Africans become the refuse place for dated textbooks, used clothes, disused weapons, decrepit aircraft, and other products which imperil human life and damage environmental health.[3]

The basic principle here is that you offend someone else's dignity when you provide for them something that they can provide for themselves. There are of course times, particularly in response to emergency situations, when direct aid is both necessary and welcomed, but at the same time we need to ensure that while trying to meet someone else's material needs, we are not simultaneously eroding the dignity that may be just as much required.

In addition to resource paternalism, there exists the recurrent problem of labour paternalism. This occurs when those in HICs undertake activities in LICs that could easily have been performed by those who live in those communities. This can easily lead to a situation in which local innovation is stifled. If one always believes that the solution to one's problems are located externally then one is far less likely to expend time and energy in finding those solutions. As Ilo has said:

> This is why the Lord did not stop at simply providing food for the hungry, and healing the sick. He also was concerned with empowering the poor so that they can take control of their lives. He did not preach or practice a dependent charity, but a liberating charity that freed the people on one hand, and gave them the impetus to transcend and change their condition on the other.[4]

The same point has recently been made by Bryant Myers, who argues that Britain developed not because of external intervention but because of internal liberation. The people were able to think and behave differently. He argues that too much development rhetoric and practice remains stuck in a model which assumes that outside intervention is the key to helping countries grow economically. In the process, we simply contribute to the lack of self-worth, innovation and creativity that ultimately will change these countries. By way of contrast, our development support needs to be much more long-term, far less interventionist and ensure that, whatever we do, it increases rather than decreases 'agency, dignity, and liberty'.[5]

It is important to note here that work was not a result of the fall but rather preceded it (Gen. 2.15). Chris Wright describes it as 'originally a good gift of God to those created in God's own image'.[6] There is an inherent dignity in a man or woman who by the sweat of their brow cultivates crops, catches food, builds a shelter or in some other way contributes to their own livelihood. The *Voices of the Poor* report expresses it well: 'As time passes . . . unemployment begins to undermine the young man's self-esteem. He starts to see himself . . . as having failed in his supreme duty as father and head of household – Gabon 1997.'[7]

One of the great myths of the late twentieth and early twenty-first centuries has been that work is necessarily toilsome. Clearly for some – perhaps those on an assembly line or in call centres – work is mere drudgery, but the myth that has crept in is that this is necessarily so. There are various historical antecedents for this view, but perhaps the real legacy lies at the feet of Aristotle. He had a complete disdain for those whose work is menial: 'the citizens must not lead the life of artisans or tradesmen, for such a life is ignoble and inimical to excellence.'[8] For Aristotle, excellence exists in the fulfilment of a good life, not a biological life. So the question is not whether work contributes to mere living – though of course that is a prerequisite – rather the right question is whether one's work contributes to Aristotle's conception of the virtuous life, and for him that does not include those who labour manually:

> Any task, craft, or branch of learning should be considered vulgar if it renders the body or mind of free people useless for the practices of virtue. That is why the crafts that put the body in a worse condition and work done for wages are called vulgar; for they debase the mind and deprive it of leisure.[9]

The obvious contrast here is the God that is presented in the opening chapters of Genesis, for this God gets his hands dirty: 'then the LORD God formed a man from the dust of the ground and breathed into his nostrils the breath of life; and the man became a living being' (Gen. 2.7). For Aristotle, such a conception would have been unthinkable. The 'gods' simply did not get their hands dirty in this way. The significance for us, however, is that it presents a picture of a God who works, even works with his hands in the dust of the earth, and as such God is rendering the very concept of work good. For Aristotle, only slaves and labourers – non-citizens – did that kind of work. For Christians and Jews, it is the privilege of us all. In developing an African theology of work, G. O. Anie comments that for Africans 'work is sweet'. She writes, 'The African concept of work as sweet is paradoxical in the sense that work is usually seen as something hard and excruciating, but the opposite is the case in Africa.'[10]

But in addition to work being good simply because God does it, work is also good because we were instructed to undertake it even before the fall. Again Anie comments:

> Work is dignifying in an African context. In Genesis 1.28, the scripture records that God blessed the male and female and said unto them: 'Be fruitful and increase in number; fill the earth and subdue it. Rule over the fish of the sea and birds of the air and over every living creature that moves on ground.' The act of rulership and subduing the earth implies dignity. God gave a good measure of power and authority to man and made him to oversee the universe and have all other creatures for food.[11]

As we have seen, there is an inherent dignity in the very nature of work that has nothing to do with the consequences of the fall. There are probably two reasons for this. The first is simply that when we work we are using the gifts, talents and resources that God has given us. In the film *Chariots of Fire*, Eric Liddell the Olympic athlete is portrayed as saying, 'I believe God made me for a purpose, but he also made me fast. And when I run I feel his pleasure.' In real life, there is no record of Eric Liddell ever saying this, but the sentiment reflects the point that I am making here, that whatever our gifts – whether physical, artistic, intellectual, relational, or whatever – when we use them we are fulfilling our God-given mandate to work, and experience the dignity that results.[12]

In addition, work is dignifying because it is how we image God to the world. Our task is to 'be fruitful', 'to subdue' non-human creation, to steward it for God's purposes. The fruit of our labour is witnessed in cultivated land, beautiful dwellings, flourishing communities. This is one of the reasons why the eschaton is not presented as a return to Eden, but as a city. Humans are meant to be productive and creative as they fulfil their role in imaging God.

One final aspect of work that Anie brings out in her African theology of work is the communal function of work, particularly in an African context. She writes:

> Work binds people together as communities in Africa. Africans live in small communities as a people. They believe in living a communal life with others of the same extended family, clan or tribe. They tend to find their identity and meaning in life through being part of their extended family and acquaintance. By so doing, there is a sense of unity and common participation in life and work, common history, and a common destiny. Communal work helps to cement African unity and community life.[13]

As a result of all this, she describes the inherent 'dignity of work' and, perhaps more significantly, suggests, 'Any theology of work fashioned in Africa that does not portray the dignity in labour lacks merit.'[14]

All of this means that when we deprive the poor of the opportunity of work – whether or not that work is remunerated – we are depriving them of the dignity and status that comes from such work. In particular, when we do something for someone that they could do for themselves we are not being generous or kind – albeit our motivation might be – rather we are taking away from them an opportunity to discover again their own sense of worth in the sight of God and themselves. Chastising a cultural change that has made begging the acceptable form of both individual and institutional requests for finance, the Zimbabwean politician Olivia Muchena has written:

> Well-intentioned development programs and their use of money can take some of the blame for this change in the culture. Where once the community felt responsibility to care for the needs of people in the community, now they look to relief and development organizations to care for those needs. Where once communities sought to improve their lot through their own work and resources, now they think that the only way to develop is to get money from someone else. Why do the work yourself when there are development agencies with more money than you will ever see in a lifetime looking for places to give it away?[15]

It is worth at this point commenting on what is undoubtedly a troubling trope in the New Testament – the concept of the undeserving poor. It was the Victorians who firmly established the idea of the undeserving poor, but we can hardly argue that they invented it. There are a range of both Old and New Testament passages that would appear to suggest the idea. In the first place, the Old Testament repeatedly warns us against the sin of idleness:

> Go to the ant, you lazybones; consider its ways, and be wise. Without having any chief or officer or ruler, it prepares its food in summer, and gathers its sustenance in harvest. How long will you lie there, O lazybones? When will

you rise from your sleep? A little sleep, a little slumber, a little folding of the hands to rest, and poverty will come upon you like a robber, and want, like an armed warrior. (Proverbs 6.6–11)[16]

The significance of the passage for our purposes is not so much its condemnation of laziness but the fact that it ties it to poverty. At least for some, the implication seems to be that laziness is the cause of poverty.

Further to this, in a number of places the New Testament advocates the value of work and admonishes those who do not work: Ephesians 4.28 encourages thieves to work with their own hands so that they have something to share; 1 Thessalonians 4.11–12 encourages something similar so that we will not be 'dependent' on anyone; 1 Timothy 5 distinguishes between widows who really do need help and those who do not. But perhaps the fullest treatment of this topic comes in 2 Thessalonians 3 where we find the following:

> Now we command you, beloved, in the name of our Lord Jesus Christ, to keep away from believers who are living in idleness and not according to the tradition that they received from us. For you yourselves know how you ought to imitate us; we were not idle when we were with you, and we did not eat anyone's bread without paying for it; but with toil and labour we worked night and day, so that we might not burden any of you. This was not because we do not have that right, but in order to give you an example to imitate. For even when we were with you, we gave you this command: Anyone unwilling to work should not eat. For we hear that some of you are living in idleness, mere busybodies, not doing any work. Now such persons we command and exhort in the Lord Jesus Christ to do their work quietly and to earn their own living. (2 Thess. 3.6–12)

At first sight, this passage would appear to endorse a deserving/undeserving poor distinction. Those who will not work should not eat. When we combine this with the numerous other passages where the Scriptures do encourage us to support the poor we can only conclude that we are to distinguish between the two groups in this way. Those who work but are still poor we should help. Those who refuse to work and are poor, we should not. However, the reality is that the passages in Thessalonians and the rest of the New Testament are more nuanced than that, particularly in light of their contextual background.

The first argument to make is that what Paul has in his sights is not so much poverty due to non-work but rather client–patron relationships. It is noteworthy that the section begins by Paul referencing a 'tradition' that he has passed on to them. Clearly, then, what he is now referring to is in respect of some body of teaching that has already been described. According to Gene Green, the most likely candidate is the kind of client–patron relationship that is suggested in 1 Thessalonians 4.11–12. He draws attention to the fact that this was not an issue of those who wanted to work, but could not. Rather, it was an issue of those who *refused* to work, at least work with their hands, that is.

These people maintained their status as dependent clients of either richer members of the congregation . . . or unconverted patrons. We do not know the exact reason why they opted to continue to live as clients . . . We can only say for sure that some of the Thessalonians decided to remain clients and were not forced into the situation against their will.[17]

Paul's issue with this situation is the dependency it bred (1 Thess 4.12). Here were members of the congregation living, we might say, with 'sugar daddies', entirely dependent on others and refusing to do the work that was on offer. Such a situation bred inequality in power and discord in the congregation. No wonder Paul objected to it.

The second possibility, and most likely the non-workers were in either or both of these camps, was those who would not work because they despised manual work. It is not accidental that in the New Testament passages on this issue the emphasis is almost always on 'work with hands'. As we have already seen, the Greek philosophical background was one in which such manual labour was despised as not worthy of the excellent life. Is it possible that, in referring to the 'tradition' that he has passed on, Paul is speaking about the Old Testament Scriptures that in contrast to Aristotle (and others) does praise the virtue of manual work? As such, the people he has in his sights here are specifically those who think they are above some menial tasks. Tying these two ideas together, Green suggests that what happened in the church at Thessalonica is that some who had previously lived as clients of wealthy patrons were now, in light of their new-found faith in Christ, being called to give up those relationships of dependency and instead work with their own hands. Some, however, were refusing, seeking to continue to live as clients – perhaps at the expense of the ecclesia rather than their previous patrons.[18] In this context, Paul's admonition is that the church should not support them. If they want to eat, they must work.

Given all this we see that what Paul is advocating here is not an unnuanced distinction between the deserving and undeserving poor. It is certainly not a charter to remove the welfare state, as some have argued.[19] However, it is at the same time an encouragement to us to avoid situations of dependency in our charitable giving. It is also a reminder that there can come a time when some will deliberately refuse work and seek to live off the generosity of others. Of this we must be wary.

A further form of paternalism that Corbett and Fikkert describe is that of 'spiritual paternalism'. This is the sense that churches in other parts of the globe are somehow dependent on the theological and spiritual insights of the Western 'mother' church. While on the ground this may still be a problem – African theological libraries remain stuffed with (usually) old theological texts from the West – there are signs that the need for and practice of self-theologizing is increasingly taking root within the church of LICs. Jesse Mugambi has encouraged the development of a reconstructive theology that is not just about aping the insights of others, but is self-created as the word and Spirit find fertile ground in African soil.[20] Similarly, Ilo gently chastises his fellow African theologians for too frequently looking to the West for their theological insights. He rightly points out:

It is also unhealthy for Africans to look outside Africa for the rich harvest of the social gospel that has the very quality and character for the imaging of a new Africa, which is within the realm of God's plan for Africa.[21]

In the process, he takes Mugambi at his word and begins to lay down the contours of what a specifically African theology might look like:

One of the challenges of doing theology in Africa is the pervasive influence of Western theological categories and frameworks that constantly lurk on the horizon for most African theologians. African theologies are still done with foreign languages, as many African languages continue to recede in usage . . . African theologians also accept as given Western distinctions and divisions of theologies, which lead to specializations into for example a dogmatic theologian, a moral theologian, a pastoral theologian, a spiritual theologian, biblical theologian, etc. . . . However, this is where the challenge of rupture arises: the danger of pursuing our field of specialization without attention to the whole picture, and seeing our areas of study in the narrow lenses of exclusivity. African theologies are mission theologies because they deal with the whole horizon of Christian consciousness in their engagement with history and new and unexplored horizons of cultural knowledge, cultural artefacts, and cultural arts in Africa. This means that the division into fields of specialization will have a unifying base in the Christian consciousness of Africans, which is the apprehension of Christ from an integrated socio-religious and cultural world.[22]

The challenge then is for those of us in the West to find the right balance between sharing our spiritual, ecclesiological and theological insights with the global Church without imposing them or assuming that our categories of understanding are appropriate or even make sense in another context. This is as much a challenge to church leaders as it is to theologians, for while the latter usually at least know the theory of contextualization, it is the former who are frequently invited to speak and lead in LIC contexts. It is imperative that we show due reticence as such invitations occur.

Corbett and Fikkert also mention 'knowledge paternalism' in which the assumption is that we in HICs have access to information and understanding that is simply not available in LICs and therefore we know best. My own experience of 'knowledge paternalism' was perhaps most evident when I worked in global health for a UK charity. I was intimately involved in setting up a healthcare project that was essentially about training East African healthcare professionals in how to apply a Western model of healthcare. The evidence for the project we were implementing was exemplary and indeed had originated in Africa with healthcare professionals from Africa. Nevertheless, it remains the case that throughout the lifetime of the project some of the attitudes and opinions that were expressed by some of the project participants were clearly paternalistic. A friend of mine from Haiti tells me that such paternalism works both ways. The West is happy to believe that we know best, but at the same time in his culture there is far too ready an acceptance that whatever is proposed by the West must be better, precisely because it comes from the West. Corbett and Fikkert give an example of how LIC farmers were chastised for not using crops that had been shown to produce the highest yields. The problem, however, was although on average these varieties produced higher yields, they did not do so sufficiently regularly. Their year-on-year yield was far too variable for an economy that did not have access to other staple crops. Given this, the farmers were reacting entirely rationally in refusing to use the higher-yielding crops.[23]

My own favourite story of knowledge paternalism concerns an Ethiopian village that was given a new borehole in the centre of the village. After a few months, the NGO that had installed the borehole returned to discover that it was hardly being used and the women were still walking miles to a nearby river to collect their water. On enquiring why, they discovered that the reason was that collecting water was not just a functional activity, but was also a social one. It provided both the men and the women in the village time to gather and talk separately from one another about the business of the village. The problem with the borehole being located in the centre of the village was that all the men could still hear what the women were talking about and the women as a result would not talk. In short, each gender needed their space and so the women chose to walk miles to get their water to provide them with the much needed social space from the men. Fortunately, in this case the NGO responded positively. They reinstalled the borehole just the right distance from the village that it gave the women the space they required without being too burdensome in terms of the distance they carried water. The fundamental problem with knowledge paternalism is that we think we see the whole of a situation and problem and in the process misapply the little we do know to what is ultimately a far more complex issue.

Finally, there exists a form of managerial paternalism. This is when the HIC tells the LIC how to run its affairs, in particular by emphasizing that the way in which the HIC runs things is the most efficient. The whole tenor of Grudem and Asmus's book, *The Poverty of Nations*, is that if only LICs ran their economies in the way that we do then they wouldn't suffer poverty at all. In contrast to this approach, Chris Wright has pointed out how in the Old Testament:

> The law typically addresses not the poor themselves but *those who wield economic or social power.* Whereas it is common to see the 'the poor' as 'a problem', and to blame them or lecture them on what *they* must do to redeem their situation, Israel's law puts the focus instead on those who actually have the power to do something, or whose power must be constrained in some way for the benefit of the poor. Thus the law addresses the creditor, not the debtor (Deut. 24.6, 10–13); employers, not day labourers (Deut. 24.14); slave-owners, not slaves (Ex. 21.20–21, 26–27; Deut. 15.12–18).[24]

In stark contrast to this, Grudem and Asmus are keen to tell the poor how to act. They write: 'To anyone in a leadership role in a poor country, the message of our book is this: there is a solution to poverty that really works . . . We are asking you to consider this solution for your own nation.'[25] I do not come from a LIC or experience poverty on a daily basis, but I suspect I would find that statement somewhat patronizing and paternalistic. It appears to be ethnocentric – the belief that one's own culture is best. Perhaps an obvious example of this concerns our relationship to time. It has frequently been pointed out that the West has a monochromic concept of time, while many in LICs have a polychromic concept. This is not so much to do with punctuality, though that may be part of it, but is more to do with how time is organized. Under a monochromic system, we do one thing at a time in a consecutive manner. We attend the meeting, then take the phone call, then answer the emails, and so on. By way of contrast, some African cultures, for instance, are said to have a polychromic concept of time, in which multiple activities can occur all at once. I can vividly remember once phoning a colleague of mine in West Africa who seemed somewhat distracted and I could hear other voices as he answered the phone. After a while, I asked what was going on, and it turned out that not only was he in a conference room listening to a speech, he was also simultaneously conducting some business negotiations with other people in the room while talking to me on the phone! Now, it would be very easy to claim – at least from a Western perspective – that this is why African countries are so poor in the way that Grudem and Asmus do. However, there is no evidence that this is what distinguishes our relative economic productivity and there is much evidence that other factors are at play. There is a huge danger in the HIC failing to appreciate that what it thinks is simply the best way to do something is in reality just our cultural norms that have no more objective value than any other norm.

One final form of paternalism that Corbett and Fikkert do not particularly mention is what I would call 'representational paternalism'. This is, when under the guise of raising funds to support LICs we depict others as poor, starving and unable to help themselves. Ilo puts it well:

There is an obvious paternalistic mind-set among non-Africans with regard to Africa. Africa is not all about naked children rummaging for food in refuse dumps or dying men and women with wasted flesh hanging on mere skeletons; Africa is not a land of violence and turmoil. There is *much more* to Africa than what is presented in the Western media; there is another face of Africa which is not easily seen in Western media. These negative images of Africa, even though sometimes stemming from pure motives, rob Africans of their dignity and give false impressions on the possibility of a better future for Africa.[26]

There does in fact exist a code of conduct for the use of images by those working in relief and development.[27] Its underlying principle is 'respect for the dignity of all people concerned', and it goes on to say that to refuse to portray negative images of poverty would be to ignore the reality of some people's lives. Nevertheless, poverty is just part of that reality and it is not the whole story. When I worked for four months among the Gogodala of Papua New Guinea, on many standard measures of poverty they were extremely poor. Yet the reality of their lives was one of community and fulfilment that many in HICs would envy. This is not to romanticize the poor but simply to say, as Ilo indicates above, that images of destitution are not the whole story and betray a paternalism that robs the poor of their dignity. It is incumbent upon us to reflect the full reality of lives, including their wider context, so that both the good and the bad are faithfully portrayed.

As already noted, the particular problem with all of these forms of paternalism is that they can compound the problem of a loss of dignity, and in this way our efforts at relief and development can make things worse. It is of course not the intention of those from HICs to make poor people feel worse, but due to a combination of ignorance and thoughtlessness this can be the result. The essence of the issue is what was indicated at the start of this section. If we think that poverty is simply material poverty, then inevitably we will pursue any effort to meet those material needs. However, if we recognize that part of the problem of poverty is the loss of dignity that arises as a result of powerlessness and feelings of inferiority, then we will make far more of an effort to ensure that our poverty alleviation efforts do not exacerbate that issue. As the South African theologian Steve de Gruchy has argued:

A great deal of development planning on behalf of the South has been undertaken by people in the North, and apart from this leading to the manifold and obvious problems of inappropriate planning and long-term dependency, the fact is that it continues to reinforce the unequal power relationship that is at the heart of poverty, neo-colonialism and globalisation.[28]

Because of this reality, we also need to recognize that poverty alleviation is as much as anything about restoring to people the sense of value and worth that they already have as image-bearers of God. If we simply treat them as, and make them feel like, objects of charity, dependent on our largesse, then it is inevitable that the sense of dignity associated with being an image-bearer will fail to flourish. If instead we recognize that together both they and we are designed to flourish, to subdue the rest of creation and to bear God's image as one body, then we can find more effective strategies to help one another do that.

Notes

1 S. Corbett and B. Fikkert, 2009, *When Helping Hurts*, Chicago, IL: Moody Publishers, pp. 109–13.

2 'Food Aid or Hidden Dumping?' Oxfam briefing paper, March 2005, p. 2. Available at: www.oxfam.org/sites/www.oxfam.org/files/bp71_food_aid.pdf (accessed 9 July 2015).

3 S. Ilo, 2014, *The Church and Development in Africa*, Eugene, OR: Pickwick Publications, p. 68.

4 Ilo, *The Church*, p. 191.

5 B. Myers, 2016, 'How did Britain Develop? Adaptive Social Systems and the Development of Nations', *Transformation* 33:2, p. 142.

6 C. Wright, 2004, *Old Testament Ethics for the People of God*, Nottingham: InterVarsity Press, p. 151.

7 D. Narayan *et al.*, 1999, *Voices of the Poor Volume 1: Can Anyone Hear Us?*, Washington, DC: World Bank, p. 142.

8 Aristotle, *Politics*, 1328b32–41, cited in C. Nederman, 2008, 'Men at Work: Poesis, Politics and Labor in Aristotle and Some Aristotelians', *Analyse & Kritik* 30, p. 21.

9 Aristotle, *Politics*, 1337a10–11, cited in Nederman, 'Men at Work', p. 22.

10 G. O. Anie, 2004, 'Christian Theology of Work: Its Implications for Nation-Building in Nigeria', *Ogbomoso Journal of Theology*, 1 December, p. 63.

11 Anie, 'Christian Theology', p. 63.

12 Consider also Jesus' parable of the talents in Matthew 25.

13 Anie, 'Christian Theology', p. 64.

14 Anie, 'Christian Theology', p. 63.

15 O. Muchena, 1996, 'Sociological and Anthropological Reflections', in T. Yamamori, B. Myers, K. Bediako and L. Reed (eds), *Serving with the Poor in Africa*, Monrovia, CA: MARC Publications, p. 177. A similar point is made by her fellow countryman Roy Musasiwa in the same volume when he describes the children of Israel as those who could 'work with their own hands and not depend on handouts. Jesus fed the hungry in emergency situations, but he taught the value of hard work as the normative way.' R. Musasiwa, 1996, 'Missiological Reflections', in Yamamori, *et al.* (eds), *Serving with the Poor*, p. 206.

16 See also Proverbs 14.23; 21.25; 23.19; 28.19; Romans 12.11.

17 G. Green, 2002, *The Letters to the Thessalonians*, Grand Rapids, MI: Eerdmans, p. 351.

18 Green, *The Letters*, p. 211.

19 W. Grudem and B. Asmus, 2013, *The Poverty of Nations: A Sustainable Solution*, Wheaton, IL: Crossway Books. A. Bradley and A. Lindsley, 2014, *For the Least of These: A Biblical Answer to* Poverty, Grand Rapids, MI: Zondervan.

20 J. N. K. Mugambi, 1995, *From Liberation to Reconstruction*, Nairobi: East African Educational Publishers.

21 Ilo, *The Church*, p. 218.

22 Ilo, *The Church*, p. 220.

23 Corbett and Fikkert, *When Helping*, p. 111.

24 Wright, *Old Testament Ethics*, p. 174. The same point is made in relation to the Psalms, where Wright states: 'Israel's worship also, like the law and the prophets, is clear about where *the prime responsibility* lies in the matter of addressing the needs and the just cause of the poor; namely, with political and social authorities – kings (Ps 72) and judges (Ps 82).' Wright, *Old Testament Ethics*, p. 177. Cf. also p. 179, where the wisdom literature is shown to echo the same theme. For this reason, I disagree with Maluleke when he criticizes Oxfam for directing a series of recommendations to wealthy internationalists. Maluleke suggests that asking multinationals not to dodge taxes is akin to 'asking cats to go and teach mice how to avoid being caught by cats'. Maluleke would seem to believe that genuine social transformation only takes place from the ground up. Historically that is simply not the case. Genuine social transformation has always involved both pressure from those who are impoverished and powerless, and from changes of heart and mind among the powerful. Certainly to address the powerful directly (as Oxfam and the Torah do) is not unwise, as Maluleke suggests, but part of the solution that is required. T. S. Maluleke, 2016, 'Christian Mission in a World under the Grip of an Unholy Trinity: Inequality, Poverty and Unemployment', in M. Auvinen-Pöntinen

and J. A. Jørgensen (eds), *Mission and Money: Christian Mission in the Context of Global Inequalities*, Boston, MA: Brill, p. 72.

25 Grudem and Asmus, *Poverty of Nations*, p. 32. See also John Schneider, who blames poverty on 'internal' processes rather than 'external' ones. J. Schneider, 2002, *The Good of Affluence*, Grand Rapids, MI: Eerdmans, p. 216.

26 Ilo, *The Church*, p. 147. This phenomenon is often now referred to as 'poverty porn'. See also D. George, 'Changing the Face of Poverty: Representations of Poverty in Nonprofit Appeals', in J. Trimbur (ed.), 2001, *Popular Literacy*, Pittsburgh, PA: Pittsburgh University Press, pp. 209–28.

27 'Code of Conduct on Images and Messages', 2006, Concord. Available at: www.concordeurope.org/publications/item/115-code-of-conduct-on-images-and -messages.

28 S. de Gruchy, 2008, 'Christian Leadership in "Another Country": Contributing to an Ethical Development Agenda in South Africa Today', in S. de Gruchy, N. Koopman and S. Strijbos (eds), *From Our Side: Emerging Perspectives on Development and Ethics*, Amsterdam: Rozenberg Publishers, p. 19.

3

The nature of poverty

In 2005, the World Bank reset the official international poverty line, defining extreme poverty as those living on less than $1.25 per day PPP (at 2005).[1] The advantages of such an economic measure of poverty is that it is clear, transparent, relatively easy to measure and it enables cross-sectional (especially cross-country) and longitudinal comparisons to be made. It enables us, for instance, to measure whether a country is getting richer or poorer and at what pace. However, for some time, a range of problems with such monetary approaches to poverty has been recognized. Perhaps the biggest issue is simply that this is not how poor people themselves – even poor people by income standards – understand their own poverty. As we have already seen in the Voices of the Poor series of reports, poverty is not just about income, but also about education, health, housing, disempowerment, unemployment, shame, humiliation and fear. A definition of poverty that is restricted to income can ignore or downplay these other facets of poverty. At the same time, different aspects of poverty are interrelated and often mutually reinforcing. So a working-age adult who is unwell due to malaria, and who cannot afford the medicines that will make him better, will also not be able to work, and might as a result lose his job, or at the very least lose some income. If a subsistence farmer, the person will also have a diminished ability to cultivate their own land or harvest their own crops and so hunger may be added to the series of interlocking problems they face. A measure of poverty that looks only at income fails to grasp the complexity of this situation. Finally, a measure of poverty that looks only at income also misdirects our approach to the solutions to poverty.

Abhijit Banerjee and Esther Duflo cite data from Maharashtra in India where the relationship between income and food expenditure in very poor families was examined. What they found was that even in families with an absolute calorie deficit extra income did not necessarily translate into buying extra food. Instead, the extra income was used to buy better tasting, more expensive calories.[2] If we think that poverty is nothing but a lack of income then our solution will be monetary. However, as the example from Maharashtra indicates, that would still leave some people starving.

For all these reasons, policy-makers have in recent years developed a new multidimensional definition of poverty. This new MPI (global Multidimensional Poverty Index) is not intended to replace the standard income measure, but it is designed to work alongside it, and to provide a richer, more complete understanding of poverty.[3] It covers three broad dimensions of poverty (education, health and living standard) and ten specific measures of poverty. They are:

1 Education
- • Years of schooling: deprived if no household member has completed five years of schooling.
- • Child enrolment: deprived if any school-aged child is not attending school in years 1 to 8.

2 Health
- • Child mortality: deprived if any child has died in the family.
- • Nutrition: deprived if any adult or child for whom there is nutritional information is malnourished.

3 Standard of living
- • Electricity: deprived if the household has no electricity.
- • Drinking water: deprived if the household does not have access to clean drinking water or clean water is more than 30 minutes' walk from home.
- • Sanitation: deprived if they do not have an improved toilet or if their toilet is shared.
- • Flooring: deprived if the household has dirt, sand or dung floor.
- • Cooking fuel: deprived if they cook with wood, charcoal or dung.
- • Assets: deprived if the household does not own more than one of: radio, TV, telephone, bike, or motorbike, and do not own a car or tractor.[4]

According to the Oxford Poverty and Human Development Initiative (OPHI), who developed these indicators, a person is poor if they are deprived in a third or more of these indicators. As will be obvious, this is a far richer understanding of poverty than the purely narrow income measures, and what is also interesting is the way in which this measure of poverty does not necessarily track income poverty. So, for instance, in Nepal in 2009/10 income poverty (less than $1.25 per day PPP) stood at 25.4 per cent, whereas MPI poverty was 64.7 per cent.[5] A similar analysis for Uganda showed that while for the country as a whole income poverty was highly correlated to MPI poverty, this was not the case for all counties or regions. Two counties in particular were in the bottom quintile for income poverty, but near the top for MPI poverty.[6] This is highly significant, because if country planners are going to invest their resources in those areas that have the highest rates of poverty then going by income poverty alone is going to potentially misdirect resources from areas that need it most.

In addition to all this, the OPHI has begun conversations about what they term the 'missing dimensions of poverty'. These include security and safety of work, empowerment, physical safety (i.e. freedom from violence and threat), relationships, freedom from shame and humiliation, and psychological well-being.[7] This work is just beginning and is not formally part of the MPI yet, partly because of the difficulties in reliably measuring these indicators. But what is interesting in this whole debate is the way in which it has tracked (perhaps unknowingly[8]) some recent biblical and theological debates about the concept of poverty.

In 1994/95, Joel Green published two chapters in two different books (with some overlapping material) that addressed the question of the "poor" in Luke-Acts.[9] He drew attention to the way in which most New Testament scholarship interpreted Luke's use of the 'poor' in largely, or even exclusively, economic terms. 'Our tendency today is to define "the poor" economically, on a scale of annual household income or with reference to an established, national or international poverty line.'[10] However, Green argues that this is to interpret Luke through our own cultural lenses and that in reality his concept of 'the poor' was far more multidimensional than that (though that is not the terminology he uses). The real issue for Luke was not so much economic prosperity but 'status honour', one's standing and acceptance within the community. He writes:

> Status honour is a measure of social standing that embraces wealth, but also other factors, including access to education, family heritage, ethnicity, vocation, religious purity, and gender. In the Greco-Roman world, then, poverty is too narrowly defined when understood solely in economic terms.[11]

In support of this argument, he points in particular to the pericope of the poor widow in Luke 21 and highlights the contrast between this 'poor' widow and the 'rich' teachers of the law oppressing her. While the latter are characterized by honour, power and standing, she is characterized by dishonour, shame and exploitation. In other words, while she certainly did suffer from economic poverty, that was not the whole of the picture that Luke presents to us, and not wholly what he means when he describes her as 'poor'.[12] In addition, he notes how Luke repeatedly juxtaposes the word 'poor' with a range of words that flesh out its meaning for him. These include: captive, blind, oppressed, hungry, mournful, persecuted, lame, deaf and leper.[13] He concludes by saying, 'The impression with which one is left is that Luke is concerned above all with a class of people defined by their dishonourable status, their positions outside circles of power and prestige, their being excluded.'[14]

While not mentioning Joel Green, Peter Oakes also proposes that we revise our understanding of the poor, based in part on his analysis of the New Testament corpus, but also incidentally on his reading of Amartya Sen, the Nobel prize-winning development economist. The object of his study was a paper by Friesen which had argued for an economic poverty scale in Greco-Roman society that would be useful in interpreting economic status in the Pauline corpus.[15] Oakes responds by saying that to focus on economic factors alone is once again too narrow, largely because the New Testament itself simply does not provide us with that kind of data in any depth. Instead, if a scale is to be useful it will have to focus on more 'sociological' and 'multidimensional' understandings of poverty.[16] The most interesting part of his analysis is where he suggests that in fact it might prove fruitful to move entirely beyond an aggregate scale towards an 'ordered poverty scale'. In such a scale, a wide range of different components of poverty are identified, and these are used to generate sub-scales for different groups of the poor. Oakes' illustrative list includes the following:

- adequate diet for survival
- adequate diet for good health
- diet suitable to status X
- adequate living space
- living space suitable to status X
- support for immediate family
- support for extended family
- provision of dowry
- purchase of medical help
- freedom to control use of time
- liberation from slavery
- liberation from abusive relationship
- freedom from likelihood of periodic want
- retention of inherited land
- carrying out of religious obligations.[17]

The parallels between this list and the MPI already described are obvious and it is probably the case that perhaps via different routes they both owe their origins to Amartya Sen's seminal work in this area.[18] Nevertheless, it is also clear Oakes is informed by his reading of the New Testament corpus, which, as indicated in Green's analysis, simply does not countenance an economic-only understanding of poverty.

It goes without saying that a similar analysis of the Old Testament would reach the same conclusion, perhaps even more so. As long ago as 1973, Richard Patterson noted not just the ubiquitous combination of the 'widow, the orphan and the poor' in the Hebrew canon, but also its ancient Near Eastern background.[19] The significance of this is that these descriptions immediately take us beyond a narrow concern with economics alone. While the widow and the orphan would have been financially destitute, they were also powerless and vulnerable to injustice and exploitation. Indeed, it is frequently these aspects of their situation that the Old Testament draws our attention to rather than their economic plight (Ex. 22.22; Deut. 10.18; 24.17; Job 24.3; Ps. 94.6; Isa. 1.17; Jer. 7.6). John Donahue writes that 'The "poor" in the Bible are almost without exception *powerless* people who experience economic and social deprivation.' They are 'victims of injustice', denied their rights, subject to lies and are 'downtrodden'.[20] In a similar vein, in his survey of the widow, the orphan, the poor and the sojourner, Donald Gowan writes this:

> The worst problem, that which these groups have in common, is powerlessness and its consequences: lack of status, lack of respect, making one an easy mark for the powerful and unscrupulous, so that those who are not poor are likely to become poor and those who are poor are going to get poorer.[21]

He goes on to say:

> It was not that all widows or resident aliens were poor. What these four groups had in common was their precarious social status. They were weak,

38

for various reasons, and thus the plight of which the Old Testament most often speaks is not hunger or lack of shelter; it is their inability to maintain their rights, so that it is possible for others to oppress them.[22]

The parallel with how we began this discussion of poverty is obvious. Chapter 1 of the second Voices of the Poor report begins in this way: 'The common theme underlying poor people's experiences is one of powerlessness.'[23] We have seen that both the Old and New Testaments understand poverty in a very similar manner. Poverty is not merely living on less than $1.25 per day, it is multidimensional, it involves issues of power, it is personal and psychological, and it incorporates issues of status within the community.

Given this, it is possible to understand the Genesis language of 'dominion' in Genesis 1.26 in a new light. That verse is not encouraging the powerful to exploit creation for their own benefit – in the way that some evangelical climate change sceptics suggest. Rather, that verse, as Richard Middleton has suggested, is given to a group of people who are themselves impoverished through exploitation and exile to encourage them to take control of their own environment in order to flourish and multiply. It chimes perfectly with the text that is undoubtedly written for the exiles, that of Jeremiah 29.5–6:

> Build houses and live in them; plant gardens and eat what they produce. Take wives and have sons and daughters; take wives for your sons, and give your daughters in marriage, that they may bear sons and daughters; multiply there, and do not decrease.

The obvious parallel with the creation mandate to subdue, be fruitful and multiply lends weight to Middleton's thesis. This then also represents the mandate given to people in LICs who are also experiencing the powerlessness that comes from economic exile and exploitation. At the same time, it challenges those of us in HICs to question whether our development activities foster that empowerment or weaken it. Gustavo Esteva, writing from a secular perspective, points out:

> For those who make up two-thirds of the world's population today, to think of development . . . requires first the perception of themselves as underdeveloped, with the whole burden of connotations that this carries . . . a life experience of subordination and of being led astray, of discrimination and subjugation . . . It impedes thinking of one's own objectives . . . it undermines confidence in oneself and one's own culture.[24]

One further way to frame this discussion is simply to understand poverty as disordered relationality. It is commonplace now, at least among theologians, to describe poverty as either having a relational dynamic, or indeed simply to be relational,[25] and this is also reflected in the OPHI work in their missing dimensions of poverty. They write:

> In research that asks poor people what matters to them, people often talk about how important relationships and social connections are for their lives.

39

Social connectedness is highly valued by people, and especially poor people, for many different reasons. People value relationships because: they bring them comfort, provide love, allow them to confide in people or feel part of a group, or because they are important for achieving other goals, such as finding a job, or learning new skills.[26]

Relationships, then, provide both intrinsic and instrumental value to people. In relation to poverty, broken relationships are implicated in a range of ways. The first of these is that poverty that is experienced for other reasons can be the cause of damaged relationships, thereby exacerbating the poverty that is already experienced. When a family is put under financial strain, perhaps because a breadwinner loses their job or income, then this can in turn lead to marital strain, domestic violence and the break-up of families. Previously, I quoted a young man from Gabon talking about the lack of esteem that resulted from unemployment. His quotation continues in this way:

As time passes . . . unemployment begins to undermine the young man's self-esteem. He starts to see himself . . . as having failed in his supreme duty as father and head of household, and this may drive him to drink and violence. When I don't know how my children are going to eat tomorrow, I tend to get drunk whenever I can. It helps me forget my problems. (Gabon 1997)[27]

The same breakdown in relationships can be the result of ill-health, in particular HIV/AIDS and mental health issues. This may be because one member of the family leaves or abandons the other, or because the community at large shuns the person who is suffering. Once again, this compounds the poverty they experience for now they add shame and humiliation to their sickness and economic plight.

In this context, Jesus' response to those thought to have leprosy in particular provides a model of restoration that should be embraced. Consider the following example:

When Jesus had come down from the mountain, great crowds followed him; and there was a leper who came to him and knelt before him, saying, 'Lord, if you choose, you can make me clean.' He stretched out his hand and touched him, saying, 'I do choose. Be made clean!' Immediately his leprosy was cleansed. Then Jesus said to him, 'See that you say nothing to anyone; but go, show yourself to the priest, and offer the gift that Moses commanded, as a testimony to them.' (Matt. 8.1–4)

At first sight, it is easy to (mis)interpret this story as a simple demonstration of Christ's healing power. The man had a skin condition, possibly leprosy, and Jesus heals him. However, that is not the substance of what is going on here. For when the man acknowledged before Jesus that he was unclean, he was not just making a physical or medical statement regarding his skin disease. Rather, he was making a social and spiritual statement regarding his access to fellowship with God and other worshippers. As an unclean man he would have been forbidden from full participation in the religious or social life of the community. It is in this context that Jesus' actions must be understood. On more than one occasion, Jesus heals people with merely a word, but on this occasion he heals by means of touch. Matthew knows that this is no accident, and so draws our attention to it by adding the phrase 'reached out his hand' (incidentally in contravention of Lev. 5.2–3). In touching him, Jesus restores not only his fellowship with God but also, to the extent that Jesus is modelling for his followers a pattern of behaviour, fellowship with others. Jesus' declaration 'be clean' is in fact translated by Donald Hagner as 'be whole'.[28] Its intent is to emphasize that, yes, the skin disease is cured, but also fellowship with God and restoration into the worshipping community is brought about.

The second way in which poverty and relationships interact is that broken or impaired relationships can lead to poverty. During my time working in East Africa, one of the people I got to know was a low-paid hospital worker. I was surprised that she was doing one of the most menial tasks in the hospital as in talking to her it became immediately obvious that she was one of the most industrious, intelligent and honest people that I had the privilege to work with. After some months, when I knew her much better, I asked why she was working in the particular job she was in and hadn't been promoted to something more reflective of her ability. Her response was that it was because she refused to have sex with one of the senior managers. As a result, she was continually blocked from further advancement. The Voices of the Poor report comments:

> Women's vulnerability in the market place takes different forms in different countries. In many of the countries in Eastern Europe expectation of sexual favors of young women seem to be widespread. This also makes it very difficult for women over 25 years to get jobs. 'Women in their early 20's who do get hired often complain of sexual harassment. Employers feel licensed to make such demands on their female employees knowing that the alternative to refusing is simply unemployment. The knowledge that young women face a tremendous uphill battle to find a steady job paying a living wage encourages employers to make outrageous demands of female employees who frequently complain only to one another.' (Ukraine 1996)[29]

Examples like these are just the tip of the iceberg. In many ways it could be argued that all poverty is in fact the result of broken or impaired relationships, including our inappropriate relationship with the planet, and this is true whether that is taking place at the individual level, such as these examples, all the way through to the global level in which multinational corporations cheat nations out of the tax revenues they are due. A recent report from Christian Aid did in fact seek to frame the whole of the problem of poverty as such a 'relational theology of development'. They discuss how 'the major issues of development, such as HIV and AIDS, climate change, taxation and the food crisis, can be formulated in terms of broken relationships between rich and poor, women and men, people and the environment and so on'.[30]

We see in this how a vicious circle can develop in which poverty can lead to poor relationships, which in turn exacerbates the poverty, which in turn leads to the further breakdown of relationships. One possible example of this at a local level is indicated in Figure 3.1.

And at an international level it could look something like Figure 3.2.

While each step could be analysed in terms of the dysfunctional relationships they imply, those highlighted indicate that dysfunctionality in particular.

The third way in which poverty and impaired relationships interact is that at times poverty just is broken relationships. Whenever someone feels shame, or inferior, or humiliated – whatever the cause and whatever the consequences – their poverty is being experienced as that of impaired relationships. This represents the intrinsic value of relationships. 'We poor people are invisible to others – just as blind people cannot see, they cannot see us' (Pakistan 1993).[31]

Of course, all of this represents a fundamental breakdown in the way things are meant to be. It is frequently noted that the fundamental problem of the fall was the way in which it disrupted relationships with God, with self, with each other and with the environment. However, more than that, a Trinitarian understanding of God teaches us that to be made in his image means that we are created as relational. The classic recent restatement of this is to be found in John Zizioulas when he writes: 'The person is no longer an adjunct to a being, a category we *add* to a concrete entity once we have first verified its ontological hypostasis. *It is itself the hypostasis of the being.*'[32] Zizioulas's point here is that Western philosophy has bequeathed to us a legacy in which we first exist as some kind of substantive being, and then secondarily relate to others

Figure 3.1.

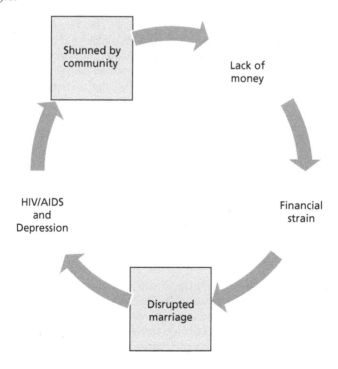

Figure 3.2.

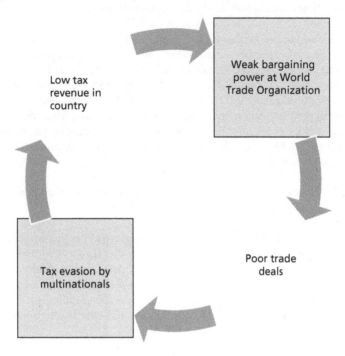

and to God. In contrast, Zizioulas takes us back to the Cappadocian Fathers and beyond to the Old and New Testaments to argue that our very existence subsists in our relationships, primarily our relationship to God. We only have our being precisely because we participate in the relationship of the Son to the Father, just as the Son's personhood subsists in his relation as Son to the Father. In Trinitarian terms, 'The Holy Trinity is a *primordial* ontological concept and not a notion which is added to the divine substance or rather follows from it.'[33] It is not just that we are created to *have* relationships as if they are a thing that comes along after our own existence/personhood is established. Rather, we are created *as* relational, and the question is not 'Should we relate?', but 'In what ways do we already relate that give honour to who we are meant to be?'

When framed in this way, we see that the impaired relationships that characterize poverty once again thwart the intentions of God. They are not how things are meant to be. Right relationships are not simply the result of obedience to some ethical command that God has given us. Rather, right relationships enable us to reflect the very nature and image of God, which is what we were created to do. And any relationship that is not right represents an impoverishment of God's image on earth.

John Klaasen, writing from an African perspective, echoes this kind of relational ontology.[34] Although he bases his argument on Trinitarian theology and definitions of personhood derived from the Cappadocian Fathers, it is perhaps not surprising that he writes his theology in that particular social context, for of course a relational ontology is precisely what is found in the African concept of *Ubuntu*, 'I am because we are.'[35] Ilo explains it thus:

> Ubuntu is today one of the most current categories from African communitarian ethics in reconciling communities, in building interdependent relationship, and encouraging the service of charity in truth. It is being embraced in international development discourse as a way of showing the mutuality of human living on earth, and the bond that could be established across racial, economic, political, and religious lines based on love and friendship. It is also another way of expressing the triple bottom line of people, prosperity, and planet (God + 3BL) as irreducibly inter-twined in any authentic and sustainable development praxis.[36]

Newbigin draws clearly the contrast between this conception and the Western individualistic model:

> For African society, the human person is seen as a partner in a whole network of relationships binding him or her horizontally across a widely extended family and vertically to the ancestors who have died and to children yet to be born. To be human is to be part of this closely woven fabric of relationships. By contrast, the Western post-Enlightenment understanding of the human person centers on the autonomy of the individual who is free to make or to break relationships at will.[37]

Returning to Ilo's description of Ubuntu, the key phrase here is 'irreducibly intertwined'. As I said in the Introduction to this book, one of the reasons I like the cover image for this book is that it acts as a reminder that the world is in our hands, that whether we recognize it or not, the decisions that all of us take have global impacts. So the coffee I choose impacts the wage earned by a day labourer in Kenya, and therefore whether his or her child can pay for the medicines they require. Ruth Valerio talks of this in terms of the idea of *detachment*. She chastises contemporary consumerism for isolating us from the process of production, the products themselves and from the producers.[38] It is particularly this separation from those who are responsible for the things that we consume that allows us to forget our responsibilities to them. But that is why *development* has not occurred when all individuals have maximal capabilities – for such a situation is theoretically, let alone practically, impossible.[39] Rather, *development* has occurred when in our relating to one another we do so with justice and righteousness. In his critique of both the political Left and political Right, Newbigin makes the same point. He notes how the Left's championing of equality is predicated on a notion of individual rights, and how the Right's advocacy of freedom is again dependent on a notion of individuality, but then how 'Both derive from the Enlightenment vision of human beings as autonomous individuals with innate and equal rights to pursue self-chosen ends to the limit of their powers.'[40] He goes on to say the following:

I believe that the Christian view of God's purpose for the human family is different from both of these and arises from a distinct belief about what human nature is. From its first page to its last, the Bible is informed by a vision of human nature for which neither freedom nor equality is fundamental; what is fundamental is relatedness.[41]

The theological significance of all this lies in the fact that the God in whose image we have been created is precisely the *relational* God, God as Father, Son and Spirit. And if we are created in his image, if what it means to be human is to reflect Father, Son and Spirit, indeed to represent Father, Son and Spirit on earth, then necessarily that means that the *imago Dei* is only realized to the extent that we model right relationships on earth. It is, in short, part of the creation mandate that we challenge inequality, remove barriers of injustice, release the oppressed and so on. To address these issues is not simply to live in obedience to a love command (though it is also that), it is rather to fulfil the implications of the creation mandate which is precisely why the author of Proverbs reminds us that 'Those who oppress the poor insult their Maker, but those who are kind to the needy honour him' (Prov. 14.31). To deny justice in the form of right relationships is not so much a failure to obey a command, it is to deny the very character of God.

The question that arises is how we go about restoring such right relationships. One way that has been dominant within development circles has been in terms of providing direct aid – food to the hungry, water and sanitation, good housing and so on. However, such direct forms of aid have come under increasing criticism from a range of sources who argue that in the long run what matters is not so much charity, but justice.[42] This is a theme that has been particularly explored by Nicholas Wolterstorff, who has argued that we often misread Old and New Testament passages to be about charity, when in reality they are about justice.

> What I have been arguing up to this point is that Jesus and the biblical writers do not think of rendering assistance to the needy of the world in terms of charity but in terms of justice. What I am now saying is that they do not primarily think of the needy of the world as unfortunates but as victims of injustice.[43]

These two frameworks – justice and charity – represent radically different ways of understanding the nature of poverty and our response to it.

Part of the reason we emphasize charity at the expense of justice is due to our misguided understanding of poverty. We tend to think of the poor as in a state of material deprivation requiring our assistance – this is the so-called needs-based approach to development. In contrast, a more appropriate response is to think of the poor in terms of the assets they already have. Our role then becomes less about making up for their lack, and more about working in partnership to help them realize the assets they already possess.[44] Ilo, in particular, is one of an increasing number of African theologians who have been critical of the needs-based approach to development work. He draws this out by challenging our use of images in the work of development:

	Charity approach	Justice approach
Attitude towards the poor person	Weak, helpless – lacking material goods in particular.	Victim of oppression, exploitation – but capable of self-transformation as injustices are righted.
Attitude towards the poverty	A tragic circumstance which rich world can help mitigate.	An injustice perpetrated by the powerful.
Attitude towards self as giver	Beneficent, generous, sharing out of love – sense of self-righteousness.	Merely doing the bare minimum required by righteousness.
Attitude towards our acts of generosity	Out of our goodness, we share with them some of the surplus we have.	We owe them justice, and a failure to address it represents sin on our part.
Relationship of poor person to giver	Giver expects gratitude from receiver.	Giver hopes for forgiveness from receiver.

Thus, the image of a dying African child will attract more sympathy than the image of a healthy African child who is studying with a kerosene lamp. These represent two ways of seeing Africa, one as a continent of needy people, and the other as a continent with people who have assets waiting to be discovered.[45]

In light of this, it is also essential that we recognize that we are all created equally in the image of God. We do not confer equality on people by means of our activities, for the only equality that ultimately matters is our status before God, and that is the same whoever we are. Having said this, it is the case that our activities can either contribute to or diminish the visible expression of that equality. When we patronize the poor by doing for them what they can already do for themselves, when we humiliate or degrade the poor by telling them that we know best, or when we fail to address the structures of injustice that keep them in poverty, then we are continuing in a system that cloaks the equality that the poor already have. In this context, Rowan Williams makes the very telling point that in contradistinction to what we might think, it is in fact the poor who liberate us when together with them we fight poverty. He writes:

> We are not trying to solve someone else's problem but to liberate *ourselves* from a toxic and unjust situation in which we, the prosperous, are less than human. The way forward is not simply the shedding of surplus wealth on to grateful recipients but an understanding that we are trying to take forward the process by which the other becomes as fully a 'giver' as I seek to be, so that the transaction by which I seek to bring about change in the direction of justice for another is one in which I come to be as much in the other's debt as they are in mine.[46]

He goes on to say that 'An unbalanced distribution of power is in the long run as damaging to the powerful as to the powerless.'[47] In the same vein, Mother Teresa is reported to have said, 'For our part what we desire is not a class struggle, but a class encounter, in which the rich save the poor and the poor save the rich.'[48] Fundamentally, seeking justice and equality for the poor is not so much an expression of compassion and care from those who are wealthy beneficently embracing the poor – however much it may seem that way. Rather, seeking justice and equality for the poor is about liberating all of us from a system which negates the God-given dignity of us all. The poor have their dignity deprived because they are prevented from fulfilling their creation mandate to be fruitful and subdue the earth; the rich have their dignity deprived because they have colluded with a system which exploits and oppresses the poor, and in this way they too fail to fulfil their creation mandate to represent the just, relational God on earth. The pursuit of justice is not fundamentally about charity; it is about seeking the restoration of the *imago Dei* on earth. But the nature of how that image was lost is the subject of our next chapter.

Notes

1 PPP = purchasing power parity, and is based on a notional basket of goods that is consistent across countries. This is to equalize measurements across countries where exchange rate fluctuations could artificially increase or decrease the purchasing value of $1.25 in any particular country. The current international poverty line is based on what could be bought for $1.25 in 2005.

2 A. Banerjee and E. Duflo, 2011, *Poor Economics*, London: Penguin Books, p. 23.

3 It is worth noting that the MPI is itself a replacement for the Human Poverty Index, which itself replaced the Human Development Index. The trajectory in all of these indices is to increasingly recognize that poverty is more than just an economic measure. The list of factors encompassed by these measures of poverty has consistently grown.

4 Oxford Poverty and Human Development Initiative (OPHI): www.ophi.org.uk.

5 R. Gaihre, 2012, 'Comparison between Multidimensional Poverty Index and Monetary Poverty for Nepal', presentation at OPHI, 21 November 2012. Available at: www.ophi.org.uk/workshop-on-monetary-and-multidimensional-poverty-measures/.

6 I. Gaddis and S. Klasen, 2012, 'Mapping MPI and Monetary Poverty: The Case of Uganda', presentation at OPHI, 21 November 2012. Available at: www .ophi.org.uk/workshop-on-monetary-and-multidimensional-poverty-measures/.

7 www.ophi.org.uk/research/missing-dimensions/.

8 It is worth noting that the most prominent scholar behind the MPI approach, Sabina Alkire, is a Roman Catholic who for her MPhil in Christian political ethics wrote on 'The Concept of Poverty Alleviation in the World Bank since 1990: A Theological Analysis'. Given this, the connection between biblical concepts of poverty and recent OPHI work may simply be unstated.

9 J. Green, 1994, 'Good News to Whom?', in J. Green and M. Turner, *Jesus of Nazareth: Lord and Christ*, Grand Rapids, MI: Eerdmans, pp. 59–74; J. Green, 1995, 'To Proclaim Good News to the Poor: Mission and Salvation', in J. Green,

The Theology of the Gospel of Luke, Cambridge: Cambridge University Press, pp. 76–101.

10 Green, *The Gospel*, pp. 79–80.

11 Green, 'Good News', p. 65.

12 Green, 'Good News', p. 67.

13 Green, 'Good News', p. 68.

14 Green, 'Good News', p. 68.

15 S. Friesen, 2004, 'Poverty in Pauline Studies', *Journal for the Study of the New Testament* 26:3, pp. 323–61.

16 P. Oakes, 2004, 'Constructing Poverty Scales for Graeco-Roman Society: A Response to Steven Friesen's "Poverty in Pauline Studies"', *Journal for the Study of the New Testament* 26:3, p. 371.

17 Oakes, 'Constructing', p. 371.

18 A. Sen, 1973, *On Economic Inequality*, Oxford: Oxford University Press; A. Sen, 1992, *Inequality Reexamined*, Cambridge, MA: Harvard University Press.

19 R. Patterson, 1973, 'The Widow, the Orphan, and the Poor in the Old Testament and the Extra-Biblical Literature', *Bibliotheca Sacra*, July, pp. 223–34. Interestingly, the one distinction between the Old Testament and the ancient Near Eastern sources on this issue is that while the Old Testament adds 'strangers' or 'foreigners' to the list of those for whom compassion should be shown, the ancient Near Eastern literature tends to limit itself to the widow, orphan and poor. Cf. D. Gowan, 1987, 'Wealth and Poverty in the Old Testament: The Case of the Widow, the Orphan, and the Sojourner', *Interpretation* 41:4, October, p. 343.

20 J. Donahue, 2004, *Seek Justice that You May Live*, Mahwah, NJ: Paulist Press, p. 55.

21 Gowan, 'Wealth and Poverty, p. 344.

22 Gowan, 'Wealth and Poverty, p. 347.

23 D. Narayan *et al.*, 2000, *Voices of the Poor Volume 2: Crying Out for Change*, Washington, DC: World Bank, December, p. 1.

24 G. Esteva, 1992, 'Development', in W. Sachs (ed.), *The Development Dictionary*, London: Zed Books, pp. 7–8.

25 S. Corbett and B. Fikkert, 2009, *When Helping Hurts*, Chicago, IL: Moody Publishers, pp. 54ff.; B. Myers, 1999, *Walking with the Poor: Principles and Practices of Transformational Development*, Marynoll, NY: Orbis Books, p. 86.

26 www.ophi.org.uk/research/missing-dimensions/social-connectedness/.

27 D. Narayan *et al.*, 1999, *Voices of the Poor Volume 1: Can Anyone Hear Us?*, Washington, DC: World Bank, p. 142.

28 Donald A. Hagner, 1995, *Word Biblical Commentary: Matthew 1–13*, Dallas, TX: Word Books.

29 Narayan, *Can Anyone*, p. 144.

30 P. Clifford, 2010, *Theology and International Development*, London: Christian Aid, p. 2.

31 Narayan, *Can Anyone*, p. 12.

32 J. Zizioulas, 1985, *Being as Communion*, Crestwood, NY: St Vladimir's Seminary Press, p. 39. For a critique of Zizioulas's Trinitarian theology, see S. Holmes, 2012, *The Quest for the Trinity: The Doctrine of God in Scripture, History and Modernity*, Downers Grove, IL: InterVarsity Press Academic, and a response to Holmes in T. Noble and J. Sexton, 2015, *The Holy Trinity Revisited: Essays in Response to Stephen Holmes*, Milton Keynes: Paternoster Press. In line

with Zizioulas's own argument, Holmes elides Zizioulas's Trinitarian theology, theological anthropology and ecclesiology and largely rejects all three. Where I differ from Holmes is that while I would part company with Zizioulas's ecclesiology entirely and his Trinitarian theology partially (and to this extent agree with Holmes), I accept Zizioulas's theological anthropology largely as written. Even though Zizioulas argues that all three flow together, it is possible to hold one without the others in their entirety.

33 Zizioulas, *Communion*, p. 17. It should of course be noted that for Zizioulas the principle of God is not 'pure relationality' but rather a person, the Father, in relation. Zizioulas, *Communion*, pp. 40–1.

34 J. Klaasen, 2013, 'The Interplay between Theology and Development: How Theology can be Related to Development in Post-Modern Society', *Missionalia* 41:2, August.

35 An equivalent concept is also found in South East Asia. Writing in a Filipino context, Fr Benigno Beltran chastises Western individualism as being thoroughly unbiblical and then states, 'The core of being human was defined not by what a living body is in itself, but by its relationship to others – "to be" is "to be in relation"'. B. Beltran, 1998, 'Towards a Theology of Holistic Ministry', in T. Yamamori, B. Myers and K. Luscombe (eds), *Serving with the Urban Poor*, Monrovia, CA: MARC Publications, p. 178.

36 S. Ilo, 2014, *The Church and Development in Africa*, Eugene, OR: Pickwick Publications, p. 265. For more on the relation of *Ubuntu* to issues of poverty, see M. F. Murove, 2008, 'Neo-Liberal Capitalism, African Elites and ICT: Challenges and Prospects for a Development Ethic based on *Ukama* and *Ubuntu*', in S. de Gruchy, N. Koopman and S. Strijbos (eds), *From Our Side: Emerging Perspectives on Development and Ethics*, Amsterdam: Rozenberg Publishers, pp. 135–50.

37 L. Newbigin, 1989, *The Gospel in a Pluralist Society*, London: SPCK, pp. 187–8.

38 R. Valerio, 2016, *Just Living: Faith and Community in an Age of Consumerism*, London: Hodder & Stoughton, p. 64.

39 This is the argument of Amartya Sen that we interact with in more depth in Part 5. See A. Sen, 1999, *Development as Freedom*, Oxford: Oxford University Press.

40 L. Newbigin, 1995, *Foolishness to the Greeks*, London: SPCK, p. 118.

41 Newbigin, *Foolishness*, p. 118.

42 For critiques of aid from a secular perspective, see W. Easterly, 2006, *The White Man's Burden*, Oxford: Oxford University Press; D. Moyo, 2009, *Dead Aid: Why Aid Is Not Working and How There Is Another Way for Africa*, London: Penguin); L. Polman, 2010, *War Games*, London: Penguin. A more positive though hardly uncritical perspective is provided by R. Riddell, 2007, *Does Foreign Aid Really Work?* Oxford: Oxford University Press. Critiques of contemporary aid from a Christian point of view can be found in G. Schwartz, 2007, *When Charity Destroys Dignity*, Bloomington, IN: Author House; Corbett and Fikkert, *When Helping*; R. Lupton, 2011, *Toxic Charity*, New York: HarperCollins.

43 N. Wolterstorff, 2006, 'Justice, Not Charity: Social Work through the Eyes of Faith', *Social Work & Christianity* 33:2, p. 136.

44 For more on needs- versus asset-based approaches to poverty, see Chapter 5 of Corbett and Fikkert, *When Helping*.

45 Ilo, *The Church*, p. 113.

46 R. Williams, 'A Theology of Development', p. 5. Available at: http://clients .squareeye.net. Fr Tissa Balasuriya (2002) makes a similar point in his 'Liberation of the Affluent', *Black Theology: An International Journal* (1:1, p. 112), and Swart makes the same point talking about a 'double movement' in our poverty alleviation efforts: a movement towards the poor and towards the rich. I. Swart, 2008, 'Meeting the Challenge of Poverty and Exclusion: The Emerging Field of Development Research in South African Practical Theology', *International Journal of Practical Theology*, 12:1, January, p. 134.

47 Williams, 'Theology', p. 6.

48 Cited in A. Bradley and A. Lindsley (eds), 2014, *For the Least of These: A Biblical Answer to Poverty*, Grand Rapids, MI: Zondervan, p. 186.

PART 2

Fall

4

The nature, depth and breadth of sin

In Part 1 of the book we noted how the doctrine of creation is not just found in the opening chapters of Genesis, but is rather to be located throughout Scripture. At the same time, the doctrine does not just provide a preamble to everything else that happens subsequently but rather sets in place a theological anthropology, doctrine of God and theology of the cosmos that continues into the present and the future. One of the dangers of the doctrines of the fall and sin – the topics of this present chapter – is that they can be thought of as obliterating all that went before, as if in the context of a fallen world we no longer bear the image of God at all. At times, the radical depravity of sin can be spoken of as if this is the case. But that is a theological mistake. Notwithstanding the numerous criticisms that have been levelled at Steve Chalke, one aspect where I think he is right is to remind us of the reality of what he terms 'original goodness'.

> Too often we fail to look at others through the eyes of Jesus. While we have spent centuries arguing over the doctrine of original sin, poring over the Bible and huge theological tomes to prove the inherent sinfulness of all humankind, we have missed a startling point: Jesus believed in original goodness! God declared that all his creation, including humankind, was very good. And it's this original goodness that Jesus seeks out in us. That's not to suggest that Jesus is denying that our relationship with God is in need of reconciliation, but that he is rejecting any idea that we are, somehow, beyond the pale.
>
> To see humanity as inherently evil and steeped in original sin instead of inherently made in God's image and so bathed in original goodness, however hidden it may have become, is a serious mistake. It is this grave error that has dogged the Church in the West for centuries.[1]

The key word in this passage, at least for my purposes, is 'inherent'. For while many have chastised Chalke for effectively denying original sin here, I'm not persuaded that is his intention. Rather, I think he is simply reminding us that we were created as good before we fell and that original goodness is not entirely displaced by the fall. This is a point that has been made by a number of theologians. Cornelius Plantinga writes, 'The glory of God's good creation has not been obliterated by the tragedy of the fall, but it has been deeply shadowed by it.'[2] Similarly, Derek Nelson writes, 'Human nature remains good even "after the fall." Human nature is one thing and sin is another thing.'[3] And again,

Henri Blocher writes, 'Sinfulness has become our quasi-nature while remaining truly our anti-nature.'[4] Perhaps most surprising – given his tendency to write negatively about the human condition – John Calvin wrote this: 'We say, then, that man is corrupted by a natural viciousness, but not one which proceeded from nature.'[5] The point that all these authors make is our inherent (the word Chalke uses) nature is not that of fallenness and sin. It is rather that of goodness. It may well be the case that the fall has corrupted that inherent nature to such an extent that it is hardly, if at all, visible. Nevertheless, our original and inherent nature remains one of goodness. This matters because if we believe that our original goodness is entirely obliterated, then it is very easy to separate ethics from anthropology. We no longer view obeying the commands of Jesus as somehow related to who we were originally created to be. They represent rather an add-on, a set of instructions we perform, until Christ comes again and redeems our entirely unredeemable bodies. What is important about the idea of original goodness is that it reminds us that the sin we see all around us is, in the words of Plantinga, 'not the way it's supposed to be'.[6] Under this guise, our ethics flow from our divinely ordained anthropology. When we work to restore the visible image of God to someone, we are not just obeying a command, we are helping to restore creation to what God always intended. We are being co-workers with Christ, builders of the kingdom and not merely obedient slaves.

The problem here is Calvin's doctrine of the total depravity of humanity. This is routinely misinterpreted to mean that there is nothing good in humanity whatsoever, or that humans can never do any good. But that is not what Calvin meant. What he meant was that every part of our lives is affected by sin, not that every single thought, feeling, attitude and action is itself sinful. It means that if we consider the various relationships we have, or tasks we undertake – the different roles and segments of our life if you will (father, husband, colleague, worshipper etc.) – then each one will to greater or lesser extents be impacted by sin. But it does not mean that everything we do is necessarily sinful. It does though mean that the whole of life in those various segments is affected. Nelson describes this as a series of ripples emanating from the centre.[7] The first of these is the individual him- or herself. We see this in the way that both Adam and Eve exploited creation for their own personal gain: 'the woman saw that the tree was good for food, and that it was a delight to the eyes, and that the tree was to be desired to make one wise, she took of its fruit and ate' (Gen. 3.6). The result of this action was that both Adam and Eve had a disordered relationship with themselves: 'I was afraid, because I was naked; and I hid myself' (Gen. 3.10). The second ripple Nelson describes, moving outwards as it were, is the impact of sin on the family. Eve encourages Adam to join with her in sinning. Adam immediately blames Eve when confronted by God (Gen. 3.6, 12). Both are complicit in disobeying God, yet their actions betray the fact that sin brings with it distorted familial relationships. The third ripple Nelson mentions is the community. He points to Genesis 6 which reads, 'The LORD saw that the wickedness of humankind was great in the earth, and that every inclination of the thoughts of their hearts was only evil continually' (Gen. 6.5–6). Nelson does not particularly mention this but we can continue to see the impact of sin beyond even the community to creation and possibly the cosmos. 'Cursed is the ground because of you; in toil you shall eat of it all the days of your life; thorns and thistles it shall bring forth for you; and you shall eat the plants of the field. By the sweat of your face you shall eat bread until you return to the ground' (Gen. 3.17–19). Of course, the immediate problem with this last point is the one highlighted by A. H. Lewis. Are we really saying that 'God added thorns to the roses or sharp teeth to the carnivorous animals'?[8] While there are a range of possible answers to that question, I think the one offered by John Bimson offers the best interpretation: that is, to understand the cosmic fall as relational rather than ontological. It is not so much that the planet suddenly functioned in a different way to how it had before, but rather how humanity related to creation is what has changed. He writes:

> In context, the essence of the curse is simply that Adam will henceforth find it harder to get his food from the soil. Note that work was already involved in acquiring a meal, as Adam was put in the garden of Eden 'to till it and keep it' (Gen. 2.15); when he is expelled, it is 'to till the ground from which he was taken' (Gen. 3.23). Hence Adam's basic activity does not change. The chief contrast he is to experience is between life in a 'garden' – implying a specially modified environment – and life among unmodified nature, where the ground brings forth 'thorns and thistles' (Gen. 3.17). In the latter his relationship with the soil will be different, because food will be harder to produce.[9]

All of this points to the most significant ripple of the fall, which is the way in which our relationship with God is disordered as a result. When Genesis 3.23–24 states that 'God sent him forth . . . He drove out the man' it is not discussing geography but theology. From this time onwards, our relationship to God is irretrievably (at least by our own efforts) affected. The whole thrust of the rest of the canon is to explore what it means to have one's relationship with God broken and how that fracture can be restored.

Throughout theological history a range of authors have located the essence of sin in an array of human faculties: for Augustine it was pride; for Luther it was unbelief; for Calvin it was disobedience. However, the foregoing discussion suggests to me that there are in fact two key ideas in sin which tie together the theological and biblical traditions more effectively. The first of these is to consider sin within the framework of disordered relationships. A number of preliminaries lead to this conclusion. One is the rather obvious point that only humans sin. Leaving aside the moral culpability of fallen angels, which I would argue we simply do not know enough about, my point is that sin is a preserve of human behaviour. Animals do not sin,[10] creation does not sin, and obviously God does not sin. While non-human creation is 'fallen', it does not have this particular privilege. Sin is a theological concept that is relevant to humanity alone. At the same time, we have already noted that humans are inherently relational beings. We are because we relate – first to God, but also to others. As image-bearers of the triune God, we do not exist outside of our relationships. At first sight, this might present a challenge. For if I only exist by means of my relationships, and if only humans can sin, then who is the 'I' that sins? When I sin, is it in fact the network of relationships in which I subsist that are somehow guilty? But if that is the case, does it remove my moral culpability and therefore render God's judgement unjust? Of course, this is not a theoretical construct. Numerous social commentators have argued that a range of inappropriate behaviour is not the result of bad moral choices, but simply the sequelae of one's early childhood or environment. And there is of course empirical evidence to support these suggestions. Child abusers tend to be those who have been abused themselves. Those guilty of violent crime have often been exposed to violence themselves from a young age. Perhaps sin is not an individual concept at all, but simply describes the network of poor relationships in which we all subsist.

The solution to this problematic is to return to the theological anthropology which we have already described. Our identity does not exist in some abstract notion of pure relationality as such. Rather, our identity exists in the particular set of relationships that have formed us and that we form. Crucially, however, we have influence both over which relationships we form and how they are conducted. Nelson summarizes Paul Ricoeur in this regard by saying: 'In my dealings with others, I do not simply enact a role or function that has been assigned to me. I can change myself through my own efforts and can reasonably ask others to change as well.' He goes on to say that this realization 'maintain[s] individual moral culpability in a relational anthropology'.[11] What this means is that sin is necessarily relational. It describes disordered relationships within ourselves and between ourselves and God, others and our environment. While the moral choices we make are impacted by those relationships, they do not reduce to pure (dis)relationality but represent instead the particular set of relationships in which we subsist and which we shape as we inhabit them. One consequence of this is that it brings to the fore the rather obvious point that the way in which we inhabit one relationship affects others. As the strings in one part of a net are strengthened or broken, so the tension in other parts of the net is changed. Prosaically, we see this when an extramarital affair impacts the marriage relationship, but we also see this when our collective purchasing decisions in London impact whether a child in Bangladesh gets to go to school. Sin then is relational disorder.

At the same time, a further helpful way to think of sin is provided by Cornelius Plantinga. He begins by drawing our attention to the pivotal concept of *shalom*. As numerous commentators have pointed out, shalom is far more than just the absence of hostilities. The English word 'peace' is far too inadequate to capture its scope. Rather:

> Shalom means universal flourishing, wholeness and delight – a rich state of affairs in which natural needs are satisfied and natural gifts fruitfully employed, a state of affairs that inspires joyful wonder as the creator and savior opens doors and speaks welcome to the creatures in whom he delights. Shalom, in other words, is the way things are supposed to be.[12]

If we consider again the full list of factors designated by the Oxford Poverty and Human Development Initiative (OPHI) in their definition of poverty – including their so-called missing dimensions of poverty – it strikes me that shalom represents the negation of all these factors. OPHI measures of poverty:

- inadequate/missing education
- poor health
- inadequate nutrition, including access to good food, clean water
- poor standard of living, e.g. no electricity and dirt flooring
- inadequate/missing sanitation
- inadequate security and safety at work
- limited empowerment with minimal decision-making over own life
- poor physical safety at risk of violence and threat
- poor relationships
- shame and humiliation
- poor psychological well-being.

Shalom is comprehensive – it is relational, physical, material, cognitive, psychological, emotional, social and spiritual. Shalom, as Plantinga likes to put it, is 'the way things are supposed to be' and he gives us a vivid description to illustrate it:

> It would include, for instance, strong marriages and secure children. Nations and people groups in this brave new world would treasure differences in other nations and people groups. In the process of making decisions, men would defer to women and women to men till a crisis arose. Then, with good humor all around, the person more naturally competent in the area of the crisis would resolve it to the satisfaction of both. Government officials would still take office (somebody has to decide which streets are cleaned on Tuesday and which on Wednesday), but to nobody's surprise they would tell the truth and freely praise the virtues of other public officials. Broadband networks would be strong enough to enable quick downloads. Highway overpasses would be graffiti free. Professors would know students' names while also leading such lively classes that students no longer felt like Facebooking their way through them. Nobody would un-friend anybody. Teachers of third graders would no longer make them sing 'I am special; I am special; look at me; look at me' to the tune of Frère Jacques. Tow truck drivers and lost motorists would be serene on city streets, secure in the knowledge that, under the provisions of government and private foundation grants, former gang members are now all in law school. Business associates would rejoice in each other's promotions. Middling Harvard students would respect the Phi Beta Kappas from the University of Southern North Dakota at Hoople and would try to learn from them. Intercontinental ballistic missile silos would be converted into training tanks for scuba divers. All around the world, people would stimulate each other's virtues. Blogs would be filled with well-written accounts of acts of great moral beauty and, at the end of the day, people on their porches would read these accounts and call to each other about them and savor them with their single martini.[13]

Bryant Myers is also helpful here. He has encouraged us to consider the impact of the fall far beyond the merely personal and spiritual. He points to the way in which some evangelicals have tended to interpret the fall purely in terms of one's own broken relationship with God, without considering its impact in the wider socio-economic arena. While in no way diminishing its significance in respect of our relationship to God, he maintains that the fall also negates God's shalom in other arenas too. He writes:

> The *economic system* was created by God to steward responsibly and justly the natural and human resources of the nation and to encourage men and women to be productive, using the gifts God has given to create wealth. Distorted by the fall, people occupying positions of influence within the economic system now act more often as owners and less as stewards. They skew the system to enhance and protect their own self-interest and insulate themselves from the impact of these distortions on the less fortunate.[14]

In similar vein, he discusses how 'the political system becomes captive to the economic order and begins to serve the powerful', and how both the political and economic collude with the religious so that 'the prophets of accountability are gradually seduced by money, power, and prestige, gradually becoming silent'.[15] It is of course possible to deny this, to state that sin is necessarily an individual concept and that the fall affects the human mind and heart but not the systems that such minds and hearts create. But I would suggest that to argue along those lines is to both fail to appreciate the full breadth of the fall and its cosmic, creational consequences, as well as to deny the relational anthropology that lies at the heart of what it means to be made in the image of the triune God. It represents a failure to take both sin and God seriously enough.

So, how does all of this relate to the concept of sin? It is in Plantinga's memorable phrase that 'sin is culpable shalom-breaking'.[16] I think this is a really helpful concept, for it takes us away from the notion that sin consists of individual acts which trespass some particular command. Of course, sin includes such acts of disobedience, but it is far more than that. Even the medieval distinction between sins of commission and sins of omission doesn't fully capture the breadth that is inherent in 'culpable shalom-breaking'. For under Plantinga's conception, we sin not just when we fail to do something we should do, but there is sin whenever something takes place that fails to promote God's full concept of shalom. As Plantinga puts it: 'God hates sin not just because it violates his law but, more substantively, because it violates shalom, because it breaks the peace, because it interferes with the way things are supposed to be.'[17]

To give a specific example, so-called structural sins are far more easily embraced by a concept such as 'culpable shalom-breaking' than they are by sin of omission, or even commission. The concept of structural sin is one that we really owe to the Latin American liberation theologians. Gustavo Gutiérrez, for instance, wrote:

> In the liberation approach sin is not considered as an individual, private, or merely interior reality . . . which does not challenge the order in which we live . . . When it is considered in this way, the collective dimensions of sin are

rediscovered . . . Sin is evident in oppressive structures, in the exploitation of humans by humans, in the domination and slavery of peoples, races and social classes.[18]

Notwithstanding the Vatican's antipathy to liberation theology at the time, Pope John Paul II picked up on the concept, writing in *Sollicitudo Rei Socialis*:

> If the present situation can be attributed to difficulties of various kinds, it is not out of place to speak of 'structures of sin' which . . . are rooted in personal sin, and thus always linked to the concrete acts of individuals who introduce these structures, consolidate them and make them difficult to remove. And thus they grow stronger, spread, and become the source of other sins, and so influence people's behaviour.[19]

Having noted this, the difference between the Latin American perspective and the Vatican, at least in the 1980s, is that the Vatican was far more intent on making it clear that structural sin is rooted ultimately in the sins of individuals. John Paul II had previously written:

> Whenever the Church speaks of situations of sin, or when she condemns as social sins certain situations or the collective behavior of certain social groups, big or small, or even of whole nations and blocs of nations, she knows and she proclaims that such cases of social sin are the result of the accumulation and concentration of many personal sins . . . A situation – or likewise an institution, a structure, society itself – is not in itself the subject of moral acts. Hence a situation cannot in itself be good or bad.[20]

Irrespective of their difference of emphasis, what is evident here is a concept which goes beyond mere 'sins of omission' – failing to do the good that one is meant to do – and instead takes us into the territory where our actions and inactions perpetuate systems that facilitate sin.

By way of example, John Paul II draws attention to the international trade system as one such example of a structure of sin. He writes:

> In this respect I wish to mention specifically: the reform of the international trade system, which is mortgaged to protectionism and increasing bilateralism; the reform of the world monetary and financial system, today recognized as inadequate; the question of technological exchanges and their proper use; the need for a review of the structure of the existing international organizations, in the framework of an international juridical order.[21]

This is helpful because if we consider sin merely in terms of sins of commission and omission then it is not at all clear whether it is my responsibility to challenge, for instance, any of the unjust practices that are perpetuated by the international trading order, or the structures that enable such practices to continue.[22] In contrast, under Plantinga's concept of 'culpable shalom-breaking', if the structure is failing to support God's shalom – and arguably certain aspects of the international trade system are guilty in this manner – then it is my responsibility to challenge that structure, at least by the way in which I participate in it. Putting this in concrete terms, it is not just sin when I fail to give to the poor – a sin of omission perhaps – it is also sin when I knowingly buy clothes or mobile phones or books or any consumer goods from a retailer that exploits its workers, fails to pay a fair price, engages in transfer mispricing, and so on. Of course, in a context where many consumer goods consist of multiple components, some of which may have been ethically sourced and some of which won't, this creates a huge practical challenge, as the example of cobalt from the Introduction indicates. Nevertheless, our responsibility is not to use that complexity as an excuse to do nothing, but as far as we are able to ensure that what we purchase reflects God's concern for the poor. As John Paul II indicates, if I fail to act as an ethical consumer out of laziness, indifference or pessimism, that still does not negate my moral culpability in participating in a structure of sin. Or as Ron Sider puts it, 'Persons sin by participating in evil systems when they understand, at least to some degree, that the system displeases God but fail to act responsibly to change things.'[23]

The unity between these two concepts of sin – sin as shalom-breaking and sin as relational breakdown – is evident when we remind ourselves, as Myers has said, that shalom simply means right relationships. He writes: 'Shalom means just relationships (living justly and experiencing justice), harmonious relationships and enjoyable relationships. Shalom means belonging to an authentic and nurturing community in which one can be one's true self and give one's self away without becoming poor.'[24]

In addition to this, however, we see the unity of this idea when we consider again the concept of the corporate *imago Dei*. As we noted in Part I, it is Jürgen Moltmann – drawing on the Cappadocian Fathers – who has developed this idea. So as Ezer Kang, discussing this in the context of HIV, puts it, 'the *imago Dei* is not a possession of a static human characteristic or trait – but rather God's "whole existence," which appears in and through right human relationships'.[25] As such, the *imago* teaches us that we are representatives of the God who instantiates perfect relationship, and as representatives, as those who image God on earth, corporately we are meant to exhibit perfect relationships on earth. Sin represents the negation of that image both in terms of the disruption of good relationships but also in terms of our failure to bring about the shalom that God's representatives are meant to exhibit. In the prayer of Jesus, we ask that his will be done, his kingdom come on earth as it is in heaven. His kingdom, his will, is precisely the shalom that followers of the King are meant to bring about. As Christopher Weeramanty points out:

The kingdom which we must seek to come is the kingdom of righteousness. That is the New Jerusalem that such conduct brings down to earth. The underlying 'thy kingdom come' interlock with those of 'thy will be done', and both interlock again with the vision enshrined in the words 'on earth as it is in heaven'.[26]

The whole of Weeramanty's book is devoted to unpacking the ethical implications of the Lord's Prayer in our current global context, and he shows how its ethical vision is not one that can be encapsulated by a set of commands, but rather, as I have argued, one that represents a call to just action in the context of an unjust world.

> In one sense, one may conceivably comply with the law of God by [mere adherence to a set of commands], but that falls far short of doing the will of God. The will of God extends much further. Beyond mere prohibitions, it is a clarion call to active service.[27]

In this context, he cites an Amnesty International advertisement which depicted images from the 1994 Rwandan genocide alongside the headline, 'Listen. Can you hear the silence?' Weeramantry points out that if we merely understand the phrase 'thy will be done' in passive terms – that is, in terms of us ensuring we do not get in the way of God's will being enacted – then we have missed the point. For there is also what he terms an active reading in which it is our duty, our responsibility, to bring about God's will, God's shalom if you like, on earth. He notes the words on the Amnesty International poster: 'Do you know what our deadliest enemy is? It's not the guns of vicious tyrants. It's the silence of good people . . . Do not be part of the killing silence.' And then he comments, 'A purely passive reading of the words "thy will be done" can lead to such a killing silence, not only in Burundi [sic] but elsewhere. The killing fields can spread.'[28]

Considering this reminds us of perhaps the most significant aspect of the doctrine of sin, and one that can be overlooked by both the political Left and political Right: it is the depth of our moral depravity. The book of Romans reminds us that 'all have sinned and fall short of the glory of God' (Rom. 3.23). Lying behind this statement, however, is a Jewish tradition that considers our (lack of) righteousness not merely as a failure to reach some moral standard, but actually in far worse terms than that. Isaiah 64.6 states, 'We have all become like one who is unclean, and all our righteous deeds are like a filthy cloth.' The phrase translated as 'filthy cloth' is, according to most commentators, that which was also used to describe menstrual rags, and so John Oswalt, commenting on this passage, writes that it was 'designed to convey the fundamental truth that sin is a not a matter of behavioural dysfunction, but an offense against the nature of creation'.[29] What we are seeing here is once again this motif that the reality of sin needs to be painted on a far wider canvas than mere obedience to commands.

If you think about it, there exists an incongruity at the heart of both the political Left and political Right in this regard. On the one hand, the political Right are fond of highlighting sin in terms of individual moral failings and less likely to point out the structural injustices that plague our political and economic systems. On this reading, then, sin exists in individuals not governments.[30] Yet, at the same time, in terms of their antipathy to big government, it would seem as if it was the government that was plagued by evil and that

individuals should be left alone in their freedom. The problem with this solution, as Walter Wink has pointed out, is that institutions also have beneficial effects. They 'socialize [people] to prevent them from doing harm to one another
and to think of the common good'.[31]

A similar incoherence affects the political Left. They have a tendency to
downplay individual moral culpability in favour of the structural, including
generational, injustices that have been experienced by the poor. For them,
people are good and it is institutions that have made them bad. In response,
one might expect them to embrace a small government agenda that allows
individuals to live with the freedom that their inherent goodness demands. Yet,
that is not what we find, and instead the far Left is characterized by a statism
that inhibits the freedom of the populace. And it is precisely because of this
tendency that the state must continually be held to account by the populace.

What all of this demonstrates is simply that sin is all-pervasive. It impacts
both individuals and the state, and each requires the other in order to hold
it in check. It is neither the case that people are evil and we need the state to
control their behaviour, nor is it the case that people are good, and so we need
no government-corralled morality. The truth is that precisely because 'all have
sinned', we need all aspects of society to hold one another to account. As Wink
sums this up, 'We are made evil by our institutions, yes; but our institutions
are also made evil by us.'[32] The reality is that the problem of sin is all-pervasive
from the individual heart to the systems enshrined by the United Nations and
the World Trade Organization, and all of it represents a breakdown in relationships and a failure to bring about the shalom that God envisages.

The significance of this broader canvas is that, contrary to Friedman, the
world is not in a just state.[33] There is a way of thinking about charity that
sees it as the remedy that is required for a few unlucky ones. The framework
here would be one in which it is thought that essentially the way the world is
structured is just, but due to the misfortune that will inevitably affect some we
need some kind of minimal safety net for those unfortunate ones.[34] By way of
contrast, a fuller appreciation of the reality of sin recognizes that we are in a
state where it is not just the case that individuals sin within a basic structure
that is righteous, but rather that the whole system we are in is one that is
unjust and unrighteous. As René Padilla argues, contra Friedman, 'Even for
an important segment of the population of the wealthiest country on earth,
the world is not flat, as Thomas L. Friedman claims, but quite uneven, and the
level playing field that he claims to exist is a myth.'[35] If that is the case – and
to deny it would be to diminish the reality of sin in our world – then charity
is no longer about helping those few unfortunates who did not quite make it.
Rather, a response of righteousness, while it might include charity, must go far
beyond mere handouts to challenge instead the very structures and systems in
which we live, recognizing that to uphold those structures is to culpably break
the shalom that God requires. In his survey of the biblical material concerning
justice, Donahue makes the same point, arguing that almsgiving within the
Scriptures is not so much viewed as an example of love, compassion or 'unself-
ish charity' towards the poor. Rather, it is framed as a work of justice, 'that is,
how one can be faithful to the Lord who has given the goods of the earth as

common possession of all and be faithful to others in the human community who have equal claim to these goods?'[36] In short, when we give to the poor we are not extending ourselves on their behalf. We are not 'going the extra mile'. Rather, we are merely undertaking some small aspect of what it means to live righteously, a full appreciation of which will also include addressing structural injustices.

Notes

1 S. Chalke and A. Mann, 2004, *The Lost Message of Jesus*, Grand Rapids: Zondervan, p. 67.

2 C. Plantinga, 2010, 'Sin: Not the Way It's Supposed to Be', Christ on Campus Initiative, p. 10. Available at: http://tgc-documents.s3.amazonaws.com /cci/Pantinga.pdf (accessed 24 July 2015).

3 D. Nelson, 2011, *Sin: A Guide for the Perplexed*, London: T & T Clark, 2011, p. 116.

4 H. Blocher, 2000, *Original Sin*, Westmont, IL: InterVarsity Press Academic, p. 30.

5 J. Calvin, *Institutes of the Christian Religion*, cited in Blocher, *Sin*, ch. 1.

6 Plantinga, 'Sin'.

7 Nelson, *Sin*, pp. 21ff.

8 A. H. Lewis, cited in H. Blocher, 1984, *In the Beginning*, Leicester: InterVarsity Press, p. 183.

9 J. Bimson, 2006, 'Reconsidering a "Cosmic Fall"', *Science and Christian Belief* 18:1, pp. 67–8.

10 For an alternative view regarding the capacity of animals to sin see D. Clough, 2012, *On Animals: Volume 1, Systematic Theology*, London: T & T Clark.

11 Nelson, *Sin*, p. 104.

12 Plantinga, 'Sin', pp. 2–3.

13 Plantinga, 'Sin', pp. 3–4.

14 B. Myers, 1999, *Walking with the Poor: Principles and Practices of Transformational Development*, Marynoll, NY: Orbis Books, p. 29.

15 Myers, *Walking*, p. 29. See also Walter Wink's trilogy for discussion of a similar theme, especially W. Wink, 1992, *Engaging the Powers*, Minneapolis, MN: Fortress Press.

16 Plantinga, 'Sin', p. 4.

17 Plantinga, 'Sin', p. 4.

18 G. Guttiérez, 2001, *A Theology of Liberation*, London: SCM Press, p. 174.

19 John Paul II, 1987, *Sollicitudo Rei Socialis*, n. 36.

20 John Paul II, 1984, *Reconciliatio et Paenitentia*, n. 16.

21 John Paul II, *Sollicitudo*, n. 43.

22 An example of this could be the limited voting rights of poorer nations in the World Trade Organization. This is a structural issue – who can vote and the relative power of national votes – but its impact is to disadvantage the poorer countries in the world.

23 R. Sider, 1997, *Rich Christians in an Age of Hunger*, London: Hodder & Stoughton, p. 115.

24 Myers, *Walking*, p. 51.

25 E. Kang, 2015, 'Human Immunodeficiency Virus (HIV) Stigma: Spoiled Social Identity and Jürgen Moltmann's Trinitarian Model of the *Imago Dei*', *International Journal of Public Theology* 9, p. 298. Kang has drawn up the implications of this corporate sense of the *imago Dei* for the Church's encounter with those with HIV. 'The divine imago also articulates a shared humanity that strives to narrow the divide between persons living with and without the virus. HIV is not simply a reality that lies beyond ecclesial margins – rather it is argued that the contemporary church or the body of Christ is inflicted with AIDS as well' (p. 297).

26 C. G. Weeramantry, 1998, *The Lord's Prayer: Bridge to a Better World*, Liguori: Liguori/Triumph, p. 215.

27 Weeramantry, *The Lord's Prayer*, p. 225.

28 Weeramantry, *The Lord's Prayer*, pp. 221–2. Weeramantry incorrectly attributes the photograph Amnesty International used to Burundi. The events depicted in the photograph took place in Kigali, Rwanda, in 1994.

29 J. Oswalt, 1998, *The Book of Isaiah Chapter 40–66*, Grand Rapids, MI: Eerdmans, p. 626.

30 See, for instance, J. Glas, 2015, 'The Gospel, Human Flourishing and the Foundation of Social Order', *The Southern Baptist Journal of Theology* 19:2, pp. 105–34.

31 Wink, *Engaging*, p. 10.

32 Wink, *Engaging*, p. 75.

33 T. Friedman, 2005, *The World is Flat: A Brief History of the Twenty-First Century*, New York: Farrar, Straus and Giroux.

34 This would seem to be the basic framework at play in W. Grudem and B. Asmus, 2013, *The Poverty of Nations: A Sustainable Solution*, Wheaton, IL: Crossway Books, and in A. Bradley and A. Lindsley (eds), 2014, *For the Least of These: A Biblical Answer to Poverty*, Grand Rapids, MI: Zondervan.

35 C. R. Padilla, 2014, 'The Globalization of Greed', *Journal of Latin American Theology* 9:2, p. 58.

36 J. Donahue, 2004, *Seek Justice that you May Live*, Mahwah, NJ: Paulist Press, p. 131.

5

Sin, taxes and debt – who owes whom?

We have been discussing the nature, depth and breadth of sin and concluded that sin is so far-reaching it encompasses a range of systemic issues that keep the poor, poor. One such example of this concerns the issue of taxation. Some evangelicals seem to view taxation as effectively the government taking what properly belongs to the individual or corporation. Angus Ritchie has described this in terms of governments taking a slice of a cake that individuals and corporations have produced. 'Often the debate about appropriate levels of taxation makes the mistaken assumption that business quite straightforwardly generates wealth, and governments then confiscate a certain proportion of that wealth.'[1]

However, as Ritchie argues, this is to fail to appreciate the way in which governments generate wealth alongside individuals and businesses. The primary way in which they do this is by providing the infrastructure that enables a business to flourish. They ensure that an educated, skilled and healthy workforce is available. They provide a transport and power infrastructure that is essential. They also provide the legal and security framework which provides, for instance, an investor with confidence that if they buy a particular piece of land or property it will not be arbitrarily seized at some point in the future. In addition to this, governments may well provide goods and services, which some individuals may not need or even consider immoral, but that does not alter the fact that in order for wealth to be created by individuals or businesses the framework provided by governments is essential. All of this means that when a government imposes levies on such business it is not taking that which is not its own, rather it is seeking payment for services already provided. Ritchie comments:

> The 'cake' of wealth is not in fact generated by business and partially consumed by the state. Rather, the state and the citizens are coproducers of that wealth in the first place, which already generates a *prima facie* entitlement to a 'slice' in order to continue to provide the environment and the public goods in which enterprise and commerce are possible.[2]

Indeed, it is interesting to note that some recent research has demonstrated that it is precisely the presence of a functioning and active tax infrastructure that is the difference between an aid recipient country growing economically and failing to grow. In other words, and no doubt to the chagrin of neo-conservatives, it is only by effectively collecting taxes that economic growth is possible.[3]

Of course, there is a legitimate debate about the particular level of tax that is levied by government, but the fundamental principle underlying taxation is one in which we (both individuals and corporations) owe the state money for goods and services from which we have already benefited and which we continue to enjoy. All of this means that if we fail to pay those taxes then arguably our moral offence is the equivalent of theft, for we have taken goods and services without paying for them.[4] It is interesting in this regard to note the particular terminology that the New Testament uses when it talks about our obligation to pay taxes:

> For the same reason you also pay taxes, for the authorities are God's servants, busy with this very thing. Pay to all what is due them – taxes to whom taxes are due, revenue to whom revenue is due, respect to whom respect is due, honour to whom honour is due. (Rom. 13.6–7)

The emphasis in this passage is on what is due, what is owed. The word used for 'due' is *opheilas* which has the same root as the word used in the Lord's Prayer for debts/sin: 'forgive us our debts/sins as we forgive our debtors/those who sin against us'. The particular focus of the word is on the obligation that exists due to the debt that is held. What is even more remarkable about this is the context in which it is said. This is not a situation when those to whom Paul was writing were governed by some democratic authority. Rather, he was writing to a mixed group of Jews and Roman citizens, some of whom would have had no rights vis-à-vis the Roman authorities. One of the more frequent arguments that is posited in defence of withholding taxes is that the government will not spend the money as wisely as we would. While that is quite possibly true today, it was even more the case in first-century Palestine and Rome where large proportions of tax would have been (mis)spent on military conquests in the further reaches of the empire. If ever there was a justification for withholding tax on the grounds of corrupt government, it existed at this time. Yet, that is not what Paul proclaims. Instead, he counsels his reader to obey the authorities and pay whatever is due.

This point is reinforced by Jesus in his response to the question of taxation. The question of context is again important.

> Taxation in Roman Palestine was extractive, that is, designed to exert elite control over agrarian production. In the society of early Roman Palestine, villagers preferred to conduct business along the lines of reciprocity; but since elites controlled taxation (land products), labour, and commerce, redistributive arrangements tended to prevail. Caesar's agents collected taxes and redistributed them to clients. The priests and the Jerusalem temple collected offerings and redistributed them. Redistribution exchanges were replicated throughout society. Their major impact was to remove most goods from the control and enjoyment of most people. The terms 'extraction', 'redistribution' and 'tribute' reflect the political nature of these distributive mechanisms. All of these terms emphasize that the benefits in ancient economy flowed 'upward' to the advantage of elites.[5]

In this context, Jesus is approached by a group of Herodians, who believed that taxes should be paid, and Pharisees, who had mixed views on the issue.

This was clearly, then, a live and practically relevant question – should we pay or not (Mark 12.13–17)? Nicholas Townsend has helpfully suggested that the literature provides three different interpretations of Jesus' answer: 'Give to the emperor the things that are the emperor's, and to God the things that are God's' (Mark 12.17). The first of these is a kind of two kingdoms balance between God and the emperor. There are two spheres of rule – one earthly and one divine – and we must render to each what is due.[6] The second interpretation is the reverse of this, that there is just one kingdom of which God is ruler, and the third is somewhat between the two. There do exist two jurisdictions, but that of Caesar is temporary and provisional. God is the ultimate ruler and Caesar is allowed his power for a time only because God permits it.[7] While the first and third of these readings would lead to the conclusion that the tax should be paid, the middle one does not.

Townsend concurs that Jesus' answer in effect means that the tax should be paid, but the most significant aspect of this passage, however, is one that Townsend chastises the commentaries for not drawing more attention to. It concerns the Greek words used in all three Synoptic Gospels by Jesus' accusers and by Jesus in response. In all three examples of this story, the Herodians and Pharisees ask whether it is lawful to give/pay (*dounai*) taxes to the emperor. In response, Jesus is very clear that they should give back (*apodote*) whatever is owed to Caesar and to God. As Reed comments, the verb used by the questioners means to give, 'whereas Jesus uses *apodote*, which carries the sense of "returning" or "restoring", as when Jesus returned the scroll to the attendant in the synagogue at Nazareth (Luke 4.20), or returned the boy with an unclean spirit to his father (Luke 9.42)'.[8] We see, then, here the same picture as we saw in Romans. Not only are we to pay taxes to those to whom they are due (irrespective of how corrupt the government is), but in doing so we are not being 'robbed' by those governments, rather we are paying back, returning what we already owe.

I have discussed this issue at length because it illustrates well the problem we have in recognizing the breadth and depth of sin. Returning to our two concepts earlier – if sin is relational breakdown expressed in culpable shalom-breaking – then anything that prevents God's shalom from being realized constitutes sin, and we are culpable for that sin to the extent that we knowingly participate in it. When a failure to pay tax deprives poor communities of money, then we are in a situation of shalom-breaking, and to the extent that we participate in that system we are also guilty of sin.

A similar argument can be made in regard to the debt that we in HICs owe to LICs. It might be considered odd to have put the issue in those terms, for the one thing that everyone knows about current development debates is that the poorer parts of the world are saddled with crippling debt that is owed to the wealthier parts of the world. According to the latest report from the Jubilee debt campaign, the problem of national debt is once again on the rise. Between 2008 and 2011, there was a modest drop in total international net debt, but since 2011, net debts have increased from $11.3 trillion to $13.8 trillion in 2014. They estimate that in 2015 this figure will rise to $14.7 trillion.[9] And, of course, the countries most at risk in this scenario are also those who are the poorest. The list of countries at high risk of a sovereign debt crisis are Bhutan, Cabo Verde, Dominica, Ethiopia, Ghana, Lao PDR, Mauritania, Mongolia, Mozambique, Samoa, Sao Tome and Principe, Senegal, Tanzania and Uganda.[10] We know that servicing external debt is crippling such countries, and in particular sub-Saharan Africa. In a ground-breaking report from 2014, a coalition of charity groups looked at the total financial flows both in and out of sub-Saharan Africa and showed that despite all the rhetoric about how aid is financing Africa, the reality is that sub-Saharan Africa makes a net loss of around $58 billion each year to the rest of the world.[11] While sub-Saharan Africa receives around $134 billion each year in official aid, government loans, remittances and foreign direct investment, it pays out around $192 billion over the same period. Of this $21 billion of this is in debt service payments, not much less than the $30 billion it receives in aid. Given all this, why am I suggesting that it is the rich world that is indebted to the poor?

The reason is because of the contribution we have made to this indebtedness by means of our colonial legacy, irresponsible lending, fostering illicit financial flows, as well as the debt we owe due to climate change. All of these represent ways in which the materially rich world has impoverished the poor, and as such have been guilty of shalom-breaking. Yet they are also ways in which we fail to acknowledge or recognize our sin.

Much has been written about the West's colonial past, but far too often it is simply seen as a dark period in our history that is of little direct relevance to today. This is particularly the case among theologians who are keen to maintain the current economic status quo. So, Grudem and Asmus write:

> It does not seem to us, however, that looking to the past and blaming colonialism does much of anything to solve the current problems, all of which have complex causes. The correct approach is to look forward and seek solutions.[12]

While at first sight, such statements sound plausible, I am not inclined to concur. A fuller appreciation of our colonial legacy helps us recognize the ways in which we *owe* the poorer parts of the world, and therefore provides a moral justification for easing the debt burden on those countries. It is as if Grudem and Asmus encounter a man whose house has been burnt to the ground by someone else and then say to him, 'It does not seem to us, however, that looking to the past and blaming the arsonist does much of anything to solve the current problems, all of which have complex causes. The correct approach is to look forward and seek solutions.' In one sense they are right. Blaming the arsonist does not get the house rebuilt. However, if the arsonist happens also to be someone to whom the house-owner owes money, then, at the very least, justice demands that such debt is forgiven, not least because it will enable the house-owner to finds the funds to rebuild. Indeed, more than that it is arguable that the arsonist should also put in several hours of free labour to help the house-owner rebuild. Perhaps even more significant, however, is the fact that repentance is the first step to reconciliation. As I will show, the West has done untold damage to many poorer parts of the world, and simply for our own collective conscience we need to acknowledge that harm and as appropriate seek to undo it. This is surely what it means to pursue God's shalom.

James Cypher, a development economist, has written what is one of the standard textbooks on development economics. In the chapters on colonialism, he describes at least five aspects of the colonial era for which the West should be ashamed and which have contributed both to Western wealth today and the impoverishment of many former colonies.

The first of these is simply the raw demographic changes that colonialism brought with it. He cites research, for instance, that suggests the population of Latin America shrank from 70 to 90 million in 1540 to 3.5 million in 1690.[13] Similarly, in Africa, almost 50 million people either died due to activities associated with the slave trade or were transported as slaves out of Africa. As a proportion of world population, Africa reduced from 18 per cent to just 8 per cent in the 200 years prior to 1850.[14] Such death and destruction inevitably had economic consequences as the smaller residual populations were more easily exploited and less able to develop their own nations economically.

Second, colonialism was often very effective in creating internal elites within countries. The frequent policy of a number of colonial powers was to separate off a small section of the local community who in return for power and wealth would become the puppets of the colonial masters. Such a process not only fostered a new authoritarianism and social divisions within these countries, but it can also be argued that it led to the culture of corruption and dictatorships that has plagued a number of former colonies. Cypher writes: 'A new economic role for African chieftains was created, that of facilitator and regional beneficiary of the slave trade. Authoritarianism was strengthened and resistance to the status quo made more difficult.'[15]

Third, and perhaps most importantly in terms of its long-term consequences, they changed the terms of trade for many of these countries. Not far from where I am writing this is Calver Mill in Derbyshire, UK. The mill opened in 1778 but reached its zenith in the 1830s when it processed cotton from India, producing textiles for both the UK market and for export back to India. This is no accident for during the nineteenth century the British government had used its military power in India to pursue a deliberate policy intent on stifling India's textile industry at the expense of the incipient British industry. During the eighteenth century, India had a thriving textile industry that wove locally grown cotton and exported it across the globe. At the same time, Britain was in the throes of the Industrial Revolution[16] and was keen to protect its developing textile industry. In order to do this, the British government imposed a tariff of 70–80 per cent on imported Indian textiles and at the same time forcibly ensured that the Indian market was open to receive British textiles at minimal cost. In combination with the increased mechanization of British industry, the impact of this was that Indian cotton growers increasingly sold their raw cotton for export while the Indian textile industry collapsed.[17] This is a pattern that has been repeated across a number of colonies, such that the nature of international trade today is one in which poorer countries export raw, unprocessed goods to wealthier countries who process the goods and then resell them on the world market. Perhaps that would not matter if the profit on raw goods was as much as it is on manufactured ones, but that is not the case. One of the injustices of the current international trade scene is that the rules of the market are set by the wealthier nations in such a way that their exports (largely manufactured goods) receive far more preferential terms than the exports (largely raw goods) of poorer nations.[18] It would also matter less if this was a pattern that the colonies had chosen for themselves, but as the Indian textile industry illustrates, this is a pattern of trade that more often than not was forced upon the former colonies, leaving a legacy that still impacts them today.

John Shao's comments from 2001 remain pertinent:

> The truth is that the global market is dominated and controlled by, and operates in the interests of, the industrial countries of the North . . . international markets are distorted by the operation of multinational corporations, government tariffs, and other restrictive practices. Is it really fair trade when pricing of commodities from Africa and the rest of the developing world is determined in the markets and/or administrations of the North Atlantic countries, while poor African countries are not involved in setting the prices for industrial goods sold to them? Can such practices in international trading be anything but unjust?[19]

The fourth aspect of the colonial legacy is that the colonizing powers in effect simply stole money from the colonized nations. This is most obvious in the Spanish acquisition of gold in Peru and Mexico, but it was also done more subtly by the Northern European powers. One example cited by Cypher is the following:

> In the 1700s, coffee was a major export crop [of Indonesia]. The Dutch guaranteed a net drain of income from their colony by forcing delivery of coffee from native cultivators and then 'paying' the cultivators for only a fraction of the total. One practice was to receive delivery of 240lb of coffee but pay the cultivator for only 14lb. The remainder the Dutch simply appropriated.[20]

Britain pursued a similar path in India, but what has only recently been shown is that these kinds of practices not only impoverished the colonies but were also one of the main determinants of colonial wealth. So for instance, in 1821, £15.2 million (5.27 per cent of England's GDP) was directly transferred from India and the West Indies to the UK. Cypher writes: 'The important conclusion to be drawn is that contemporary scholars, using detailed quantitative analysis, conclusively find that the critical years of Britain's economic ascendancy are strongly and causally linked to forced colonial resource extractions, particularly in India.'[21] In short, at least part of the reason Britain is wealthy today is because we stole from India during the eighteenth and nineteenth centuries.

Finally, and inevitably, we cannot ignore the slave trade. Not only were millions killed or forcibly removed as part of this trade, but the practice is one that directly led to the wealth enjoyed by many in the West today. It is estimated for instance that British profits from the slave trade during the eighteenth century amassed to around £50 million and that profits from the plantations themselves were around £200 to £300 million.[22] Cypher writes:

> There can be no doubt that a portion of these funds entered the British banking system, thereby adding to liquidity, driving down interest rates, and releasing a flow of investment funds which could be tapped by the early British industrialists for their industrialization projects.[23]

To put it in more prosaic terms, the Calver Mill mentioned earlier is now a six-storey building of high-class flats for the middle class of the UK Peak District. Arguably, their comfort today is at least in part the result of the unpaid-for efforts of Indian cotton farmers from two hundred years ago.

There is a scene in the US TV series *The West Wing* in which a political adviser (Josh Lyman) to the President is discussing the issue of slavery reparations with a putative Assistant Attorney General nominee (Jeff Breckenridge):

Jeff   Dr Harold Washington, who's chief economist at the Manchester Institute, calculated the number of slaves held, multiplied it by the number of hours worked, multiplied that by the market value of manual labour and came up with a very conservative figure.

Josh   What is it?

Jeff   1.7 trillion dollars.

Josh   Okay. Listen, this is probably a better discussion to have in the abstract, don't you think?

Jeff   No.

Josh   What do you mean?

Jeff   I mean someone owes me and my friends 1.7 trillion dollars.

. . .

Josh   Jeff, the committee is going to be looking for a certain degree of practicality. We don't have 1.7 trillion dollars. To raise 1.7 trillion dollars, we would have to sell Texas and the US Navy.

Jeff   I understand the predicament and I'm willing to give you a break. We'll take our money in tax deductions and scholarship funds, how 'bout that?

Josh   How about you take it in affirmative action and empowerment zones and civil rights acts?

Jeff   Three things which we wouldn't have needed in the first place.

Josh   [stands, getting ticked] You know, Jeff . . . I'd love to give you the money, I really would. But I'm a little short of cash right now. It seems the SS officer forgot to give my grandfather his wallet back when he let him out of Birkenau.

Jeff   Well, your beef's with the Germans.[24]

I have included this exchange because it illustrates a problem whenever we try to draw on history to make a case about the present. Josh tries to dismiss Jeff's claim by pointing out that atrocities have been committed by all sides in the past, and implicitly he raises the question of how far back we need to go. Do the Italians owe the rest of the world something for Roman imperialism? Do the Greeks before them? Do the Ottomans? Yet, what is missing in Josh's analysis is what development economists call 'path dependency'. On moral (and therefore theological) grounds, we can argue that the colonial era has much to answer for, but even on purely economic grounds it matters because it set in train a sequence of events that are part of the economic problem today.

> The term 'path dependence' has been used to describe the important role which historical events and historically informed institutions have in determining the future range of possibilities for a nation. Once institutions have been formed, they tend to lock in a certain evolutionary path for the nation.[25]

As we have seen, by means of depopulating their countries, creating internal elites, changing the terms of trade, stealing money and assets, and the slave trade, the West has become rich while many former colonies have remained poor. This argument has recently received some significant empirical support. Cypher cites a study by Shahid Alam, which explored the economic growth rates of former colonies following independence with those countries that had not been colonized in the same way or to the same degree. As Cypher puts it, 'The results, then, tend to confirm that colonialism matters in a negative way . . . after formal independence the institutions and path dependence established by colonialism continued to exert an influence which constrained growth.'[26] My point is that it is hard to argue that in any substantial fashion the Greek, Roman or Ottoman empires have led to impoverishment in the West today; it is also hard to argue (to draw on *The West Wing* example) that the Holocaust has impoverished the West today.[27] However, as I have argued, it is clear that a number of former colonial nations are poorer today than they would have been had it not been for our activities during the colonial period. This is the argument of path dependence.

One final point is worth noting here. Some conservative evangelicals are very fond of telling former colonies that the reason they are poor now is because they have not pursued the same free trade principles that we in the West have done. Specifically, they tell Christian leaders in those countries to 'encourage their own nations to change any import tariffs' and 'to stop the agricultural price support programs'.[28] What makes these proposals particularly galling is that, as we have seen, the West did not grow its wealth by means of free trade. Whether in relation to Indian textiles or Egyptian industrialization,[29] the West maintained its economic power precisely by opposing free trade principles and protecting its own infant industries. The fact that some African countries may wish to do the same today is surely up to them.

This extensive discussion of colonialism has been important primarily because of the West's ongoing failure to acknowledge how its past crimes continue to have an impact today. Of course, why any particular country is poor is a highly complex subject, but at least part of the reason is because of the enduring legacy of what we in the West have done. Such behaviour constitutes shalom-breaking, and the only theologically responsible response to it is one of repentance.

In addition to the colonial legacy, we also need to explore how many of the poorer countries became indebted in the first place. The short answer to this is that the debt that was incurred was one that was aggressively encouraged by wealthier nations. The problem began in the 1970s when OPEC countries raised the price of crude oil by 500 per cent.[30] There were two consequences to this: one was that oil-dependent nations (which essentially meant all countries) needed to find extra funds to pay for the higher costs; the other was that the oil-producing nations found themselves in a position of excess liquidity. Their solution to this was to deposit the funds in the international banking system. They in turn needed to find a market for these funds in order to finance the interest on the deposits, and the obvious market was the least developed countries who required extra funds to pay for the more expensive oil.[31] This whole charade was termed 'petrodollar cycling', but the ones who suffered most as a result were the poorer countries who, according to Cypher, 'became the recipients of aggressive efforts' to receive these loans. So, for instance, the total external debt of Brazil, Kenya and Pakistan was respectively 3.3, 0.2 and 3.1 billion dollars in 1970. By 2000, this had risen to 238, 7.5 and 32.1 billion dollars respectively – an average increase of nearly 4,000 per cent.[32] The obvious response to this is to say that the poorer countries were not forced to take these loans. However, that is like saying a starving man is not forced to sell his house to buy a loaf of bread. It is his free choice. The problem the poorer countries faced was the complete collapse of their own infant industrialization if they did not manage to continue to import oil, albeit at exorbitant prices. In that sense, they had no real choice – particularly when the international banking system was so forceful in trying to get them to receive the funds.

This initial phase of petrodollar cycling was then exacerbated by the structural adjustment policies of the IMF during the 1980s and 1990s. The assumption of the IMF was that the primary reason poorer countries remained poor was because of a range of structural macroeconomic issues related to how the country organized its financial sector. In response, the IMF offered loans at favourable rates consequent upon the countries adopting a range of policies that the IMF dictated to these countries. In particular, countries were expected to devalue their currency, control the money supply, reduce government spending and reduce real wages. In current debates, this whole package would be called an austerity package. Cypher cites a large study conducted between 1982 and 2009 which explored the impact of such packages on 86 low- and middle-income countries. The results were damning: 'In the 1982–2009 period (1) poverty increased, (2) the severity of poverty rose, and (3) the distribution of income became more unequal during the period of an IMF stabilization program.'[33]

Supporters of the IMF say that the reason the programmes were not successful is because countries did not follow IMF advice to the letter, and this was certainly true. But the usual reason is because the countries were seeking to mitigate what they perceived to be the disastrous consequences of the IMF approach. Nevertheless, the fact remains that over a 30–40-year period, high-income countries, either via the Bretton Woods institutions or via the international banking system, have loaned significant amounts of capital to poorer countries in a way that has either exploited their weaknesses or imposed poverty-inducing conditionalities. Our collective policy on loans has not been judicious and has not had the welfare of the poor as its primary concern.

A further example of the way in which we owe the poorer countries of the world concerns the international tax system. In 2015, the United Nations held its third international conference on 'Financing for Development'. Prior to the conference, a number of stakeholder countries had been calling for significant changes to the way in which the current tax system operates. The fundamental problem is that under the current system, it is extremely easy for large multinational corporations to avoid paying tax in low-income countries – where the tax rate may be higher – and instead pay tax in low-tax countries, including offshore havens where the tax rate might be zero. Such a system would be fair if what we were talking about was economic activity that had taken place in these low-tax countries, but that is not the situation. Rather, what is taking place is that even when the relevant economic activity has taken place in a low-income country – for instance Zambia – the tax on that activity is paid, for instance, in Switzerland. This is called 'transfer mispricing' and is precisely what is happening with the copper-mining industry in Zambia.[34] While this activity is largely legal, it remains thoroughly immoral, for it is cheating poor countries out of the tax that they and their citizens are due. In response to this, a global coalition of tax experts and other stakeholders had issued a unanimous report to the United Nations conference on Finance for Development, arguing for major reform of the current corporation tax system. In the words of a commission member, Nobel prize-winning economist and former chief economist of the World Bank, Joseph Stiglitz:

> We unanimously agreed that the current system is broken, and that minor tweaks will not fix it. We proposed an alternative – similar to the way corporations are taxed within the US, with profits allocated to each state on the basis of the economic activity occurring within state borders.[35]

Such a proposal seems fair, modest and reasonable. Yet, under pressure from the USA in particular, the UN conference rejected these proposals and did not include them in any form in the final communiqué.[36]

According to the *Honest Accounts* report, sub-Saharan Africa loses $35.3 billion per year in tax-evasion and tax-avoidance manoeuvres like these.[37] A system which allows corporations to pay tax not in the country where the economic activity took place but where the corporation can get the lowest tax rate is clearly prejudicial to the economic welfare of the original country. When we consider that the countries in question are those that are the poorest, then the moral imperative to challenge this system is even greater.

One final way in which HICs owe LICs is in respect of climate change. Three facts are, it would seem, irrefutable:

1 Due to industrialization in the West, greenhouse gases are increasing.
2 Average global temperatures are rising.
3 The rise in global temperature is very likely due to the increase in greenhouse gas.

Hence, humans – and in particular the West – are responsible for global warming. What is more contentious is whether this average rise in global temperatures will cause significant harm or not. However, even in that respect there is very much now a scientific consensus that due to the rise in temperatures, many millions of poor people will die. Indeed, *The Lancet*, Britain's premier medical journal, calls it 'the biggest global health threat of the 21st century'.[38] In the most recent Intergovernmental Panel on Climate Change (IPCC) report, the committee concluded:

> People who are socially, economically, culturally, politically, institutionally, or otherwise marginalized are especially vulnerable to climate change . . . Impacts from recent climate-related extremes, such as heat waves, droughts, floods, cyclones, and wildfires reveal significant vulnerability.[39]

As already noted, this problem is largely one that has been created by the West. While of course the BRIC (Brazil, Russia, India, China) countries are now increasing their production of greenhouse gases, the historical burden of greenhouse gas production has been the preserve of the early industrializing nations. Yet, the effects of climate change are going to disproportionately affect the poor. According to one report, Africa loses each year $36.6 billion in climate change adaptation. They point out that sub-Saharan Africa is responsible for just 4 per cent of climate change emissions, yet in 2010 there were 400,000 additional deaths globally due to climate change, the majority affecting African countries.[40] The reasons for such deaths are heatwaves, crop failures, diarrhoeal diseases (due to inadequate potable water) and increases in vector-borne diseases. As Kirk Smith has commented, 'The rich will find their world to be more expensive, inconvenient, uncomfortable, disrupted and colourless; in general, more unpleasant and unpredictable, perhaps greatly so. The poor will die.'[41]

In order to mitigate these effects, sub-Saharan Africa is going to need to spend billions to adapt and prevent further climate-related disasters. Such adaptations include:

> better drainage, irrigation, and sanitation systems to manage increasingly uncertain water supplies; and more disaster-resilient buildings and transport systems. The restoration of the natural infrastructure . . . for example,

rehabilitating water sources or replanting forests to provide flood breaks. Improved systems of food and water storage will be necessary to safeguard against droughts, crop failures, and extreme weather events. New, sustainable livelihoods may also be needed in areas where the changing climate means that traditional forms of agriculture, fishing, or pastoralism can no longer support local communities. Early warning systems and resources for disaster relief are also essential.[42]

The cost of all this will run into tens of billions of dollars per year, and yet the reason this is required is not because of the behaviour of African countries, but because of the behaviour of the industrialized nations which are responsible for over 90 per cent of greenhouse gas emissions to date.

Putting together climate change adaptations and debt repayments as well as illicit financial flows and other factors it has been estimated that sub-Saharan Africa suffers a net loss of around $58 billion each year.[43] This puts in stark perspective the issue of debt repayments. Economists in HICs are fond of pointing out the moral hazard involved in wiping out the debts of poorer countries. All that will happen, it is argued, is that we will encourage them to borrow irresponsibly again. But what is noteworthy in this argument is that such moral hazard did not seem to operate in the same way in the 2008/09 banking crisis. At that time, banks in the UK for instance were bailed out to the tune of $500 billion and yet few of the same economists worried that the banks would behave irresponsibly again.

I have described our colonial legacy, our irresponsible lending, the sequelae of climate change and the way in which the West supports an international finance system that deprives LICs of billions of dollars, in order to make the point that although on paper many poorer countries owe the West significant sums of money, there is a clear moral case that can be made that our debts to them are just as great, if not greater. Ilo has written, 'The world today owes Africa a debt in justice more than Africa owes a debt in capital.'[44] Yet, as I have hopefully shown, the reality is that even in respect of capital, the greater debtor is the West. Such a realization reframes how we consider the issue of charity. Sometimes, we can be very proud of what we do in giving to LICs, but I wonder if Cynthia Moe-Lobeda actually speaks the truth when she says, 'When I donate money to an agency working in Mozambique, dare I consider a gift what is frankly "stolen goods"?'[45]

Notes

1 A. Ritchie, 2004, 'Tax and Government', in *Tax for the Common Good: A Study of Tax and Morality*, Christian Aid, p. 25.

2 Ritchie, 'Tax and Government', p. 26.

3 M. Prasad and A. Nickow, 2016, 'Mechanisms of the "Aid Curse": Lessons from South Korea and Pakistan', *The Journal of Development Studies*, May.

4 This of course contrasts with those who argue that governments imposing taxes constitutes theft. Cf. M. Rothbard, 1998, *The Ethics of Liberty*, New York: New York University Press.

5 K. C. Hanson and D. Oakman, 1998, *Palestine in the Time of Jesus: Social Structures and Social Conflicts*, Minneapolis, MN: Fortress Press, p. 116.

6 N. Townsend, 2014, 'Surveillance and Seeing: A New Way of Reading Mark 12:17, "Give back to Caesar . . ."', *Studies in Christian Ethics* 27:1, p. 80.

7 Townsend, 'Surveillance', p. 80.

8 E. Reed, 2014, 'Tax and International Justice', in *Tax for the Common Good*, Christian Aid, p. 12.

9 'The New Debt Trap', 2015, *Jubilee Debt Campaign*, July, p. 3. Available at: http://jubileedebt.org.uk/wp-content/uploads/2015/07/The-new-debt-trap-report.pdf. See also R. Culpeper and N. Kappagoda, 2016, 'The New Face of Developing Country Debt', *Third World Quarterly* 37:6, pp. 951–74.

10 'The New Debt Trap', p. 13.

11 *Honest Accounts: The True Story of Africa's Billion Dollar Losses*, July 2014, Health Poverty Action *et al.* Available at: http://jubileedebt.org.uk/wp-content/uploads/2014/07/Honest-Accounts_Final-Version.pdf.

12 W. Grudem and B. Asmus, 2013, *The Poverty of Nations: A Sustainable Solution*, Wheaton, IL: Crossway Books, p. 89.

13 J. Cypher, 2014, *The Process of Economic Development*, 4th edn, Oxford: Routledge, p. 86.

14 Cypher, *The Process*, p. 87.

15 Cypher, *The Process*, p. 87. Interestingly, the same policy was pursued by the British in India where they created a number of Maharajas for precisely this purpose. See also P. Vallely, 1990, *Bad Samaritans*, London: Hodder & Stoughton, pp. 95ff.

16 The spinning jenny, for instance, was invented in 1764 by James Hargreaves.

17 Cypher, *The Process*, p. 97.

18 J. Stiglitz and A. Charlton, 2007, *Fair Trade for All*, Oxford: Oxford University Press.

19 J. Shao, 2001, 'Alleviating Poverty in Africa', in D. Belshaw, R. Calderisi and C. Sugden (eds), *Faith in Development*, Oxford: Regnum Books, p. 23. For more on contemporary imbalances in trade, see R. Mshana, 2013, *The European Union, the United States and China in Africa: The Development Dialogue*, Geneva: World Council of Churches.

20 Cypher, *The Process*, p. 94.

21 Cypher, *The Process*, p. 95.

22 Cypher, *The Process*, p. 92.

23 Cypher, *The Process*, p. 93.

24 'Six Meetings Before Lunch', 2000, dir. C. Johnson, *The West Wing*, Season 1, ep. 18.

25 Cypher, *The Process*, p. 87.

26 Cypher, *The Process*, pp. 101–2. Cf. M. S. Alam, 2000, *Poverty from the Wealth of Nations*, London: Macmillan.

27 This is not to deny that clearly many individual families are impoverished today partly as a result of losing assets during the Holocaust. My point is that no particular nation or even region has been so impoverished.

28 Grudem and Asmus, *Poverty of Nations*, p. 90.

29 Between 1820 and 1840, Muhammed Ali pursued a path of industrialization for Egyptian cotton. In response, the British fought a war against him and in the

process de-industrialized the country, forcing it to become a typical exporter of raw cotton. Cypher, *The Process*, pp. 98–9.

30 Cypher, *The Process*, p. 614.

31 Cypher, *The Process*, p. 616.

32 Cypher, *The Process*, p. 618.

33 Cypher, *The Process*, p. 662.

34 Methodist Tax Justice Network, *Tax Justice in Zambia*. Available at: http://methodisttaxjusticenetwork.nationbuilder.com/zambia (accessed 14 October 2015).

35 J. Stiglitz, 2015, 'America is On the Wrong Side of History', *Guardian*, 6 August. Available at: www.theguardian.com/business/2015/aug/06/joseph-stiglitz-america-wrong-side-of-history (accessed 26 August).

36 'Addis Ababa Action Agenda of the Third International Conference on Financing for Development', 2015, United Nations, New York. Available at: www.un.org/esa/ffd/wp-content/uploads/2015/08/AAAA_Outcome.pdf (accessed 26 August 2015).

37 *Honest Accounts*, p. 12.

38 A. Costello *et al.*, 2009, 'Managing the Health Effects of Climate Change', *The Lancet* 373, p. 1693.

39 'IPCC, 2014: Summary for Policymakers', 2014, in C. B. Field *et al.* (eds), *Climate Change 2014: Impacts, Adaptation, and Vulnerability. Part A: Global and Sectoral Aspects. Contribution of Working Group II to the Fifth Assessment Report of the Intergovernmental Panel on Climate Change*, Cambridge: Cambridge University Press, pp. 1–32.

40 *Honest Accounts*, p. 24.

41 K. Smith, 2008, 'Symposium Introduction. Mitigating, Adapting, and Suffering: How Much of Each?', *Annual Review of Public Health* 29, pp. 11–25.

42 *Honest Accounts*, p. 25.

43 *Honest Accounts*.

44 S. Ilo, 2014, *The Church and Development in Africa*, Eugene, OR: Pickwick Publications, p. 183.

45 C. Moe-Lobeda, 2013, *Resisting Structural Evil*, Minneapolis, MN: Fortress Press, p. 92.

6

Structural sin – are we really guilty?

We have been discussing the nature, depth and breadth of sin and come to the realization that who owes whom is not always as clear-cut as might at first seem to be the case. In order now to explore this issue in more depth we need to deal more clearly with the question of structural sin and individual culpability. As already noted, the concept of structural sin is one that the Catholic Church in particular has bequeathed to us, but within it two distinct conceptions are at play. The first of these, advocated largely by the liberation theologians, is that sin exists within structures of society, and we are both individually and collectively responsible (in some sense) for those structures. The contrasting view is that provided by the Catholic encyclicals (at least prior to Pope Francis) that when we talk of structural sin we are, in the end, talking about the actions and attitudes of individuals in supporting structures of oppression. The Jesuit theologian John Donahue puts this in terms of structural sin being in 'an analogous or extended' relationship to individual, personal sin.[1] It is worth noting that though at first glance it might seem as if Schleiermacher's concept of original sin is useful here in that he defines original sin in terms of its social dimensions, his concept does not particularly help our understanding. This is because Schleiermacher is equally clear that original sin does not confer any guilt, whereas *both* the pre-Francis Catholic social teaching and the liberationists do ascribe guilt to our participation in structural sin.[2]

A helpful way through this morass has been provided by Kenneth Himes in a paper written some 30 years ago.[3] Himes discusses three related terms. The first of these is responsibility. He distinguishes between four different senses of the word, but for our purposes only two of them are particularly relevant. The first of these is responsibility in the sense of causal responsibility. Event X is responsible for outcome Y. In this sense, no moral blameworthiness or culpability is ascribed. It is merely a description of how one thing has been caused by another. We can, for instance, state that the tsunami caused someone's death, without implying in any sense that the tsunami itself is guilty of some moral failure. The second sense of responsibility, however, is about moral blameworthiness, or culpability. This is when we are responsible not just in a causal sense but also in the sense that we hold guilt because of the outcomes of our actions. The murderer is responsible for killing the innocent victim. Himes suggests that if we are talking about responsibility in this sense then we should always refer to it as culpability or 'moral responsibility'.[4]

The second term he clarifies is that of liability. Once again, he points out that it is possible for one to be liable for something without any sense of moral blameworthiness. The example he gives is of an insurance policy which states that someone is liable to pay for a proportion of damages whether or not they are responsible (either causally or morally) for them. In such a setting someone may be liable for the cost of damages without being either responsible or culpable for those damages.[5]

The third term is that of culpability and, as we have indicated, equates to moral responsibility. It is when we can rightly be ascribed blame for some outcomes and are guilty in respect of that blameworthiness.

The question Himes then asks is in respect of structural sins, what he terms social sins: in what sense are we guilty? Are we responsible, liable, culpable – or all three? His response is to point out that in differing circumstances any or all of the three may apply, even when the 'sin' committed is the sin of a collective. Consider the example of historical slavery. We are not causally responsible – we were not the ones kidnapping and chaining the slaves; nor are we culpable – we have not personally participated in any morally blameworthy behaviour in respect of the slaves who are now many generations dead. But, as I have already indicated, we could certainly argue that we are liable for the injustice that was committed by our forebears. The reason we bear that liability is simply that we enjoy the fruits of that slavery. The houses we live in, the infrastructure we enjoy, the wealth of our nations is, in part, built upon the backs of former slaves. For that reason, we are liable – for at least some of those costs – even if we are not responsible or culpable.

In the same way, in respect of historic climate emissions, we are again liable, but neither responsible nor culpable. It was not our decision to burn millions of tons of coal in changing our countries from pastoralists to a fully industrialized nation, but we once again reap the benefits of that industrialization and as such we are liable. An example of this principle at work is evident in the Old Testament laws:

> If someone's ox hurts the ox of another, so that it dies, then they shall sell the live ox and divide the price of it; and the dead animal they shall also divide. But if it was known that the ox was accustomed to gore in the past, and its owner has not restrained it, the owner shall restore ox for ox, but keep the dead animal. (Exod. 21.35–36)

In the first scenario, an ox that is not known to be violent kills another ox. Given that it was unknown, the owner of the ox is clearly neither responsible nor culpable for the death of the neighbour's ox. Yet despite this the owner is liable to some extent, which is why the assets of both are divided equally between the two. If the Old Testament had assumed that liability only worked in tandem with culpability, then the owner of the live ox would have retained his live ox and it would simply have been hard luck that the owner of the dead ox had had his asset base reduced (I am assuming that a live ox is worth more than a dead ox). But that is not what happens. Instead, the asset base of both owners is reduced, thereby demonstrating that the owner of the violent ox bears liability even though he bears no responsibility or culpability. This is confirmed in the second narrative, where the owner of the violent ox bears both culpability – he knew the ox was violent – and liability. For, in this scenario, he does not just end up with the value of half a live ox plus half a dead ox, but instead the significantly less sum of one dead ox. His liability has increased in proportion to his culpability. The significant point, however, is that even when he bears no culpability there is still some liability that is owed.

We have established that we can be liable without being culpable, but if that is the case then in what sense might we be involved in structural (or social) sin? Again, Himes is useful here for he points out that sin – at least personal sin – does not reside in our liability as such, but it does lie in our failure to respond adequately to that sin. Having pointed out that we should challenge structural sin, he suggests that to do so does not necessarily mean that those who inhabit those structures are engaged in what he terms 'formal sin', which would be the 'intentional creation and preservation of structures that oppress'. Having said that, though, he then makes this telling point: 'Only after a person comes to see the material sinfulness of a societal practice and *still does nothing to eradicate* the social sin, is the threshold of formal sin approached' (Emphasis mine).[6]

To give a prosaic example, if our car is crashed into while stationary, we are not responsible for the damages or culpable for them, but we may remain liable for any excess that is payable. However, if we fail to pay those damages, then at that point we become responsible and culpable and remain liable. In short, failure to pay for damages for which we are liable constitutes sin. In the same respect, we are not responsible or culpable for our colonial legacy, but if we deliberately choose to do nothing about those historic injustices – if we continue, for instance, to demand debt repayments from countries to whom we owe so much – then at that point we are not facing up to our own liabilities and as such are engaged in sin, personal sin expressed in a structural manifestation. As Ron Sider has stated, 'If we are members of a privileged group that profits from structural evil, and if we have at least some understanding of the evil yet fail to do what God wants us to do to change things, we stand guilty before God.'[7] Perhaps even more challenging are these words from the Fathers of the Church:

> This also is theft, not to share one's possessions. Perhaps this statement seems surprising to you, but do not be surprised. . . . I beg you remember this without fail, that not to share our own wealth with the poor is theft from the poor and deprivation of their means of life; we do not possess our own wealth but theirs. (John Chrysostom)

> Will not one be called a thief who steals the garment of one already clothed, and is one deserving of any other title who will not clothe the naked if he is able to do so? That bread which you keep belongs to the hungry; that coat which you preserve in your wardrobe, to the naked; those shoes which are rotting in your possession, to the shoeless: that gold which you have hidden in the ground, to the needy. Wherefore, as often as you were able to help others, and refused, so often you do them wrong. (Basil of Caesarea)[8]

Of course, the economic counter-argument to what Basil and Chrysostom have stated is that if anything I produce beyond mere subsistence is legitimately the property of another, then where is my incentive to produce more? Such an argument has cogency if one assumes the reality of *homo economicus,* namely that each one of us is primarily motivated by the economic gain we can accrue to ourselves. However, why should we make such an assumption? Moreover, the problem we face is that because *homo economicus* is assumed, markets are constructed in such a way as to foster the development of such thinking. What Basil and Chrysostom are proposing is an economic system in which self-accrual does not become the marker of human flourishing, but rather something else. To create a market in which the kind of behaviour that is encouraged is to imagine a wholly different economic world. The challenge before us is that so often we are blind to such possibilities. Chris Wright has pointed out how the predominant concern of the Old Testament prophets was simply that people '*saw what was going on*' in relation to the poor.[9] He continues: 'They were the mouthpiece of the God who sees . . . A major part of the problem is that poverty becomes invisible and the poor inaudible. But not to the God of Israel. "I have been watching! declares the Lord" (Jer. 7.11).'[10]

This motif is also prevalent in the teachings of Jesus. In many of the gospel stories, the issue we are presented with concerns someone who is blind to the purposes of God and in particular blind to their own sin. This is especially evident in Jesus' repeated condemnation of the Pharisees:

Let them alone; they are *blind* guides of the *blind.* And if one *blind* person guides another, both will fall into a pit. (Matt. 15.14)

Woe to you, *blind* guides, who say, 'Whoever swears by the sanctuary is bound by nothing, but whoever swears by the gold of the sanctuary is bound by the oath.' (Matt. 23.16)

You *blind* guides! You strain out a gnat but swallow a camel! (Matt. 23.24)

You *blind* Pharisee! First clean the inside of the cup, so that the outside also may become clean. (Matt. 23.26)

In saying all this, Jesus is simply repeating a trope that was present in the Old Testament also. 'Israel's sentinels are blind, they are all without knowledge; they are all silent dogs that cannot bark; dreaming, lying down, loving to slumber' (Isa. 56.10). It is my contention that such blindness is the most significant aspect of our collective sin today. Many sins are obvious and are frequently commented upon both by the media and the Church, but the more fundamental problem today is the sins – both personal and corporate – to which we are blind.

Speaking of the UK Methodist Church today, Michael Tapper recently wrote: 'Regrettably, Methodists have historically participated in social sin – for example, injustices related to slavery, apartheid, and missionary activity associated with colonialism. Undoubtedly, Methodists today continue to be blind to their participation in other unjust structures and institutions.'[11] In saying this, Tapper draws on Gregory Baum's analysis of social and structural sin. He notes in particular Baum's description of a false consciousness:

82

> As their society promoted increased personal comfort and financial gain, members of the upper classes could not see how their actions adversely affected other people. They often traced the plight of the poor to either the will of God or the low morals and behaviour among the lower classes.[12]

He links this to a point that Wesley had made attacking the rich for their wilful ignorance of the lives of the poor.

> Hence it is that . . . one part of the world does not know what the other suffers. Many of them do not know because they care not to know; they keep out of the way of knowing it; and then plead their voluntary ignorance as an excuse for their hardness of heart.[13]

It is clear that the same point could be made today. We do not address the structural injustices that perpetuate the consumer lifestyles of HICs and the poverty of LICs because our sin is expressed in an unwillingness to recognize our own complicity in the shalom-breaking that this represents.

One particular example of such blindness is evident in the idolatry of greed. Lesslie Newbigin rightly reminds us that 'Traditional Christian ethics had attacked covetousness as a deadly sin, and Paul had equated it with idolatry.'[14] Chris Wright makes the same point when he says, 'Paul was not the first to teach that covetousness is tantamount to idolatry, which is as much as to say that to break the tenth commandment is to break the first.'[15] Yet, the logic of unfettered capitalism is that it only works to the extent that it is characterized by unrestrained desire. The goal is no longer sufficiency, it is permanent growth. Commenting on Michael Novak's acknowledgement of this fact, Newbigin writes: 'The capitalist system is powered by the unremitting stimulation of covetousness. The apostolic advice that a person should be content with food and clothing (1 Tim. 6.8) is not compatible with the development of our kind of society.'[16] While it is not surprising that Novak adopts this view, it is not one we would expect in an evangelical theologian. Yet this is precisely what Grudem and Asmus give us. They write: 'In order to solve the problem of poverty in a poor nation, it is important to have the correct goal in mind . . . the correct goal is that a nation continually produces more goods and services per person per year.'[17] In this context, they present a somewhat tortuous defence of the covetousness that is required for free-market capitalism to thrive. In the first place, they note that the world will never 'run out of new products to make and new job opportunities' because 'human beings have limited needs (food, clothing and shelter) but unlimited wants'.[18] The idea that such unlimited wants need not be equated with greed or covetousness is dismissed by suggesting that 'the basic idea of wanting new and better products is not wrong in itself. It is part of how God created the human race – with a drive to continually subdue the earth.'[19] A similar argument is made by Albert Mohler Jr when he writes in defence of contemporary neoliberal economics: 'That which accrues value is honourable, and the impulse to accrue that value is honourable . . . The increase of things can be a sign of the glory of God and the fulfilment of the dominion mandate.'[20]

Such an approach seems to be in stark contrast to the advice provided in Deuteronomy:

When you have eaten your fill and have built fine houses and live in them, and when your herds and flocks have multiplied, and your silver and gold is multiplied, and all that you have is multiplied, then do not exalt yourself, forgetting the LORD your God. (Deut. 8.12–14)

Or even Ecclesiastes:

The lover of money will not be satisfied with money; nor the lover of wealth, with gain. This also is vanity. When goods increase, those who eat them increase; and what gain has their owner but to see them with his eyes? (Eccl. 5.10–11)

In addition, this approach is to ignore the fact that the creation mandate to subdue the earth was for the sake of corporate human flourishing. If my subjugation of the earth causes your poverty, or even ignores your poverty, then my subjugation is wrong.

In a recent article for *The Southern Baptist Journal of Theology*, David Kotter has explored this, trying to delineate the precise point where legitimate self-interest changes into idolatrous greed. He suggests at least three different tests in respect of income to help in this. The first of these is whether our acquisitiveness is accompanied by other sins. Lying and stealing would be obvious examples. However, inappropriate greed is also exemplified when 'a merchant desired gain to the point of making misleading claims or employing a false balance', or when they were involved in fraudulent behaviour or oppression of others.[21] He cites with approval Walter Bauer who described greed as to 'take advantage of, outwit, defraud, cheat'.[22] In addition to this, Kotter says greed is also present when in the process of seeking greater income we neglect our other duties to the Church or the family. If this really is a test of greed, then one could argue that it is impossible to earn significant incomes without it being greed, for apart from money that is inherited almost every role that commands a high salary also demands excessive working hours. Having noted the responsibilities that we have outside of work, he writes:

If such a person instead chose to spend long hours on the job to advance and earn money such that his wife felt abandoned and his children ran riot, then this likely is evidence of greed as the motivation to work.[23]

Kotter's final test of greed in relation to income is when our love of money outstrips our love of God, when money becomes in short our 'god'. He suggests this is evident when our desire to earn more is driven by a desire for wealth for its own sake, rather than wealth for the good it can do in respect of others.[24] This would seem to contrast strongly with Grudem and Asmus, who see no problem in desiring more irrespective of the motivation for that want.

Helpfully, Kotter also addresses a similar spectrum in respect of our possessions, and again he tries to delineate a crossover point between having possessions that merely reflects our appropriate self-interest – a roof over our heads, for instance – and having possessions to the extent that we are guilty of sinful

greed. On the legitimate self-interest side of this continuum he places possessions that we have as a means of sustenance (being able to live), utility (materials we need in order to fulfil our professions), security (being able to provide
for others and ourselves in an emergency situation) and enjoyment (life is not
just about mere sustenance). However, at the greed end of the line are possessions for the sake of indulgence and signalling. The former of these is defined
as 'enjoyment to a degree that is personally harmful, impinges on the interests
of other people, or replaces the pleasure of knowing Jesus Christ'.[25] The latter
is when we have possessions purely for the sake of displaying our wealth to
others. He gives the example of the person who buys a Rolls Royce instead of
a Ford Fusion when, from a functional point of view, they both get you from
A to B. The expensive car is clearly part of a status symbol. For Kotter, that
characterizes the idolatrous sin of greed. He writes: 'Paul seems categorically
to reject possessions that merely signal riches without adding to sustenance,
utility, or security.'[26]

There is much that is helpful in Kotter's analysis, but the part I want to pick
up on is the way in which he defines greed as acquisitiveness and affluence that
impacts the well-being of others. For this is where the blindness of capitalist
greed is most evident. Grudem and Asmus write:

> Sometimes people think that poor nations are poor because of things done
> by outside factors and entities, such as colonialism, large banks, large cor-
> porations, rich nations, or the world economic system. The basic problem
> with blaming poverty on such outside factors is it does nothing to solve the
> problem.[27]

What this quotation illustrates is a blindness that so often characterizes sin.
The authors seem unwilling to acknowledge that the factors they mention
both have and continue to have an impact on the wealth of poorer nations.
Recognizing this, seeing it, is the first step in providing a solution. To give a
very mundane example, if more people in HICs – and especially the USA –
recognized that the excess emission of greenhouse gases leads to the deaths of
poor children around the globe, then maybe they would support a much more
aggressive green policy in the US Congress. But blindness to the impact of our
own actions on others, coupled with blindness to our own greed and idolatry,
leads us to unrestrained consumer desire, the essence of which is idolatry. For
all these reasons, Himes encourages us, 'The first step is to assist the individual
in seeing how he is responsible for perpetuating human sinfulness by unwit-
tingly accepting the prevailing false consciousness transmitted by the social
setting.'[28] He notes that 'many people will not see themselves as particularly
blameworthy for the existence of political and economic institutions that permit world hunger, legal structures that enshrine sexist practices, or educational
systems that deny equal opportunity for blacks'.[29] It is that failure to see, to
recognize the sin within, that is a feature of our current corporate blindness to
structural sin.[30]

One further way this issue of blindness to sin impacts us concerns the peren-
nial issue of corruption in other countries. One of the most frequent arguments

made by those wishing to stop all aid to other countries is that their governments and officials are corrupt and will simply misappropriate the funds. And,
of course, there is evidence that to some extent this is true.[31] Transparency
International (TI) produces a regular perception of corruption index, and perhaps not surprisingly those countries listed as most corrupt are also those who
are among the poorest.[32] Similarly, the ten least corrupt countries are among
the wealthiest.[33] We have all heard individual stories of corrupt dictators who
have plundered their nation's wealth before settling down to a comfortable
retirement on some off-shore island. For all these reasons, Dambisa Moyo has
infamously argued in *Dead Aid* that all bilateral aid should be stopped. She
begins her chapter on aid and corruption in this way:

> In 2004, the British envoy to Kenya, Sir Edward Clay, complained about
> rampant corruption in the country, commenting that Kenya's corrupt min-
> isters were 'eating like gluttons' and vomiting on the shoes of the foreign
> donors. In February 2005 (prodded to make a public apology for his state-
> ments given the political maelstrom his earlier comments had made), he
> apologized – saying he was sorry for the 'moderation' of his language, for
> underestimating the scale of the looting and for failing to speak out earlier.[34]

However, as Padilla points out, while it is undoubtedly the case that many poorer
countries do suffer from serious corruption among their political elite what is often
ignored in this analysis is the corruption that is endemic among many wealthier
nations.[35] Switzerland represents a particular case in point. In 2014 this country
came fifth least corrupt on Transparency International's corruption perception
index. Yet, at the same time Switzerland is involved in what is arguably a far
more corrupt practice than many nations further down the Transparency index.
According to the Tax Justice Network, Switzerland ranks top on its financial
secrecy index.[36] There are a number of reasons for this, but one of them is the way
in which some of its cantons effectively operate as off-shore tax havens, charging
minimal tax in return for large transnational corporations depositing significant
assets there, while paying no attention to the origin of those assets.

According to research undertaken by the Methodist Tax Justice Network,
BHP Billiton represents just one example of this. They are one of the largest
mining companies in the world. Between 2006 and 2012, BHP Billiton made
$114 million per year from the Mozal Aluminium smelter in Mozambique.
Throughout this time the government in Mozambique (and therefore the
people of Mozambique) received just 1 per cent in tax from the smelting works,
while BHP Billiton subsidiaries deposited huge sums in the Swiss canton of
Zug, which has an effective corporate tax rate of 0 per cent.[37] Of course, there
is nothing currently illegal in any of this, but a country that allows transnational corporations to deposit profits made in another part of the world in
their highly secretive banking system certainly calls into question our current
definitions of corruption. The primary reason why activities such as these do
not impact Transparency International's corruption index is that TI tends to
focus on corruption within the public rather than the private sector. In a media
interview, in which a TI representative defended their approach, they said this:

Widening the definition of corruption to include tax evasion and capital flight would in our view dilute the concept. If we included tax evasion in the corruption perception index, that would mean no longer focusing on the main actors but introducing into the index elements not directly related to corruption. For example, it would make no sense to include in the corruption perception index a German dentist who places income on a foreign account so as to conceal it from the tax authorities.[38]

It is not immediately clear to me why a tax-avoiding dentist should not contribute to an index of corruption, but what is particularly interesting is how the TI representative goes on to defend this approach. She says:

The OECD Anti-Bribery Convention takes the same line. Before coming into effect in 2000, the fight against corruption occurred strictly within national borders. It took a major decade-long effort to convince the international community of States that corruption should be fought globally. Broadening the scope to include other offences such as tax evasion would have made this more difficult if not impossible.[39]

In other words, the OECD – who are after all the rich countries' club – did not want concepts of tax avoidance and capital flight included in a compendium of corruption. It seems likely that the reason for this is because their member countries benefit from these forms of corruption and so don't want the spotlight put on them. All of this just indicates that concepts of corruption are highly contextual and possibly culture specific.

Consider the following. Which of these behaviours is corrupt?

1 Paying a member of waiting staff a large tip in response to faster service and attention.
2 Offering to pay a member of waiting staff a large tip for fast service and attention.
3 Offering to pay a visa official a large tip for fast service and attention.

In most Western cultures (1) is not just not corrupt but expected; (2) may be unusual but again no one will consider it corrupt. However, (3) would definitely be considered corrupt behaviour. But why is this the case? If the scenario I am imagining is one in which the recipient qualifies for a visa anyway, then all we are talking about is a faster approach to a service that was already due. If we argue that this is corrupt because if the official serves us more quickly then someone else will be served more slowly, then that same argument applies to the restaurant scenario. So, what makes (3) corrupt? Perhaps it is the fact that the visa official is a public official and not a private one. But does that mean that if we were in a government building receiving service in a publicly owned restaurant, we should not offer the waiting staff tips?

This point has been made by Jason Tan in exploring the socio-cultural aspects of bribery and corruption in the Philippines. He begins by noting that 'what is considered a bribe or extortion differs in various contexts'.[40] He continues:

What is considered a bribe or an extortion in Singapore or elsewhere may well be acceptable in the Philippines. In the latter, policemen in some provinces may take or receive a 'love gift' or 'donation' from a grateful patron after responding to a call or an emergency at night. These gifts are given as tokens of appreciation by patrons who know that many public servants have to pay for the fuel when responding to an emergency call. So the act of giving gifts for services rendered by the police, which is not acceptable in many countries, is legitimate in this circumstance in the Philippines.[41]

Tan's approach contrasts sharply with that of a report written by Paula Gooder for the UK Bible Society. In that report, the assumption seems to be made that we all know what corruption is and it is universally a bad thing: 'It is clear that because God is impartial and takes no bribes, officials should be the same. Corruption is an anti-God word.'[42] In the course of this discussion, she tells us that 'The Hebrew word "sehad" often translated as gift or bribe describes an action that is regularly condemned throughout the Hebrew Bible'.[43] What is interesting about this is that Tan has a very different perspective on the same term. He writes:

> Even the Old Testament does not have a word for 'bribe', but instead uses the word *kopher*, which means 'ransom', or *shachad*, translated as 'gift' or 'present'. These two Hebrew words are not equivalent to the English word 'bribe', but may be interpreted as such depending on the context. For instance [in Proverbs 17.23] *shachad* is rightly interpreted as a bribe, but in Proverbs 17.8 the same word should be interpreted as meaning a gift instead.[44]

I am not particularly convinced of Tan's interpretation of Proverbs 17.8 here, but the broader point that the Hebrew word is open to both meanings – bribe and gift – is undeniable, and therefore the context of any individual passage is what will determine which understanding should be employed. Indeed, Daryl Balia goes even further, drawing attention to the 'double message' that is evident in the Scriptures in relation to bribery.[45] Having noted a number of passages that appear to condemn bribery, he then points to Proverbs 18.16 and 21.14 in which bribery is at the very least accepted as the norm, if not actually condoned:

> A gift opens doors; it gives access to the great. (Prov. 18.16)

> A gift in secret averts anger; and a concealed bribe in the bosom, strong wrath. (Prov. 21.14)

Balia concludes:

> Weighed together with the overall lack of sanctions against the practice of bribery, it might be more plausible to assume that the Old Testament as a whole, including Proverbs, reflects the state of affairs in a permissive and tolerant society.[46]

The reason this matters is that it shows, as Tan argues, that there was not a univocal concept of bribery in the Hebrew language in the same way that there is in English. Gifts could be used for both positive and negative ends and discernment is required to determine which is operative in any particular situation.[47]

My point in all of this is not to argue that corruption does not happen or that it does not have a devastating impact on the development of many LICs. Rather, as with so much sin, while we are very quick to point to the corruption that occurs in other countries and so blame their poverty on such corruption, we are often blind to our own corruption and the contribution it makes to global poverty. While the Western Church is fond of highlighting the daily peccadilloes that make travel and dealing with officialdom in poorer countries difficult as the root cause of poverty, they often simultaneously ignore the massive tax avoidance and evasion that ultimately robs those countries of billions of dollars of revenue. As Padilla argues:

> Why are so many people in these countries poor? The ready-made answer to this question – an answer oftentimes taken for granted in the West – is synthesized in one word: *corruption*. That is quite correct, I retort, but then I raise another question: Whose corruption? . . . all the emphasis is laid on corruption as a problem in the developing countries, but no attention is given to the other side of the coin: 'the role of the multinational corporations and the governments of the industrialized countries in the shocking corruption that has shaken the region'.[48]

This chapter has explored the doctrine of the fall and the sin that ensnares us. I have drawn on concepts of sin as relational breakdown and culpable shalom-breaking to argue that we need to embrace a far wider and deeper idea of sin than is usually the case. If we limit 'sin' to merely command-breaking, then we will inevitably avoid facing our own complicity in the structures of sin that keep the poor in poverty. It is our blindness (either accidental or deliberate) to those structures that prevents us from facing our own culpability. In the words of William Wilberforce, 'You may choose to look the other way but you can never say again that you did not know.'

Notes

1. J. Donahue, 2004, *Seek Justice that You May Live*, Mahwah, NJ: Paulist Press, p. 34.

2 W. Wyman, 2005, 'Sin and Redemption', in J. Mariña (ed.), *The Cambridge Companion to Friedrich Schleiermacher*, Cambridge: Cambridge University Press, pp. 134ff.

3 K. Himes, 1986, 'Social Sin and the Role of the Individual', *Annual of the Society of Christian Ethics* 6, pp. 183–218.

4 Himes, 'Social Sin', p. 189.

5 Himes, 'Social Sin', p. 189.

6 Himes, 'Social Sin', p. 214.

7 R. Sider, 1997, *Rich Christians in an Age of Hunger*, London: Hodder & Stoughton, p. 114.

8 Basil of Caesarea, cited in V. Ramachandra, 2008, *Subverting Global Myths*, Downers Grove, IL: InterVarsity Press, p. 107.

9 C. Wright, 2004, *Old Testament Ethics for the People of God*, Nottingham: InterVarsity Press, p. 176 (emphasis in original).

10 Wright, *Old Testament Ethics*, p. 176.

11 M. Tapper, 2013, 'Social Sin and Needed Corporate Reform in the Wesleyan Tradition', *Wesleyan Theological Journal* 48:2, September, p. 207.

12 Tapper, 'Social Sin', p. 196. Cf. G. Baum, 2006, *Religion and Alienation*, 2nd edn, Toronto: Novalis Publishing.

13 Tapper, 'Social Sin', p. 200.

14 L. Newbigin, 1995, *Foolishness to the Greeks*, London: SPCK, p. 109.

15 Wright, *Old Testament Ethics*, p. 152.

16 Newbigin, *Foolishness*, p. 113. Cf. M. Novak, 1982, *The Spirit of Democratic Capitalism*, New York: Simon and Schuster.

17 W. Grudem and B. Asmus, 2013, *The Poverty of Nations: A Sustainable Solution*, Wheaton, IL: Crossway Books, p. 45.

18 Grudem and Asmus, *Poverty of Nations*, p. 173.

19 Grudem and Asmus, *Poverty of Nations*, p. 173.

20 R. Albert Mohler Jr, 2015, 'Economics and the Christian Worldview: 12 Theses', *The Southern Baptist Journal of Theology* 19:2, pp. 9–16, at p. 14. To be fair to Mohler, he goes on to encourage thrift as what distinguishes Christian economic thinking from purely capitalist economic thinking among other critiques of capitalism. Nevertheless, the primary impulse to acquisition is not only not critiqued but praised.

21 D. Kotter, 2015, 'Greed vs. Self-Interest: A Case Study of How Economists Can Help Theologians Serve the Church', *The Southern Baptist Journal of Theology* 19:2, p. 29.

22 Kotter, 'Greed', p. 45, n. 62.

23 Kotter, 'Greed', p. 30.

24 Kotter, 'Greed', pp. 30–1.

25 Kotter, 'Greed', p. 36.

26 Kotter, 'Greed', p. 39.

27 Grudem and Asmus, *Poverty of Nations*, p. 82.

28 Himes, 'Social Sin', p. 192.

29 Himes, 'Social Sin', p. 193.

30 For more on the idolatry of greed, see also Chapter 8, 'Need for Greed', in T. Sedlacek, 2011, *Economics of Good and Evil*, Oxford: Oxford University Press.

31 D. Agbiboa, 2014, 'Under-development in Practice: Nigeria and the Enduring Problem of Corruption', *Development in Practice* 24:3. M. Lang, 2014, 'The Patterns of Corruption in Christian Churches of Cameroon: The Case of the Presbyterian Church in Cameroon', *Transformation: An International Journal of Holistic Mission Studies* 31:2, pp. 132–44.

32 www.transparency.org.

33 In 2014, they were, in order, Denmark, New Zealand, Finland, Sweden, Norway, Switzerland, Singapore, Netherlands, Luxembourg, Canada.

34 D. Moyo, 2009, *Dead Aid: Why Aid is Not Working and How there is Another Way for Africa*, London: Penguin, p. 48.

35 C. R. Padilla, 2014, 'The Globalization of Greed', *Journal of Latin American Theology* 9:2, p. 59.

36 www.financialsecrecyindex.com/PDF/Switzerland.pdf (accessed 17 September 2014).

37 M. Jones, 2014, *Investigating our Investments*, Methodist Tax Justice Network, p. 3.

38 B. Gurtner, 2007, 'Disputed Transparency International Index', AllianceSud, Autumn. Available at: www.alliancesud.ch/en/policy/finance disputed-transparency-international-index (accessed 17 September 2015). Interestingly, Balia, in his otherwise excellent study of corruption and its impact on economic development, also chooses to exclude illicit financial flows from his definition of corruption. He writes: 'It is important . . . to distinguish corruption from other forms of criminal conduct that do not involve the misuse of public office. These would include cases of tax evasion, insider dealings on the stock market, production of counterfeit money, subsidy fraud, and contraband, all of which are excluded from our focus.' D. Balia, 2009, *Make Corruption History*, London: SPCK, p. 9.

39 Gurtner, 'Disputed'.

40 Jason Richard Tan, 2015, 'Christian Mission Amidst the Cultural and Socioeconomic Dynamics of Bribery and Extortion Practices in the Philippines', in J. Cheong and E. Meneses (eds), *Christian Mission and Economic Systems*, Pasadena, CA: William Carey Library, p. 88.

41 Tan, 'Christian Mission', p. 88.

42 P. Gooder, 2014, *Thirty Pieces of Silver: An Exploration of Corruption, Bribery, Transparency and Justice in the Christian Scriptures*, London: Bible Society, p. 4.

43 Gooder, *Thirty*, p. 4. Balia draws attention to the lack of theological engagement on the issue by quoting a US judge, J. T. Noonan, who wrote: 'It was as though at a certain level of theological sophistication or at a certain level of class consciousness it was agreed that everyone knew what constituted bribery, that everyone knew that bribery was wrong, and that no problems existed worthy of debate or discussion.' Noonan, as cited in Balia, *Make Corruption*, p. 23.

44 Tan, 'Christian Mission', p. 95.

45 Balia, *Make Corruption*, p. 115.

46 Balia, *Make Corruption*, p. 117.

47 See also B. Waltke, 2005, *The Book of Proverbs: Chapters 15–21*, Grand Rapids, MI: Eerdmans, p. 48, n. 81. In addition to this, Kumalo, writing from a South African perspective, notes that cultural differences are also at play in how we respond to corruption even when everyone agrees the person is guilty. He points out that while the North responds with public critique, 'most Black African cultures . . . are built on a cultural norm of shame' in which 'citizens do not criticize any person in public' but instead 'follow certain channels to call them to order and even punish them'. S. R. Kumalo, 2008, 'Paying the Price for Democracy: The Contribution of the Church in the Development of Good Governance in South Africa', in S. de Gruchy, N. Koopman and S. Strijbos (eds), *From Our Side: Emerging Perspectives on Development and Ethics*, Amsterdam: Rozenberg Publishers, p. 181.

48 Quoting A. Oppenheimer, in Padilla, 'The Globalization', p. 59.

PART 3

Israel

7

Israel's mission

In turning to the topic of Israel, it would be relatively easy to undertake a survey of the Hebrew Scriptures and proof text a series of quotations from the whole corpus to make the point that God has a concern for the poor. From the book of Genesis through to Malachi, the Old Testament screams God's compassion for the poor, a point which incidentally reveals the shallowness and naivety of any reading of the Bible that suggests the God of the Old Testament is all about violence while the God of the New is about love. The biblical canon is far more complex than such Marcionite tendencies. So, for instance, the Torah is replete with injunctions that we are to protect and serve the poor (Ex. 22.21–23; Lev. 25.35–36; Deut. 10.17–19; 24.17–22). This motif continues in the Psalms and Wisdom literature (Ps. 9, 10, 37, 49, 72, 73; Prov. 13.23; 17.8; 18.5) and is an especial concern of the prophets (Isa. 3.14–15; 10.1–2; Amos 2.6–8; 8.4; Mic. 3.1–3).

However, rather than take such a proof-texting approach, I want in this chapter to consider Israel in a wider theological frame. What was their purpose? How was God achieving his purposes through them? How does Israel fit into the whole canon of Scripture and into the whole plan of salvation? My reason for this is the problem of simply quoting Leviticus 19.13–15 in support of compassion for the poor:

> You shall not defraud your neighbour; you shall not steal; and you shall not keep for yourself the wages of a labourer until morning. You shall not revile the deaf or put a stumbling-block before the blind; you shall fear your God: I am the LORD. You shall not render an unjust judgement; you shall not be partial to the poor or defer to the great: with justice you shall judge your neighbour.

The problem being that it is not immediately obvious why Leviticus 19.19 does not also apply today: 'you shall not sow your field with two kinds of seed; nor shall you put on a garment made of two different materials'. Of course, the standard evangelical response to this is to divide the Old Testament law into civil, cultic and moral requirements and to argue that only the moral continues to have normative force. However, as with a growing number of evangelical scholars, I find this response unpersuasive for the simple reason that this is not how the Old Testament presents itself.[1] Given this, I want to draw much more heavily on the approach taken by Chris Wright in his monumental *The Mission of God*. In this work, Wright eschews a proof-texting approach to God's work in the world and instead draws us into what the subtitle of his book calls 'the Bible's grand narrative'. I want to explore this narrative as it pertains to God's work in and through Israel and as it touches on God's compassion for the poor.

In briefest summary, my argument (following Wright) is this: Israel's mission is primarily a continuation of and participation in God's mission to the world (*missio Dei*). This mission was that Israel might be God's representatives to the whole earth and as God's representatives (*imago Dei*) bring blessing to all the nations. This blessing is holistic – spiritual, material and social – and this purpose is indicated in the whole of the Hebrew canon and is exemplified in God's pivotal actions in establishing the nation, releasing them from slavery in Egypt, giving them the law and, through the prophets and exile, recalling them to their primary calling: *acting as God's agents to be a holistic blessing to all the nations.*

We begin, then, with the concept of the *missio Dei*. One of the more remarkable aspects of Wright's work is his unashamed embrace of this concept. He begins by gently chastising his earlier self for having to teach a course at All Nations Christian College on the 'The Biblical Basis of Mission'. Wright's point is that mission is not so much something we *do* for which the Bible is a guidebook and motivation. Rather, *'the whole Bible is itself a "missional" phenomenon. The writings that now comprise our Bible are themselves the product of and witness to the ultimate mission of God.'*[2] He goes on: *'Fundamentally, our mission . . . means our committed participation as God's people, at God's invitation and command, in God's own mission within the history of God's world for the redemption of God's creation.'*[3] This of course represents a classic restatement of the doctrine of *missio Dei*.

As Wright points out, the concept goes back to Karl Barth and his emphasis on the primacy of God in mission. However, it primarily gained ground following the 1952 Willingen World Mission conference. According to David Bosch, it was at that conference that the 'idea (not the exact term) *missio Dei* first surfaced'.[4] Bosch summarizes the idea thus:

> In the new image, mission is not primarily an activity of the church, but an attribute of God. God is a missionary God . . . Mission is thereby seen as a movement from God to the world; the church is viewed as an instrument for that mission. There is church because there is mission, not vice versa. To participate in mission is to participate in the move of God's love toward people, since God is a fountain of sending love.[5]

Wright critiques the fact that for some (presumably within the World Council Churches) *missio Dei* became essentially an activity of God and not an activity of the church in any meaningful sense.[6] Whether or not that criticism is fair, it certainly cannot be levelled at the original 1952 conference whose framing theme was 'The Missionary Obligation of the Church'.[7] This is why Wright's embrace of the concept is so significant. Wright is a significant evangelical theologian who is known for his evangelical credentials. He is a former principal of a major evangelical Bible college in the United Kingdom, is currently the international director of an evangelical mission agency and, perhaps most significantly, he chaired the theology working group for the third Lausanne Congress on World Evangelization (2010). He was also the primary author of its communiqué, *The Cape Town Commitment*. Throughout much of the later twentieth century, conservative evangelicals have been at odds with the kind of theology emerging from the World Council of Churches, particularly on the nature and importance of evangelism. Hence, for a card-carrying evangelical to embrace a concept of mission that emerged from such circles is of itself significant. Yet it reminds me of the point that John Stott made when he embraced, albeit tentatively, the doctrine of annihilationism instead of eternal conscious torment for the damned. Stott said this:

> As a committed Evangelical, my question must be – and is – not what my heart tells me, but what does God's word say? And in order to answer this question, we need to survey the Biblical material afresh and to open our minds (not just our hearts) to the possibility that Scripture points in the direction of annihilationism, and that 'eternal conscious torment' is a tradition which has to yield to the supreme authority of Scripture.[8]

It would seem that it is this same yielding to Scripture that is characteristic of Wright's theology. Even if *missio Dei* is a concept that has been brought to the fore by 'ecumenicals' (Wright's term) this is not a reason to dismiss it if it is grounded in Scripture. He writes:

> To read the whole Bible in the light of this great overarching perspective of the mission of God, then, is to read with the grain of this whole collection of texts that constitute our canon of Scripture . . . [This] is nothing more than to accept that the biblical worldview locates us in the midst of a narrative of the universe behind which stands the mission of the living God.[9]

In the sections that follow, I will spell out in more detail what this means both for Israel and for us. But the point I wish to establish at this stage is simply this: Israel's mission and ours is nothing more than a participation in the mission that God has already begun. As such, the contours of Israel's mission (and our own) are provided by God. This does not mean that each generation does not do something new, for each generation finds itself in a unique environment, and God's mission is always contextual. But at the same time, it does mean that there are unifying themes and tropes that we can trace throughout the whole of God's mission, from creation to consummation, and it is these themes that we will explore in what is to follow. As a signal, however, of the direction I will be going, consider the following point made by Wright in relation to economic ethics:

> In broad terms, covenant-based economics called for economic relationships to be based on love and mutual support, not just on self-interest. Indeed, some of the economic regulations of Israel called for the sacrifice of self-interest in favour of the needs of a fellow Israelite. And all this was placed within a more fundamental call to trust their creator-redeemer God, even in the face of economic 'common sense'.[10]

The reason I have included this quotation at this point is because it illustrates a number of key themes as we consider the *missio Dei* and its relationship to the poor. The first of these is that participation in God's mission means that we set aside our own interests for the sake of the other. This idea reaches its apotheosis in the sacrifice of God for us, but as a theme it is evident in God's provision in the garden, his calling of a people, his forgiveness of sin and his promise of eternity with him. God has extended himself on our behalf and so we also must extend ourselves on behalf of the other. However, what differentiates such self-sacrifice from mere masochistic immolation is that we undertake it within a framework of God's provision for us. We give of ourselves both because we are following the example of the God who gave himself for us, but also, and perhaps more fundamentally, because in giving of ourselves we discover ourselves in the life of the triune God. In short, we find ourselves precisely because we lose ourselves.

'Those who find their life will lose it, and those who lose their life for my sake will find it.' (Matt. 10.39)

'Very truly, I tell you, unless a grain of wheat falls into the earth and dies, it remains just a single grain; but if it dies, it bears much fruit. Those who love their life lose it, and those who hate their life in this world will keep it for eternal life.' (John 12.24–25)

It is only in the context of the *missio Dei* that those verses from Jesus make any sense. In the absence of a notion that this is God's mission in which we participate, mission becomes simply raw obedience to a divine despot. But this is not the mission to which we are called. Rather, our calling is to be part of a much wider mandate – to be part of God's own mission – in which as we give of ourselves we find our true home in the purposes of God, and therein lies life.

So how does that mission express itself in terms of the life of Israel? The pivotal text here is found in God's calling of Abraham:

Now the LORD said to Abram, 'Go from your country and your kindred and your father's house to the land that I will show you. I will make of you a great nation, and I will bless you, and make your name great, so that you will be a blessing. I will bless those who bless you, and the one who curses you I will curse; and in you all the families of the earth shall be blessed.' (Gen. 12.1–3)

In this text, we do not merely find the calling of an individual – Abraham – but the establishment of a nation. More than that, we are also told what the purpose of this nation is to be – the blessing of all nations. This theme of blessing is one that is repeated and emphasized throughout the passage:

I will bless you . . .
    so that you will be a *blessing.*
I will *bless* those who *bless* you . . .
    and in you all the families of the earth shall be *blessed.*

We begin by noting that Abram's blessing of others is contingent upon his receipt of blessing from God. 'I will bless you . . . so that you will be a blessing.' Chris Wright notes how the second half of this phrase is in fact an imperative – 'be a blessing' – but how, when two imperatives occur together, the sense can be that the second is a fulfilment of the first. Hence, what we read is a command to Abram in which the imperative to go is fulfilled or completed by Abram's being a blessing to those he will reach. 'The message of the combined halves of the text . . . is that if Abraham does what he is told, and if God does what he says he will do, the result will be blessing all round.'[11] In this we see echoes of the *missio Dei* idea already described. Abraham's blessing to the nations is the result of God's blessing of him. But what is the nature of this blessing? In what does it consist?

According to Wright, the blessing is creational, relational, missional, historical, covenantal, ethical, multinational and christological.[12] I will pick up on just a few of these themes as they relate to our overall purpose. By creational, Wright's intent is to remind us of the blessing bestowed by God on creation on days five, six and seven. According to Wright, such creational blessing is found in 'fruitfulness, abundance, fullness and rest'.[13] It represents, in other words, the creational mandate to be fruitful and multiply. This includes 'increase of family, flocks, wealth or all three. God's blessing means enjoying the good gifts of God's creation in abundance.'[14] Blessing is material. This is important because conservative evangelicals in particular have a tendency to interpret the Abrahamic covenant as referring merely to spiritual blessing, and in the process restrict their responsibilities to the nations to nothing but evangelism. Even when they do recognize their mandate to assist the poor in practical terms, this is frequently understood as a response to Jesus' love command, and as such it is merely an act of obedience or mercy, but not as such foundational to what it means to participate in the mission of God.

What these verses indicate is that if our mission is to participate in God's mission, and if God's mission is exemplified in God's call upon Abraham, then being a blessing to the nations, and so participating in God's mission, includes as a foundational element fostering material fruitfulness in the nations. Having concern for, and acting on behalf of, the global poor is not just an act of obedience or love, it is instead to be in partial fulfilment of the mission to which we are called. This is not to argue for some form of prosperity theology in which knowledge of God is automatically linked to material prosperity. Rather, it is to talk in terms of what it means for us to take the good news (gospel) of Christ to all the nations – and to argue that this is done just as much by drilling a bore hole or campaigning for tax justice as it is by verbally proclaiming the death of Christ for us.

In addition to this holistic understanding of blessing, the crucial point to realize is that the call of Abraham was to be such a blessing to all the nations. Clearly, this cannot simply mean that Abraham as an individual was to traverse the world taking the message, or blessing, of YHWH with him. Rather, it means that through him, and that means through the nation of Israel (and subsequently through Christians), all the nations of the world were to be blessed holistically. In the first place, Wright points out how this trope is repeated whenever the Abrahamic covenant appears:

Genesis 12.3: 'in you all the families of the earth shall be blessed'.

Genesis 18.18: 'all the nations of the earth shall be blessed in him'.

Genesis 22.18: 'by your offspring shall all the nations of the earth gain blessing for themselves'.

Genesis 26.4: 'all the nations of the earth shall gain blessing for themselves through your offspring'.

Genesis 28.14: 'all the families of the earth shall be blessed in you and in your offspring'.[15]

However, more than this, Wright adumbrates a series of passages from the rest of the Pentateuch (Ex. 9.16; Deut. 28.9–10), the historical texts (Josh. 4.23–24; 1 Sam. 17.46), the Psalms (Ps. 22.27–28; 67.1–2) and the prophets (Isa. 45.22–23; Jer. 4.1–2; Zech. 8.13) to make the point that Abraham's call to be a blessing to *all the nations* was in fact a call to the nation of Israel, and through Christ a call to subsequent generations of Christians.[16] He concludes:

> Beyond doubt, then, there was a universal purpose in God's election of Abraham, and therefore also a universal dimension to the very existence of Israel. Israel as a people was called into existence because of God's mission to bless the nations and restore his creation.[17]

When we combine this point with the one noted earlier, that this blessing was meant to be material as well as spiritual, then we can only conclude that our missional mandate is to bless the whole earth holistically.

Such a conclusion may seem unsurprising, but one of the sequelae of this point is that it highlights our ethical responsibility not just to those who are proximal but also to those who are distant. We are meant to be a blessing to the whole earth, not just those we know. It is on this point that Wright distances himself from Stott, who had criticized the World Council of Churches for interpreting the Exodus as a paradigm 'for all the downtrodden'.[18] Wright's response is important:

> There is a lot of force in this objection, and it is of course correct to point out the uniqueness of Israel and the emphasis on God's promise to Abraham. I have stressed the same things repeatedly. However, it is not the whole truth. For while I agree with John Stott's point, I do not think it goes far enough in recognising the paradigmatic nature of the exodus, on the basis of the paradigmatic significance of Israel itself for the rest of humanity.[19]

He continues: 'We must remember that God's promise to Abraham was never intended for Israel's exclusive benefit.' And Wright's only criticism of political interpretations of the Exodus is simply that they do not go far enough, that by limiting their interpretation to the political and economic and ignoring the spiritual, they do an injustice to what it means to be a holistic blessing to the whole world.[20]

The reason this matters is because there remains within certain circles the idea that assuming we do have an ethical responsibility to others such responsibility can be delimited proximally. In a book that is subtitled *A Biblical Answer to Poverty*, Glenn Sunshine writes of 'the importance of moral proximity' in our relations to the poor:

> Scripture is clear that our first responsibility is to our family . . . From there, we have responsibilities to those in our churches and our communities, in concentric circles outward. This is not to say we have no responsibilities to those dying of AIDS in Africa or of starvation in South Asia, but any such responsibility is secondary to the needs of those closer to us.[21]

> The principle of moral proximity states that we have responsibilities to others in proportion to our relationship with them: those who are closer to us have more of a claim on us than those who are distant . . . Jesus understood the commandment, 'Honor your father and mother,' to mean that we need to provide for our parents even ahead of giving to the temple (Mark 7.9–13); and Paul tells us that we are responsible to take care of our grandparents rather than passing them off to the church (or the state) to take care of them (1 Timothy 5.4) . . . the church's first concern must be for the needy within its own community. But this does not preclude the church from taking on other charitable work further afield, whether in poor areas in our own nation or overseas. This is important work as well, but it must not replace meeting local needs.[22]

In *The Good of Affluence*, John Schneider defends this notion of moral proximity that our economic responsibilities vary according to how close others are to us. Somewhat surprisingly, he finds support for this notion in the narrative of Israel. He writes: 'it seems that something like this moral principle operated in the ethics of Ancient Israel. For one thing, the people within Israel had no developed system of obligations in their ethics towards people living outside their national boundaries.'[23] As we have already seen, this is far from the truth. At its original moment, when Abraham was called, God made it clear that the establishment of the nation was precisely so that they would be a blessing to all the nations. This idea was then repeated in the Exodus and jubilee narratives. The idea, then, that Israel had no notion of ethical responsibility beyond its borders is simply without foundation. The implication, however, of Schneider's notion of moral proximity is that it is not others – including one's workers – that are one's primary responsibility, but rather one's kith and kin.

Leaving aside the fact that the particular verses cited by Sunshine may not actually lend support to the idea of moral proximity,[24] the biggest problems with his and Schneider's analyses are the very clear passages that they both ignore. In the first place, Jesus makes it abundantly clear that being his disciple includes putting him and his kingdom ahead of our families: 'Whoever comes to me and does not hate father and mother, wife and children, brothers and sisters, yes, and even life itself, cannot be my disciple' (Luke 14.26). But more than that, Jesus stated that all of the law and prophets could be summed up in just two commands, that we are to love God and love our neighbour as ourselves. If we interpret our neighbour as merely those to whom we have 'moral proximity', then Sunshine and Schneider's analyses are correct. However, the whole parable of the good Samaritan is given to demonstrate the fallacy of that understanding. The teacher in the law came to Jesus seeking to justify a notion of moral proximity, but Jesus' response destroys the idea. By placing a Samaritan – the enemy of the Jews – at the epicentre of the story, and as the one who shows mercy, Jesus is exploding the notion that the category of neighbour can be delimited by any kind of proximity. And if we recall that Jesus also commanded us explicitly to love our enemies, then we are left with the startling conclusion that those who are most distant from us – our enemies – are to be loved in the same way as the one who is closest to us, namely ourselves. This challenges the concept of moral proximity and moreover fits in with the whole tenor of the mission of God as expressed in the canon.

Of course, this truth has been known throughout Christendom. Rodney Stark has pointed out how one of the reasons the early Church thrived was because of its concern, in the context of plagues, not just for their own, but for their pagan neighbours as well. He quotes with approval Cyprian, who wrote in the third century that 'there is nothing remarkable in cherishing merely our own people with the due attention of love . . . Thus the good was done to all men, not merely to the household of faiths.'[25] Our moral responsibility then is to all the nations without qualification. Moe-Lobeda has written of how our individualized culture has given birth to a moral individuality in which 'I am not *individually* culpable in another's suffering, I am innocent.' However, she goes on, 'What I eat, how I heat my home, what I purchase, where I vacation, how I speak *as part of a society in which these ways are common practice* has moral impact even if my individual piece, isolated, does not.'[26]

Of course in practice we cannot love everyone in precisely the same way. We have to make choices. But that is not the point. Those choices are not made on the basis of some dubious notion of moral proximity, but on the basis of the calling which each one of us receives. Whether that calling is to an AIDS sufferer on another continent or to one's own mother, the important point is that we evaluate such callings according to the will of God for our lives and not according to any misplaced notion of moral proximity. Advocates of moral proximity theology might respond at this point by saying that each one of us is called first to serve our immediate family, then our extended family, then local community, and so on in ever-diminishing circles. No doubt that will be true for some, but we cannot conclude that it is a blanket requirement for everyone. Moreover, it is worth noting that somewhat conveniently the notion of moral proximity also enables Sunshine to argue that the solutions to the problems of the poor should also come from those closest to them. In one stroke he has evacuated any idea that HICs have any kind of significant moral responsibility to the global poor.[27] This is the fundamental problem with the doctrine of moral proximity. It is used to suggest that we have minimal responsibility towards the global poor and justifies an ethnocentrism that is impossible to square with Abram's call to be a blessing to *all the nations*, let alone Jesus' command to love neighbour and enemy without qualification.

It is also worth noting in passing that if the concept of neighbour does extend even to our enemies, then it certainly includes not just those who are geographically, ethnically or relationally distant now, but also those who are temporally distant, in other words future generations. This of course has obvious implications for our response to climate change.

As Cynthia Moe-Lobeda writes:

> My conclusion . . . is that neighbor-love, as seen in Jesus' life and teaching, *pertains to whomever one's life in some way impacts or whose life impacts one's own.* Jesus' actions demonstrate the infinite value of loving care between known individuals. At the same time, given the current realities of globalization and climate change, North American's lives impact people around the world. The call to love pertains also to relationship with these distant neighbors. In stark terms, if I am proximate enough to join in taking another's land, water, or livelihood (through collective actions), I am proximate enough to be neighbor.[28]

One further point regarding the universal scope of this blessing is important to consider. That is the fact that such universality was to be achieved via particularity, namely, the particular nation of Israel, and through Israel, the particular servant Jesus Christ.[29] The significance of this is that even if other nations or people groups are failing to be a blessing to *all the nations*, that does not at all affect the manner in which Israel, and subsequently we as Christians, are meant to be a blessing to all. One of the more frequent arguments one hears in respect of global justice is that if we do not engage in some morally questionable behaviour – perhaps tax avoidance or trade tariffs – that it will make no difference because everyone else is engaging in it anyway.[30] But that is to miss the point. The call on Israel to be a blessing to all the nations was *meant* to be particular. The other nations were not meant to behave in the same way, and it was precisely by means of their *particular* approach that the God of Israel would be honoured throughout *all the nations*. In short, Israel, and subsequently ourselves as Christians, are meant to be an example to the world (Deut. 4.6–8). Of course, as is well known, Israel failed spectacularly in this purpose. It was intended to be a 'light to the peoples' (Isa. 51.4), but in reality became just like the rest. Commenting on Jeremiah's condemnation of such sin, Wright states, 'Far from bringing him praise and honour, they brought him disgrace and contempt.'[31] The argument that it is acceptable to engage in some particular practice irrespective of its moral worth because everyone else is similarly complicit is to fail to understand the particular calling that has been placed upon us. We are meant to be distinct, we are meant to engage in the world differently, and when we do not, we fail in our missional purpose, we fail to bring honour to God.

Notes

1 While I may not agree with his alternative conclusion of principlism, J. Daniel Hays sets out well the problems with the traditional civil, cultic and moral approach. J. Daniel Hays, 2001, 'Applying the Old Testament Law Today', *Bibliotheca Sacra* 158: 629.

2 C. Wright, 2006, *The Mission of God: Unlocking the Bible's Grand Narrative*, Nottingham: InterVarsity Press, p. 22 (emphasis in original).

3 Wright, *The Mission*, p. 22 (emphasis in original).

4 D. Bosch, 2011, *Transforming Mission: Paradigm Shifts in Theology of Mission*, Marynoll, NY: Orbis Books, p. 399.

5 Bosch, *Transforming*, p. 400.

6 Wright, *The Mission*, p. 63.

7 Bosch, *Transforming*, p. 399.

8 D. Edwards, 1988, *Evangelical Essentials*, Downers Grove, IL: InterVarsity Press, p. 314.

9 Wright, *The Mission*, p. 64.

10 C. Wright, 2004, *Old Testament Ethics for the People of God*, Nottingham: InterVarsity Press, p. 157.

11 Wright, *The Mission*, p. 201.

12 Wright, *The Mission*, pp. 208–20.

13 Wright, *The Mission*, p. 208.

14 Wright, *The Mission*, p. 209.

15 Wright, *The Mission*, p. 216.

16 Wright, *The Mission*, ch. 7. The same point is also made in relation to the kings and the Temple (pp. 344ff.).

17 Wright, *The Mission*, p. 251.

18 J. Stott, as cited in Wright, *The Mission*, p. 282.

19 Wright, *The Mission*, p. 282.

20 Wright, *The Mission*, p. 284.

21 G. Sunshine, 2014, 'Who are the Poor?' in A. Bradley and A. Lindsley (eds), 2014, *For the Least of These: A Biblical Answer to Poverty*, Grand Rapids, MI: Zondervan, p. 21.

22 Sunshine, 'Who are the Poor?', p. 35.

23 J. Schneider, 2002, *The Good of Affluence*, Grand Rapids, MI: Eerdmans, p. 89.

24 It is fair to say that 1 Timothy 5.8 would appear to suggest some notion of moral proximity. However, the Greek *malista*, which is often translated 'especially', probably means 'namely' or 'that is' in the Pastoral Epistles. Hence, 1 Timothy 5.8 should read, 'If anyone does not provide for his own people, that is, his household . . .' The emphasis then is not some universal notion of moral proximity, but the rather mundane point that each of us has a responsibility to provide for those under our roofs – which in the first-century would have included the extended family and slaves. Cf. C. Blomberg, 1999, *Neither Poverty Nor Riches*, Leicester: Apollos, p. 208.

25 R. Stark, 2011, *The Triumph of Christianity*, New York: HarperCollins, p. 113.

26 C. Moe-Lobeda, 2013, *Resisting Structural Evil*, Minneapolis, MN: Fortress Press, p. 118.

27 Sunshine, 'Who are the Poor?', p. 24. See also Schneider's epilogue, 'Being Affluent in a World of Poverty', in Schneider, *The Good*.

28 Moe-Lobeda, *Resisting*, p. 175.

39 Wright, *The Mission*, pp. 254ff.

30 Cf. W. Grudem and B. Asmus, 2013, *The Poverty of Nations: A Sustainable Solution*, Wheaton, IL: Crossway Books, p. 99.

31 Wright, *The Mission*, p. 259.

8

Exodus

If Abram's call to be a blessing to the nations sets the scene for what the nation of Israel is meant to be about then the narrative of the Exodus reprises that scene in redemptive terms. By the time of the Exodus, things have changed significantly. Israel is no longer one man, but pictured as a numerous people.[1] However, they find themselves in a state of slavery in Egypt and they cry out to God for deliverance. It is clear from the rest of the Old Testament that this narrative of plea and redemption by God's mighty arm is significant in the nation's identity. Beginning with Miriam's song, the nation repeatedly defines itself in terms of what God has done for them in the Exodus. Psalm 136 is typical of many in drawing attention to this motif:

> who struck Egypt through their firstborn,
>   for his steadfast love endures for ever;
> and brought Israel out from among them,
>   for his steadfast love endures for ever;
> with a strong hand and an outstretched arm,
>   for his steadfast love endures for ever;
> who divided the Red Sea in two,
>   for his steadfast love endures for ever;
> and made Israel pass through the midst of it,
>   for his steadfast love endures for ever;
> but overthrew Pharaoh and his army in the Red Sea,
>   for his steadfast love endures for ever. (Ps. 136.10–15)

In this way, the Exodus provides a paradigm for the nation as to the nature of redemption, and it is this paradigm that is worthy of further exploration.[2] Though not the first to do so,[3] the Latin American liberation theologians have of course drawn extensively on the Exodus narrative for their own theology of liberation. Having drawn a close parallel between the doctrine of creation and the historical reality of the Exodus – both representing an act of salvation – Gutiérrez then makes this point: 'The liberation of Israel is a political action.'[4] In doing this, he sets the tone for much of his interpretive framework. He continues:

> It is the breaking away from a situation of despoliation and misery and the beginning of the construction of a just and comradely society. It is the suppression of disorder and the creation of a new order. The initial chapters of

Exodus describe the oppression in which the Jewish people lived in Egypt, in that 'land of slavery' (13.2; 20.2; Deut. 5.6): repression (Exod. 1.10–11), alienated work (5.6–14), humiliations (1.13–14), enforced birth control policy (1.15–22). Yahweh then awakens the vocation of a liberator: Moses.[5]

We see in this list many of the key facets that characterize a political theology of liberation – harsh working conditions, political oppression, shame and powerlessness – and as such, it is no surprise that Guttiérez chooses to frame much of his theology around that narrative.[6] Indeed, Norbert Lohfink argues that this political liberation is what distinguishes Israel's response to the poor from the rest of the ancient Near East. While many other ancient near Eastern documents demonstrate concern for the poor, in the Exodus we are presented with a paradigm in which the poor are delivered from the *system* that keeps them poor, and that is unique.[7]

An even stronger opinion is expressed by Enrique Dussel who describes the Exodus paradigm as the 'fundamental schema' of liberation theology.[8] Within this he discerns eight key relations that comprise the paradigm. These are:

- domination or sin
- cry of the people
- conversion, the call of the word to the prophet
- challenge to the people of God
- departure, liberation
- critical prophetic action
- entry, the building of the new system
- salvation, the kingdom, the community of life.[9]

As Dussel's analysis progresses, however, it is clear that what he has in mind is an almost exclusively political, indeed Marxist, interpretation of the Exodus. He writes: '"the poor" – thanks to the mediation of the social sciences and the political commitments of Christians – were now seen as a "class", and even more, "the people". The idea of "the poor" had been filled out, made historical, identifiable.'[10] And it is at this point, of course, that the liberation theologians have met their detractors.

Peter Hebblethwaite helpfully charts the way in which the papacy of the 1980s and 1990s responded to the political interpretations of the Exodus presented by liberation theology.[11] He draws attention to Pope John Paul II's instruction, *On Certain Aspects of Liberation Theology*, and in particular its comment on the Exodus as a (non)political event.

The exodus, in fact, is the fundamental events in the formation of the chosen people. It represents freedom from foreign domination and slavery. One will note that the specific significance of this event comes from its purpose, for this liberation is ordered to the foundation of the people of God and the covenant cult celebrated on Mt Sinai. That is why the liberation of the exodus cannot be reduced to a liberation which is principally or exclusively political in nature.[12]

As this quotation illustrates, while there is a nod to historical, political liberation – *foreign domination and slavery* – the emphasis, both implicit and explicit, is that what matters is the spiritual and religious liberation that is enacted in the event. Its *raison d'être* is not political freedom but rather the 'foundation' of the nation and its worship of God on Mt Sinai. As such, the Vatican had no problem with the language of liberation as long as everyone understood that what they meant by liberation was thoroughly spiritual. 'In this exodus experience God is recognised as the liberator. God will enter into a new covenant with his people. It will be marked by the gift of God's spirit and the conversion of hearts.'[13] And so Hebblethwaite concludes his article by noting the Vatican's declaration that 'liberation theology was not only opportune but useful and necessary', as long as the theology we are talking about is 'one that has been purged of Marxism'.[14]

There is an interesting parallel that can be observed between the spiritualizing of the Exodus by the Vatican in the 1980s and 1990s and the same tendencies by some conservative evangelicals. Chris Wright picks up on this when he talks about the spiritualizing of the Exodus that he was taught as a child:

The problem is that, having rightly affirmed this spiritual and Christocentric interpretation of the exodus in the New Testament, popular preaching of the exodus then tends to dismiss or ignore the historical reality that constituted the original event for Israel, namely, the actual deliverance out of real, earthy, injustice, oppression and violence. The thought process goes something like this . . .
- In the exodus, God delivered the Israelites from slavery to Egypt
- And through the cross of Christ, God delivered us from slavery to sin.[15]

We can find an almost exact copy of this approach – to such an extent that I wondered if they had read Wright on this – in a book by a group of scholars from Oakhill Theological College, a conservative Anglican evangelical college in the UK. They write:

In this way, the exodus is a paradigm for God's deliverance of his people from hostile powers. Just as the Lord set his people free from slavery to Pharaoh, their oppressor, so also the Lord Jesus Christ has set us free from slavery to sin, the world and the devil, those hostile powers that once held us in bondage.[16]

In saying this, Steve Jeffery *et al.* are not necessarily denying the political interpretation of the Exodus. They write, for instance, that the Israelites 'did not yet enjoy a land of their own' and that the event did constitute delivery 'from the tyranny of the Egyptians'.[17] However, the emphasis, which Wright suggests is typical, would seem to be the spiritual liberation that the Exodus represents.

Wright's response to this kind of spiritual interpretation is not to deny it in any respect whatsoever. He is firmly committed to the idea that the Exodus does function in this way. However, his point is that to interpret the Exodus solely or even chiefly in that way is to do a disservice to the scriptural narrative. For Wright, the Exodus is both spiritual and political, and we are mistaken whenever we adopt either end of that polarity. He quotes with approval Walter Brueggemann in respect of this:

> There is no doubt that the Old Testament witness concerns real socioeconomic and political circumstances, from which Yahweh is said to liberate Israel. There is also no doubt that the rhetoric of the New Testament permits a 'spiritualizing' of Exodus language, so that the liberation of the gospel is more readily understood as liberation from sin, in contrast with concrete socioeconomic political bondage . . . Thus we must not argue, in my judgement, that deliverance is material rather than spiritual, or that salvation is spiritual rather than material. Rather, either side of such dualism distorts true human bondage and misreads Israel's text . . . The issue of the Bible, in both Testaments, is not one of either/or but of both/and. It will not do to be reductionist in a materialist direction. Conversely it is simply wrong to refuse the material dimension of slavery and freedom in a safe spiritualizing theology, to which much Christian interpretation is tempted.[18]

Wright draws out the implications of all this by restating the classic Lausanne Covenant call to combine social action with evangelism. He denigrates both social action without evangelism and evangelism without social action as partial accounts of the gospel and what it means to be missional to the world.[19] Yet even here he would seem to repeat what at least to me is one of the errors of the Lausanne movement in this regard.[20] That is, far too often evangelism and social action are understood as discrete activities which the well-rounded Christian will combine by ensuring that they undertake both, at least to some extent. Bosch describes the problem with this kind of approach:

> The moment one regards mission as consisting of two separate components one has, in principle, conceded that each of the two has a life of its own. One is then by implication saying that it is possible to have evangelism without a social dimension and Christian social involvement without an evangelistic dimension. What is more, if one suggests that one component is primary and the other secondary, one implies that one is essential, the other optional.[21]

The problem with this approach is that churches frequently interpret integral mission to mean that they must have a balanced list of activities. Evangelism team – check. Social action team – check. As long as the Church is both verbally proclaiming the gospel and feeding the hungry then it is *doing* integral mission. But theologically this is untenable. If we return to the Exodus, Jeffery *et al.* rightly point out that one of the reasons God wanted to liberate his people was so that they could worship him aright.[22] And Pope John Paul II was similarly right to say that liberation in the Exodus was 'ordered to the foundation of the people of God'.[23] In other words, when God liberates politically there are indeed direct spiritual implications of that liberation. We do not have to think of spiritual liberation as some parallel activity *alongside* that of political liberation. Rather, spiritual liberation is one of the *fruits* of political liberation.

But at the same time, the reverse is also true – political liberation can itself be the *result* of spiritual liberation. Hebblethwaite draws attention to the way in which the Exodus was viewed by Polish Catholics during the 1980s. Just as much as their Latin American brothers and sisters, they also desired a political liberation, suffering as they were under the brutal oppression of a communist state, but for them the Marxist interpretations of the Exodus, beloved of some liberation theologians, seemed exactly the wrong kind of solution. Marx was not the liberator; he was the oppressor. As Hebblethwaite comments, Polish prelates 'found the Latin American fascination with Marx . . . naïve, alarming, uncritical, bewildering, inaccurate and above all theoretical . . . The Latin Americans failed to judge the tree of Marxism by its bitter fruits.'[24] The Polish response to this, however, was not so much to despair but rather to embrace a spiritual freedom that was real irrespective of one's particular political situation. Hebblethwaite quotes Helmus Juros:

> To be free, [Poles] did not have to be liberated by the collapse of 'socialist conditions'. It was rather that his individual, Christian-oriented autonomy endowed him with a freedom that would eventually win through in society and would thus overcome the political 'unfreedom' of the state, and free itself and others from dictatorship.[25]

What we see here is the notion that spiritual freedom in Christ generates a dignity and confidence that enables a community to in turn seek their own political liberation. It is no accident that many of the reform movements across the globe – from the Levellers through to the South African Kairos document – were not just motivated by a Christian concept of equality in some abstract sense, but also reflected the inherent dignity that their participants experienced in Christ.

A relatively recent example of this is found in the Zimbabwean Kairos Document. Written in 1998, it begins thus:

> Man and woman were created in God's own image and likeness. God looked upon them as worthy of dignity and value. The Israelites were especially chosen, their cries in slavery were heard and they were liberated to form a nation, governed according to the precepts of Yahweh through the Ten Commandments and the law which emanated from them.[26]

It then goes on to spell out a series of injustices that were perpetrated by the Zimbabwean government of the time and issues a call for justice and equality to reign instead. The subtitle of the document reads as follows:

> A call to faith communities, civic organisations and all movements and individuals that are working for positive, social, political and economic change to build solidarity to work for social, economic and political transformation of society for delivery from poverty, social inequality and to promote good governance.

What we have here is another example of how spiritual freedom leads in turn to calls for political liberation. In all of this my point is that in interpreting the Exodus we must move away from the notion that there are two possible interpretations and that somehow we need to hold both together or keep both side by side. Rather, I want to argue that there is in fact just one interpretation – that the God of Israel rescued his people – but that just as Abraham's call was to be a holistic blessing to all the nations so God's liberation of his people has multiple dimensions, which reinforce one another. In short, I want to suggest that the political and spiritual cannot be divided, as is so often assumed. The so-called political liberation has spiritual consequences. The spiritual liberation has political consequences. Indeed, each is intertwined with the other in what is effectively a perichoretic fashion, so that it is not just bad hermeneutics to talk of the political without the spiritual or the spiritual without the political, but rather it is impossible. And the reason for all this is because it reflects the character of the redeemer God, a God who created us to live holistic lives of complete flourishing: spiritually, politically, relationally, economically and so on. This is what shalom means. It was the call to Abraham, and it is now identified in this founding narrative of the nation.

Both the previous chapter and this one have been seeking to establish just two points: that Israel was called to be a *holistic blessing* to *all the nations*. Both of these points – holistic blessing and all the nations – have been exemplified though the narratives of the call of Abraham and the Exodus from Egypt and are reprised throughout the whole of the rest of the Old Testament. They are fundamental to our understanding of who Israel was, and what she was called to be. It is important to recognize this broad canvas, for in the rest of Part 3 of the book we shall be dipping into a range of teaching, from the Levitical laws through the wisdom of the sages to the proclamations of the prophets, to illustrate these two points. However, it is imperative that we recognize the hermeneutical gap between the passages we shall be exploring and any application for the Church today. As I have already indicated, one of the problems with simply taking Leviticus 19.13–15 and applying it to just trade is that it is not obvious why Leviticus 19.19 does not also apply to the clothes we wear today. The answer to that problematic is to see the whole picture of what Israel was called to be and do, and to understand those verses within the framework that I have outlined. For now, my purposes are simply to delve into the laws and prophets of Israel to provide a richer and more finely grained picture of what it means for them to be a *holistic blessing* to *all the nations*. I am not, at this stage, arguing simplistically that because Leviticus 19 says x, we must also do y. In the next chapter, I will be arguing that, as the people of God, Christians do have the duty to continue the mission that was given to Israel – namely to be a *holistic blessing* to *all the nations*. And given that, I shall throughout the rest of this Part of the book be indicating what I believe might be the implications of any particular passage for the way we construct our socio-political lives today – much as I did in Chapter 6 when I drew on Exodus 21.35–36 to help us understand the interrelationship of culpability and liability. Nevertheless, it is imperative that we recognize that when any particular passage is drawn upon, especially when it is applied to today, that it is first interpreted through the framework of Israel's grand narrative and then, second, interpreted through the framework of the extent to which Israel's call is also our own. While hermeneutics remains a highly contested topic, the approach I am indicating shares greatest affinity with a 'redemptive-historical' approach.[27] The strength of this view is that while it recognizes the importance of understanding any text within its own historical-grammatical context it prioritizes the event of Christ such that ultimately the whole of the canon is interpreted through the lens of Christ and his redemptive work. With those caveats in mind, we will now proceed to explore one of the more remarkable commands given to the nation.

Notes

1 I will ignore as not relevant to my purposes the ongoing debates as to whether the numbers given in the book of Exodus for the size of the nation are historically accurate or not.

2 It is worth noting that some commentators have suggested that the Exodus represents even more of a definitive event for the establishment of the nation than the call of Abraham. P. Hebblethwaite, 1993, 'Let My People Go: The Exodus and Liberation Theology', *Religion, State and Society* 21:1, p. 105.

3 C. Wright, 2006, *The Mission of God: Unlocking the Bible's Grand Narrative*, Nottingham: InterVarsity Press, p. 281, n. 12.

4 G. Gutiérrez, 2001, *A Theology of Liberation*, London: SCM Press, p. 154.

5 Gutiérrez, *A Theology*, p. 154.

6 D. Stephen Long has questioned the significance of the Exodus for Gutiérrez. He wrote, 'Concerning the Exodus, Gutiérrez has stated that the importance attributed to it for liberation theology is overrated. It is 'not a major theme in our theology of liberation' (*The Truth Shall Make You Free*, p. 29).' D. S. Long, 2000, *Divine Economy: Theology and the Market*, London: Routledge, p. 298, n. 41. This, however, is both a misquotation and consequent slight misrepresentation of Gutiérrez's own position. The correct quote in context is the following: 'The theme of the exodus has been and still is an important one for us, but I think it an over-statement to say that it was the major theme in our theology of liberation. It is important because the exodus has been the basic historical experience of the Jewish people and has set its mark on the entire Bible. But I think that we have also treated other themes as important.' He then goes on to talk of how poverty as a theme has been more important than the Exodus. G. Gutiérrez, 1990, *The Truth Shall Make You Free*, Marynoll, NY: Orbis Books, p. 29.

7 N. F. Lohfink SJ, 1987, *Option for the Poor: The Basic Principle of Liberation Theology in the Light of the Bible*, Berkeley: BIBAL Press, pp. 16–32.

8 E. Dussel, 2003, 'Exodus as a Paradigm in Liberation Theology', in E. Mendieta (ed.), 2003, *Beyond Philosophy: Ethics, History, Marxism, and Liberation Theology*, New York: Rowman and Littlefield, p. 116.

9 Dussel, 'Exodus', p. 117.

10 Dussel, 'Exodus', p. 122.

11 Hebblethwaite, 'Let My People Go', pp. 105–14.

12 John Paul II cited in Hebblethwaite, 'Let My', p. 108.

13 Hebblethwaite, 'Let My People Go', p. 109.

14 Hebblethwaite, 'Let My People Go', p. 113.

15 Wright, *The Mission*, pp. 276–7.

16 S. Jeffery, M. Ovey and A. Sach, 2007, *Pierced for Our Transgressions*, Nottingham: InterVarsity Press, p. 36.

17 Jeffery, Ovey and Sach, *Pierced*, p. 35.

18 W. Brueggemann, 1997, *Theology of the Old Testament: Testimony, Dispute, Advocacy*, Minneapolis, MN: Fortress Press, p. 180. See also, Wright, *The Mission*, p. 286.

19 Wright, *The Mission*, pp. 286–8.

20 J. Thacker, 2009, 'A Holistic Gospel: Some Biblical, Historical and Ethical Considerations', *Evangelical Review of Theology* 33:3, July.

21 D. Bosch, 2011, *Transforming Mission: Paradigm Shifts in Theology of Mission*, Marynoll, NY: Orbis Books, p. 405.

22 Jeffery, Ovey and Sach, *Pierced*, p. 35, n. 2.

23 John Paul II, cited in Hebblethwaite, 'Let My People Go', p. 108.

24 Hebblethwaite, 'Let My People Go', p. 110.

25 Hebblethwaite, 'Let My People Go', p. 110.

26 *A Call to Prophetic Action: Zimbabwean Kairos Document*, 1998, Harare: Ecumenical Support Services. Available at: http://ujamaa.ukzn.ac.za/Libraries /manuals/The_Kairos_Documents.sflb.ashx (accessed 15 October 2015).

27 For a useful introduction to this approach, see R. Gaffin, 'The Redemptive-Historical View', in B. M. Stovell and S. E. Porter (eds), 2012, *Biblical Hermeneutics: Five Views*, Downers Grove, IL: InterVarsity Press Academic, pp. 89–110.

9

Jubilee

While many of God's commands have been set aside, ignored or repudiated over the centuries, probably none have been more so than the precepts contained in Leviticus 25. For while many admire its ethos, the practicalities of living it out have only rarely been followed.[1] I will quote the text at length:

> You shall count off seven weeks of years, seven times seven years, so that the period of seven weeks of years gives forty-nine years. Then you shall have the trumpet sounded loud; on the tenth day of the seventh month – on the day of atonement – you shall have the trumpet sounded throughout all your land. And you shall hallow the fiftieth year and you shall proclaim liberty throughout the land to all its inhabitants. It shall be a jubilee for you: you shall return, every one of you, to your property and every one of you to your family. That fiftieth year shall be a jubilee for you: you shall not sow, or reap the aftergrowth, or harvest the unpruned vines. For it is a jubilee; it shall be holy to you: you shall eat only what the field itself produces.
>
> In this year of jubilee you shall return, every one of you, to your property. When you make a sale to your neighbour or buy from your neighbour, you shall not cheat one another. When you buy from your neighbour, you shall pay only for the number of years since the jubilee; the seller shall charge you only for the remaining crop-years. If the years are more, you shall increase the price, and if the years are fewer, you shall diminish the price; for it is a certain number of harvests that are being sold to you. You shall not cheat one another, but you shall fear your God; for I am the LORD your God.
>
> . . . The land shall not be sold in perpetuity, for the land is mine; with me you are but aliens and tenants. Throughout the land that you hold, you shall provide for the redemption of the land.
>
> If anyone of your kin falls into difficulty and sells a piece of property, then the next-of-kin shall come and redeem what the relative has sold. If the person has no one to redeem it, but then prospers and finds sufficient means to do so, the years since its sale shall be computed and the difference shall be refunded to the person to whom it was sold, and the property shall be returned. But if there are not sufficient means to recover it, what was sold shall remain with the purchaser until the year of jubilee; in the jubilee it shall be released, and the property shall be returned.
>
> If anyone sells a dwelling-house in a walled city, it may be redeemed until a year has elapsed since its sale; the right of redemption shall be for one year. If it is not redeemed before a full year has elapsed, a house that is in a walled

city shall pass in perpetuity to the purchaser, throughout the generations; it shall not be released in the jubilee. But houses in villages that have no walls around them shall be classed as open country; they may be redeemed, and they shall be released in the jubilee. (Lev. 25.8–17, 23–31)

Arguably, no other biblical text has had as much impact on the politics of global poverty as this one. A whole movement – Jubilee 2000, now the Jubilee Debt Campaign – was founded on the principles outlined in this section of Scripture. A number of fundamental principles would seem to be evident within the passage. Perhaps the first of these is simply that God owns everything. This is made especially clear in verse 23, which states, 'The land shall not be sold in perpetuity, for the land is mine.' The underlying idea is that because God created the land and gave the land to the Israelites, their 'ownership' of such land is but provisional. They are stewards rather than absolute owners, and as such when the land is passed around from one to another these transactions are more about transfer of stewardship than ownership, for ultimately the land belongs to God. It shall not be sold in 'perpetuity' because it cannot be – the steward-owners simply do not have that right. Wright says:

> One of the central pillars of the faith of Israel was that the land they inhabited was YHWH's land. It had been his even before Israel entered it (Ex. 15.13, 17). This theme of the divine ownership of the land is found often in the prophets and Psalms. Far more often than it is ever called 'Israel's land', it is referred to as 'YHWH's land'.[2]

The ethical impact of this for those holding the land is twofold. First, it places restrictions on what they can do with the land. The one who holds property absolutely can do with it what they want, but the one who is holding the property as a steward may well make decisions regarding its use, but they act within a limited set of freedoms regarding that land. This point would appear to be denied by Arthur Lindsley in his discussion of this passage. He helpfully titles the relevant section, 'Myth #3: Jubilee Shows the Relative Nature (Relativisation) of Private Property', and then goes on to say:

> According to this myth, since God owns the land (Leviticus 25.23) there are no absolute rights to private property . . . If you have been following the argument of this chapter, you will see that Leviticus 25 argues the exact opposite. God owns the land, but he has given the Promised Land to the tribes and families of Israel with the condition that private property cannot be sold, squandered, or permanently given away. The property rights remain in the hands of the tribe or family who were given the land in the first place.[3]

But that is precisely not what the passage says. The reason given in verse 23 for why the land cannot be sold in perpetuity is not because it must be permanently owned by the original title-holders. Rather, the reason that is provided in verse 23 for why land cannot be permanently sold is because it is precisely not the sellers' to sell, they are but stewards; the land belongs to God. As William Cavanaugh has argued:

> The very distinction between what is mine and what is yours breaks down in the body of Christ. We are not to consider ourselves as absolute owners of our stuff, who then occasionally graciously bestow charity on the less fortunate. In the body of Christ, your pain is my pain, and my stuff is available to be communicated to you in your need.[4]

Moreover, as Bryant Myers notes, even the fruit of our work does not truly belong to us but represents the fruit of God's work in us. As such, one impact of the fall is that we ignore 'the claim of God on all things in creation or the transcendent responsibility each has for the well-being of the larger community'.[5]

The second principle for us that emerges from these jubilee regulations is that because God's ownership of the land relativizes our rights as owners, God is also at liberty to instruct us how we should *use* the land. This flows immediately from the fact that God is the ultimate title-holder, not us. The question then arises as to how God might want us to use the property that he has bequeathed to us. Again, Wright is helpful here. He makes the point that the Jubilee provisions are not some special requirement, somehow unrelated to God's overall missional purpose, but as with everything else God's purpose in these jubilee regulations is that the nation might be a holistic blessing to all the nations. In practice, the way we use property must be for the benefit of the whole community.

> Just as the right of access to, and use of, the *resources* of the earth is a shared right that sets moral limitations to the right of private ownership of resources, so too the right to consume or enjoy *the end product* of the economic process is limited by the needs of all. We are all responsible to God for what we do with what *we* produce, as we are for what *God* has given us 'raw'. There is no mandate in the creation material either for private *exclusive* use, or for hoarding or consuming at the expense of others.[6]

This interpretation is challenged by John Wind when he argues that 'Wright's claim that Genesis 1–2 teaches corporate human ownership of material goods as taking precedence over individual human ownership is a weak textual claim.'[7] But this is categorically not what Wright is claiming. He is not at all advocating 'corporate human ownership'. Indeed, he explicitly states that the jubilee 'stands as a critique not only of massive private accumulation of land and related wealth, but also of large-scale forms of collectivism or nationalization that destroy any meaningful sense of personal or family ownership'.[8] Wind's argument is one that is frequently followed by those who, on capitalist grounds, wish to avoid the obvious implications of the jubilee principles. They set up a false polarity, arguing that the only options available are either unfettered capitalism, and therefore absolute private ownership, or communist or socialist collectivism. This is especially clear in Grudem and Asmus' *The Poverty of Nations*, and in Bradley and Lindsley's *For the Least of These*. But, as Wright makes clear, those are not the only options. Wright is not arguing against private ownership in favour of state-organized collectivism. Rather, he is arguing for relativized private owner-stewardship, which is to be administered for the benefit of the whole community. Another contemporary example that avoids both absolute private ownership and nationalization are Community Capital Trusts, which are non-profit trusts that hold capital for the sake of cultural and social benefits.[9]

It would seem, though, as if capitalist hermeneutics ignores these options because it ignores the prior truth that God owns everything. But if one takes seriously the prior claim that absolute ownership is indeed the preserve of God alone, then that relativizes our ownership and also means that God can indicate to us how we should use those goods we currently own/steward. And it is here, Wright says, that we should use them for the good of all:

> Private dominion over some of the material resources of the earth does not give us a right to consume the entire project of those resources, because dominion always remains trusteeship under God and responsibility for others. There is no necessary or 'sacrosanct' link between what one owns or invests in the productive process and what one can claim as an exclusive right to consume as income in return. There is a mutual responsibility for the good of the whole human community, and also for the rest of the non-human creation.[10]

It is in this sense that 'the right of all to *use* . . . seems to be morally prior to the right of any to *own*'.[11] Wind misinterprets this to be a statement supporting collectivism, but that is not Wright's point. It is a moral argument regarding how God wishes us to steward the resources that he has put at our disposal.

With this framework in mind, the precise features of the jubilee laws now make complete sense. God's overall purpose in them is to ensure that the whole people of God are blessed. God was not enumerating a socio-economic-political principle as such – whether capitalist or socialist. Rather, God's approach was effectively pragmatic. He recognized that, for a range of reasons, some of the people will inevitably fall on hard times – they might have suffered an accident and so be unable to work, perhaps their crops were blighted by some disease, maybe they suffered a raid from a nearby tribe, and possibly even they had been lazy and not worked the land appropriately – the precise reason does not matter, but as a result they had sold their land or even themselves to deal with their acute economic crisis. However, God's intention was that the people should not remain in that situation of destitution and impoverishment for ever. He also recognized that there was no way in which they could bring themselves out of the situation, and so he provided the jubilee principles to ensure that every 50 years those who are poor would be brought out of poverty by having their land restored. This is especially clear in verses 25–28, which begins with the person who, due to 'difficulty', sells their property. If a relative is able to redeem their property then so be it, but if not – in other words, if there is no other way for this person to find their feet again – then after 50 years their 'property shall be returned'. Wright correctly points out that at the heart of the jubilee principle is not so much a redistributive political ethic, but rather a question of restorative justice: 'It was not a handout of bread or "charity", but a restoration to family units of the *opportunity and the resources to provide for themselves again.*'[12] Within a political framework where the only options are individual private ownership or state ownership then jubilee makes no sense. However, within a theological framework in which none of us ultimately own anything, and in which *all* that we have is given for the benefit of all, then it makes complete sense that there are these moments of periodic restoration in which those who cannot help themselves are provided with sufficient resources to begin the journey of restoration again.

The contemporary practical implications of this are obvious. It is no accident that the original Jubilee 2000 campaign was a campaign regarding international debt. As I have already argued, the question of international debt, and in particular forgiving those debts, is not a matter of redistribution but of restorative justice. When I previously argued this it was in relation to the indebtedness of the West to low-income countries. However, even if those arguments are not fully accepted then a similar practical outcome – that is, forgiving international debts – can be made on the basis of the jubilee principles. Applied at the national level – and of course Leviticus 25 is written for a nation – the responsibilities it enshrines are that we use the wealth we have accumulated to be a blessing to *all the nations*. In particular, in relation to the jubilee principles, if a nation finds itself impoverished for any reason, we have a responsibility to use our wealth to assist that nation by means of providing it with a mechanism to restore its wealth. In the sixth to fifteenth centuries BC,[13] that meant restoration of land rights so that a family/tribe could continue to cultivate produce and farm animals for slaughter. In the twenty-first century, that might mean forgiveness of debts and adoption of trade policies that do not harm LICs but allow them to make the most of the natural resources with which they have been endowed. In regard to this, the following passage from further on in Leviticus is also instructive:

> If any of your kin fall into difficulty and become dependent on you, you shall support them; they shall live with you as though resident aliens. Do not take interest in advance or otherwise make a profit from them, but fear your God; let them live with you. You shall not lend them your money at interest taken in advance, or provide them food at a profit. I am the LORD your God, who brought you out of the land of Egypt, to give you the land of Canaan, to be your God. (Lev. 25.35–38)

The clear injunction in these verses is that when people fall on hard times, while it is perfectly possible to take advantage and make profit from their hardship, this is categorically outlawed. Moreover, the reason it is outlawed is because this is not in line with the character of God. In appealing to the Exodus narrative, the point of the author is to reprise all that we have said before – that God has created this nation not for its own sake, but so that it can be a benefit to all the nations. The purpose of the Exodus was not just to rescue the nation, but, as we have already noted, to rescue the nation so that it can be a blessing to the nations. Therefore, if an Israelite takes advantage of the hardship of another Israelite they are failing to act in line with God's purposes for the nation, namely to be a blessing to all. Given all this, I find it simply bewildering that Mark Isaac can argue that the kind of profiteering condemned in Leviticus is somehow acceptable for a Christian. He writes:

> One of the ways for an economist to become unpopular at a cocktail party is to defend, upon the basis of mutual benefit, the merchant who sells gasoline for $20 a gallon following a hurricane. Although I am one of those economists who would do so, as a Christian can I really argue that mutual benefit by itself is just? Yes.[14]

Isaac's argument is that the 800 per cent increase in price is justified because the resource is now scarce and demand is extremely high, and he says that any alternative to such a mark-up would represent a 'race headlong toward the slippery slope of "just price" theology, price controls, and all of the bad economics those views entail'.[15]

There are innumerable problems with this argument. In the first place, such unrestricted capitalism inevitably leads to gross inequalities (see the last chapter), and even if such inequalities were not in themselves morally reprehensible, they contribute, as Joseph Stiglitz has argued, to a stagnant economy.[16] However, more to the point is that such restrictions on economic behaviour seem to be precisely what the author of Leviticus envisages. Isaac might dismiss such Levitical economics as 'bad economics' – though, as I have indicated, Stiglitz and I would argue with this – but what is less clear is how he can ignore such injunctions when they are contained in the pages of the Scriptures that he indicates he follows. The author of Leviticus is indeed insisting on 'price controls' at this point, and whether or not Isaac agrees with him economically he should agree with him theologically.

What is clear about Isaac's point, however, is that he is at least being consistent with a neoliberal argument that suggests market restrictions are always inappropriate. What is less clear is why other Christian free-market capitalists do not follow him in suggesting that profiteering in the context of a natural disaster (or presumably war) is not entirely justifiable. Isaac seems to be ploughing a lonely furrow in this regard, which suggests that other Christians who do espouse free-market capitalism are perhaps not entirely being consistent to their free-market principles when they recognize the moral reprehensibility of profiteering in this context. My point is that with very few exceptions no one believes in completely free markets. The question is not whether we restrict capitalism, but how and in what manner. The Levitical injunctions would seem to indicate that it is restricted in a pro-poor direction, and this provides a framework for us to follow.

Lying behind this is a difference between how we understand the goal of economics. For Isaac, as for any free-market fundamentalist, the purpose of economics is to ensure that the nation as a whole grows its economic output, its GDP. This is particularly clear in Grudem and Asmus' treatment of the topic. They begin their book by outlining for us what is the correct goal of economic policy: 'The correct goal is that a nation continually produces more goods and services per person each year.'[17] Stated like that, one might not have too much of an argument with them, particularly if one assumes that such increasing goods and services are distributed relatively equally. But that is not what

Grudem and Asmus mean at all. For in practice what they mean by this goal is an increase in a country's GDP irrespective of its impact on economic equality. They write:

The most important question, then, is this: What will increase a country's GDP?[18]

The goal must be to increase a nation's GDP.[19]

When government forces economic equality (for example through heavy taxes on the rich), it can actually diminish economic incentives and harm the GDP.[20]

This last quote is particularly telling, for it illustrates the way in which Grudem and Asmus would seem to prioritize a nation's overall GDP ahead of its economic equality. This is significant because there is only one way in which a nation can overall become wealthier while its level of economic equality worsens, and that is by the wealthiest members of that country becoming even more wealthy than the poorest, in other words by wealth accumulating to the rich. But the goal of the jubilee principles is precisely the opposite – that the poor get richer while the rich get poorer. Anyone who has lost land and who is destitute will inevitably find their asset base improved by having that land restored. And anyone who owns lots of land and who is forcibly required to relinquish some of it at no cost will find themselves poorer. The goal, it seems to me, is not redistribution in the ideological sense that everyone should have an equal share of wealth. The fact that houses within cities can remain the property of the rich in perpetuity indicates that fact (Lev. 25.29–30). Rather, the goal is that everyone, each person, has a chance to flourish as a human being. That is the problem that is being addressed by the jubilee principles. The poor, landless peasant simply has no opportunity to flourish precisely because they have no assets at their disposal – nothing with which they could make money even if they had the industry and initiative to achieve it. The goal, as I have indicated repeatedly, is that the nation should be a blessing to all the nations, and within the nation that means a blessing to all the people. Keeping someone in a permanent state of servitude does not enable them to live the life that God intended. Enabling them to live that life is then a question of justice, not one of politics.

Returning then to the international scene, if our trade and tax practices prevent these poorer nations from flourishing, then, irrespective of any questions or indeed politics of redistribution, we are failing to be the people that God has called us to be. That is the issue before us. It is not so much a question of redistribution in an ideological, political sense. It is much more a question of human flourishing – and which economic policy, will enable *all* nations and *all* people to flourish. Very clearly, unfettered (or growth) free-market capitalism is not that policy, for while it definitely does make nations *qua* nations richer, it does this by paying no attention to the impoverished at the bottom of the income and wealth scale, and that is to ignore the whole purpose of Leviticus 25.

One final point that crops up in the literature to dismiss the idea that Leviticus 25 has any moral hold on us is that historically it probably was never followed. This is an argument that is pursued by a number of authors[21] and the implication seems to be that because it never actually happened we are not obliged to follow their non-example. However, as Wright points out, 'there is no historical record of the Day of Atonement, either'.[22] Moreover, since when has obedience to God's commands been a matter of historical precedent – we are only obliged to follow those commands that have successfully been obeyed by others! In reality, I suspect that those who point out the non-historicity of the narrative are in fact trying to make another rather subtle point. What they are trying to suggest without actually saying so is that its non-historicity indicates that it represents some form of later interpolation, and implicitly what is being suggested is that it should not be part of the canon at all. That is a perfectly intelligent position to hold, but if that is the reason why we should ignore Leviticus 25 then it behoves those critics who point to its lack of historical evidence to state that clearly – and that is what they do not do.

Notes

1 Of course, some Christian communities, such as the Levellers and Diggers, have tried with varying success to live out the kind of radical equality described in Leviticus 25. For discussion and examples, see M. Hoek, J. Ingleby, A. Kingston-Smith and C. Kingston-Smith (eds), 2013, *Carnival Kingdom: Biblical Justice for Global Communities*, Gloucester: Wide Margin.

2 C. Wright, 2006, *The Mission of God: Unlocking the Bible's Grand Narrative*, Nottingham: InterVarsity Press, p. 292.

3 A. Lindsley, 'Does God Require the State to Redistribute Wealth? An Examination of Jubilee and Acts 2–5', in A. Bradley and A. Lindsley (eds), 2014, *For the Least of These: A Biblical Answer to Poverty*, Grand Rapids, MI: Zondervan, p. 84. For a similar argument, see also J. Glas, 2015, 'The Gospel, Human Flourishing and the Foundation of Social Order', *The Southern Baptist Journal of Theology* 19:2, pp. 105–34.

4 W. T. Cavanaugh, 2008, *Being Consumed*, Grand Rapids, MI: Eerdmans, p. 56.

5 B. Myers, 1999, *Walking with the Poor: Principles and Practices of Transformational Development*, Marynoll, NY: Orbis Books, p. 28.

6 C. Wright, 2004, *Old Testament Ethics for the People of God*, Nottingham: InterVarsity Press, p. 149.

7 J. Wind, 2015, 'Not Always Right: Critiquing Christopher Wright's Paradigmatic Application of the Old Testament to the Socio-economic Realm', *The Southern Baptist Journal of Theology* 19:2, p. 94.

8 Wright, *Old Testament Ethics*, p. 207.

9 M. Large, 2010, *Common Wealth: For a Free, Equal Mutual and Sustainable Society*, Stroud: Hawthorn, pp. 156–60.

10 Wright, *Old Testament Ethics*, p. 149.

11 Wright, *Old Testament Ethics*, p. 148.

12 Wright, *Old Testament Ethics*, p. 207.

13 The dating of Leviticus is irrelevant to the argument I am making here.

14 R. M. Isaac, 'Markets and Justice', in Bradley and Lindsley (eds), *For the Least of These*, p. 129. It is noteworthy that Kotter would appear not to share Isaac's conclusion here. D. Kotter, 2015, 'Greed vs. Self-Interest: A Case Study of How Economists can Help Theologians Serve the Church', *The Southern Baptist Journal of Theology* 19:2, Summer, p. 23.

15 Isaac, 'Markets', p. 129.

16 J. Stiglitz, 2012, *The Price of Inequality: How Today's Divided Society Endangers our Future*, New York: Norton & Co.

17 W. Grudem and B. Asmus, 2013, *The Poverty of Nations: A Sustainable Solution*, Wheaton, IL: Crossway Books, p. 45.

18 Grudem and Asmus, *Poverty of Nations*, p. 48.

19 Grudem and Asmus, *Poverty of Nations*, p. 50.

20 Grudem and Asmus, *Poverty of Nations*, p. 50.

21 Grudem and Asmus, *Poverty of Nations*; Lindsley, 'Does God Require'.

22 Wright, *The Mission*, p. 295.

10

Laws

In a recent article exploring the question of economic justice and the Bible, Richard Horsley suggests that there can be found three distinct paradigms within Scripture on the issue. The first is what he terms 'radical insistence on economic justice',[1] in which the Pentateuch, in particular, plus some of the early prophets set out a series of measures which are designed to ensure 'the economic viability of each component family/household in a village community (if not economic equality)'.[2] The second of his paradigms, which he identifies as existing within monarchical texts, essentially accepts the economic injustice which exists when power is centralized, but nevertheless calls for reform to bring about a greater degree of justice. So, for instance, he points to Nehemiah who 'forced the predatory Judean aristocracy to restore the people's land and family members who they had seized as debt-slaves (Neh. 5.1–3). But he did not relax the Persian imperial demand for tribute that had drawn them into poverty in the first place.'[3] The final paradigm that Horsley describes is that of 'divine blessing on institutionalized injustice'. While it is relatively easy to recognize in Scripture the first two of Horsley's frameworks, this third one is much harder to see. The evidence he adumbrates for such divine blessing on injustice is essentially the royal psalms where YHWH is seen to be advocating and empowering a monarchical system. For Horsley, such a system necessarily involves a situation of economic injustice, and so if God blesses the monarchy then God is also necessarily blessing injustice.[4] I find this reading hard to maintain, primarily because even within the royal psalms what is clear is that YHWH honours the ruler who rules with justice, not without it. Psalm 2 tells those in authority, 'Now therefore, O kings, be wise; be warned, O rulers of the earth. Serve the LORD with fear' (Psalm 2.10–11). Psalm 89 speaks of how 'righteousness and justice' are the foundation of God's throne and how therefore judgement will come on those who forsake God's law (Ps. 89.30–32). Hence, to suggest that the very establishment of a monarchy necessitates an economic injustice is to confuse how things turned out with how God intended them to be.

The point of this discussion though is that, while contexts change, the consistent line throughout the whole of Scripture is the one indicated by Horsley's first paradigm, namely that the Scriptures provide economic wisdom so that *all* may live lives of economic security. We have already seen that this is in reality the motif exemplified in the creation narratives and in the call of Israel. God's intention is that *all peoples* may experience shalom. This then sets the background to a series of Old Testament laws that we will now explore. Their purpose is not to instantiate or describe a particular economic system – whether capitalist, socialist or anything else. Rather, they are there simply to ensure or promote God's shalom for all.

However, as well as indicating the overall moral purpose of these commands, it is also necessary to provide some principle for their relevance today. I have previously noted that we must avoid at all costs any kind of shortcut from 'the Bible said so, therefore we must do it today', particularly in respect of the kinds of commands found within the Pentateuch. A helpful approach in this respect is that outlined by Charles Cosgrove in his *Appealing to Scripture in Moral Debate: Five Hermeneutical Rules*. I am particularly drawn to the first of these rules, 'the rule of purpose'. According to this rule, the moral weight of a particular command does not lie in the specific instruction that is outlined but rests rather on the moral purpose that lies behind the command. For Cosgrove, the specific instructions were never given to exhaustively describe our moral responsibilities but rather to illustrate some broader moral goal.[5] He provides the example of Jesus' instruction to walk the extra mile, and his point is that 'biblical moral rules impinge on us not in their rulish formulations but in their justifications, which may be principles'.[6] His further point is that precisely because these principles (or justifications) carry more weight than the particular formulation, they may in fact be used to counteract the formulation if in a specific circumstance to obey the formulation would be to deny the principle.[7]

Perhaps a more obvious example of this can be found if we consider the following injunction: 'When you build a new house, you shall make a parapet for your roof; otherwise you might have blood-guilt on your house, if anyone should fall from it.' The precise form of this command is not what matters – it clearly pertains to the type of dwellings that existed at the time – but the broader principle of protecting others from harm is where the moral weight lies. To pick up on the point that I made in Chapter 8, to read this instruction through a christological hermeneutic is to see it as an expression of what it means to love your neighbour. Loving your neighbour – Christ's command – involves doing no harm to your neighbour, which includes ensuring their safety. In the twenty-first century, this means everything from ensuring the brakes work on your car, to complying with building regulations when a new house is built. It would also include ensuring that the conditions in which your workers labour are safe.

In April 2013, the Rana Plaza building in Savar, Bangladesh, collapsed, killing over 1,000 workers and injuring another 2,500. The reason for the collapse was subsequently identified to be a structural deficit. What makes this tragedy even more shocking was that it was entirely avoidable. The day before the collapse, workers had identified a series of major cracks that had appeared. Nevertheless, the workers were told that they must continue working and return the next day. When they did so, the building failed and many lives were lost. The global dimensions of this tragedy were indicated by the fact that the factory made garments for many Western household names, including Benetton, Monsoon, Accessorize, Matalan, Primark and Walmart. We can see a direct line from Deuteronomy 22.8 to the victims of Savar. However, that hermeneutical path goes via the principle of protecting others and the christological command to love one's neighbour.

In the same vein, as I explore a series of commands below, I am not simply pulling commands out of the Old Testament and applying them to a series of economic concerns today. Rather, I am adopting Cosgrove's rule of purpose and the christological hermeneutic described previously to discuss what the relevance of such commands might be for today. In terms of Cosgrove's approach, the purpose of all these commands, or at least the purpose I would wish to highlight, is the one that we have already noted, namely that God's desire is for *all* to flourish. This is a purpose highlighted in creation, lost in the fall and recapitulated in the calling of the nation. Many of these commands can be viewed as particular illustrations of the kinds of actions that are required in order to bring about a situation of shalom for all. Moreover, the christological dimension of that purpose is once again seen in the command to love one's neighbour. It is in essence about bringing about the well-being of others. With that framework in mind, we will now explore some of these specific instructions.

Within the Old Testament, we find a series of commands concerning the way in which slaves, servants and, more broadly, workers are treated. Wright classifies these instructions into three specific categories: conditions, payment and rest.[8] He points out that owners of slaves were put under uncharacteristic (for the time) constraints in how they were to treat their slaves, with Leviticus 25.43 declaring in relation to Hebrew servants that 'You shall not rule over them with harshness, but shall fear your God.'[9] Perhaps clearer are the numerous instructions to ensure prompt and fair payment of workers:

- You shall not keep for yourself the wages of a labourer until morning. (Lev. 19.13)
- You shall not withhold the wages of poor and needy labourers, whether other Israelites or aliens who reside in your land in one of your towns. You shall pay them their wages daily before sunset, because they are poor and their livelihood depends on them; otherwise they might cry to the Lord against you, and you would incur guilt. (Deut. 24.14–15)
- Woe to him who builds his house by unrighteousness, and his upper rooms by injustice; who makes his neighbours work for nothing, and does not give them their wages. (Jer. 22.13)
- I will be swift to bear witness against the sorcerers, against the adulterers, against those who swear falsely, against those who oppress the hired workers in their wages, the widow, and the orphan, against those who thrust aside the alien, and do not fear me, says the LORD of hosts. (Mal. 3.5)

This is not just an issue about prompt payment, but also about the level of pay that is appropriate. It is the Catholic Church that has done most of the thinking about the issue of just wages. Building on Aquinas' concept of the just price, Catholic social teaching has continued this trajectory by developing the concept of the just wage. This is most explicit in Pope Leo's encyclical *Rerum Novarum*, and was then followed in John Paul II's 1981 encyclical *Laborem Exercens*. In it he notes the inherent injustice in merely setting wage levels according to market mechanisms, which in practice means the lowest possible one can get away with, and instead proposes that 'Just remuneration for the work of an adult who is responsible for a family means remuneration which will suffice for establishing and properly maintaining a family and for providing security for its future.'[10] He states that the level of wages that is supplied is a means of checking the justice of the whole socio-economic system. Behind these statements lies a theology that recognizes our corporate responsibility to ensure the flourishing of all. Of course, the retort of some might be that they are not running a charity but a business, but that is entirely to miss the point of where our ultimate responsibility lies. If the salary level that is set does not facilitate the flourishing of one's employees, then such a salary level is not in tune with God's purposes. This is not to argue for entirely flat salary structures, but it is to say that in choosing a level of remuneration the flourishing of all should be the primary consideration and not merely the lowest that will be accepted. It is perfectly obvious that a starving person will undertake work for significantly less than the work warrants, and to pay a fair wage is an issue of justice, for in paying a just wage the inherent dignity of the employee is being recognized. To fail to pay such a wage is to fail to recognize the *imago Dei* in one's brother or sister.

The third dynamic that Wright identifies is the importance of rest for employees.

> But the seventh day is a sabbath to the LORD your God; you shall not do any work – you, or your son or your daughter, or your male or female slave, or your ox or your donkey, or any of your livestock, or the resident alien in your towns, so that your male and female slave may rest as well as you. (Deut. 5.14; cf also Ex. 20.10)

Of course, part of the injunctions regarding Sabbath rest was to demonstrate honour to God who set this pattern in train, but far more significant was that it provided the practical rest and relaxation that is required for humanity. Once again, this links to the idea that God's goal is that all of us are meant to flourish. The person who works 12-hour days, 7 days a week may be existing but is not flourishing. God's purpose is that life is enjoyed, not just subsisted. This also relates to the level of wages that are set, for if the salary level for one's employment is set at such a level that the employee has no choice but to take two or three jobs, working every weekend with no rest, then once again we are violating the commands of God. James Cypher gives the example of a couple who worked for a company to whom Nike had subcontracted their labour. Working full time, the couple earned a total of $82 per month and their single room occupancy is described thus:

> A single bare bulb dangles from the ceiling, its dim glare revealing a plain bed, a single gas burner, and a small plastic cabinet. Their room, one of a dozen in a long cement building, is provided with one container of water daily. If they want more water, each jug costs around 5 cents.[11]

In fact, there are two issues at stake here. To deny workers fair treatment is both to negate the image of God in them, to strip away the dignity that is conferred on them by creation, *and* it is to fail to uphold the creation mandate to bring about flourishing in all the nations. Of course, within a neoliberal economic system these concerns simply do not figure at all. The primary responsibility of businesses is to their shareholders not to their employees; the argument proffered in support of this notion is that unless shareholders are not duly reimbursed they will not invest, and without investment there is no economic growth. These arguments have merit, and so in suggesting that part of an employer's responsibility is to consider the flourishing of all of its employees, I am simply making the case for what has recently been called the 'triple bottom line'. This phrase was coined by John Elkington in 1994 and essentially it encourages businesses to account not simply for their profits and losses, but also for their environmental and social impact.[12] The three bottom lines are often described as people, planet and profit. The social impact aspect of the three bottom lines includes therefore the employees of any business, as well as the wider social community affected by the business. To argue that business should be reporting in this way represents a fairly modest measure, but that is certainly achievable. It might be argued that merely reporting a triple bottom line does nothing to change the circumstance of employees. That is correct. However, at the same time, by reporting a triple bottom line, a business and its shareholders are forced to confront the human and environmental impact of the conduct of their business. The easiest way to ignore poor treatment of workers is to refuse to acknowledge the issue – the triple bottom line disavows that approach.

In addition to arguing for a triple bottom line, the Old Testament principle that would encourage human flourishing also mandates some form of minimum wage. The Old Testament does not tell us what level a minimum wage should be, but the clear intention of the passages quoted above is that the reason for prompt and fair payment is so that the employee has sufficient to meet their daily needs for sustenance and livelihood.

This focus on the well-being of all is also evident in another of the Old Testament commands to which we must turn our attention, namely provision for the poor. As Wright correctly points out, an underlying principle here is that we are not wholly responsible for the wealth we have created. We noted earlier how the wealth any of us have produced is in part a product of the general system of government in which we live (and for that reason taxes are justifiable), but that is even more the case if we consider the contribution of God to the labour of our hands. For it is God who gave us life, skills, resources and time in order to produce the wealth that we now enjoy. 'Do not say to yourself, "My power and the might of my own hand have gained me this wealth." But remember the LORD your God, for it is he who gives you power to get wealth' (Deut. 8.17–18).

It is precisely for this reason that for Christians there is no absolute notion of private property, but rather a relative one, for ultimately everything belongs to God. This then provides the rationale for the Old Testament gleaning laws.

When you reap the harvest of your land, you shall not reap to the very edges of your field, or gather the gleanings of your harvest. You shall not strip your vineyard bare, or gather the fallen grapes of your vineyard; you shall leave them for the poor and the alien: I am the LORD your God. (Lev. 19.9–10; cf also 23.22)

When you reap your harvest in your field and forget a sheaf in the field, you shall not go back to get it; it shall be left for the alien, the orphan, and the widow, so that the LORD your God may bless you in all your undertakings. When you beat your olive trees, do not strip what is left; it shall be for the alien, the orphan, and the widow.

When you gather the grapes of your vineyard, do not glean what is left; it shall be for the alien, the orphan, and the widow. (Deut. 24.19–21)

It is very easy to interpret these verses as the Old Testament equivalent of *noblesse oblige*, but that is not what is taking place here. To leave one's gleanings was not an act of charity, but rather one of justice. It was to recognize, first, that all the fruit of one's labour ultimately belongs to God, and therefore God can dispose of it as he wills. But it was also to recognize that God's purpose in blessing us with the ability to work and harvest goes hand in hand with God's desire to see all peoples blessed, to see every individual flourish. The significance of the poor, the widow, the orphan and the alien is not that these people are objects of charitable giving, it is simply that because of their particular life circumstances they are currently in a situation where they cannot sow seed and till land in order to produce their own crop. As such, they are dependent on the produce grown on the land of others.

One of the great lies of neoliberalism is that we have somehow earned the livelihood we now enjoy and therefore it is up to us to decide how we spend that excess. These Old Testament commands remind us that everything belongs to God, even the so-called fruit of our labour, and therefore ultimately it is up to him how it is spent. In her novel *The Poisonwood Bible*, Barbara Kingsolver draws out this clash of world-views. The novel tells the story of an American missionary family who travel out to the Belgian Congo in 1959. They struggle to adapt to Congolese life in numerous ways, but repeatedly throughout the novel one of the aspects that they find odd is the way in which the villagers routinely share their excess with one another. 'Whenever you have plenty of something, you have to share it,' declares one character, and the following exchange occurs between one of the missionary children and a Congolese teacher:

'When one of the fishermen, let's say Tata Boanda, has good luck on the river and comes home with his boat loaded with fish, what does he do? . . .

'He sings at the top of his lungs and everyone comes and he gives it all away.'

'Even to his enemies?'

'I guess. Yeah. I know Tata Boanda doesn't like Tata Zinsana very much, and he gives Tata Zinsana's wives the most.' . . .

'That is just how a Congolese person thinks about money.'

'But if you keep on giving away every bit of extra you have, you're never going to be rich.'

'That is probably true.'

'And *everybody* wants to be rich.'
'Is that so?'[13]

Perhaps it is that last line that reveals the main difference between individualistic and communitarian cultures. Within the latter, it is not charity to share with one another, it is just what one does. Within an individualistic culture, the only possible type of sharing is that done as charity. It is for that reason that we can struggle to understand fully the Old Testament gleaning laws. We tend to see them as a means of charitable giving or even as a social safety net, but that is not their primary function. They were instead about re-establishing justice in the community, ensuring that all – whether stranger or native-born – were able to flourish in the way that God intended. In short, they were about the people of God being the people of God. This is why these verses are interspersed with many other aspects of the holiness code that make little sense today. These verses are about the kind of people, the kind of nation, Israel was going to be – and God's intent was that it was a nation characterized by justice for all.

All of this means that it is not immediately obvious how such gleaning laws should be translated into practice today. As I've indicated, some would argue that the relevant contemporary practice is welfare provision, and depending on how one views welfare this does indeed make sense. The problem I am trying to avoid is the approach to welfare that views it as an issue of charity rather than one of justice. This is clearly the mindset that pervades many of the authors in Bradley and Lindsley's *For the Least of These*. Lawrence Reed writes: 'Government welfare or "relief" programs encourage idleness, break up families, produce intergenerational dependency and hopelessness, cost taxpayers a fortune, and yield harmful cultural trends that may take generations to cure.'[14] Further on, he opines, 'It is wrong to take a dollar from the responsible and give it to the irresponsible.'[15] For Reed, then, state-sponsored welfare is a waste of money. Notwithstanding the fact that his assertions are highly questionable, the principal issue here is what kind of community we are meant to be. Authors such as Reed believe strongly in the individual ethic of the self-made man. In a section where he encourages his readers to emulate 'lives of self-improvement', he also tells them 'to stand on our own two feet as far as our abilities allow'.[16] He describes all of this as what it means to pursue a biblical character, but what seems to be absent is that a biblical character is only about self-improvement to the extent that it blesses all. The call to Israel was not to be the most prosperous, numerous nation that it could be, but to be a flourishing nation so that in turn all nations would be blessed through her. The purpose of self-advancement (if there is such a thing) is only for the sake of others. Hence, if there are others who, for whatever reason, are struggling it is simply a matter of justice that we share with them out of the abundance that God has given us.

In reality, at a global level, we not only do not do this to any meaningful extent, we actually pervert the course of justice and in effect not only prevent them from gleaning from our fields, but prevent them from gleaning even from their own. The commands that speak to this are the numerous ones that counsel us to show justice to the poor. Their unifying feature is not about charity but once again about justice, simply that we do not exploit the inherent weakness that comes from powerlessness. There are at least four different ways in which this is expressed. The first of these concerns the price that is set for various goods and services.

> If any of your kin fall into difficulty and become dependent on you, you shall support them; they shall live with you as though resident aliens. Do not take interest in advance or otherwise make a profit from them, but fear your God; let them live with you. You shall not lend them your money at interest taken in advance, or provide them food at a profit. (Lev. 25.35–37)

In a short while, I shall deal with the thorny issue of usury, but for now I want to consider what this passage says about the just price. The context is where one of your kin has fallen into financial difficulty. The passage does not indicate the reason for this difficulty. Indeed, it seems to be of no consequence to the author what the cause of the impoverishment has been. What matters is how we respond in this situation. Due to their difficulty, the family member has become dependent and the instruction in the passage is that we should support them. What makes this particularly interesting is that in telling us we should support them, the passage clearly indicates that we do this by treating them as 'resident aliens'. The clear implication of this is that this kind of behaviour was not restricted to extended family members. Indeed, the implication is that the author does not need to repeat the numerous injunctions telling the Israelites they are to take care of aliens. Rather, what is new in this situation is the need to take care of someone from the extended family. If we think about it for a moment this makes sense. As I have already indicated, what links the orphan, the widow and the alien is that they are powerless and vulnerable to exploitation. For differing reasons, they are without the power that is needed to work and provide for themselves, and so the Israelites are commanded to take care of them. What is unusual in the situation described in Leviticus 25.35ff. is that this would appear to be a person who under normal circumstances can provide for themselves. We need to note that this is a person who has fallen into difficulty, therefore indicating that at some previous point in time they were not in difficulty – they were financially stable. But now, they find themselves on hard times. This is why it is different to the orphan, the widow and the alien. Presumably, they were perennially destitute, and therefore needed to be looked after in some way continually. Not so with this kin person – they have found themselves poor, perhaps a failed harvest, perhaps a raid by some nearby enemies, perhaps sickness in the family. Whatever the situation, they were secure, now they are poor, and what is the God-fearing Israelite instructed to do in this situation? They are to provide for them, not taking a profit, specifically not selling food at a profit. Once again, then, we have evidence that God is more concerned that all are able to flourish than he is that someone in particular take advantage and make a quick buck.

In the previous chapter we encountered Isaac's argument in favour of market-set prices, even in the context of local disasters. The argument he pursues is essentially this: the price of any good or service should be determined by supply and demand. Goods in high demand but low supply (such as his post-hurricane gasoline) should be priced accordingly high. And goods in low demand and high supply should be priced proportionately low. The apparent justification for such market-derived valuations is simply that the free market is the best way to organize an economy and no other mechanism has been shown to be beneficial for a nation as a whole. Throughout *For the Least of These*, this is the form of argument that is consistently put forward whenever any challenge is put towards neoliberalism. If we don't pursue as aggressively as possible a free-market approach then we end up with communism, or some form of state socialism. We know that doesn't work, so it has to be neoliberalism that is pursued.

At least one of the problems with this argument is that it is simply not true. Many economists predicted that a minimum wage would inevitably lead to a rise in unemployment. The most recent meta-analysis of this issue in the USA has demonstrated the falsity of this prediction, with the minimum wage having minimal or no effect upon employment rates.[17] In the same vein, supporting some form of just price, or at the very least making illegal exploitation of the kind supported by Isaac, is very unlikely to collapse an economy. The reason I say this is because a number of highly successful European countries do enjoy some form of price controls in relation to essential utilities, for instance, and yet have not collapsed into the communist dystopia that neoliberals predict.

I am not arguing that all goods and services should be controlled in this way. My point, rather, is that it is perfectly possible to set ceilings on certain essential goods and services that mean the powerless are not exploited and that don't collapse the whole of the economy. This is precisely what it seems that Aquinas meant in his definition of the just price, which is not absolutely fixed but 'there is a justice in exchange that is not reducible to market rates'.[18] Once again, the rationale for all of this is simply that all enjoy the opportunity to flourish. In the absence of such price controls, a starving man will sell his house or land for a loaf of bread, and thereby deprive himself of the ability to make future income via his livelihood. The same principle is at work in Deuteronomy 24.6: 'No one shall take a mill or an upper millstone in pledge, for that would be taking a life in pledge.' While the person in desperate circumstances might be willing to sell or pawn their livelihood for the sake of some much needed cash, it is incumbent upon us not to take advantage of others in this way. The overriding principle seems to be that even when taking advantage is possible, we must not do this. This stands in sharp contrast to the neoliberal ethic that at all times one must maximize profit – it is merely business is the cry that goes up, but such practices leave a trail of impoverishment in their wake.

The same approach is evident in the issue of usury. As Chris Wright has pointed out, the ban on interest was not an outright ban but limited to loans between Israelites. Given everything else that has been said about God's purpose being a blessing on all nations, this contrast cannot be because God is unconcerned with the economic plight of non-Israelites. It seems much more likely that this differential is because different kinds of loans are in view. Between nations, and therefore when the Israelites were trading with other nations, what was in mind was the kind of commercial trading with which we are familiar today. However, between Israelites, the kinds of loans that were in question were loans born not of comparative advantage, but loans born of necessity. We can see this in the various commands that discuss the use of such loans and the goods put up as collateral:

> When you make your neighbour a loan of any kind, you shall not go into the house to take the pledge. You shall wait outside, while the person to whom you are making the loan brings the pledge out to you. If the person is poor, you shall not sleep in the garment given you as the pledge. You shall give the pledge back by sunset, so that your neighbour may sleep in the cloak and bless you; and it will be to your credit before the LORD your God. (Deut. 24.10–13)

And so Wright comments:

> Deuteronomy's permission to charge interest to a 'foreigner' probably has that kind of commercial trading in mind. But the other laws clearly specify that the loan is required because of *need*, primarily for the annual necessities of agricultural life, for example the loan of seed corn. The ban on interest is thus not concerned with economic growth in itself, but with growth achieved by taking unscrupulous advantage of another's need.[19]

The final way in which the poor were not to be exploited was in respect of justice before the law.

> You shall not pervert the justice due to your poor in their lawsuits. Keep far from a false charge, and do not kill the innocent or those in the right, for I will not acquit the guilty. You shall take no bribe, for a bribe blinds the officials, and subverts the cause of those who are in the right.
> You shall not oppress a resident alien; you know the heart of an alien, for you were aliens in the land of Egypt. (Exodus 23.6–9)

Once again, the issue is one of powerlessness. The poor – the widow, the orphan, the alien – simply did not have the economic resources to ensure that they were dealt with fairly. God's command is that despite their impoverished state they must be treated equitably. This also highlights the final point in this section, that frequently in respect of issues of poverty the people who were addressed were not the poor themselves but the powerful, the wealthy. It is they who must use honest weights and measures (Lev. 19.36), it is they who must pay their workers promptly and fairly, it is they who must set a just price, and it is they who must not exploit the poor in the courts. Much of Isaac's chapter in *For the Least of These* is addressed to the poor themselves, telling them how they should not be so indigent, lazy, irresponsible, and so on.[20] In contrast, we have already noted Wright's comment that the Old Testament does not portray the poor as the problem and instead focuses on the rich and powerful, those 'who actually have the power to do something, or whose power must be constrained in some way for the benefit of the poor'.[21] Perhaps the clearest way in which such truth to power was spoken was not the law, however; it was in the

LAWS

mouths of the prophets who in essence called the leaders and the nation back to the law that they had ignored. The prophets, then, are the topic of our final chapter in this part of the book.

Notes

1 R. Horsley, 2015, 'You Shall Not Bow Down and Serve Them: Economic Justice in the Bible', *Interpretation: A Journal of Bible and Theology* 69:4, p. 417.

2 Horsley, 'You Shall Not', p. 418.

3 Horsley, 'You Shall Not', p. 420.

4 Horsley, 'You Shall Not', p. 420.

5 C. Cosgrove, 2002, *Appealing to Scripture in Moral Debate: Five Hermeneutical Rules*, Grand Rapids, MI: Eerdmanns, pp. 12–50.

6 Cosgrove, *Appealing*, p. 17.

7 Cosgrove gives the example of the person who discovers that carrying the burden an extra mile is in fact facilitating some other evil act – carrying stolen goods for instance.

8 C. Wright, 2004, *Old Testament Ethics for the People of God*, Nottingham: InterVarsity Press, p. 159.

9 Of course, the whole question of why they were allowed to keep slaves in the first place comes to the fore here. However, what is clear is that the Israelites were commanded to look after their slaves in a way that the surrounding nations were not.

10 John Paul II, 1981, *Laborem Exercens*, n. 19.

11 J. Cypher, 2014, *The Process of Economic Development*, 4th edn, Oxford: Routledge, p. 535.

12 J. Elkington, 1997, *Cannibals with Forks: The Triple Bottom Line of 21st Century Business*, Oxford: Capstone.

13 B. Kingsolver, 1998, *The Poisonwood Bible*, London: Faber and Faber.

14 L. Reed, 2014, 'A Poverty Program that Worked', in A. Bradley and A. Lindsley (eds), *For the Least of These: A Biblical Answer to Poverty*, Grand Rapids, MI: Zondervan, p. 194.

15 Reed, 'A Poverty Program', p. 208.

16 Reed, 'A Poverty Program', p. 209.

17 H. Doucouliagos and T. D. Stanley, 2009, 'Publication Selection Bias in Minimum-Wage Research? A Meta-Regression Analysis', *British Journal of Industrial Relations* 47:2, pp. 406–28; see also D. Oliver, 2014, 'The Evidence is Clear: Increasing the Minimum Wage Doesn't Cost Jobs', *Guardian*, 11 June.

18 B. Brock, 2015, 'Globalisation, Eden and the Myth of Original Markets', *Studies in Christian Ethics* 28:4, p. 415.

19 Wright, *Old Testament Ethics*, p. 165.

20 R. M. Isaac, 2014, 'Markets and Justice', in Bradley and Lindsley (eds), *For the Least of These*.

21 Wright, *Old Testament Ethics*, p. 174.

133

II

Prophets

It almost goes without saying that the prophetic texts continue to demonstrate God's concern for the poor that we have already evinced in the law and the founding of the nation. Indeed, the frequent reprise of these books is that the nation needs to return to the God whose primary concern is the orphan, the widow the alien – in short, the powerless. Donald Gowan draws attention to the injustice that was at the heart of the prophetic concern:

> For Old Testament writers the cause of poverty which produced the most concern and true indignation was not what the poor do or do not do but what others have done to them . . . There were ways to deal with the problems of being hungry and ill-clothed and homeless; but all of them could be thwarted by injustice, and it is that against which the Old Testament rages. Those people who do not have the power to insist on justice for themselves are thus held up as a special concern for the whole community . . . Nowhere does the Old Testament hold up as an idea a complete equality in the distribution of wealth. It assumes throughout that there will always be some with relatively more possessions. This is no scandal, for wealth is to be prized as one of the good gifts of God (Prov. 22.4). What is a scandal, as many texts have shown us, is when those who do have so much are deprived of what is rightfully theirs by those whose consciences do not bother them.[1]

Gowan puts his finger here on what is at the heart of the prophetic lament. It is not that the rich are not being sufficiently charitable or philanthropic, it is that the rich and powerful are exploiting and oppressing the poor. This is the refrain that keeps on returning throughout the prophetic books:

> For if you truly amend your ways and your doings, if you truly act justly one with another, if you do not oppress the alien, the orphan, and the widow, or shed innocent blood in this place, and if you do not go after other gods to your own hurt, then I will dwell with you in this place, in the land that I gave of old to your ancestors for ever and ever. (Jer. 7.5–7)
>
> Hear this word, you cows of Bashan, who are on Mount Samaria, who oppress the poor, who crush the needy, who say to their husbands, 'Bring something to drink!' The Lord GOD has sworn by his holiness: The time is surely coming upon you, when they shall take you away with hooks, even the last of you with fish-hooks. (Amos 4.1–2)

Render true judgements, show kindness and mercy to one another; do not oppress the widow, the orphan, the alien, or the poor; and do not devise evil in your hearts against one another. But they refused to listen, and turned a stubborn shoulder, and stopped their ears in order not to hear. They made their hearts adamant in order not to hear the law and the words that the LORD of hosts had sent by his spirit through the former prophets. (Zech. 7.9–12)

There are many possible reasons for this being the emphasis within the prophetic texts, not least the fact that the nation would appear to have abandoned, if not forgotten entirely, the law which was first given to them. However, in addition to this, a number of authors have suggested that with the passage of time, and in particular in post-exilic Israel there is evidence of increasing social stratification. Marvin Chaney discusses how changes in trading patterns during the eighth century BC 'widened the already gaping economic chasm between the wealthy urban elite and most peasants and artisans. It also pauperized portions of those already poor.'[2] He also discusses the agricultural intensification that developed during this period and the consequent changes in loan practices from what was effectively a social insurance mechanism to what became predatory loaning.

Wealthy landlords could first squeeze every last drop from a peasant family's labor, and then foreclose, thereby creating a growing pool of landless day laborers and debt-slaves. Foreclosure on peasant land rights for non-payment of survival loans granted on impossible terms was also a mechanism of land consolidation. More and more land rights passed into fewer and fewer hands, as those few wealthy enough to grant survival loans foreclosed upon the desperate many who had no choice but to take them out. Land consolidation and an increase of landless day-laborers and debt-slaves walked hand in hand.[3]

Focusing on the post-exilic period, Albino Barrera draws attention to the archaeological evidence of increasing social stratification evidenced in house size. In pre-exilic Israel most houses were of a simple four-room design. There was, of course, some variation in house size with some with larger rooms and some as small as two or three rooms, but the degree of variation appears to have been strictly limited. In contrast, in post-exilic Israel, there was a rapid and marked transformation whereby these four-room houses disappeared, to be replaced by 'large agricultural estates' replete with peasant or slave workers.[4] In this context, the condemnation of Micah makes poignant sense:

Woe to those who plan iniquity, to those who plot evil on their beds! At morning's light they carry it out because it is in their power to do it. They covet fields and seize them, and houses, and take them. They defraud people of their homes, they rob them of their inheritance. (Mic. 2.1–2, NIV)

If this analysis is true, then the picture we are painted is one in which increasing inequality arises precisely because those with power and authority are failing to fulfil their covenantal duties and in the process exploiting the poor and the powerless, thus building wealth for themselves at the expense of the less well off.

We see here a very different response to poverty to that which is employed either by the political Left or the political Right. For too often the main response of some on the political Left is essentially that of philanthropy. Luke Bretherton has chastised this approach calling it the age of humanitarianism. He suggests that such assistance is frequently accompanied by a paternalism that denies the agency of the person we are helping. We have already noted the dangers of such paternalism earlier in this book. Bretherton writes:

> Even if what we do to help is not intentionally paternalistic or colonial in orientation, our interventions are more often than not an attempt to govern the lives of others . . . we end up removing their agency in order that they might conform to our notions of what is good and right and proper.[5]

As we have also seen, however, on the political Right the response is to chastise those who are poor for not working hard enough, being irresponsible, failing to be sufficiently entrepreneurial. What links both of these responses is that the object of their attention is the poor themselves – on the one hand to help, perhaps in a paternalistic fashion; on the other, to chastise. Perhaps counter-intuitively both are guilty of what Bretherton describes, that is, neglecting the agency of the poor themselves. The humanitarian does this by effectively claiming that they have the solution to poverty, the Right does this by claiming that the poor have not demonstrated sufficient agency already. What both sides ignore is what the prophets seem to have grasped – that the problem is not the poor, but the rich and the powerful. The poor do have agency and if only they were no longer exploited and oppressed, if only the rich and powerful would get off their backs, then they would enact their own solutions to poverty. This seems to be the context in which the prophets write.

> The people of the land have practised extortion and committed robbery; they have oppressed the poor and needy, and have extorted from the alien without redress. And I sought for anyone among them who would repair the wall and stand in the breach before me on behalf of the land, so that I would not destroy it; but I found no one. (Ezek. 22.29–30)

This is what the prophets have done. They have sought to stand in the breach, to plead the cause of the powerless to ensure they are released from their oppression. What makes this trope particularly interesting is that it is one that very clearly continues into the New Testament. The role of the prophet becomes the role of the Church in its task to speak truth to power, and in particular to cast down empires that set themselves up against the Lordship of Christ. In *Colossians Remixed*, Brian Walsh and Sylvia Keesmat provide an alternative interpretation of the letter to Colossae, drawing out its anti-imperial rhetoric. They point, for instance, to Paul's description of the fruitfulness of the gospel in Colossians 1.5–6 and comment:

The Colossian community was surrounded by a claim of fruitfulness and fertility, a claim rooted in the oppressive military might of the empire, in the controlling social structures of the empire, and in evocative images of lush fertility found on the building, statues and household items that shaped their visual imagination . . . If the empire encodes in the imagery of everyday life – on public arches, statues and buildings – the claim that Rome and its emperor are the beneficent provider and guarantor of all fruitfulness, then can a claim that the 'gospel' is bearing fruit 'in the whole world' be heard as anything less than a challenge to this imperial fruitfulness?[6]

Walsh and Keesmat argue that throughout the book of Colossae what can be found is an alternative narrative that challenges the imperial rhetoric of Rome. Caesar is no longer Lord; Christ is. Caesar does not bring salvation; Christ does. Caesar is not the source of hope; Christ is. Their point is that the gospel of Jesus Christ is far more than a ticket to heaven, it is the blueprint of an alternative empire – one that is ruled by peace and justice for all, or, perhaps another way of putting that, the flourishing of all nations. In their book, they draw out the contemporary implications of this by pointing to the current practice of economic processing zones (EPZs). EPZs exist in a number of LICs as a means to allow multinational corporations to avoid paying tax or adhering to labour laws in that country. In effect, the Zone – a geographical area usually on the edge of one of these countries – becomes an area where the employment rights of workers can be ignored and tax on the economic activity within the zone is minimal. Governments of LICs facilitate such zones because they fear that without them the multinational would simply take their investment and employment elsewhere. It is also suggested that bribes frequently accompany the setting up of such zones. Nevertheless, as Walsh and Keesmat point out, the conditions within the zones are frequently atrocious. Naomi Klein captures this well:

Regardless of where EPZs are located, the workers' stories have a certain mesmerizing sameness: the workday is long – fourteen hours in Sri Lanka, twelve hours in Indonesia, sixteen in Southern China, twelve in the Philippines. The vast majority of the workers are women, always young, always working for subcontractors from Korea, Taiwan or Hong Kong. The contractors are usually filling orders for companies based in the United States, Britain, Japan, Germany or Canada. The management is military style, the supervisors often abusive, the wages below subsistence, the work low-skill and tedious.[7]

Walsh and Keesmat comment:

Every time we step into a Wal-Mart or Niketown or Gap or Winners and exclaim over the great deal we can get on an article of clothing, or how trendy we now look, we've made sweatshop workers our slaves . . . The language of inevitability is the language of empire . . . The truth is we have many choices. The simplest action anyone can take is to stop purchasing these products . . . You might decide to lobby these corporations to end their oppressive labour practices. Or you might decide to join one of the projects of campaigns that work to end child labour and support workers' rights. Maybe you will lobby your government to withdraw from trade agreements that legitimate oppression and call on your political leaders to draft new legislation that seeks to end the global markets equivalent of slavery.[8]

This is what being prophetic is about. It is about recognizing injustice, exploitation and oppression – particularly of the vulnerable – and denouncing those practices, refusing to take part in them and working to change them. The nation of Israel was called to be a blessing to all nations, it was not called to an ethic of individual freedom. The challenge for us is to recognize that an alternative world is possible. As I have already pointed out, the argument of the political right is that the only options are neoliberal capitalism or communism, and because we must reject the latter we are only left with the former. But these are not the only options. In their book drawing out the anti-imperial rhetoric of Revelation, Wes Howard-Brook and Anthony Gwyther point out that one of the ways in which the Roman Empire sought to maintain its power was to convince the population that change was impossible. What we see in the prophetic texts and in the anti-imperial denunciations of the New Testament is that another world is possible, and it is to this world that we are called.

Ultimately, as with the illusions propagated by the Roman Empire, the primary illusion generated and maintained by the global capital empire today is that the world is largely as it should be and that efforts to change it are misguided at best and dangerous at worst . . . Thus, as Revelation underscores, a key aspect of being true to our Christian vocation today is to name and resist this illusionary power of empire.[9]

Notes

1 D. Gowan, 1987, 'Wealth and Poverty in the Old Testament: The Case of the Widow, the Orphan, and the Sojourner', *Interpretation* 41:4, October, pp. 349–50.

2 M. Chaney, 2014, 'The Political Economy of Peasant Poverty: What the Eighth-Century Prophets Presumed but Did Not State', *Journal of Religion & Society* 10, p. 37.

3 Chaney, 'The Political Economy', p. 43.

4 A. Barrera, 2013, *Biblical Economic Ethics*, Plymouth: Lexington Books, pp. 53–4.

5 L. Bretherton, 2015, 'Poverty, Politics, and Faithful Witness in the Age of Humanitarianism', *Interpretation: A Journal of Bible and Theology* 69:4, p. 448.

6 B. Walsh and S. Keesmat, 2004, *Colossians Remixed: Subverting the Empire*, Downers Grove, IL: InterVarsity Press, pp. 74–5, at p. 72.

7 N. Klein, 2000, *No Logo: Taking Aim at the Brand Bullies*, Toronto: Village Canada, p. 205.

8 Walsh and Keesmat, *Colossians*, pp. 213–14.

9 W. Howard-Brook and A. Gwyther, 1999, *Unveiling Empire: Reading Revelation Then and Now*, Marynoll, NY: Orbis Books, p. 254. A similar argument has also recently been made by Whitlark in relation to the book of Hebrews,

namely that the primary purpose of the book was to encourage an anti-imperialist stance among the nascent Christian community. J. Whitlark, 2014, *Resisting Empire: Rethinking the Purpose of the Letter to 'the Hebrews'*, London: T & T Clark. Interestingly, Macaskill indicates that Revelation is not so much a critique of Rome 'as a challenge to a potentially complicit church'. G. Macaskill, 2009, 'Critiquing Rome's Economy', in B. Longenecker and K. Liebengood (eds), *Engaging Economics*, Grand Rapids, MI: Eerdmans, p. 259.

PART 4

Redemption

12

The gospel and salvation

We have been tracing this theme of a corporate *imago Dei* throughout this book. If one conceives of the *imago* in individualistic terms then it makes sense that our state as fallen beings can also be conceived of individualistically, and similarly our redemption is then an individual act – the single sinner saved by the grace of Christ. However, if one conceives of the *imago* corporately then, as we have seen, our fallen nature consists of a corporate failure to display the relationships of justice and righteousness that will facilitate human flourishing for all, and consequently our redemption consists of a corporate redemption, or at least our redemption has a corporate dimension.

Not long after the Reformation, the Protestant Church wedded its theology of salvation to the emergent Enlightenment individualism. Indeed, some would trace the roots of Enlightenment individualism to the Reformation. It is a short step from 'all are now priests' to 'each of us stands in a direct relationship with God' to 'each of us is redeemed as an individual'. In saying this, I am not arguing that there is not any individualistic element to the gospel of Jesus Christ. It is indeed the case that as an individual I am a sinner and as an individual I will stand before the judgement seat of Christ and give an account of my life as an individual. However, the New Testament (and the Old) balances this individual account of redemption with a strong emphasis on its corporate dimension. The image of the living God is not the head of a group of individuals, but the head of the body, that is, the Church. If one part suffers, all parts suffer. The problem with contemporary Protestantism is that our individualism has become unchecked. We have thrown out any sense of corporate salvation. We have no idea what such words would even mean. Salvation consists of my journey to heaven – it does not involve anyone else at all. In this chapter, I want to recover a more corporate sense of redemption, and I do this not because I am rejecting an individualistic concept of salvation but rather because I view it as a necessary corrective to that individualistic conception.

In his book *After Our Likeness: The Church as the Image of the Trinity*, Miroslav Volf spends some time arguing that salvation is necessarily a communal phenomenon. He presents two particular arguments in this regard. The first is to draw attention to the manner in which we receive our faith. He points out that each one of us who has heard the gospel has heard that gospel through the Church – in the sense that we have heard it through other believers. None of us have imagined this gospel by ourselves through direct relationship with God, rather we have received the word of salvation as it was spoken by others who have in turn received that word. As such, our reception of faith has been mediated by others and in that sense we cannot be an individual believer, for our very beliefs have come to us though others. He comments:

> Ratzinger has emphasized that one receives faith precisely as a gift of God *from* the church . . . indeed, the actual believing subject or 'I' is the collective 'I' of the church . . . Because the church has an essential role in the mediation and discharging of faith, salvation itself possesses an indispensable social dimension.[1]

He goes on to point out the sacramental aspect of this, noting that no one can 'self-administer' the sacraments and that as such, the sacraments demonstrate 'the essentially communal character of the mediation of faith'.[2]

In addition to drawing attention to the way in which faith is received, Volf also constructs an argument based on the nature of faith itself. In essence, his argument is that in relating to God through faith, we do not relate as isolated individuals, but only as a communal entity. We do not first of all believe and then come to join the Church as some kind of associative group made up of members with mutual interests. The Church is categorically not the spiritual or religious version of some single-interest 'club'. Rather, the faith that is born in us by the Spirit is at the same time a faith that establishes our relationship to God and to one another. Our fellowship with God is simultaneously a fellowship with one another. 'Those who say, "I love God", and hate their brothers or sisters, are liars; for those who do not love a brother or sister whom they have seen, cannot love God whom they have not seen' (1 John 4.20). The significance of this verse is that it does not say that we need to add obedience to our faith in God, as if we first of all love God and then, in some subsequent ethical move, love our neighbour. The intent of the verse is that if we do not love our brother or sister then, by that very fact, we cannot at the same time love God. Of course, experientially, this is not what seems to be the case. All of us will have had the sense of a deep, profound faith in God while at the same time a deep resentment (even hatred) towards particular brothers and sisters. However, while experientially we may think we can love the one without loving the other, the Johannine witness is that ontologically this cannot be. Indeed, the fact that our experience is divorced from the reality that the author of 1 John describes simply suggests that our experience (not for the first time) is misleading us. The reality is that we have misunderstood what it means to say 'we love God'. For the Johannine verse would appear to suggest that loving God is only possible as we love our neighbour. This is not to collapse love of God into love of neighbour. God remains a distinct being in whom we put our trust independently, as it were, of our love for neighbour. Rather, the point being made is that there is something in the very nature of faith that means that when we love God we are, at the same time, predisposed to love our neighbour.

This simultaneous love (of both God and neighbour) is not an ethical addition – of one love to another love – but an ontological state of affairs in which there is one love which arises from faith and which when directed towards God issues in love of God, and when directed towards neighbour issues in love of neighbour. The one faith therefore has both divine and corporate dimensions. Quoting Eberhard Jüngel, Volf writes:

> Communion with this God is at once also communion with those others who have entrusted themselves in faith to the same god. Hence one and the same act of faith places a person into a new relationship both with God and with all others who stand in communion with God. These others 'are discovered *equiprimally* with the new communion with God as one's neighbours, as those who belong to the same communion'.[3]

Volf makes two further points in support of this argument. The first is that precisely because we believe the Church to be the outcome of God's work, rather than the product of our efforts in mutual collectivism, we must believe that to be part of that Church is a primary rather than secondary effect. As God brings us into fellowship with himself, he also brings us into fellowship with others. Anything else reduces the Church to being merely a club.[4] Second, the Church stands as a sign and foretaste of the eschatological communion that is yet to be. But as such, faith must necessarily involve an ecclesial identity. To allow for the possibility of an individual faith outside the Church is to allow for the possibility of an isolated believer in the eschaton, but that is not the hope to which we look forward. As Volf comments:

> To experience faith means to become an ecclesial being. Nor can it be otherwise if the church is to be the proleptic experience within history of the eschatological integration of the *entire* people of God into the communion of the triune God.[5]

Volf mentions this in passing,[6] but it is also noteworthy that one of the primary metaphors used in the New Testament for the Church is that of the family. In becoming Christians, we are *born* (again) into this family, we separate from our human relatives (Matt. 12.48; Luke 14.26), and we identify those who share our faith as brothers and sisters (1 Tim. 5.2). The significance of the family, however, is that by definition one cannot be a member of a family as an isolated individual. The family necessarily involves some criteria for entry – that one is born or adopted into it – but in the very same moment of entry one also relates to a range of others. One is not born/adopted, and then at some later date *choose* to become the brother/sister, son or daughter. Rather by being born/adopted, one does *at the very same time* become brother/sister, son/daughter and so on. In the same way, in becoming members of God's family through faith, we become brothers and sisters to the whole worldwide community of faith. Salvation is necessarily corporate. We are not first saved and then an ecclesial identity is added as some subsequent movement. Rather, to be saved just means having an ecclesial/communal identity as members of the whole Church of God.

The preceding discussion has sought to argue that salvation is not of the isolated individual, but of the individual in relationship, and as such salvation is of the Church as the corporate image-bearer. In order to apply this understanding to a theology of poverty, however, we need to explore further the nature of the salvation that is enjoyed by the Church. Is it present? Is it future? Is it about our souls? Or does it involve in some sense our whole bodies? Perhaps even the whole of creation? It is to these questions that we now turn our attention.

The Western, and in particular the Protestant, and even more especially so the evangelical, parts of the Church have for some time tended to interpret salvation this way: to be saved means that I, as an individual, have been rescued from sin and death and one day I will go to spend eternity with God in heaven. In the meantime, my role is to convince as many people as possible of the truth of this great rescue plan so that they in turn can go to heaven when they die. This kind of thinking is standard evangelical fare – it was the gospel on which I was raised. However, as numerous authors have pointed out, such a 'gospel' is a travesty of the biblical witness. According to N. T. Wright, there are at least four distinct problems with this approach, and we shall discuss each of them in turn.

The first is that it pictures salvation as affecting a disembodied soul rather than a whole human being. As Wright has extensively pointed out, resurrection does not mean revivification of a corpse, neither does it mean the ongoing eternal existence of the soul in some spiritual realm. Rather, 'resurrection means bodily life *after* "life after death", or, if you prefer, bodily life after the *state of* "death"'.[7] This was the single, coherent meaning for the Greek term *anastasis* and its cognates among pagans, Jews and Christians. Whether the person in question was affirming or denying the reality of such resurrection, this was simply what the word meant. If, then, the Christian hope is of resurrection from the dead, this cannot mean anything other than an embodied existence in a new heaven and new earth. This is precisely where the biblical witness lies and what the relevant Greek terms mean. As Wright goes on to say:

> This explains at a stroke the otherwise puzzling fact that the New Testament often refers to 'salvation' and 'being saved' in terms of bodily events within the present world. 'Come and save my daughter,' begs Jairus; as Jesus is on his way to do so, the woman with the issue of blood thinks to herself, 'If I can only touch his clothes I will be saved'; 'Daughter,' says Jesus to her after her healing, 'your faith has saved you.'[8]

Salvation, then, is not about a disembodied existence but rather a material existence in a renewed or new heaven and earth.

But if, as those passages indicate, it is embodied, then it is also about the present, not the future. Frequently – especially in evangelical circles – salvation is talked of in terms of a future hope, and of course there is a future dimension to salvation. The eschaton is not yet fully realized. But at the same time, we must emphasize that there is a 'now' aspect to the salvation that we enjoy. It is not entirely about the future. We see that in the ministry of Jesus. When John the Baptist was doubting whether or not Jesus was the one to come, Jesus' reply was to point to the outworking of the gospel in the present: 'the blind receive their sight, the lame walk, the lepers are cleansed, the deaf hear, the dead are raised, the poor have good news brought to them' (Luke 7.22). Commenting on this passage, Joel Green notes that 'good news to the poor' both 'interprets and is amplified by these other designations'.[9] In other words, the gospel that

Jesus brought was in part the good news of miraculous healings in the here and now. Salvation, then, is not merely about the future; it is also an aspect of what we see now.

> A proper grasp of the (surprising) *future* hope which is held out to us in Jesus Christ leads directly and, to many people, equally surprisingly, to a vision of the *present* hope which is the basis of all Christian mission. To hope for a better future in this world – for the poor, the sick, the lonely and depressed, for the slaves, the refugees, the hungry and homeless, for the abused, the paranoid, the downtrodden and despairing, and in fact for the whole wide, wonderful and wounded world – is not something *else*, something extra, something tacked on to the 'gospel' as an afterthought.[10]

Far too often, Christian salvation is viewed solely in terms of rescue from this dead and decaying world, but that is not the Christian hope. The Christian hope is that as we grasp the nature and certainty of the *future* hope that motivates us to bring about a better world in the *present*.

Third, Christian salvation is not individualistic, but as we have already argued necessarily corporate. An individualistic gospel frequently reduces to what is effectively a selfish individualism. Indeed, it is often preached that way. 'Come to Jesus and you too can be saved and spend eternity with him.' But that is not the Christian message at all. Wright provides a telling analogy in which he asks us to imagine a child that is given a cricket bat for Christmas.[11] To peddle a selfish, individual gospel is equivalent to such a child proclaiming, 'I won't play with anyone else; this bat has been given to me, and it is *mine*.' To make such a point is to completely miss the purpose of the gift, and for us to think that the purpose of the gospel is merely so that we, as individuals, can go to heaven when we die, is also to miss its purpose. Its purpose is for us to make this world a better place; to foster relationships of hope, justice and mercy; to encourage human flourishing for all. As Tom Wright comments:

> [God] did not want to rescue humans *from* creation, any more than he wanted to rescue Israel *from* the Gentiles. He wanted to rescue Israel *in order that Israel might be a light to the Gentiles,* and he wanted thereby to rescue humans *in order that humans might be his rescuing stewards over creation.*[12]

While such a corporate emphasis to salvation might seem unusual to Western ears, it is far more naturally embraced by other parts of the world. Fr Benigno Beltran has spent much of his life working as a parish priest among the urban poor who live on the Smokey Mountain garbage dump in Manila, Philippines. He charts the individualistic, atomistic culture and theology that pervades the West, contrasting it with the more integrated anthropology and theology of South East Asia, before commenting that for Filipinos, 'Salvation was communitarian, understood as participation in the future Lordship of Yahweh over the whole earth.'[13] A similar anthropology is articulated by the Ghanaian theologian Kwame Bediako, and he also draws out the missional and soteriological implications of this:

The Great Commission is not about the percentages of national populations that we may consider to have 'reached' or remain 'unreached' with the gospel, important as these considerations are. Our Lord did not say, 'Go make disciples of some people or even of a large percentage of the people of the nations.' What he commanded was, 'Go make disciples of the nations, go make the nations my disciples.'[14]

And he continues:

The task of the gospel is not the salvation of our 'souls' apart from the cultural embodiment of our lives. Rather, the purpose and goal of the gospel is the redemption of cultures and the cleansing of all cultural forms of life and expression so that they come to express praise and adoration of the one Living God and our Lord Jesus Christ.[15]

Returning to Tom Wright, we can see how this way of conceiving things pulls together what otherwise is frequently held apart – namely our doctrine of atonement and Jesus' ministry on earth, and this represents our fourth critique of the model under scrutiny. For if the atonement is essentially about how we get to heaven when we die, then Jesus' very clear emphasis during his earthly life on the socio-political transformation of society is somewhat embarrassing. If all that matters is what happens when we die, why did Jesus bother challenging the ruling authorities or heal the sick or feed the hungry and so on? But if, on the other hand, all that matters is Jesus' political kingdom ministry then his death and resurrection becomes something of an embarrassing afterthought, and certainly not worthy of the weight that Paul, in particular, seems to place on them. In contrast to these two options, a *Christus Victor* understanding of the atonement, coupled with a kingdom theology that draws its contemporary application from the not yet, enables us to view Christ's work (his life, death and resurrection) as a unified whole. Jesus Christ was fulfilling what first Adam and then Israel had failed to achieve, that is, the inauguration of God's rule on earth. Such rule would be manifest in the embodied flourishing of all as they enjoy stewardship of the earth's resources and relationships of righteousness with one another – in short as they experience shalom, all under the just and merciful guidance of their creator God. Christ inaugurates this through his healings, signs of mercy and reversal of status dishonour among the poor. In so doing, he is communicating to all both that they are welcome in God's kingdom and the nature of that kingdom. But Christ also brings this about through his death and resurrection which defeats evil and the powers that hold us captive to death. Christ does not work alone, though, because in defeating evil he opens the way for us – his body – to continue this ministry of reconciliation, to be his ambassadors and so extend this worldly flourishing that he has inaugurated to as many as possible. And all of this is an anticipation of the full and complete shalom that shall be enjoyed in the age to come. This is the gospel of Jesus Christ and this is what salvation means.[16]

The significance of the preceding section for the topic before us is widespread. In a short while, I will examine a range of theories and theologies of international development and investigate them in conversation with the doctrine of redemption I have just outlined. After all, if salvation is concerned with bringing about the mutual flourishing of all the nations then at least to some extent the goal of salvation should be aligned with the goal of international development work. However, before I examine those broad theories and theologies of development there are some specific development practices that I want to explore in light of the understanding of salvation I have just described.

Lying behind the practices I will explore is our tendency to privilege the individual over the community or wider structural issues. We have already seen the evangelical/Protestant tendency to view conversion as an individual activity of saving souls. It will then be no surprise to discover that in respect of international development it is frequently evangelical development agencies that are at the forefront of programmes that favour the individual. This is particularly obvious in respect of child sponsorship programmes. World Vision and Compassion are two leading international aid agencies, both of which have an evangelical foundation, and both headline child sponsorship as a significant part of their efforts. While there do exist secular development agencies that incorporate child sponsorship into their work, there is not a single major British secular development agency that has individual child sponsorship as a significant aspect of its work.[17] In contrast, there are a number of Christian – and especially evangelical – development agencies for whom child sponsorship represents a major part. I am not convinced that this is accidental and wonder if the evangelical propensity to save the individual soul is simply being transferred to a desire to save the individual child. Having said this, it is important to recognize that rarely do child sponsorship programmes literally channel funds from a particular donor to a particular child. More common is a process whereby child sponsorship funds are pooled and spent on projects in the community in which the child lives. This is definitely the case for World Vision, though for Compassion at least some of the funds are spent directly on the school fees for the individual child.

The ethical issues with this approach have been well attested, however, and have not changed much since *New Internationalist* outlined nine problems with child sponsorship in a famous article from 1989, 'Simply . . . Why You Should Not Sponsor A Child'.[18] More recently, in a review of the topic, Willem van Eekelen summarized ten conceptual and practical issues associated with child sponsorship. His review concluded that those agencies engaged in child sponsorship have significantly improved their practices since the 1980s and 1990s and that many (if not all) of these residual problems are at least conceptually solvable, and so child sponsorship programmes can make a valuable and worthwhile contribution to the aid portfolio.[19] Nevertheless, it is worth exploring from a theological point of view some of the issues that he raises. Some of these – such as fostering relationships of dependency – are generic to international development work, and therefore I will focus for now on those issues he identifies that relate in particular to child sponsorship and the individualism it involves.

The first of these is that such programmes can be discriminatory. Van Eekelen points out that this can be the case in at least two distinct ways. First, some child sponsorship work can isolate an individual child within the family. One child has their school fees paid while another does not. One child receives gifts and letters from their sponsors and another does not. The second form of discrimination is that one family receives sponsorship while another family does not. As van Eekelen comments, 'At both levels, the programme potentially creates a miniature us and them, where sponsored children and families are privileged but also potentially stigmatised, and their unsponsored peers may be jealous or have a sense of superiority.'[20] Of course, this kind of problem can affect all development work. A development agency that raises none of its funds via child sponsorship will choose, for whatever reason, to work in one locality rather than another. In a context of finite funds, decisions need to be taken on how to allocate those funds – and an absolute needs assessment in which every single family is mapped so that funds can be allocated most judiciously is simply impossible. Therefore, the specific issue that relates exclusively to child sponsorship is when only one child within a family is sponsored and others are not. This is a significant issue because the family unit is meant to be just that – a unit. When one child is favoured over another, for whatever reason, the sibling tensions that result could be catastrophic for family unity. In a much trumpeted piece of research, Bruce Wydick et al. pointed to the efficacy of child sponsorship by highlighting the impact of a Compassion programme on a range of outcomes in adult life. One of these outcomes was years of schooling in which they compared sponsored children to non-sponsored siblings within the same family. Unsurprisingly, the report authors found a significant difference in the number of years of schooling between these two groups and highlighted this as evidence of the programme's efficacy.[21] My own interpretation of the same findings is somewhat different. It seems to me that a core component of appropriate parenting is that we do not privilege one child over another, but instead treat all of our children equally. In saying this, I am not for a moment criticizing the parents of the children in the LICs, for they are being forced into an impossible situation when they are offered sponsorship for some, but not all, of their children. Of course such parents will accept these offers, but I am unconvinced that we in HICs should be fostering such inequity. As one development worker put it to me, 'One child is favoured, the others are not; one child gets shoes at Christmas, the others do not. What does that say to the other siblings in the family?'[22] Indeed, as we have noted in a previous chapter, one of the long-term negative sequelae of colonialism was its practice of creating internal elites that divided communities. Is it possible that a parallel could be drawn with some child sponsorship practices today whereby we are encouraging divided families?

In 2 Corinthians 8.14, Paul indicates that the primary goal of his fundraising approach is unity and equality in the church. One of the reasons why Paul rejected the patronage model of fundraising where only a few would have supported the church is precisely because of the impact such practices would have had on unity in the church. Ben Witherington notes that for him to have accepted funds from one particular donor 'would also mean that he would be perceived as taking sides with one of the factions in Corinth'.[23] We already know that the church suffered from various divisions along personality (1 Cor. 3) and wealth lines (1 Cor. 6.1–11; 11.17–22) and hence Paul has a particular desire to bring unity to the church. It is possibly for this reason that in describing the benefits of giving, his emphasis is not on the needs of the Jerusalem church (though he could easily have done that) but on the unity that results from the church sharing its resources (2 Cor. 9.12–14). One aspect of this disunity centred on Paul himself, and it is quite possible that this also fed into his rejection of personal support from the Corinthian church (1 Cor. 9.1–18; 2 Cor. 11.5–10). Paul then rejected patronage for its ability to sow discord in the church. The same argument can, of course, be made in respect of the family. Patronage of one child but not of another creates precisely the kind of disunity that Paul is keen to avoid in his engagement with charitable giving for the Jerusalem church. Returning to our earlier discussion regarding our ontological status as persons-in-communion, we can see that the reason such favouritism is so problematic is because it directly damages the constitutive relationships that contribute to our identity. The fact that someone else is my familial brother or sister does not have the same identity-constitutive function as the fact that someone is my geographical neighbour. Both are my theological neighbour, but the former has a far greater identity-constituting function. Therefore, when I am separated from my siblings because they have school fees and Western pen friends, and I do not, the donor is not merely privileging one child over another, the donor is tearing at my identity as a full member of this family. Of course, there is a ready solution to this problematic, which is that child sponsorship agencies insist that monies will only ever be spent at the level of the nuclear family (or wider community) and never on the individual child. Most do this, but unfortunately not all.[24]

The second issue to be considered is the problem of targeting and use of imagery. International aid agencies engaged in child sponsorship need to find some mechanism to decide which children will be sponsored and which will not. Of particular concern is when such targeting takes place via donor choice. I routinely attend a large UK Christian conference where one of the child sponsorship agencies usually has a stand in which photographs of individual children are prominently displayed under the tag line 'Sponsor a child today'. The potential donor is meant to scan these different photographs with the minimal information provided and then decide which child/children will be the beneficiary of their donation. I would love to think that such decisions are based on entirely random factors, but we are being naive if we do not imagine that certain types of faces are likely to induce greater concern than others. As such, our choice of who to sponsor is far from 'random' and is almost certainly biased towards certain types of children. The fact that such favouritism is unintentional does not justify us being complicit in its reality.

The third problematic that van Eekelen identifies is that child sponsorship never really addresses the underlying causes of poverty. It remains restricted to the level of addressing the symptoms. There is an increasing cacophony of voices from LICs arguing that what is wanted is not more aid but greater emphasis on the wider structural issues that keep the poor in poverty. One such example is the Filippino theologian Melba Maggay, who has written:

Evangelicals are unfortunately stuck in merely providing discrete services to the poor, without addressing the larger context of why people are poor. There is a reluctance to engage in advocacy, to create a public voice and insert the cause of the poor into political space.[25]

Similarly, Ignatius Swart, writing from a South African perspective, talks of a 'mode of involvement that reveals the churches' inability – and unwillingness – to engage in more sustainable and long-term modes of action that would deal competently with the more deep-seated issues of society'.[26] And van Eekelen, referencing child sponsorship in particular, concludes:

These programmes do not and can never amount to sustainable or integrated socio-economic development. The reason is that sponsorship programmes neither address nor outweigh the many and mutually reinforcing root causes of poverty at the level of the individual family (caste, social strata, orphan-related stigma, HIV), community (environmental degradation, gender-related obstacles, systems of land ownership, heritage conventions), country (oppressive regime, geographical and urban biases, infrastructure), and international realities (trade system, wars). A consequence is that sponsored children are unlikely to escape a life of poverty.[27]

There are two related issues here. The first is that child sponsorship programmes are notoriously inefficient in the way they use funds. Inevitably, there are larger overhead costs with child sponsorship. As van Eekelen points out, the children need to be identified, tailored reports then need to be written and transmitted between donors and children, and lastly significant time is taken up with administration around children whose donors drop out of the programme, or children who drop out themselves. In addition to this, other programmes require letters to be translated and distributed, or staff members to sit with the children to either write the letters for them or at least help the child write it themselves. Another development practitioner working in sub-Saharan Africa commented, 'We are so caught up having to fulfil the obligations [of the child sponsorship program] that other more important activities are missed. We can't do the work we need to do because we're doing the admin for the program.'[28] All of this leads to significantly raised overheads compared to other forms of humanitarian giving.[29] In addition, and as already suggested, these programmes are inefficient in the broader sense that they do not address at all the underlying causes of poverty. One of the primary weaknesses of the Wydick study that apparently demonstrated the impact of child sponsorship is that they used the wrong comparator. In their study, they compared outcomes of sponsored children with outcomes of non-sponsored children.[30] If there had not been a difference then there would have been something markedly wrong with child sponsorship. But comparing sponsored with unsponsored children is not the correct comparison. What they should have done is compared the outcomes in a community that received child sponsorship with the outcomes in a community that received funding at the whole community level. Of course, if you compare individual child with individual child you will see a benefit from sponsorship, but what matters is the impact of that funding on the whole family and community, and whether giving in the way of individual sponsorship is more or less cost effective than giving at a community level.

In a previously published article I have argued that part of the reason we prefer this individualistic approach is due to the well-described *identifiable victim effect*. This is a psychological phenomenon in which people will give more to charitable causes where individual people are identified than to charities that stick to broad statistics – even if those broad statistics make it clear that the need they are addressing is more pressing and extensive than the one where particular victims are identified.[31] When I wrote that article, my proposal was largely speculative, but interestingly I have since found confirmation – at least for one child sponsor – in a blog written by a Christian theologian on the ethics of child sponsorship. In the course of defending the child sponsorship in which he was engaged he wrote the following in response to the challenge that child sponsorship involves 'poverty pornography':

> How do you overcome this problem, and yet maintain the level of human concern that the mawkish videos unquestionably generate? By humanising the problem. By putting people in touch with people, in real and genuine ways. And this is what child sponsorship does. I have no problem with supporting generic relief and development work (and we give more to other charities working in this area each year than we do to Compassion in sponsorship); but it matters to me that in a couple of cases I am not thinking about 'poor people' – I am thinking about Karen, and Jennivieve – and Karen's grandmother, Doris, who is sick just now, and so on.[32]

In this comment, Holmes confirms that what justifies his child sponsorship (at least in part) is the *identifiable victim effect*. By 'humanizing' the problem, by knowing their names and specific situations, this somehow provides a greater impetus to engage in the child sponsorship approach. As an empirical fact, Holmes is of course correct. It is indeed the case that by knowing and thinking about Karen and Jennivieve, as opposed to a nameless statistic, Holmes and others are far more likely to donate their funds. My difficulty with this approach is that I question whether this should be the case. In other words, is the identifiable victim effect simply a result of our fallen nature because what it speaks to is our relative inability to have compassion for those we do not know? And is not our calling as followers of Christ to be directed towards the one that is unknown: the stranger, the foreigner, the Samaritan neighbour, indeed our enemy?

There does exist something of an irony in me making this point for evidence exists that when you point out to people that they should really base their giving not on identifiable victims but on the actual need that exists, their response is an overall decrease in giving. Much of our actual giving is driven more by emotion than reason, and if by highlighting issues such as the identifiable victim effect you remove the emotional impact then the outcome seems to be reduced funding. In short, whether I like it or not poverty porn works.[33]

Having said this, Christian ethics is not (or should not) be driven by mere consequentialism but is rather to be theologically informed, and it is here that my concerns about the known nature of the victim remain. For as far as I can tell the approach described by Holmes would seem to share some affinity with the moral proximity argument advanced by Schneider and Sunshine. Our greatest moral responsibility lies towards those we know – in ever-diminishing circles. But as I indicated when we discussed that argument in Chapter 7, Jesus' love ethic towards the unknown neighbour and unloved enemy would appear to challenge the notion that our responsibility is in proportion to our felt relationship. Indeed, I would suggest that Jesus is explicitly seeking to challenge that way of thinking. The point of the parable of the good Samaritan is the man who was helped was not just 'unknown', but an enemy. He was doubly removed from the Samaritan who helped – removed both filially and religiously/ethically. Yet, the Samaritan still helped, and we in turn are commanded 'Go and do likewise'. The question we need to struggle with is not so much how we love those we know – for most likely we will do that naturally – but how we show love to those we do not know. As one development worker said to me, 'It feels shallow of us in the West that to raise funds we need to focus on an individual child. Wouldn't it be better to support a project which benefits a community as a whole?'[34]

In the course of his argument, Holmes draws an analogy with someone arriving on the scene of a train crash. He comments:

[S]uppose I am trained in first aid and arrive quickly at the site of a train crash, where there are dozens of injured people. Should I attempt to split my time equally between them, or should I help one until she is stable and then move on to the next? I think we all know the answer to that one.[35]

While Holmes clearly puts his finger on an important practical problem here – we cannot fund every project that comes to our attention or support every person in need, and therefore choices have to be made – I remain unpersuaded by his solution. For the truth is that in the scenario he describes the correct response is not simply to treat one person at a time, almost at random. Rather, the correct response – especially if you are trained and one of the first on the scene – is to conduct some form of triage. I speak from personal experience. While working in Kenya as a doctor, I was involved in a major incident in which a bus carrying about 100 passengers had plunged over a ravine after its brakes had failed. The hospital became inundated with patients and on arriving at the scene it was a situation of utter chaos. Together with others, I immediately began a process of triage in which the patients were divided into the four categories of:

- Immediate – life-threatening injuries that require treatment now.
- Urgent – serious injuries that require intervention in the next few hours.
- Delayed – not serious injuries that will require intervention, but not immediately.
- No priority – dead or dying for whom no treatment option is possible.

As indicated, this is standard medical practice and the decisions as to which category to put the patient in is made in seconds.[36] The rationale behind this system is that it enables the limited resources to be focused on where they will make the most difference.

Of course where Holmes is correct is that if a non-professional arrives at the scene of a train crash then it is understandable that they simply move from one victim to another after stabilizing each one, but he is incorrect to suggest that someone who is trained should do that. In precisely the same way – and this is the parallel that Holmes is drawing – as we encounter the huge problem of global poverty I do not think it is enough for professionals simply to say that as long as we are doing something it does not really matter what we do. It is entirely understandable for non-professionals to adopt that approach, but those engaged in international development have a responsibility to ask the question: what is the most efficient and effective form of development work? My point in this is not that all child sponsorship work is inappropriate. And certainly, there is evidence that some forms of child sponsorship can do much good. Rather, my point is that some forms of child sponsorship may in the long run do harm to the community that outstrips the benefit to the individual child. I also fear the impact it has on us as donors – it seems to involve a system in which my motivation to give is in part dependent on what I get out of the giving process, instead of being driven entirely by the need that is being addressed. I am not convinced that it is a recipe for sustainable giving, especially for the nameless, voiceless poor. Finally, I wonder if this approach has been embraced by evangelicals in particular because it reflects an individualistic gospel and individualistic salvation.

International Justice Mission (ISM) is another Christian development agency that, while not engaged in child sponsorship, would seem to emphasize the individualistic approach to development work. Their mission is to pursue justice for the poor across the globe. Using a casework model, they work with lawyers, campaigners and the criminal justice system to seek redress for individual victims of injustice. Lack of fair access to the law is a major issue in many poor countries, and so the work of IJM in this regard is absolutely necessary, important and ground-breaking. However, it is note-worthy that in writing about the work of IJM, Gary Haugen, the President of IJM, advocates this casework model to the possible detriment of other approaches.

> We have found that working a critical mass of *individual cases* of violent abuse with the criminal justice authorities (from beginning to end, over sev-eral years, with *specific* victims and perpetrators) is the most effective way to accurately diagnose what is broken in the criminal justice 'pipeline' and precisely understand how the victims and perpetrators actually experience this system.[37]

To be fair to Haugen he does also recognize the value of what he terms 'issue-based advocacy (public policy research, awareness campaigns and lobbying)'[38] and part of his rationale seems to me that the most effective way to get at the system is via individual cases. Certainly in respect of the work that IJM actually undertakes, there seems to be an increasing emphasis on structural issues – perhaps based on the fact that they now have a large repository of cases which speak to those structural concerns. Nevertheless, in his writings, Haugen continues to promote the individual approach, stating that we must not 'leapfrog over the victims' in our attempts to secure justice.[39] I find this a very strange way of putting things because to direct one's attention to the systemic issues in the judicial and legal systems is not to leapfrog over victims but is simply to advocate for the victims that one does not already know. It is to pay attention to the victims of injustice who, for whatever reason, have not crossed our pathways. If one were to follow Haugen's logic then Wilberforce should not have put all of his energies into campaigning in Parliament for a change to the law, but should have instead redeemed the slaves one by one. I think it is clear that while such an approach would have brought rapid short-term gain, in the long run it would have been far less effective at ending the transatlantic slave trade and thereby freeing millions of slaves. In saying this, I am not arguing against the case-based model, which is clearly very effective for those it addresses. Rather, my point is that Christians sometimes seem reluctant to address the systemic causes of violence, injustice and poverty, and so have a tendency to revert to the individual when a wider perspective would also be of value. Not least, one of the reasons I argue this is that to take the systemic approach does more justice to Jesus' imperative to love the stranger we do not know, rather than the friend we do.

As I have suggested, more and more voices are calling for the same transfer of attention from individual acts of charity to the wider systemic causes of poverty. Allan Boesak quotes with approval a famous sermon by Martin Luther King Jr:

> On the one hand, we are called to play the good Samaritan on life's roadside: but that will only be an initial act. One day we must come to see that the whole Jericho Road must be transformed so that men and women will not be constantly beaten and robbed as they make their journey on life's highway. True compassion is more than flinging a coin to a beggar: it is not haphazard and superficial. It comes to see that an edifice which produces beggars needs restructuring.[40]

Similarly, Cynthia Moe-Lobeda has written that individual acts of charity 'may individualize or privatize the causes of social problems, obscuring their systemic roots'.[41] And Paul Vallely has written, 'Individual donors, in common with many aid agencies and journalists, find it easier to relate to the drama of a particular event than to address the more deep-seated causes of the problem.'[42]

Robert Davis has pointed out how evangelicals in particular are especially prone to prioritizing the proximate at the expense of the more distal causes of poverty. He writes:

> While development practitioners know that these larger structural sins exist, the fact that they are so large, so 'macro', and so complex in terms of their operation makes it difficult to analyse them and to understand how to deal

effectively with them. In the end, agencies may settle for a more basic message about the need to deal with immediate (proximal) causes of poverty without a clear sense of what do about the larger structural sins.[43]

It is noteworthy that precisely the same critique has been offered from a secular stance by Jason Hickel. In an essay entitled 'The Death of International Development', he writes that the reason it has failed is because of development agencies' failure to tackle the structural causes of poverty.

> There have been attempts by some NGOs to campaign on these more structural issues . . . But such efforts toward global justice are quickly drowned out by the dominant framing of charity and aid that the same NGOs promote. The charity paradigm obscures the real issues at stake. Poor countries don't need our aid – they need us to stop the plunder.[44]

Charles Elliot goes even further when he says, 'There is a curious, one might almost say pathological, discontinuity between an intense emotional commitment to a particularly dramatic symptom and a continuing neglect of the chronic disease of which the symptom is a part.'[45]

As I have indicated, this emphasis on structural issues is one that is increasingly emanating from leaders in LICs and so it behoves us in the wealthier parts of the world to listen. In *Christianity, Poverty and Wealth*, Michael Taylor charts the responses of numerous voices from LICs in regard to poverty, aid and wealth. The comments of one Chilean pastor are telling: 'If you will permit me the comparison, I think that we have a sick person with a very serious infection and we are administering aspirin to lower the fever, but are losing sight of the illness itself.'[46] To continue with this analogy, my plea here is not that we stop administering aspirin, but that we turn our attention to the underlying causes as well. That is what a corporate gospel and corporate salvation would demand.

Notes

1 M. Volf, 1998, *After Our Likeness: The Church as the Image of the Trinity*, Grand Rapids, MI: Eerdmans, p. 162.

2 Volf, *After*, p. 163.

3 Volf, *After*, p. 173. For an extended discussion of the nature of faith as directed both to God and to neighbour, see J. Thacker, 2007, *Postmodernism and the Ethics of Theological Knowledge*, Aldershot: Ashgate.

4 Volf, *After*, p. 176.

5 Volf, *After*, p. 174 (emphasis mine).

6 Volf, *After*, p. 180.

7 N. T. Wright, 2003, *The Resurrection of the Son of God*, Minneapolis, MN: Fortress Press, pp. 108–9.

8 T. Wright, 2007, *Surprised by Hope*, London: SPCK, p. 211.

9 J. Green, 1995, *The Theology of the Gospel of Luke*, Cambridge: Cambridge University Press, p. 297.

10 Wright, *Surprised*, p. 204.

11 Wright, *Surprised*, p. 212.

12 Wright, *Surprised*, p. 215 (emphasis in original).

13 B. Beltran, 1998, 'Towards a Theology of Holistic Ministry', in T. Yamamori, B. Myers and K. Luscombe (eds), *Serving with the Urban Poor*, Monrovia, CA: MARC Publications, p. 182.

14 K. Bediako, 1996, 'Theological Reflections', in T. Yamamori, B. Myers, K. Bediako and L. Reed (eds), *Serving with the Poor in Africa*, Monrovia, CA: MARC Publications, p. 184.

15 Bediako, 'Theological Reflections', p. 187.

16 Wright, *Surprised*, p. 217.

17 Plan UK and ActionAid both have child sponsorship as significant parts of their work, but in terms of secular development agencies they are relatively small.

18 'Simply . . . Why You Should Not Sponsor A Child', 1989, *New Internationalist* 194. Available at: https://newint.org/features/1989/04/05/simply/ (accessed 4 June 2016).

19 W. van Eekelen, 2013, 'Revisiting Child Sponsorship Programmes', *Development in Practice* 23:4, p. 480.

20 Van Eekelen, 'Revisiting', p. 473.

21 B. Wydick, P. Glewwe and L. Rutledge, 2013, 'Does International Child Sponsorship Work? A Six-Country Study of Impacts on Adult Life Outcomes,' *Journal of Political Economy* 121:2, April, pp. 393–436.

22 Personal communication from a former staff member at a development charity involved in child sponsorship.

23 B. Witherington III, 1995, *Conflict and Community in Corinth*, Grand Rapids, MI: Eerdmans, p. 417.

24 Another alternative is always to ensure that whenever an individual child is sponsored all their siblings are similarly sponsored. However, I am not aware of any agency that adopts this approach because to do so would concentrate funds in particular families to the exclusion of others, and may anyway be unworkable logistically.

25 M. Maggay, 2008, 'Justice and Approaches to Social Change', in J. Thacker and M. Hoek (eds), *Micah's Challenge: The Church's Responsibility to the Global Poor*, Milton Keynes: Paternoster, p. 125.

26 I. Swart, 2008, 'Meeting the Challenge of Poverty and Exclusion: The Emerging Field of Development Research in South African Practical Theology', *International Journal of Practical Theology* 12:1, January, p. 125, n. 89.

27 Van Eekelen, 'Revisiting', p. 474.

28 Personal communication.

29 Van Eekelen, 'Revisiting', p. 475.

30 Wydick, Glewwe and Rutledge, 'Does International', pp. 393–436.

31 J. Thacker, 2015, 'From Charity to Justice Revisited', *Transformation* 35:2, p. 121.

32 S. Holmes, 'The Ethics of Child Sponsorship'. Available at: http://steverholmes.org.uk/blog/?p=6980 (accessed 6 June 2016).

33 D. A. Small, G. Loewenstein, P. Slovic, 2006, 'Sympathy and Callousness: The Impact of Deliberative Thought on Donations to Identifiable and Statistical Victims', *Organizational Behavior and Human Decision Processes* 102:2, pp. 143–53.

34 Personal communication from a former staff member at a development charity involved in child sponsorship.

35 Holmes, 'The Ethics'.

36 W. Smith, 2012, 'Triage in Mass Casualty Situations', *Continuing Medical Education* 30:11, pp. 413–15.

37 G. Haugen, 2014, *The Locus Effect: Why the End of Poverty requires the End of Violence*, Oxford: Oxford University Press, p. 247 (emphasis in original).

38 G. Haugen, 2002, 'Integral Mission and advocacy', in T. Chester (ed.), *Justice, Mercy and Humility*, Carlisle: Paternoster, p. 198.

39 Haugen, 'Integral Mission', pp. 198–9.

40 M. L. King, 1967, 'Beyond Vietnam', sermon from Riverside Church, 4 April, cited in A. Boesak, 2015, *Kairos, Crisis, and Global Apartheid: The Challenge to Prophetic Resistance*, New York: Palgrave Macmillan, ch. 1.

41 C. Moe-Lobeda, 2013, *Resisting Structural Evil*, Minneapolis, MN: Fortress Press, p. 90.

42 P. Vallely, 1990, *Bad Samaritans*, London: Hodder & Stoughton, p. 32.

43 R. Davis, 2009, 'What about Justice? Toward an Evangelical Perspective on Advocacy in Development', *Transformation: An International Journal of Holistic Mission Studies* 26:2, p. 93. For a Christian defence of advocacy, cf. *The Prophetic Church*, Christian Aid. Available at: www.christianaid.org.uk/resources/churches /the-prophetic-church.aspx (accessed 14 July 2016).

44 J. Hickel, 2015, 'The Death of International Development'. Available at: www.redpepper.org.uk/essay-the-death-of-international-development/ (accessed 14 July 2016).

45 C. Elliot, 1987, *Comfortable Compassion*, London: Hodder & Stoughton, pp. 10–11.

46 Chilean pastor, quoted in M. Taylor, 2003, *Christianity, Poverty and Wealth*, London: SPCK, p. 41.

13

Secular theories of development

Having provided a framework for the gospel, and having indicated the way in which some of our contemporary responses to poverty mimic some of the problems associated with some versions of the gospel, it is now time to turn more specifically to a range of development theories, and to discuss these in interaction with the redemptive motif that we have already adumbrated. We shall begin this chapter by discussing four distinct secular theories of development, before turning to discuss a further five theological approaches, and in each case we shall dialogue with them in light of the framework for salvation that has already been introduced.

Modernization theory

In his book *Missions and Money*, Jonathan Bonk suggests that the current approach to development is merely aping an earlier generation of Christians who sought 'civilization through Christian conversion'. We now see civilization – or economic development, which is the secular equivalent – through capitalist conversion.

> The confident, sometimes breathless, and often patronizing tone of nineteenth-century missionary apologists migrated and is now found almost exclusively in the language and agendas of contemporary nonreligious organizations such as the United Nations, the World Bank, and the International Monetary Fund.[1]

This is the essence of modernization theory. It is the belief that the West has followed an inevitable path of progress that the rest of the world now needs to follow. In other words, the solution to poverty is for the rest of the world to adopt the consumer-driven growth capitalism that the West has embraced. The classic description of this approach goes back to Walt Whitman Rostow, an American economist and political theorist with close ties to President Lyndon Johnson's administration in the 1960s. In 1960, Rostow published *The Stages of Economic Growth: A Non-Communist Manifesto*, which described a five-stage model for economic development. The first of these was 'the traditional society', characterized by limited growth and technology. This was followed by a stage in which commercial, in contrast to subsistence, exploitation of agriculture and extractive industries began to develop. As these commercial operations expanded, they were accompanied by a developing infrastructure of roads, power and communication networks. All of this led to the third stage – 'the take-off' stage. This was when the developing country increasingly grew its manufacturing sector and began to tap into the emerging consumer markets. As the country continued to invest in its manufacturing base, becoming less dependent on agriculture, and as it developed stable political and social institutions, so it progressed into the penultimate stage or 'drive to maturity', before finally arriving at the fifth and final stage of economic development, high mass consumption and exploitation of comparative advantage in international markets.[2]

The details of Rostow's model have inevitably been extensively criticized. Alain de Janvry and Elisabeth Sadoulet point out that though Rostow is proposing this model for all countries, in essence all he has actually provided is a historical description of what happened in the West during the eighteenth and nineteenth centuries. There is no reason why we should presume that the economic development trajectory pursued by the West in that period will also be applicable to countries with very different social, cultural and economic histories in the twentieth or twenty-first century.[3] As such, Rostow represents a form of cultural imperialism that must be challenged.

The broader point, however, is that Rostow's overall framework – in which the path of development is essentially to follow the map laid out by the West – remains one that impacts much development discourse today. The fundamental assumption here is that there is one road to development and, while there may be local variations, any country that is going to avoid the multiple traps of poverty needs to follow this Western model. While Rostow presented his model in economic terms, we can see the same neo-imperialistic attitude at play when the West demands that African countries adopt the same human rights agenda as they, or when the World Bank and IMF demand that other countries adopt the same social and political institutions as the West has done. In each case, what is assumed is that there is one single path of progress – the Western trajectory – and the rest of the world will be developed once it has aped this Western model of economic, ethical and political modernization. So, for instance, Paul Gifford, quoting David Landes in the latter part of this excerpt, writes:

The assumption behind the whole notion of 'development' in the latter part of the twentieth century was the former colonized lands would 'modernize' and take their place alongside the nations earlier industrialized . . . It is fashionable now in some circles to challenge this assumption, in the name of 'postmodernism' and 'multiple modernities' . . . The expression 'multiple modernities' is invoked to indicate that different people can take their place in the twenty-first century without becoming 'occidentalized'; they have their own way of being modern . . . I have never considered the concept of 'multiple modernities' very helpful in Africa. To be clear, by 'modern' I mean more than just existing in the twenty-first century. Modernization means something like 'that combination of changes – in the mode of production and government, in the social and institutional order, in the corpus of knowledge, and in attitudes and values – that make it possible for a society to hold its own way in the twenty-first century; that is, to compete on even terms in the generation of material and cultural wealth, to sustain its independence, and to promote and accommodate to further change'.[4]

While I have a number of criticisms of this position, Gifford is right to point out that in respect of scientific knowledge some truths are in practical terms culture free. He rightly points out that it is not culturally imperialistic to teach basic algebra for instance. The problem then with Gifford's and Landes' approach is that they would appear not to recognize any distinction between those facets of modernity that are especially culturally loaded and those that are not. I am not, I should make clear, seeking to endorse a facts v values binary opposition here. Rather, all aspects of knowledge are on a continuum. At one end of that continuum is, as Gifford rightly points out, physics. At the other end might be conceptions of art, beauty and music. And everything else is in between. So while it may not be culturally imperialistic to insist that modern medicine is taught in the same way in Kampala as it is in Birmingham,[5] it is culturally imperialistic to insist that Ugandans have the same 'attitudes and values' as the British populace, or that their political institutions look exactly the same as UK political institutions. Gifford's failure to appreciate this distinction is problematic.

Gifford writes from a secular point of view, but according to Elliot the Church has been guilty of 'swallowing . . . the modernisation paradigm' and in the process failing to develop its own theologically appropriate account of development.[6] He rightly points out that it can never be correct 'for the work of [secular] organisations to *define* an adequate Christian response to the pro-cesses of impoverishment, oppression and dehumanisation'.[7] Yet, that is what we have so often succumbed to, in the process becoming 'indistinguishable from an enlightened liberal humanism'.[8]

Increasingly, however, resistance to this approach is being voiced in both the Christian and secular literature. From a Christian point of view, Melba Padilla Maggay has argued effectively that sovereign nations must define their own path to development. 'What seems clear . . . is that nations would do well to jump off the rails of "development" as a uni-linear path to prosperity, and chart their own course based on the contours of their own unique geographical features, historical traditions and cultural resources as a people.'[9] Similarly, Molefe Tsele, critiquing the modernization thesis, writes:

We need to assert that from the African perspective, which is a perspective we subscribe to, our model of development has to be more than a catching up exercise, more than a struggle to climb the development ladder to the commanding heights already reached by countries in the North. We must state from the beginning that our development is concerned with something qualitatively different, something that has to do with the totality of our social well-being. This kind of development seeks to achieve a more human society and greater equity in the distribution and sharing of resources. In particular, we need to measure development by its ability to sustain healthy and dignified standards of living without excessive destruction or abuse of people and ecosystems.[10]

Returning to secular critiques of modernization theory, Tim Kelsall in a recent article argued that Western attempts to impose Western norms of leadership on African patrimonial systems were ineffective and instead more would be achieved if we worked 'with the grain' rather than against it in African development.[11] Brian Levy has argued similarly in respect of governance. For 23 years, Levy worked at the World Bank where he led work on the Bank's governance and anti-corruption strategy. That experience taught him that much of what passes for good governance speak is merely Western 'hubris'.[12] In Chapter 1 of his book he describes how 'Good governance is nothing less than an institutional embodiment of the values of the Western enlightenment'.[13] He continues:

> There is a deeply rooted tendency for people to find ways of thinking well of ourselves by setting standards, viewing ourselves without much self-critical reflection as worthy exemplars of those standards – and then judging others for their supposed shortcomings . . . As a growing number of scholars were pointing out, there was something truly extraordinary about coming up with a comprehensive governance reform program for low-income countries by describing the characteristics of the world's most affluent and most open societies and then reverse engineering them.[14]

Speaking of the political and economic development of the West, he writes:

> Vast sweeps of history brought these countries from there to here – no smooth arc of progress but a history that includes war, revolution, and economic depression. Ignoring this long sweep, and instead turning the outcomes into a blueprint for immediate action, seems like a breathtaking combination of naiveté and amnesia.[15]

Levy's point is not that there can be no universal goals for good governance, or indeed economic development, but his contribution to the debate is that there are multiple routes to those goals. He thinks that the problem of much Western-led development is that we have tried to short-circuit the particular historical and cultural pathways that each country has taken, and in the process sought to impose a Western model of governance that simply does not fit. Instead, we need to – in the title of his book – 'work with the grain' of national development. As can be seen, this is far from Rostow's development model with which this chapter began.

Politically and economically, the weakness of the modernization thesis is that it has proven to be ineffective. During the 1980s and 1990s in particular, the IMF and World Bank pursued Structural Adjustment Programs (SAPs) with a range of LICs. These were designed to ensure that these countries grew economically as they followed the path of economic development that had been pursued by the West. The impact of these SAPs was, however, devastating. In Chapter 5, we noted Cypher's summary of the impact of SAPs in terms of increasing poverty, increasing inequity and diminished growth.[16] All of this is charted by the former chief economist of the World Bank, Joseph Stiglitz, in his *Globalization and Its Discontents*. He writes:

> The result for many people has been poverty and for many countries social and political chaos. The IMF has made mistakes in all the areas it has been involved in . . . Structural adjustment programs did not bring sustained growth even to those . . . that adhered to its strictures.[17]

Theologically, the fundamental problem with the modernization thesis is that, as Levy suggests, it is characterized by 'hubris' and pride. The modernization aficionados believe that they have arrived and that every other country simply needs to follow in their footsteps if they also are to achieve wealth and prosperity. So consider Grudem and Asmus' quite astonishing statement in the opening chapter of their book, which purportedly addresses the issue of national poverty:

> The solution we propose explains practical steps that any poor nation can take. These steps will lead the nation out of the poverty trap and into a path of ever-increasing prosperity that will often lift *almost everyone* in the nation to a better standard of living.[18]

As I read those words, the immediate parallel that comes to mind is the parable of the Pharisee and the tax-collector in Luke 18. While the Pharisee prides himself on his achievements, the tax-collector simply looks to God for help. The problem with the modernization thesis is that it fails to address the plank in our own eyes while focusing on the splinter in someone else's. In the first place, it assumes that the path we have trod to prosperity is the only path that can be trod. It fails to take into account the particular historical contingencies that made our path possible that may not be available to other countries today – the slave trade being an obvious example as was discussed in Chapters 5 and 6. It also assumes that the high mass consumption on which our economies depend is necessarily worthwhile. In an era of climate change and over-consumption, it is not just questionable that the route we took to our prosperity may not be the right one to follow, but the goal itself might be wrong.[19] In short, the modernization thesis fails to take seriously its own sin and blindness. It assumes – like the Pharisee – that it and only those like it are saved – and that the path to that salvation is the one that it has followed.

Dependency theory

The second secular theory of development that I wish to explore is to a large extent the complete opposite of the first. This is the proposal known as dependency theory. At the outset, it is important to emphasize that dependency theory is entirely unconnected to the problem of aid dependency that we have already discussed in an earlier chapter. Dependency theory became popular in the 1960s in Latin America, roughly at the same time as liberation theology. Interestingly, its most popular form shared many of the Marxist overtones of liberation theology. Its central tenet is that the world is divided into *core* and *peripheral* (and sometimes semi-peripheral) nations. The core, wealthier nations are not accidentally wealthy but wealthy precisely because the peripheral nations are poor. There is some single mechanism that enables the core to become rich at the expense of the poor.

A range of so-called path-critical factors have been suggested to explain this co-dependency. One of the more obvious ones is the slave trade. As we saw in Chapter 5, it is unquestionable that significant assets, in terms of human lives, were stripped from Africa during the colonial period. As Janvry and Sadoulet remind us, this amounted to approximately 18 million individuals during the 400 years of the trade.[20] Olaudah Equiano wrote one of the first slave narratives during the eighteenth century and in it he makes it clear that such export not only deprived Africa of its human resources, but also contributed directly to the coffers of the Western powers.[21] One of the points that Equiano repeatedly makes in his autobiography from 1745 is that frequently when, either as a slave or as a freed man, he was able to scrape together small sums of money and via trade and hard work increase those sums, they were often summarily requisitioned by a white person in a position of power. The following story is typical and concerns a time when Equiano had been freed and chose to work:

On the 14th of October the Indian Queen arrived at Kingston in Jamaica. When we were unloaded I demanded my wages, which amounted to eight pounds and five shillings sterling; but Captain Baker refused to give me one farthing, although it was the hardest-earned money I ever worked for in my life. I found out Doctor Irving upon this, and acquainted him of the Captain's knavery. He did all he could to help me to get my money; and we went to every magistrate in Kingston, but they all refused to do anything for me, and said my oath could not be admitted against a white man.[22]

It is not just the case, however, that historically the West has grown rich at the expense of various African nations. Rather, a particular facet of dependency theory is the phenomenon of *path dependency*. According to path dependency, particular countries have been set on a historical trajectory because of the way in which the West engaged with them historically. So Janvry and Saboulet describe a study by Nunn which explored GDPpc in 2000 with historic slave exports controlled for by land area. The study found 'a strong negative . . . relationship between the number of slaves exported . . . and current economic performance'.[23] In other words, it is not just the case that previous historical atrocities impacted the economic development of the country during the seventeenth and eighteenth centuries; it is that this economic impact reverberates today.

Cypher mentions two other mechanisms by which African countries in particular may have been locked into a particular economic trajectory by the colonial period. The first of these is the fostering of internal elites by the colonial powers. Such local elites helped the colonists by administering the territories under their jurisdiction and thereby minimizing the requirement for direct colonial rule. However, such elites were not chosen on the basis of merit, but on the basis of loyalty to the colonial power. Moreover, they were supported – at times militarily – by the colonial power. In this way, it was the colonists who encouraged a form of authoritarianism that is reflected in today's 'big man' rule in Africa. It is arguable, therefore, that the ongoing problems associated with patrimonialism and corruption that plague many African states are a problem that at the very least was encouraged by the colonial powers.[24]

In addition to this, Cypher points to the influence of the colonists on incipient agricultural and manufacturing industries. Frequently it was the case that the colonists encouraged/forced the colonized to focus on the export of raw produce: cotton from India, food products from Africa and the Caribbean, at the expense of manufactured products. This stifled the development of a robust manufacturing industry – to the subsequent benefit of the colonial powers and detriment of the colonized.[25]

Dependency theory remains controversial, however. For some, it has been subsumed under the category of world systems theory. According to this idea, it is undoubtedly the case that how one country develops has an impact on other countries – in that sense, national economic development is never an isolated phenomenon. However, world systems theory would argue that dependency theory is too simplistic. The world is not neatly divided into core, semi-peripheral and peripheral countries. Rather, there are bilateral trading relationships that in some respect may be harmful to one partner, but in another respect may be beneficial. The influence of one country's or one block's economic development on another is not as simple as dependency theory would suggest.

For others, dependency theory should be abandoned as it is an insufficient diagnosis of the chronic economic problems facing Africa. So Sara Marzagora writes:

> The upheavals of the 1970s and 1980s made dependency theory seem increasingly insufficient to explain the continent's political woes. It was apparent that there was a very strong internal, African agency to the economic collapse of many African states, and that the crisis could not only be blamed on neo-colonial exploitation.[26]

For others, the problem was that it didn't help alleviate the current crisis. Jephias Matunhu, writing from an African perspective, argues that both modernization theory and dependency theory may have some truth within them, but they have failed to help Africa develop, and therefore attention needs to be paid to other factors.[27] His view is that despite some of the reality of dependency theory, it has distracted Africans from facing realistically their own contribution to the problem of African underdevelopment. He argues that the right approach is to recognize

> Africans to be part of the development problem as well as being part of the solution to the continent's underdevelopment. This is no longer the time to cry foul but to act decisively, knowing pretty well that the west has become even more sophisticated in their plan to keep Africa under economic and political bondage.[28]

By way of contrast, Arno Tausch, writing from a European perspective, continues to believe that the lessons from dependency theory should not be forgotten. He remains a strong advocate, arguing that Europe should 'finally learn that dependence indeed has had a critical impact on the overall long-term development trends of a nation'.[29]

Dependency theory remains, then, a contested space, and it is perhaps no accident that those I have cited in support of the idea are from the former colonial powers, while those I have cited against it are from the colonized. To some extent, this represents the competing values of postcolonial guilt (with which the West is struggling) and pragmatic concerns for actual economic development (with which Africans are struggling).

Theologically, our response – as was the case with modernization theory – has to be nuanced. While the fundamental problem of modernization theory was that of ethnocentric pride, the fundamental problem with dependency theory can be that of reverse or inverted pride. With modernization theory, the nations in the West consider themselves better because they have arrived – economically, politically and culturally. With dependency theory, the nations on the periphery consider themselves better because they have not participated in the exploitation and subjugation of others. While under modernization theory, the West looks down on the economic and political underdevelopment of the rest of the world; under dependency theory, the peripheral nations look down on the West for their lack of moral development.[30]

The problem with this outlook is that it is a short step from such reverse ethnocentrism to a victim mentality that denies agency. This is the problem that Marzagora and Mutunhu would seem to be alluding to. If the problem is entirely external, then where is the internal agency that will rectify it? In this sense, the theological problem with dependency theory is the same as that with modernization theory: both are insufficiently blind to their own sin. For while it is undoubtedly the case that much of the poverty experienced in LICs today is the result of both historic colonialism and contemporary neocolonialism, that does not mean that there are not issues within LIC cultures that require addressing. To turn to another of Jesus' parables, it is indeed the case that the West has a huge plank of wood in its own eye, but that does not mean that a splinter does not remain in the eye of some within LICs.

In short, both theories have been too ethnocentric and failed to recognize the full corporate boundaries that Christ sought to bring. The concept of the corporate image is that we only image God to the extent that we *all* flourish, which means not just stewardship over creation, but also right and just relationships with one another. While the West is certainly guilty of trampling those relationships, it does not serve LICs to adopt a moral superiority that, though warranted, is pragmatically ineffective.

Human rights approach

One of the more noticeable features of development discourse over the last 30 years has been the growing prevalence of rights-based language. Throughout the 1970s and early 1980s, development theory had been dominated by the basic needs approach (BNA). Drawing on Abraham Maslow's hierarchy of needs, BNA emphasized what was absolutely required in terms of water and sanitation, nutrition, health and education. It was felt that if these basic needs could be met then the fundamentals of development would at least be addressed.

As the 1980s progressed, however, the BNA began to lose support. There were a number of reasons for this, including the newly imposed structural adjustment programmes of the IMF and World Bank, the fact that in practice the BNA was insufficiently participatory – often the basic needs were defined by donors rather than recipients – and a growing realization that the BNA was not achieving the development outcomes that were hoped for.[31]

Into this conceptual space emerged the human rights approach to development.[32] Of course, modern human rights discourse had been in existence since the 1948 United Nations Universal Declaration of Human Rights. However, in 1986 human rights landed on the development agenda with the UN Declaration on the Right to Development. Article 1 of that declaration reads as follows:

> The right to development is an inalienable human right by virtue of which every human person and all peoples are entitled to participate in, contribute to, and enjoy economic, social, cultural and political development, in which all human rights and fundamental freedoms can be fully realized.[33]

For the first time, development was now an 'inalienable human right', taking its place alongside rights to freedom, self-determination, recognition before the law and so on. Such rights-based development discourse has shown remarkable resilience since the 1980s. Neoliberal approaches to development have come and gone and come again, as have dependency approaches, but rights-based language has existed as a continual backdrop to these ongoing development debates.

The supporting documentation for the 2000 Millennium Development Goals was replete with rights-based language, and more recently the 2015 Sustainable Development Goals (SDGs) continue this practice of framing development in terms of rights. Consider for instance the following targets, all of which are an integral part of the 17 SDGs:

> By 2030, ensure that all men and women, in particular the poor and the vulnerable, have equal rights to economic resources, as well as access to basic services, ownership and control over land and other forms of property, inheritance, natural resources, appropriate new technology and financial services, including microfinance. (Target 1.4 of Goal 1)

> By 2030, ensure that all learners acquire the knowledge and skills needed to promote sustainable development, including, among others, through education for sustainable development and sustainable lifestyles, human rights, gender equality, promotion of a culture of peace and non-violence, global citizenship and appreciation of cultural diversity and of culture's contribution to sustainable development. (Target 4.7 of Goal 4)

Ensure universal access to sexual and reproductive health and reproductive rights as agreed in accordance with the Programme of Action of the International Conference on Population and Development and the Beijing Platform for Action and the outcome documents of their review conferences. (Target 5.6 of Goal 5)[34]

Similarly, the preamble to the SDGs states that these new goals are 'grounded in the Universal Declaration of Human Rights, international human rights treaties, the Millennium Declaration and the 2005 World Summit Outcome Document [and] . . . informed by other instruments such as the Declaration on the Right to Development'.[35]

What is interesting about this framework for development is the way in which some development experts view such rights-based language as the normative and explicitly secular counter to any religious theory of development. In May 2014, the UN hosted a major consultation to explore the issue of religion and development, involving a range of UN agencies, donors and faith-based NGOs. The report of that meeting wrote this regarding the language of rights:

A question was raised about the Universal Declaration of Human Rights: To what extent is it viewed as a 'sacred text', at least in some quarters of the UN and secular development contexts? There is a strong alignment between the global conversation and what religious traditions have carried, one participant said. Many concurred that International Conventions and frameworks are reflections of universal values and traditions, accumulated by humanity over time, and enshrined in the Universal Declaration of Human Rights. Centering the post-2015 process on human rights is a means of countering the technocracy noted above. Human rights are at the core of what several UN development agencies are committed to. Through this focus on the Declaration, the unifying confluence of religion and values is being respected. The starting point, some maintained, must be secular development discourse. This requires, simultaneously, an acknowledgement that all actors speak from clear normative positions. Thus, secular development actors are themselves speaking from an ideological paradigm, which is a human rights discourse.[36]

This last sentence is the most interesting one as it indicates that at least among some development professionals, there is an ideological framework to development, and it is a secular one, and that framework is human rights.

We do not have sufficient space to undertake a thorough theological analysis of human rights theory, though interested readers can review these texts.[37] However, let me summarize some of the main criticisms of a human rights approach from a theological perspective, and then we will tie this more closely to the particular theological focus of this chapter. The first critique is simply that to claim universal human rights – as the UN declarations do – is to deny the particularity of cultural values. According to this critique, human rights discourse is simply a Western framework imposed on the rest of the world. Second, rights are viewed as inherently individualistic. Their focus is not on the community as such, but on individuals. Third, and this is a particular critique from theologians, human rights assert some kind of power for individuals, but they do not make any correlating demands. Indeed, as Vinoth Ramachandra has noted:

> In late modern societies a pervasive victim mentality has undermined any sense of moral obligations, and human rights talk has assumed the status of secular religion: every misfortune or disappointment is now responded to with litigation and every grievance couched in the language of rights.[38]

Fourth, the justificatory ground of human rights remains ambiguous, particularly when framed as a secular motif. As Michael Perry has argued, 'there is, finally, no intelligible secular version of the idea of human rights, that the conviction that humans beings are sacred is inescapably religious'.[39] Fifth, again from a theological perspective, human rights seem to be a rather minimal commitment compared to the demand of love that is encapsulated in many religious texts. Lastly, and perhaps most significantly, 'The greatest problem associated with human rights is the universal failure in the actual implementation of human rights.'[40] It is all well and good declaring that all people have the right to education, for instance, but if it is not at the same time clear whose duty it is to ensure that right is enabled then the declaration simply becomes a piece of wishful thinking.

To be fair to the 1986 UN Declaration on the Right to Development, this document did spell out a series of duties, as well as rights. So, for instance, Article 4 indicates that 'States have the duty to take steps, individually and collectively, to formulate international development policies with a view to facilitating the full realization of the right to development.'[41] This is a welcome development from statements that only enumerated rights but not duties. Nevertheless, the problem is that 'the state' is an incredibly vague term. In international law, the state is not merely the head of state or even the ruling party but encompasses in some sense the way in which society is ruled, incorporating the government, laws, the judiciary, the police, tax-collecting mechanisms, and so on. All of this makes it clear that when a UN document declares that a state has a duty to protect or advance some right, it is virtually meaningless – it doesn't indicate what that means in practice. For this reason, rights may well be enumerated, but more often than not they are not enacted. In this sense, a declaration of rights may well be something that keeps those in the West, who already have their rights largely protected, comfortable; it helps us feel that we are doing a good thing. In reality, a declaration of rights makes very little difference to those who are poor.

Christian Aid is a major international development agency, and we shall come on to discuss their underpinning theological framework shortly, but in a recent report they have defended the human rights approach as an appropriate Christian framework for development work.[42] In the process, they outline the six criticisms of rights that I have already noted. Their response to these criticisms is, however, rather unconvincing. So, in regard to the philosophical ground of human rights, they simply state that these challenges have now been met – without especially telling us how or where they have been met.[43] Similarly, in response to the accusation of individualism, they merely point to a comment by Kofi Annan that '*victims* of suffering and exploitation' never make this critique. Yet, in the same publication, the two sources they provide for this critique are from the Sri Lankan theologian Vinoth Ramachandra and a Portuguese scholar who has conducted extensive fieldwork in the exclusion and oppression of those in Brazil, Cabo Verde, Macau, Mozambique, South Africa, Colombia, Bolivia, Ecuador and India.[44] In other words, there is ample evidence that victims of poverty do indeed criticize rights approaches as too individualistic. Many of their other responses to criticisms of rights language were similarly unpersuasive. Christian Aid is correct to point out that 'participants in this conversation often stereotype each other',[45] but the problem which remains unaddressed is that some in both the secular and Christian development world wish to make rights-based language *the* framework for international development. If Christians wished to view rights language as an adjunct to a fully worked out theology of international development, then certainly such language has a place. But what is insufficient is to argue that rights language becomes the dominant paradigm for international development discourses. Theologically, this will not do.

For if we turn to our own model of restoration as articulated in the kingdom of God, the problem with the language of rights is, despite appearances, its lack of egalitarianism. The fundamental framework of all rights language is that the state (whatever that might mean in practice) has duties towards individuals, and those individuals have claims upon that state (namely their rights). In contrast, under the theological framework we are proposing here everyone has both the same ontological status – a person in communion with others – and everyone has both the same duties and rights in respect of others. This division between those who have duties and those who have rights simply does not exist. At the same time, the whole focus of the redemption we have in mind is that of the whole community flourishing, and flourishing as one connected community. As was noted in Chapter 1, this is what distinguishes the framework I am outlining here from eudaemonism, where the focus is on the individual and their well-being. What I am talking about here is flourishing from the perspective of the whole community, and that necessarily means that a relational dynamic is embedded from the start. It also means that the community cannot be flourishing if the community experiences deep inequalities. The problem with rights-based language is not that it cannot contribute to our moral dialogue. Even the Bible talks of rights, and there is an obvious biblical basis to a notion of human rights that is derived from the *imago Dei*. The problem is when human rights language becomes the sole or governing discourse. Human rights cannot on their own govern the moral framework for society; they are only ever an adjunct. Referring to the tyranny of rights-based language, Ramachandra comments:

> It should be clear by now that respect for the dignity and freedom of the individual, especially those most threatened by the political and technological forces unleashed in recent times, requires that a wider matrix of social practices and moral beliefs be held in place than the mere assertion of fictitious 'autonomy'.[46]

Capability approach

The final secular theory of development that I wish to discuss is Amartya Sen's capability approach. In the last ten years, this approach to development has become increasingly popular among both secular and Christian commentators. His framework is based upon the notion that we as individuals should choose the capabilities that we as individuals particularly value. He writes: 'The analysis of development presented in this book treats the freedom of individuals as the basic building blocks.'[47] 'Development can be seen . . . as a process of expanding the real freedoms that people enjoy',[48] which he goes on to explain are 'the capabilities – to choose a life one has reason to value'.[49] For Sen, development consists in maximizing the freedoms that individuals have to pursue the capabilities that they consider worthy of merit. In saying this, Sen is explicitly distancing himself from the kind of pure economic approach to development that characterizes modernization theory for instance. He provides the putative example of a state which has brought about full economic development by entirely centralized means with every decision made by a dictator. And then he writes:

> It is not hard to argue that something would be missing in such a scenario, to wit, the freedom of the people to act as they like in deciding on where to work, what to produce, what to consume and so on.[50]

What matters in development, then, is not what outside bodies think, but what the individual has 'reason to value', whatever that might be. Development occurs when such capabilities are maximally expanded.

There is much to admire in Sen's analysis and in particular his de-emphasis of a purely economic understanding of development. However, what is problematic in his approach is the individualism that characterizes it. What is almost entirely absent from his description is any concept that our very existence is necessarily relational, and therefore in choosing the capabilities that I have reason to value I simply cannot avoid the relational aspects of those choices.[51] Even if I want to make 'individual' choices, I am in fact making 'relational' ones; to pretend that somehow my choice does not have relational implications is misleading. Consider, for instance, the decision as to whether I drink tea or coffee, which would at face value be nothing but a matter of individual concern. Yet, the reality is that the choices I make as a consumer do have implications for the tea or coffee producer, including whether or not they get a fair price for their efforts and therefore their level of income and so on. Sabina Alkire and Séverine Deneulin, who are two of Sen's greatest advocates, try to avoid this critique, calling it a misunderstanding, by claiming that Sen is only arguing for ethical and not ontological or methodological individualism.[52] They define this as the view 'that individuals, and only individuals, are the *ultimate* units of moral concern'.[53] Their argument in support of such 'ethical individualism' is that too frequently it has been the case that when the focus of analysis has been groups of any size then inevitably individuals and inequalities within those groups have usually been overlooked.[54] I am very sympathetic to that concern, which as an empirical point is hard to argue with. However, what it demonstrates is a Western anthropology that conceives of relationships as some additional factor to our individuality, and as such betrays the ontological individualism that is denied. For if we subsist only as a network of relationships then it is not so much that ethical individualism should be rejected, it is rather that such individualism is impossible.[55]

In regard to this, Klaasen has recently juxtaposed the Alkire/Sen definition of development, in which he says 'there is not a strong sense of mutually enriching interaction', with one developed in South Africa: 'a process of planned social change designed to promote the wellbeing of the population as a whole'.[56] He goes on to comment:

> Sen's definition of development restricts development to the increase of the choices of the individual . . . Unlike the capability approach that compartmentalizes the person, development of the person happens in relationships with other persons and the rest of creation, including structures, societal units or material resources.[57]

Moreover, I am not convinced that the situation that Alkire and Deneulin are concerned about – individuals and inequalities being overlooked – is mitigated by protecting individual freedoms. It is far more effectively mitigated by evaluating any putative development work in terms of its impact on relationships, including relationships of inequality. To put this in concrete terms: imagine a cash transfer programme when an NGO is distributing a particular sum of money to a community. Alkire and Deneulin would seem to be arguing that the best way to avoid trampling on individual freedoms would be to distribute the money equally between all members of the community, and that the only locus of evaluation should be whether the money has been distributed equitably in this fashion. By way of contrast, a relational approach to the same problematic would ask where the relations of power and coercion existed in the community. They would also ask what the current inequities are. They would then ask how can we distribute this money most effectively to bring about benefits for all, *plus* more equitable and less coercive relationships as a whole. The latter task is clearly more difficult, but my point is that those are the questions that should, at least in theory, be asked if what we seek is full development. It is in passing worth noting that those involved in statecraft have often failed to ask such questions about existing power relationships, and that is why democracy has struggled to work effectively in a number of countries where its introduction has been new. Theologically, then, the critique of Sen's capability approach is that it remains too individualistic. It is certainly far better than neo-imperialist modernization theory but shares some of the weaknesses of the human rights approach that we have already discussed.

Notes

1 J. Bonk, 2006, *Missions and Money*, Maryknoll, NY: Orbis Books, p. 32.
2 W. Rostow, 1960, *The Stages of Economic Growth: A Non-Communist Manifesto*, Cambridge: Cambridge University Press, ch. 2.

3 A. de Janvry and E. Sadoulet, 2016, *Development Economics: Theory and Practice*, London: Routledge, p. 132.

4 P. Gifford, 2015, *Christianity, Development and Modernity in Africa*, London: Hurst & Co., pp. 152–4, quoting D. Landes, 1969, *The Unbound Prometheus*, Cambridge: Cambridge University Press, p. 6. For a similar view, see F. Fukuyama, 2011, *The Origins of Political Order: From Prehuman Times to the French Revolution*, New York: Farrar, Straus and Giroux.

5 Though having said that, while the empirically derived content of medicine may be unchanged from Birmingham to Kampala, the method of teaching and underlying pedagogy might well be very different.

6 C. Elliot, 1987, *Comfortable Compassion*, London: Hodder & Stoughton, p. 45.

7 Elliot, *Comfortable Compassion*, p. 179.

8 Elliot, *Comfortable Compassion*, p. 180.

9 M. Maggay, 2013, 'The Influence of Religion and Culture in Development in the Philippines', in M. Hoek, J. Ingleby, A. Kingston-Smith and C. Kingston-Smith (eds), *Carnival Kingdom: Biblical Justice for Global Communities*, Gloucester: Wide Margin, p. 202.

10 M. Tsele, 2001, 'The Role of the Christian Faith in Development', in D. Belshaw, R. Calderisi and C. Sugden (eds), *Faith in Development*, Oxford: Regnum Books, p. 207.

11 T. Kelsall, 2008, 'Going with the Grain in African Development?', *Development Policy Review* 29:s1, pp. 223–51.

12 B. Levy, 2014, *Working with the Grain: Integrating Governance and Growth in Development Strategies*, Oxford: Oxford University Press, p. 7.

13 Levy, *Working*, p. 6.

14 Levy, *Working*, pp. 6–7.

15 Levy, *Working*, p. 7.

16 J. Cypher, 2014, *The Process of Economic Development*, 4th edn, Oxford: Routledge, p. 662.

17 J. Stiglitz, 2002, *Globalization and Its Discontents*, New York: W. W. Norton, p. 18.

18 W. Grudem and B. Asmus, 2013, *The Poverty of Nations: A Sustainable Solution*, Wheaton, IL: Crossway Books, p. 25.

19 For theological critiques of consumer capitalism, see R. Valerio, 2016, *Just Living: Faith and Community in an Age of Consumerism*, London: Hodder & Stoughton.

20 Janvry and Saboulet, *Development Economics*, p. 114.

21 A. Constanzo (ed.), 2001, *The Interesting Narrative of the Life of Olaudah Equiano*, Ontario: Broadview Literary Texts (first published 1745).

22 Constanzo (ed.), *The Interesting*, p. 234. In light of this, Ngugi wa Thiong'o's provocative novel has a point when he writes, 'History shows us that there has never been any civilisation that was not built on the foundations of theft and robbery. Where would America be today without theft and robbery? What about England? France? Germany? Japan? It's theft and robbery that have made possible the development of the Western world.' N. wa Thiong'o, 1983, *Devil on the Cross*, London: Heinemann, p. 79.

23 Janvry and Sadoulet, *Development Economics*, p. 114. See also N. Nunn, 2008, 'The Long-Term Effects of Africa's Slave Trades', *Quarterly Journal of Economics* 123:1, pp. 139–76.

24 Cypher, *The Process*, pp. 86–8.

25 Cypher, *The Process*, pp. 86–8.

26 S. Marzagora, 2016, 'The Humanism of Reconstruction: African Intellectuals, Decolonial Critical Theory and the Opposition to the "Posts" (Postmodernism, Post-structuralism, Postcolonialism)', *Journal of African Cultural Studies* 28:2, p. 165.

27 J. Matunhu, 2011, 'A Critique of Modernization and Dependency Theories in Africa: Critical Assessment', *African Journal of History and Culture* 3:5, pp. 65–72.

28 Matunhu, 'A Critique', p. 72.

29 A. Tausch, 'Globalisation and Development: The Relevance of Classical "Dependency" Theory for the World Today', *International Social Science Journal* 61:202, p. 467.

30 Understandably, this is particularly clear in Equiano's contemporary description where his contempt for the 'civilization' of slave traders is hardly concealed. 'When you make men slaves you deprive them of half their virtue, you set them in your own conduct an example of fraud, rapine, and cruelty, and compel them to live with you in a state of war; and yet you complain that they are not honest or faithful!' Constanzo (ed.), *The Interesting*, p. 128.

31 V. Desai and R. Potter, 2014, *The Companion to Development Studies*, 3rd edn, Oxford: Routledge, pp. 29–30.

32 Gerrie ter Haar tries to draw a distinction between a 'human rights' approach to development, which emphasises the legal aspects, and a 'rights-based' approach, which is a broader conception covering issues of equity and fairness. While technically ter Haar may be correct, this distinction is not followed in much of the development (as opposed to legal) literature and therefore I have not rigidly followed it here. G. ter Haar, 2011, 'Religion and Human Rights', in G. ter Haar (ed.), *Religion and Development: Ways of Transforming the World*, London: Hurst & Co., p. 296.

33 *Declaration on the Right to Development*, 4 December 1986, United Nations. Available at: www.un.org/documents/ga/res/41/a41r128.htm (accessed 10 June 2016).

34 *Transforming Our World: The 2030 Agenda for Sustainable Development*, 2015, United Nations. Available at: https://sustainabledevelopment.un.org/post2015/transformingourworld (accessed 10 June 2016).

35 *Transforming Our World*.

36 *Religion and Development Post-2015*, 2014, UNFPA, p. 8. Available at: www.unfpa.org/sites/default/files/pub-pdf/DONOR-UN-FBO%20May%202014.pdf (accessed 10 June 2016).

37 N. Wolterstorff, 2008, *Justice: Rights and Wrong*, Princeton, NJ: Princeton University Press; J. Milbank, 2012, 'Against Human Rights', *Oxford Journal of Law and Religion* 1:2, pp. 203–34; S. Hauerwas, 1991, *After Christendom*, Oxford: Abingdon Press; A. MacIntyre, 1981, *After Virtue: A Study in Moral Theory*, Notre Dame, IN: University of Notre Dame Press.

38 V. Ramachandra, 2008, *Subverting Global Myths*, Downers Grove, IL: InterVarsity Press, p. 121.

39 M. Perry, 2000, *The Idea of Human Rights*, Oxford: Oxford University Press, p. 35.

40 T. Lorenzen, 2000, 'Towards a Theology of Human Rights', *Review and Expositor* 97, p. 58.

41 *Declaration*.

42 S. Durber, 2016, *Putting God to Rights: A Theological Reflection on Human Rights*, London: Christian Aid.

43 Durber, *Putting*, p. 13.

44 Durber, *Putting*, p. 11.

45 Durber, *Putting*, p. 16.

46 Ramachandra, *Subverting*, p. 124.

47 A. Sen, 1999, *Development as Freedom*, Oxford: Oxford University Press, p. 18. See also S. Deneulin and L. Shahani (eds), 2009, *An Introduction to the Human Development and Capability Approach: Freedom and Agency*, London: Earthscan.

48 Sen, *Development*, p. 3.

49 Sen, *Development*, p. 74.

50 Sen, *Development*, p. 27.

51 In the final chapter of his book, Sen does address the interrelation of individual freedoms with social commitments. In this chapter, he recognizes to some extent the social aspects of individual responsibility, but in the final analysis he is still working with an ontological individualism rather than a relational one. Cf. 'Individual Freedom as a Social Commitment', in Sen, *Development*.

52 S. Alkire and S. Deneulin, 2009, 'The Human Development Capability Approach', in Deneulin and Shahani (eds), *An Introduction*, p. 35.

53 Deneulin and Alkire, 'The Human', p. 35.

54 Deneulin and Alkire, 'The Human', pp. 35–6.

55 To some extent Martha Nussbaum's version of the capability approach can be argued to be less individualistic than that of Sen. This is particularly the case in regard to her willingness to outline ten 'central capabilities' that are common to all people, and in particular in the way in which she frames one of these–that of affiliation–as having a structural role in coordinating and influencing the others. M. Nussbaum, 2011, *Creating Capabilities: The Human Development Approach*, London: Harvard University Press, Chapter two.

56 J. Klaasen, 2013, 'The Interplay between Theology and Development: How Theology can be Related to Development in Post-Modern Society', *Missionalia* 41:2, August, p. 185.

57 Klaasen, 'The Interplay', p. 192.

14

Theologies of development

Liberation theology

Having explored a number of predominantly secular theories of development, it is now time to investigate a range of more explicitly Christian theologies of development. The first of these is Latin American liberation theology.[1] While liberation theology is well known for its emphasis on the poor, what is less well known is that both in its original and more recent form liberation theology has consistently viewed Western approaches to international development as fundamentally at odds with its own 'option for the poor'. So the Boffs criticize two approaches that in theory address the plight of the poor: 'What is the action that will effectively enable the oppressed to move out of their inhuman situation? . . . [I]t has to go beyond two approaches that have already been tried: aid and reformism.'[2] By aid, the Boffs mean the sticking-plaster approaches of the international community that address the symptoms of poverty, but not the underlying structural injustices that keep the poor, poor.

> Aid remains a strategy for . . . treating [the poor] as objects of charity, not as subjects of their own liberation. The poor are seen simply as those who have nothing. There is a failure to see that the poor are oppressed and made poor by others.[3]

In a similar way, Gustavo Gutiérrez also critiques aid as a means to address poverty:

> In this situation we would have to give serious thought again to the meaning of the aid that the Churches in the opulent nations offer to the Churches in the poor nations. This economic aid, if not well oriented, could easily be unproductive in respect of the witness to the poverty which they could offer; it may also lead them to a reformist position producing superficial social changes which in the long run will only help to prolong the situation of misery and of injustice in which the marginated (*sic*) people live. This aid might also be able to offer, at a cheap price, a good conscience to Christians, citizens of countries that control the world economy.[4]

In this way, Gutiérrez would seem to be echoing Marx's point regarding the role of religion in keeping the masses quiescent. Aid serves the opulent world by appeasing our guilt and preventing us from genuinely addressing the structural injustices that both keep the poor in poverty and keep the rest of us rich. This same theme has been explored at book length by Thia Cooper who explicitly contrasts the approach of liberation with the approach of development. 'Development and liberation . . . are opposites. People who are poor need liberation from development as well as other forms of oppression.'[5] In this way, Cooper seems to be going even further than the arguments of the Boffs and Gutiérrez. For them, aid is a relatively well-meaning but clearly misguided approach to the problem of poverty. It may even be counter-productive because it distracts us from the real task of economic and political revolution. Cooper's language of 'oppression' would seem to take this one step further, and she explains her rationale:

> Charity is only needed when a situation of injustice exists. On its own, charity is not enough; it leaves the person 'giving' with the power. It does not ask how to achieve a just system, where no one holds greater economic, political, racial, gender, or other types of power over another human being.[6]

In other words, aid itself instantiates a structural imbalance that also characterizes the global economic community. In this way, aid can be a tool of oppression and it helps foster the imbalance of power that is at the root of all poverty.[7] For Cooper, the solution is clear – we must reject aid in favour of fostering the process of liberation.

The problem of course is what does that mean in practice? Ivan Petrella, while situating himself within the liberation movement, criticizes it for its lack of concrete projects on the ground.[8] And this has remained one of the main critiques of liberation theology even as it has transitioned to other contexts. So in an African context, Jesse Mugambi, explicitly building on Latin American liberation theology, has called for a 'theology of reconstruction' arguing that this is the next step beyond mere liberation.[9] Such a theology will be

> Reconstructive rather than destructive; inclusive rather than exclusive; proactive rather than reactive; complementary rather that competitive; integrative rather than disintegrative; programme-driven rather than project-driven; people-centred rather than institution-centred; deed-oriented rather than word-oriented; participatory rather than autocratic; regenerative rather than degenerative; future-sensitive rather than past-sensitive; co-operative rather than confrontational; consultative rather than impositional.[10]

While we might applaud many of those sentiments, the question remains, what does any of that mean in practice? As Petrella has rightly argued regarding Latin American liberation theology, the absence of concrete examples which are genuinely transformative and which instantiate the theology being articulated renders the theology effectively moot. Whether or not the same could be said of the South African version of liberation theology is arguable.

Such South African liberation theology certainly echoes many of the themes evident in Latin American liberation theology. Yet, at the same time, there would appear to have been a greater emphasis on the practical outworkings of this theology, at least compared to its Latin American sibling. This was especially evident in its stand against apartheid and the 1985 Kairos document, which weaved beautifully together theological affirmation with concrete political demands and helped bring an end to the apartheid regime, thereby liberating millions from political oppression. Such pragmatism is also evident in the most recent examples of South African liberation theology. Ignatius Swart has described this as the fourth-generation approach to development, and its focus is on mobilizing a people's movement towards emancipatory change.[11] Such language might sound highly speculative, but its pragmatic note is evident in its attitude to consumer capitalism. While the original Latin American liberation theology had called for (?revolutionary) overthrow of capitalism, contemporary South African liberation theology would seem to be much more comfortable with what the Boffs criticized as 'reformism'. Swart writes:

> In terms of a more informed discourse on the kind of renewal that would be at stake in the newfound focus on the world of the rich and privileged, one could here also point out how we have been moving from an initial, rather vague 'alternatives to capitalism' position to one where we more assertively begin to speak about the idea of an 'alternative capitalism' . . . Over against prevailing fixed 'radical anti-capitalist' and 'conservative pro-capitalist' positions, an approach is more specifically pleaded for that overcomes [these dichotomies] . . . In essence, therefore, it points to a frame of mind whereby 'we want to reconsider positively the idea that there might be much good and beneficial also in the system of capitalism and that the best and most viable alternative might in fact be to work for an alternative form of capitalism.'[12]

What is interesting about this development in thought is that it echoes a parallel development in Latin American liberation theology. Jung Mo Sung is a Brazilian who in recent years has been arguing for a very different approach to capitalism to that of the original liberation theologians. While the Boffs called for revolution[13] and Gutiérrez criticized 'developmentalism',[14] Sung can write the following:

> To affirm the existence of the excluded, the fundamental dignity of them all, and to hear their clamour and to witness – with the visible presence of the Church in the midst of the poor in concrete struggles on their behalf – that God is among them, is the best way of denying the absolutizing of the market, of unveiling concretely and practically its limits. However, to deny the idolatry of the market and to show its limits is not to deny the market in an absolute way – that would be reverse idolatry. What we need is an adjustment of the market in line with the objective of a dignified and enjoyable life for all human beings.[15]

Interestingly, in his otherwise excellent book *Comfortable Compassion*, Charles Elliot argues for what he terms 'total transformation, not ameliorative reform', and in the process acknowledges that this might be 'utopian' but that the call of Christ is to no other.[16] As well as some theological critiques of such utopianism, which I discuss in the final part of this book, the practical issue is that Elliot fails to provide any concrete examples where such total transformation in structures has actually taken place – this is despite providing an apparent list of these. Echoing Tinyiko Maluleke's point regarding cats and mice,[17] Elliot writes somewhat provocatively, 'If you believe that *capitalism* is the problem there is not too much point in asking capitalists to be more humane capitalists.'[18] The argument of this book, in concert with contemporary liberation theology as articulated by Swart and Sung, is that yes there is.[19]

Of course, the precise nature of these adjustments is still continually being worked out (though see the Epilogue to this book for some suggestions). However, what is evident from this discussion is that if liberation theology is going to have a future it will only do so to the extent that it can transform its utopian ideals into practical action. Swart and Sung have begun to signal a direction in which this might take place, and from a Western perspective the whole purpose of this book is also to point in the same reformist direction. Theologically, it is arguable that the problem with the original liberation programme was simply that it was too over-realized. Latin American liberation theology was certainly not shy of proclaiming its utopian credentials. The Boffs talk of translating 'the eschatological hope of the kingdom for the full freedom of the children of God into historical hopes in the personal and social spheres',[20] and Mario Aguilar, quoting Felix Wilfred, says:

One of the greatest possibilities of liberation theology has always been the possibility of utopia, the possibility of dreaming that a better world can eventually come because 'utopias are not illusions' but 'they are imaginative and creative, but realistic possibilities for the future'.[21]

However, the problem with such utopianism is evident in two particular ways. The first is simply that, this side of the new heaven and new earth, there is no perfect and just political and economic system. Of course, the current system is grossly unjust and can be improved upon with the adjustments and reforms that Swart and Sung speak of, but the problem with the original Latin American liberation theology is that it seemed to assume a perfect political order could be articulated and enacted. A far more helpful approach is articulated by Christopher Rowland, a significant British advocate of liberation theology. He writes: 'The apocalyptic and eschatological in the New Testament and indeed the Bible more generally are visionary in character but not utopian. There is no detailed blueprint of a New Age and the ways it should be implemented.'[22] As is the case with all revolutionary movements, the original Latin American liberation theology promised far too much and delivered far too little. But, at the same time, it also failed to take into account the reason why such a perfect political order is not possible – and that is the reality of sin.

While change is possible . . . *complete, lasting and sustainable* social transformation on this side of eternity will never be a reality, because we live in the in-between times where evil and the kingdom of God coexist in this world . . . It is disconcerting to see a new generation of Christians naively believe that this world can be transformed on this side of eternity, as it shows a lack of understanding of the concept of sin and how insidious, corrosive and destructive evil is.[23]

To some extent, this critique also applies to Swart's fourth-generation development initiative. For while he advocates mass mobilization of the people, what we must not forget is that all too easily the people can become the mob. As Tyler Wigg-Stevenson has put it, 'Those who have aimed at utopia have often been the most effective at unleashing hell on earth.'[24] I am not suggesting that a rebalancing of power between the people and the state, and in particular the people and the global economic system, is not required – it is – but we must never be so naive as to think that all that is required for a regime of justice and peace to be realized is for the people to be liberated. Genesis 3 and George Orwell's *Animal Farm* indicated the vacuity of that mistruth. If, then, the poor are truly to be served, this will not be done by utopian idealism but only by patient revolution. Indeed, Taylor goes so far as to say 'that it is no longer very useful to talk about "revolution", if ever it was', and 'The debate is not about capitalism, for or against. It is not about the replacement of capitalism. It is about the form that capitalism should take.'[25] I would concur.

A possible alternative to this reformist perspective is provided by Walter Wink. He writes that Jesus

> was not a reformer, bringing alternative, better readings of the Law. Nor was he a revolutionary, attempting to replace one oppressive power with another (Mark 12.13–17 par). He went beyond revolution. His assault was against the basic presuppositions and structures of oppression itself. Violent revolution fails because it is not revolutionary enough. It changes the rulers but not the rules, the ends but not the means.[26]

I have a lot of sympathy with Wink's position, here agreeing that Jesus changed the rules and not merely the rulers. Whether or not it is appropriate to describe that as a more revolutionary approach is debatable and hinges on how we understand the term 'revolutionary'. I would probably prefer the term 'radical', which suggests wholesale change from the roots, but radical change undertaken in a patient, reformist manner. Volf describes this approach as 'internal difference', Maggay terms it 'not so much revolutionary as subversive',[27] and I have more sympathy with this articulation than that of Wink.[28] We turn now to another theology of development that arguably commits the same fallacy as liberation theology. Indeed, it could be argued that this represents the people movement that Swart speaks of. Yet, I fear that it is plagued by the same over-realized eschatology that affected liberation theology.

Pentecostal theologies of development

In her edited book *Pentecostalism and Development*, Dena Freeman makes the case that Pentecostalism has been good for economic development. The focus of her study is a rural population in the Gamo Highlands of Ethiopia where she undertook anthropological research in the 1990s and 2000s. Freeman describes the way in which the embrace of Pentecostal theology and new business opportunities fostered by a development NGO led to remarkable 'social, economic and spiritual transformation' for the people of Masho.[29] What is noteworthy about Freeman's analysis is not so much the details of the transformation in Masho – which undoubtedly were profound – but the way in which Freeman builds on that particular experience to articulate what she calls 'the Pentecostal ethic'.[30]

Max Weber had famously argued that the growth of capitalism was fostered by a Protestant work ethic. In particular, that ethic had encouraged hard work, thrift and a distinction between business relationships and family relationships. All of this had ensured that the growing economies of Northern Europe, in particular, had sufficient capital available for further investment and such investment led to the development of those capitalist economies.[31] Freeman draws on Weber's thesis – the historical accuracy of which is not the point under discussion here – to argue for a similar Pentecostal ethic.[32] In particular, she suggests that Pentecostalism is characterized by the same 'hard work, saving and a limitation on certain types of consumption'.[33] While she acknowledges that African Pentecostals may not have quite the abstemious lifestyles that were characteristic of eighteenth- and nineteenth-century Protestants, nevertheless, 'There is a marked limitation of "wasteful consumption" and reorientation towards investment and accumulation.'[34] Similarly, while Weber's Protestant ethic understood hard work to be motivated by a desire to demonstrate that one is part of the elect, so the Pentecostal ethic motivates hard work because the fruits of such labour demonstrate that one is achieving God's blessing, the elect on earth as it were.[35] Finally, just as Weber had indicated that separating business from family was essential to enable saving for investment, so Freeman argues that Pentecostalism moralizes 'separation from more distant kin' and so allows the accumulation of capital for similar purposes.[36] One further feature of Pentecostalism that Freeman describes and that was less evident in Weber's thesis is that Pentecostalism directly encourages the spread of entrepreneurial behaviour. She quotes a Pentecostal pastor who preached, 'It's not enough just to give the "sacrifice" and cross your arms. You have to leave your job and open a business, even if it's only selling popcorn on the street. As an employee you'll never get rich.'[37]

In contrast to Freeman, Paul Gifford, another anthropologist, is far less sanguine about the contribution of Pentecostalism to economic development. He shares Freeman's view that Pentecostalism is motivating and encourages entrepreneurial behaviour.[38] However, he suggests that African Pentecostalism has a range of other features that to his mind render it less than congenial to economic development. There are three particular features of African Pentecostalism that he points to that indicate this. The first is the enchanted world-view that characterizes African Pentecostalism. While modernity would teach that business success depends on hard work, good financial control and wise investments, Pentecostalism would teach, at least in part, that such success depends on the relative blessings of God and cursings of the spirit world. I have said 'in part' because Gifford acknowledges that Pentecostalism does at times encourage human agency and responsibility and calls for hard work, savings and investments. But at the same time, and as Gifford points out, sometimes in the same communication, it also indicates that we are at the mercy of the spirit world. As Paul Hiebert explained in his classic article, one of the problems of the Western missionary endeavour is that it failed to take into account what Hiebert called 'the excluded middle', that realm of reality which is neither scientific nor religious in the sense of God, the divine, the sacred. The excluded middle is that realm where the spirit world impacts human life, and it is in that realm where many African Christians find answers to many of life's imponderables. Hiebert comments:

> What are the questions of the middle level? Here one finds the questions of the uncertainty of the future, the crises of present life and the unknowns of the past . . . the crises and misfortunes of present life must be handled: sudden disease and plagues, extended droughts, earthquakes, business failures and the empirically unexplainable loss of health.[39]

Gifford's thesis is that as long as African Pentecostalism maintains such an enchanted view of the world, as long as the budding entrepreneur believes that their business success is as much down to the vagaries of the spirit world as it is to sound business practices, then such beliefs will always act as a brake on any economic development that might otherwise have taken place.

The second issue that Gifford identifies is that African Pentecostalism 'militates against any form of community or social capital; it breeds fear and distrust'.[40] In defence of this thesis, Gifford cites numerous examples where Daniel Olukoya, a particularly prominent Nigerian Pentecostal, encourages rifts in families by pointing to one family member or another as the cause of some personal disaster. So, for instance:

> A woman saw a frog on the yam she was pounding: when she struck it she became paralyzed in an arm and a leg; on praying a 'return to sender', she was cured but her sister became paralyzed immediately, revealing that the sister was responsible.[41]

While the particular examples that Gifford cites are indeed odd and no doubt bred family disunity, as a general thesis characterizing Pentecostalism and against modern economic development this seems a rather misplaced accusation to make. In the first place, it is immediately obvious that if there is a problem with African Pentecostalism, families and economic development, the problem is exactly the reverse of that which Gifford suggests. In his seminal work, Weber had already suggested that economic development requires 'the separation of business from the household',[42] going so far as to suggest that a new child entering the household is primarily thought of as a 'potential business partner of the rationally managed enterprise',[43] rather than by their social and familial relationships. Weber wrote: 'Even where the household unit remains outwardly intact, the internal dissolution of household communism by virtue of the growing sense of calculation goes on irresistibly in the course of cultural development.'[44] For Weber, then, modern capitalism *required* the dissolution of the family, at least in an economic sense.

This point of course is well known by those who live in cultures where ideas of the extended family require all members of the family to support one another. The problem is that when such economic ties are prevalent, it is very hard for any individual member of the family to save enough for a meaningful invest-ment. Some friends of mine in Uganda, who are seeking to establish a maize-milling business, have told me of their need to hide financial wealth from their family members in order to save enough for the next large piece of machinery and hook up to the electrical grid. Similarly, Abhijit Banerjee and Esther Duflo, referring to a couple from Kenya who were trying to save for fertilizer, wrote: 'Saving at home is difficult, they explained, because there is always something that comes up that requires money (someone is sick, someone needs clothes, a guest has to be fed), and it is hard to say no.'[45] The only way, then, for such families to save enough to invest is precisely by curtailing the extended family ties that tend to draw away any potential funds for saving. Freeman recognized this and saw it as a strength of African Pentecostalism. The odd thing about Gifford's analysis is not that he recognizes it but that he seems to think it mili-tates against economic development. One wonders if the reason Gifford has done this is because the view he is especially keen to critique is the enchanted, spirit-filled and animistic African view and so whenever he encounters it – even if it does some economic good – he cannot help but criticize it.

Where Gifford seems on stronger ground is in the ambivalent attitude that much African Pentecostalism has to hard work. Freeman suggests that this is a real strength and is consistently encouraged, at least among the groups she observed. However, it is hard to argue with Gifford's point that in much African Pentecostalism, business and financial success is frequently portrayed as being the product of God's blessing or spiritual forces and totally uncon-nected to one's own effort and industry. So a Nigerian friend of mine who has been educated in a Western environment recently shared this post on his Facebook wall: 'God will give you a job making more money than you've ever imagined with a position you're not even educationally qualified for. It's called favour.' Similarly, Gifford lists a series of examples in which economic progress is made not just in spite of weak endeavour, but sometimes because the recipient has refused to work hard like others. Quoting David Oyedepo, he writes:

Remember [prosperity] is a supernatural act of God. It is not something to labour for ... You never get rich through sweat, at least not in the kingdom ... We are commanded not be idle, but your strength is inadequate to guarantee you riches; so don't sweat over it, the sinners are the ones sweating over it. If we join the world in the struggle for survival, we will fail the way they fail. The knowledge and the practice of the truth make you a sweatless winner. Not all winners sweat to win. Sweating is a curse. It symbolizes struggle ... It is the blessing of God that make rich without adding any sorrow. They are released through obedience. Your expertise will not make rich (*sic*).[46]

184

Yet at the same time, Gifford rightly points out a tension (if not contradiction) in this theology, for once again he quotes Oyedepo on the value of work: 'There is no substitute for hard work . . . Hard work is the key to distinction. Without hard work, your destiny will decay. So, go and work.'[47] Clearly, then, both sentiments are present in African Pentecostalism.

One final criticism that Gifford mentions, though somewhat surprisingly does not make much of, is the conspicuous consumption that plagues many African Pentecostal leaders. Gifford suggests that this is merely a sacralized version of the well-known phenomenon of the African 'big man', and if that is correct it could be traced back to the colonial heritage as we previously discussed. He notes how Oyedepo owns thirty-two cars and four private jets rivalling any of Nigeria's top businessmen.[48] What is unusual about the wealth of African Pentecostal leaders, at least in comparison to Western wealthy religious leaders, is the way in which such wealth is ostentatiously displayed. Part of the theology of prosperity teaching is that it is important that one demonstrates visibly the signs of God's blessing; for that reason wealth is not to be hidden, but rather ostentatiously displayed. This aspect of African Pentecostalism is explicitly criticized by Kwakena Asamoah-Gyadu, who contrasts the values of materialism and consumerism which characterize it with the values of the cross:

> God is certainly a God of prosperity but definitely not a God of consumerist values and materialism. The materialistic orientation of the Gospel of Prosperity means that the triumphs, glory and honour of the Cross are emphasized to the neglect of its representation of pain and suffering.[49]

Such ostentatious consumerism is of course completely counter to Weber's ethic, in which the priority of saving for investment and restricted consumption is evident. The only sermon I have ever walked out of in my life was in a small, rural Kenyan church where a visiting speaker was telling a group of a hundred or so subsistence farmers, some of whom were suffering from malnutrition, that the reason he needed to eat meat while they survived on ground maize was that he was so busy preaching the word of God that he couldn't spend the time chewing ground maize in the way that they did!

There are, then, aspects of African Pentecostalism that certainly foster the capitalist spirit as Weber would understand it. It encourages – at least some of the time – hard work, entrepreneurship, saving to invest and restrictions on some consumption. Yet, at the same time, there is also much in African Pentecostalism that militates against economic development: sweatless work, conspicuous consumption, collectivist economics within the family and an animist world-view that tends to see spirits rather than human factors behind a range of life circumstances. It is a conundrum, and in one sense no surprise, that Freeman and Gifford come to such starkly different conclusions. It is very likely that in some locations, among some groups (if not some families), the positives of Pentecostalism are emphasized and a sense of human agency and responsibility dominates in a way that leads to sound economic growth. And no doubt, there are other places (and other families/individuals) where a less than Weberian ethic predominates and opportunities for entrepreneurship are mishandled or misapplied. Africa and African Pentecostalism is simply too large a phenomenon for any simple conclusions to be drawn – whether positive or negative.[50]

Catholic social teaching

Throughout this book, I have already had cause to refer to the Catholic Church's teaching in regard to poverty and development. However, it is worth pausing to examine somewhat more systematically the approach that is taken by the Catholic magisterium. When one reads Catholic social teaching (CST), particularly in contrast to evangelical pronouncements on public theology, what immediately strikes one is the depth of theological and historical comment. While it often feels as though evangelicals shoot from the hip, scattering a few well-chosen verses to make some political point to which they are committed for other reasons, the same accusation cannot be levelled at the Catholic Church, at least in its official pronouncements. This is not to say that I agree with everything that emerges from the papacy – far from it, but it certainly has a quality of biblical, theological and social reflection that the rest of the Church could learn from.

One of the guiding principles of CST is the principle of subsidiarity. The Catholic Church understands society to be comprised of successive levels, from the individual, though the family unit, the community, to local and national government. The principle of subsidiarity states that decision-making should take place at the lowest possible level that is appropriate so that as far as possible decisions are made by those who are closest to the people. To varying degrees, this approach is also reflected in CST itself.[51] Papal pronouncements have a tendency to be high-level without much detailed policy guidance, with the more specific implications of such papal utterances being worked out at a local or at least national level.

The first Catholic encyclical to explicitly and comprehensively deal with issues of development was *Populorum Progressio*, in which development is described as 'the new name for peace'.[52] The encyclical acknowledged that more needed to be done to address the problems of poverty than had hitherto been the case. Quoting a previous Vatican report, the encyclical stated: 'What we mean, to put it in clearer words, is that our charity toward the poor, of whom there are countless numbers in the world, has to become more solicitous, more effective, more generous.'[53] As indicated, however, Catholic encyclicals do not emerge *de novo,* but self-consciously build on what has previously been written, and a number of significant 'development' themes had already been addressed in previous encyclicals.

Perhaps the first of these was the condition of the working person, which had been an explicit concern in the first papal encyclical, *Rerum Novarum.* What is interesting about this encyclical is the way in which it steers a middle ground between communism/socialism and the emergent capitalism. This is a pattern that has been followed by almost every encyclical since, with the

Catholic Church offering critiques of both polarities. So, on the one hand, *Rerum Novarum* states this in regard to socialism:

> Socialists, therefore, by endeavouring to transfer the possessions of individuals to the community at large, strike at the interests of every wage-earner, since they would deprive him of the liberty of disposing of his wages, and thereby of all hope and possibility of increasing his resources and of bettering his condition in life.[54]

Yet, at the same time, it is clear that the primary concern of this encyclical is the exploitation of workers by employers who 'too often treat them with great inhumanity and hardly care for them outside the profit their labour brings'.[55] It is in this encyclical that we find an explicit defence of just wages. It notes the typical capitalist answer, which is that the employer should be free to offer any wages they want as long as the employee is free to accept or reject that work. But it then points out that this is insufficient, for it fails to address the fact that 'without the result of labour a man cannot live'.[56] In other words, the poor man is not free to accept or reject work that is being offered at low wages; he must live, therefore he must work – even if the wages are insufficient for his needs. As a result, the encyclical states 'that wages ought not to be insufficient to support a frugal and well-behaved wage-earner'. Anything else makes the worker 'the victim of force and injustice'.[57]

This theme is then picked up in *Populorum Progressio* and expanded to include the economic development of nations through free trade:

> In Rerum Novarum this principle was set down with regard to a just wage for the individual worker; but it should be applied with equal force to contracts made between nations: trade relations can no longer be based solely on the principle of free, unchecked competition, for it very often creates an economic dictatorship. Free trade can be called just only when it conforms to the demands of social justice.[58]

We see in this the carefully nuanced position of the Catholic Church in regard to economic development. Long before the third way became fashionable in British political circles, the Catholic Church had been arguing for their own moderate position. Yes, they believe in free trade and certainly disavow complete state ownership of the means of production. Nevertheless, that does not mean that capitalism should be unbridled or that it is not beholden to the demands of social justice. A reformed capitalism is the solution to economic development.

Lying behind all of this is a natural law theology that understands itself to be applicable to all people. In other words, the Church is not specifying some particular 'religious' doctrine, but one that in principle is persuasive to all. Yet at the same time, CST does make explicit appeals to the creation mandate as the basis for fair treatment of workers and just trade. *Populorum Progressio* discusses the way in which creation is ordered for human flourishing, which in turn brings glory to God, and then states:

All other rights, whatever they may be, including the rights of property and free trade, are to be subordinated to this principle. They should in no way hinder it; in fact, they should actively facilitate its implementation. Redirecting these rights back to their original purpose must be regarded as an important and urgent social duty.[59]

Two further concepts within CST are worthy of our attention as they relate to the issue of poverty. The first of these is the Catholic concept of the dignity and sanctity of life. It is well known that Catholics have emphasized this teaching in respect of abortion and end-of-life care, but what is less frequently appreciated is that the Catholic concept of the dignity of life is not restricted to those extremes of life, but applies equally to the conditions in which everyone might find themselves. *Populorum Progressio* had stated that development must not be 'restricted to economic growth alone. To be authentic, it must be well rounded; it must foster the development of each man and of the whole man.'[60] What this means is that the dignity and sanctity of life are not being upheld when a child suffers from malnutrition in Angola, when a worker is unfairly dismissed in São Paulo, when an Indian woman is held in debt slavery, when a Ugandan girl is deprived of the opportunity for education, or when a sweatshop worker in the Philippines fails to receive wages that enable life. The concept of dignity, then, extends to the whole of our human condition. It speaks to the issue of whether we are able to mutually flourish. In saying all of this, we are simply saying that the Catholic concept of dignity is one that is holistic. Frequently this is described as 'integral human development'.[61] Moreover, it is one that also embraces the spiritual dimension of humanity's existence, not as some add-on to our material existence, but rather as the ultimate telos for our lives. Interestingly, in his 2009 encyclical, Pope Benedict XVI drew attention to the dangers of a despiritualized humanity being exported by HICs to LICs in their drive for economic development:

> *God is the guarantor of man's true development,* inasmuch as, having created him in his image, he also establishes the transcendent dignity of men and women and feeds their innate yearning to 'be more'. Man is not a lost atom in a random universe: he is God's creature, whom God chose to endow with an immortal soul and whom he has always loved. If man were merely the fruit of either chance or necessity, or if he had to lower his aspirations to the limited horizon of the world in which he lives, if all reality were merely history and culture, and man did not possess a nature destined to transcend itself in a supernatural life, then one could speak of growth, or evolution, but not development . . . In the context of cultural, commercial or political relations, it also sometimes happens that economically developed or emerging countries export this reductive vision of the person and his destiny to poor countries. This is the damage that 'superdevelopment' causes to authentic development when it is accompanied by 'moral underdevelopment'.[62]

Very much related to the concept of human dignity or integral human development is the Catholic idea of the common good. The common good is essentially the concept that the welfare of all members of a society is important and needs to be considered in efforts at development. This involves the belief that humans are necessarily relational, and that 'the good of the community formed by these relationships and the good of each individual are mutually implicating'.[63] It means that in formulating and enacting new policies, the welfare of all – not just as a group of isolated individuals, but as a community – needs to be taken into account.

> It implies that every individual, no matter how high or low, has a duty to share in promoting the welfare of the community as well as a right to benefit from that welfare. 'Common' implies 'all-inclusive': the common good cannot exclude or exempt any section of the population. If any section of the population is in fact excluded from participation in the life of the community, even at a minimal level, then that is a contradiction to the concept of the common good and calls for rectification.[64]

The common good demands then that even if a principle such as 'development', 'freedom' or 'rights' is espoused, the practical application of that principle is subject to its impact on the common good. The common good ensures that no one is left behind, no one is forgotten in the pursuit of some other goal. The common good would imply that the tax regimes of countries would be set so as to facilitate not just individual human flourishing (and presumably therefore low taxes) but also mutual human flourishing (and therefore a sufficiently high tax base to ensure adequate provision of services to all, and minimal inequality). The common good would ensure that working conditions are just and fair to ensure employment for as many as possible, while an adequate standard of living is enjoyed by those who can't work. Applied at the international level, the common good would insist that my country's economic development is not at the expense of some other country through unfair trade deals, tax injustice or asset stripping. And applied towards those not yet born, the common good would ensure that we do not leave an environmental legacy that takes decades, if not centuries, to mend. In summary, the common good stands opposed to the excessive individualism that is only concerned with my rights or my freedoms, but requires all of us to consider all in the pursuit of human development.

Strongly linked to the idea of the common good is the concept of solidarity. Pope John Paul II defined this not as

> a feeling of vague compassion or shallow distress at the misfortunes of so many people, both near and far. On the contrary, it is a firm and persevering determination to commit oneself to the common good; that is to say to the good of all and of each individual, because we are all really responsible for all.[65]

Theologically, the fundamental principle that lies behind most of this teaching is a robust doctrine of creation, which insists upon mutual human flourishing, the dignity of humanity and the glory of God through such flourishing as the end of humanity. Catholics are happy to embrace a relational personhood, though not perhaps with the same vigour as the Orthodox Church, and they also have a strong doctrine of sin as that to which we are blind and that which prevents the full realization of the mutual flourishing to which we are called. Less noticeable is any emphasis on salvation as won through the death of Christ. As it relates to issues of development, the emphasis would seem to lie more on a moral influence Christ than on a *Christus Victor* motif, though having said that the motif of victory in Christ has been more prominent in one of Pope Francis' recent encyclicals.[66] There is much, then, to be praised in CST. Their socio-political affirmations are strongly rooted in Scripture and theology, they are appropriately nuanced in their findings and at their core is a strong desire to see the mutual flourishing of all peoples irrespective of nationality or status. They are also a good example of what it means to speak truth to power.

Practitioner theologies of development

By their own admission, the Orthodox Church has not particularly reflected on issues of development, though this is not to say that in practice they have not been extensively engaged.[67] And there are of course a range of other Christian theologies of development that could be discussed.[68] However, in this final section I want to focus on two theologies of development as articulated by two leading British development agencies, one ecumenical and one evangelical: Christian Aid and Tearfund.

Christian Aid

Christian Aid (hereafter CA) are a major ecumenical British and Irish development agency. In 2014/15 they had a turnover of approximately £100 million, working with 568 partners in 39 countries with just under 900 full-time equivalent staff (national and international).[69] In the section that follows I shall be offering some critiques of CA's theology of development. I want to preface that analysis by indicating, however, that in terms of their actual practice on the ground the work of CA is exemplary. Nothing in what follows should be understood to mean that as an organization they are not worthy of financial support. I am proud to have worked with them and supported them financially myself. Indeed, one of the reasons why I have examined their theology of development is because they are one of few Christian development agencies that have invested time and energy to produce such a theology, and for this they are to be commended.

In the last few years, they have produced a series of reports which describe the theology by which they work. The first of these, written in 2010 by Paula Clifford, entitled *Theology and International Development*, set out the relational framework by which Christian Aid understood its development work. This was followed in 2012 by *Theology from the Global South*, which sought to highlight the voices of a range of Global South theologians and their perspectives on Christian Aid's work. Other reports have been more specific, exploring from a theological point of view issues such as climate change, HIV/AIDS, tax justice, human rights, prophetic advocacy and gender.[70]

The analysis I shall present here is informed by the two broader reports – *Theology and International Development* and *Theology from the Global South*. The introduction to the first of these reports indicates that it represents the fruit of consultation with many of CA's staff and supporters and that the second report, *Theology from the Global South*, will represent the outcome of a similar exercise with churches and partners in the Global South. The first report, then, describes itself as a 'synthesis of previous work' and 'an overarching theology of development' that underpins all that CA does.[71] It begins with a discussion on the nature of poverty and in the process draws on a liberation paradigm, the capabilities approach and human rights discourse.[72] The report does not seem to recognize the tensions between these paradigms or the fact, as we have already indicated, that many within the liberation movement would view some of the development work in which CA is engaged as opposed to their agenda. In a telling phrase, the report acknowledges two distinct approaches to international development – needs based and rights based – and then says, 'In reality, the work carried out under each approach is more or less the same.'[73] Pragmatism is of course the scourge of activists the world over and it would seem that the pragmatist spirit is impacting CA's work too – even in a report that ostensibly is about the theological underpinnings of its work. In short, in the spirt of the times, it would seem as if CA has adopted a bricolage approach to their work: if a bit of liberation theology helps, we will use that; if some capability language serves us, we'll draw on that, and if, at another time, rights-based discourse is effective we'll use that. The problem, of course, with such pragmatic approaches is that while pragmatism claims to have no underlying theory, the real problem with pragmatism is that it does have an underlying concept – it is simply one that is unexamined and insufficiently explored. Towards the end of the first chapter, the report states that the approach they take is one that is 'grounded in the Christian gospel but that is also distinct from Christian mission'.[74] As a theologian, it is hard to know what to make of that statement – for the Christian gospel simply is missional. It is theologically incoherent to have work that is grounded in the gospel but distinct from mission. To be fair to CA, as the conclusion continues it seems that what they have in mind by 'mission' is proselytism and so what they are trying to say is that their development work is somehow motivated by the good news of Jesus Christ, but will not involve any direct or indirect efforts at conversion. In the process, they explicitly say that what they will not do is seek to transmit 'their beliefs directly to the people they help'.[75] What is interesting about this phrase is that it betrays a confusion that frequently plagues discussions of evangelism or proselytism. Because, of course, CA is in the business of 'transmitting their beliefs'. When they do any kind of health-promotion work, I am fairly sure that they tell the people to wear condoms, practise safe sex, get their children vaccinated against measles, boil water before consumption and so on. All of that is transmitting beliefs, so presumably what they mean is that they won't transmit their Christian beliefs. But even then the separation between sacred and secular is not quite as clear as they seem to imagine. Consider an animist who believes that their malaria is caused by their dead aunt's curse. Will CA encourage that person to believe it is caused by a bite from the anopheles mosquito and so bed nets are a good thing, or will they leave the person believing in ancestral spirits? In the process, will they indicate that the aunt's curse is not the cause? If so, isn't that a case of transmitting their religious, or at the very least world-view, beliefs? The same could be said of someone struggling with issues of self-esteem. Is it really the case that to point to the hope in the gospel that God loves and cares for such a one is beyond the remit of a CA worker? The relevant code of conduct for international humanitarian work requires far less than CA seem to offer. It states:

> Aid will not be used to further a particular political or religious standpoint. Humanitarian aid will be given according to the need of individuals, families and communities. Notwithstanding the right of Non Governmental Humanitarian Agencies to espouse particular political or religious opinions, we affirm that assistance will not be dependent on the adherence of the recipients to those opinions. We will not tie the promise, delivery or distribution of assistance to embracing or acceptance of a particular political or religious creed.[76]

Of course, I am well aware why CA are taking the line that they do. It is of a piece with the pragmatism that appears to dominate their use of development theory and theology. If they were to indicate that they might share some of their Christian beliefs at some point then all kinds of grant money might be in jeopardy. But as Paul Bickley, in his excellent report on proselytism and faith-based actors indicates, the word itself remains undefined, and possibly undefinable. Moreover, he argues that while there have been some extreme and obvious cases, in the vast majority of situations proselytism is in practice no issue at all. 'If we understand it properly and respond to it maturely, the problem of proselytism should be recognised for what it is – no problem at all.'[77]

In the second chapter of the report, they draw on notions of justice, the *imago Dei* and the Trinity to argue for a relational concept of development, and from here on the rest of the report frames all of its discussion within this relational concept. The fundamental argument seems to be that poverty and injustice can be primarily characterized as disordered relationships.

> As before, several types of relationship may contribute to overall injustice. In the case of HIV, for example, the unjust treatment of women by men is a key cause of the spread of infection; but so, too, is the injustice done to poorer people by the rich within the community, either in denying them treatment or by increasing their vulnerability (where, for example, poverty means that people living with HIV cannot afford the nourishing food that they need). At a global level, the unjust relationship between human beings and the created world has led to climate change. But again the relationship between rich and poor is a factor, as the disproportionate levels of carbon emissions from rich countries have a particularly adverse effect on the lives of people in poor countries.[78]

Inevitably, the solution to all this is to seek the restoration of right relationships. Although clearly very wary of abandoning the language of rights, the report at this point juxtaposes the restoration of relationships and the promotion of rights as the appropriate kind of response.[79] The obvious and practical tension between these two approaches – demands for rights often leads to fractured relationships – is not especially addressed.

In exploring how the Church undertakes this task of restoring relationships, the report draws on Hauerwas' understanding of the Church as distinct from the world and that which holds the world to account, and in the process somewhat surprisingly states, 'This means that the church is required to do more than hold the world to account: it cannot challenge the world's values and actions without stating its own values and without itself taking action.'[80] I say 'surprisingly' because previously the report had argued that CA was not in the business of 'transmitting their beliefs' to those they serve. Indeed, the report goes on to advocate CA's 'prophetic voice' as that which 'is not afraid to challenge what has gone unchallenged, or to say things which might make people uncomfortable'.[81] I indicated earlier that the problem with pragmatism is not so much its absence of theory, but the fact that its theory is so often hidden and unexamined. And that seems to be what is going on with CA in this report. Clearly, there is a set of Christian beliefs which, in the name of CA, should not be propagated – presumably an exclusivist understanding of salvation and perhaps some aspects of traditional Christian morality. And there is another set of beliefs – presumably to do with challenging structures of injustice and the fact that aunts' curses don't cause malaria – that are to be promoted. The problem is not that CA has these two different sets; it is that they are not transparent about which beliefs should be advocated and which cannot. One also fears that CA are doing precisely what Hauerwas cautions against, namely failing to offer something distinctive over against the world. They had previously quoted Hauerwas with approval to the effect that the Church must be different from the world,[82] but in their hidden lists of beliefs that can be promoted and those that cannot, it would seem that they are doing the precise opposite of this in that the beliefs that can be promoted are those that are acceptable to, indeed indistinguishable from, those promulgated by the mainstream development community. Whereas, the views that cannot be promoted are those that would not be acceptable to the secular development community. In what sense, then, is CA holding the world to account by 'pointing to the reality of God's kingdom'?[83] As CA note, to not do that would allow 'ethical differences to become blurred – it would begin to merge into the world and be incapable of a clearly definable relationship with it'.[84] Molefe Tsele has written of the need for Christian development agencies to demonstrate their distinctive nature in contrast to the world: 'We want to stake a legitimate place for faith as part of the Church's option for the poor, but also to liberate the development enterprise from its secular and material captivity and crisis.'[85] It is not entirely clear how CA is doing this.

I want to suggest that the fundamental problem with CA's theological basis for their work is the near complete absence of any doctrine of redemption. It is noteworthy that the word atonement appears nowhere in the report, redemption (and cognates) a mere 5 times, crucified (and cognates) just twice and Christ only 13. By way of contrast, God appears 169 times and church 139. Indeed, it is noteworthy that out of the 46 mentions of Jesus almost all are about his moral example of compassion and mercy. Just three could be said to have anything to do with his death. Given that the New Testament devotes so much space to the history and meaning of Christ's death on the cross its near absence in this report is telling. The fundamental theological framework which is articulated by CA is essentially a moral influence theory. The world was created by God then marred by human sin, which is exemplified in disordered relationships between God and humanity, humanity and creation and between humans. God called out a people to restore those broken relationships – the Church – and Jesus lived, taught and died in order to provide an example of how such disordered relationships can be restored. The world is a mess; Jesus was a peacemaker and we who follow him should be so too.

In one sense there is nothing wrong with this framework, and as I have indicated nothing I say should be taken as a criticism of CA's actual work. In terms of serving the poor, and in particular in terms of their focus on structural issues of tax and trade justice, CA are doing exemplary work that puts the majority of other development agencies to shame. Having said that, there are a number of problems that result from this theological framework. The first is simply that CA seem to be unaware that moral influence is the conceptual category that is governing their work. I have already said that the problem with pragmatism – and with their blend of liberation theology, capability approach, human rights language, Barth, Hauerwas *et al.*, CA are clearly being pragmatic – is that the underlying conceptual categories are usually hidden and unexplored. I think that is what is going on here. CA simply haven't recognized that an exclusive moral influence theory is what underpins their theology of development. Now, perhaps that wouldn't matter if the moral influence theory by itself was sufficient to articulate a Christian doctrine of redemption. But it is here that CA run into problems. For while in the nineteenth century, moral influence as the sole theory of atonement was fashionable – at least among a certain group of German intellectuals – most contemporary theologians view moral influence as playing a part but not the whole story of redemption for Christians. And because for CA moral influence seems to be the only understanding at play, it means that significant aspects of the Christian story are left out or ignored as too hard to handle, and these missing pieces do have an impact on CA's actual work on the ground.

One consequence of adopting an exclusively moral influence position is that Jesus Christ is reduced to one figure among many. We Christians look to Christ's example, but there are many other moral characters who provide an example for us to follow. This explains why CA are so ambivalent about evangelism and mission. If Christ is merely one among many, then of course CA has no right (or even duty) to proclaim the uniqueness of Christ in any sense whatsoever. Practically, however, the problem remains on what basis do they, for instance, challenge an animist world-view that believes malaria is caused by the aunt's curse? It cannot be on Christian grounds – for the animist might well find their own moral influence in their ancestral spirits – so it can only be by imposing a secular, scientific framework of thought. I suspect (and hope) that in practice that is what happens, but such an approach renders CA as essentially a secular development agency motivated by a good Christian guy – Jesus Christ. In what sense are they still *Christian* Aid?

More significant, however, is that if Christ's work on the cross becomes essentially redundant (except as an example of self-sacrifice) then one is left with an under-realized concept of sin and an over-realized eschatology, and both of these impact development practice on the ground. Turning to the first of these, the CA report does acknowledge that God 'looks at the poor, but not always with unqualified approval; yes, he looks at the rich, but not always with unqualified condemnation'.[86] Yet, at the same time they fail to recognize the weaknesses discussed earlier in relation to liberation theology, human rights and the capability approach. All of these are let down in one way or another by a failure to take sin sufficiently seriously and to recognize that sin impacts all human beings – whether rich or poor, oppressed or victimizer. CA's borrowing of these ideas without qualification is in part because they have failed to identify and address the sinful weaknesses of each one.

The reason this matters is that if you combine a moral influence theory with an understanding of poverty as merely disordered relationships, then the solution becomes the restitution of those relationships. In order to bring about that restitution, one turns to the moral example of Christ and in particular his love ethic. Now, there is much that is commendable in this framework, but the problem is that it is not strong enough to support the weight that is placed upon it. Poverty will not be solved merely by looking to the moral example of Christ. Poverty will only be solved by looking to the objective work of Christ in defeating evil and death. Somewhat inevitably, therefore, CA end up with an over-realized eschatology believing, as they must, that simply by following the example of Christ the challenge of poverty can be solved. I discuss this in more detail in the next chapter, but for now let me simply point out that CA seem to interpret Christ's statement 'the poor will always be with you' either as a sign of defeat – why bother tackling poverty if we cannot solve it? – or by effectively ignoring its empirical content and claiming that, in the words of one of their slogans, *we can end poverty*.

The reason CA are forced into this false polarity is because they have an insufficient doctrine of the kingdom. If you take away Christ's victory on the cross over sin, death and the devil, then all you are left with is hope in humanity, at most inspired by the great moral example that is Jesus. And if all you are left with to give you hope is humanity, then, as history has repeatedly shown, one either gravitates to nihilism or false utopianism. This has been the history of the eighteenth through twentieth centuries in particular. If instead one brings Christ and his victory back into the equation, then a much more hopeful solution is possible. For with a firm trust in Christ's defeat of the powers of darkness (not merely subjectively via moral influence but objectively, actually) then one can cope with the reality that the poor will indeed always be with us because one knows for certain that one day, when Christ's kingdom is fully realized, there will then no longer be any poor among us. A recognition of Christ's victory on the cross and the inauguration but not completion of the kingdom to come prevents one from lapsing into false utopianism – for the kingdom is not yet fully come. But at the same time it also prevents one from lapsing into nihilistic defeat – the kingdom one day will fully come and in the meantime my job is, in the words of Tom Wright, to 'build for the kingdom'.

> What you *do* in the present – by painting, preaching, singing, sewing, praying, teaching, building hospitals, digging wells, campaigning for justice, writing poems, caring for the needy, loving your neighbour as yourself – all these things *will last into God's future* . . . They are part of what we may call *building for God's kingdom.*[87]

Of course, it might be asked, what's wrong with a bit of utopianism as long as it motivates people to action on behalf of the global poor? I will say a lot more about this in the next chapter, but for now let me highlight just one issue. A false utopianism in international development work leads to over-reach in what we think we can achieve. It leads us to do things that in the long run are not that helpful because in the short run we are trying to solve some problem that is in fact intractable. CA are right to say that we must 'do all that we can to put an end to the poverty that afflicts so many of the world's population',[88] but where I differ from them is in their belief that only a belief in the ultimate success of such human endeavours is sufficient to motivate that action. Ter Haar goes so far as to describe such forms of development as

> one of the many coercive utopias of the twentieth century . . . It can be seen as the secular translation of the Christian belief that the kingdom of God, in which all things will be perfect, will eventually arrive. However, this future kingdom is no longer seen to be in heaven but is believed to take the form of a utopia that can be created on earth . . . This [thinking] stands in stark contrast to a religious worldview that recognizes human imperfection and therefore generally accepts that life will never be perfect.[89]

Another way is possible, and on that note I turn to an exploration of Tearfund's theology of development.

Tearfund

In contrast to CA, Tearfund, another UK-based Christian development agency, has developed a far more christological theology of development. This is perhaps not surprising as they are explicitly evangelical in ethos and indeed were founded as The Evangelical Alliance Relief Fund (TEARFund). They are a slightly smaller organization than CA, bringing in just over £60 million in 2014/15. In 2015, they published a discussion paper, *The Restorative Economy*, which outlines an alternative economic future. The authors draw attention to the progress that has been made over the last 50 years or so in terms of poverty reduction, but argue that such improvements are at risk unless we chart an alternative social and economic path from the consumerist, capitalist one in which HICs are currently stuck. Their alternative is – perhaps unsurprisingly – rooted in the Old Testament jubilee principles and in particular the concepts of shalom, justice, love, righteousness, wisdom and atonement. It is the last of these that merits particular attention, for it is the fact that Tearfund put a doctrine of the atonement up front and centre that distinguishes their theological reflections from that of CA. They write: 'The overarching story of the Bible – from the fall in Genesis, through Jesus' death and resurrection, to the arrival of God's kingdom on earth in Revelation – is a story about mending broken relationships *through the process of atonement*.'[90] Every word of that sentence could have been found in the CA report except for the final clause in italics. For CA, the fundamental problem is disordered relationships and so the fundamental solution is restoration of those relationships by following the example of Christ in seeking justice, peace, love and so on. By way of contrast, for Tearfund, the fundamental problem is the same – broken relationships – but the solution is somewhat different. Tearfund undoubtedly do pursue the same moral influence concept that CA track, in that for Tearfund, as for CA, Jesus Christ is a great example to be followed especially in terms of self-sacrifice.[91] Tearfund, however, also add something else – a robust doctrine of atonement that incorporates objective as well as subjective elements.

Essentially, what Tearfund provide is a *Christus Victor* model of atonement. In a section entitled, 'How to restore broken relationships', they write, 'Jesus' death on the cross was about both dealing with sin *and* ushering in "his kingdom come" on earth.'[92] They quote Colossians 1.19–20 (NIV):

> For God was pleased to have all his fullness dwell in him, and through him to reconcile to himself all things, whether things on earth or things in heaven, by making peace through his blood, shed on the cross.

And then continue:

> So for Christians, the death of Christ is a decisive moment in the reconciliation of creator, humanity and creation . . . We catch a glimpse here of the reconciliation of all things: God's kingdom on earth, 'thy kingdom come'. God's intimate and personal contact with his people in a heavenly city speaks of a reconciled community, and the restored creation within which this city is located speaks of the completion of the šalom that was intended in creation and damaged by the fall. This image of the victory of God's purposes – an apocalypse in the strict sense of being a revelation in which things are made clear – is a deeply sustaining vision.[93]

While CA seem a little ambivalent about the kingdom, in particular about Christ's death being the decisive victory, Tearfund have no such hesitancy. The fundamental difference this brings is that Tearfund would seem to have a clear sense that on the cross Christ has really defeated evil. That victory has inaugurated his new kingdom, but that new kingdom is not yet complete. In the meantime, our purpose as the Church is to draw on that vision of the new kingdom to cause us to act and work for justice and peace, knowing that our endeavours are not in vain because ultimately the victory has been won. Sean Doherty articulates this idea in these terms: 'It provides a perpetual motor for reformist activity, in refusing to accept the way things are, while equally refusing to identify the outcomes of any given reform with the perfection of the Kingdom.'[94] While for CA it seems as if we are the saviours of the world, or can be if we work that bit harder for justice, for Tearfund it is much clearer that Christ is the saviour, but that we can participate in his kingdom-building work as we join in the movement for justice and peace. In many ways, the Tearfund theology is simply much more hopeful, much more confident that our work for justice is not pointless because the ultimate victory is secure. This is the difference that an objective understanding of atonement can bring.[95]

It is also worth noting that the Tearfund report has much less talk of secular theories of development, in particular the capability approach or human rights language. They are also much more comfortable talking of sin and its impact on us, as well as with the importance of evangelism as a part of our missional strategy. While abhorring any notion of proselytism that is conditional, manipulative or coercive, they have no problem in declaring:

> Tearfund exists to show and tell the good news of God's love in Jesus Christ and we long to see people's lives transformed as a result of an encounter with Jesus. As our Statement of Faith puts it: 'We commit to make known to all nations the gospel of God's grace through his son Jesus Christ, calling people to faith, repentance and discipleship.'[96]

In many ways, though, where they are most innovative in this work is in the recommendations that they offer. At this point, it strikes me that Tearfund are somewhat brave, for instead of pointing people to the traditional staple of development agencies – water and sanitation projects, education initiatives, healthcare and so on – they make a robust plea that sustainable economic development is the most effective route out of poverty.

> While aid remains crucial for development, especially in least developed countries, it is markets that have the most power to drive really transformative change . . . So we think some of the biggest potential in the UK's development agenda is in supporting private sector development and inclusive growth.[97]

This statement is accompanied by a series of policy recommendations that will make such economic development easier for poorer countries, including for instance a range of tax and regulatory measures that would rebalance the global economy in the direction of jubilee principles.[98] As will have been obvious throughout this book, it is this kind of shift from an aid to advocacy model that I am particularly seeking to encourage. In the long run, I think Tearfund are absolutely right that aid will not bring a lasting solution to poverty; it is only economic development that will. The problem in the meantime is that so much of the global economic system disadvantages poorer economies from taking part fully in that development. It is commendable that Tearfund (and

CA) have shone a spotlight on this issue. Yet for both organizations, challenging the unjust global economic architecture remains a relatively minor activity. In 2014/15 Tearfund spent around 19 per cent of their funds on such work, and in the same year CA spent 13 per cent, though I note that it is hard to make a direct comparison between the two organizations in this regard as their Charity Commission returns categorize their finances somewhat differently.[99] My hope is not that such work becomes the sole activity of these organizations, but that it grows in prominence and significance.

I also wonder if the theological reason that Tearfund have this emphasis is again related to the issue of hope. If one has a robust doctrine of the now and not yet, then the imperative to solve all problems immediately is somewhat less. One can take the long view and genuinely ask the question: what is going to be in the long-term interests of this group that I am working with as opposed to what is going to solve my guilty conscience in the meantime? Having said that, elsewhere in the Tearfund report, they are guilty of the kind of utopianism that I criticized CA for. So, they write for instance that their alternative economic path 'leads to a place where poverty is eliminated, where catastrophic climate change is averted, and where all human beings . . . have the chance to flourish'.[100] My theological riposte would be that such activities might lead us there, but due to sin we will never arrive, at least in this life.

The purpose of this chapter has been to explore the relevance of our doctrine of redemption for poverty-alleviation work. Through a discussion of various secular theories of development and two prominent Christian development theologies of development, I have hoped to show the relevance of a robust understanding of atonement. In the absence of Christ, secular theories tend towards individualism and utopian visions of what can be achieved that in the long run may do more harm than good, or at least fail to address adequately the primary issues. I discuss these problems in more detail in Chapter 17: the problem of aid utopianism. Recognizing Christ merely as a good moral example is better than that, but still falls short of the ideal. But trusting in Christ as the one who ultimately has won the victory, and therefore having a certain knowledge that we can have hope for the future, is what ensures our work is appropriate, long-term and hopeful.[101]

Notes

1 I have not in this book specifically addressed the so-called ecumenical approach to poverty especially as articulated by the World Council of Churches. This is largely because it echoes much of the approach taken by Latin American liberation theology, though updated in line with new capitalist realities. The classic articulation of this position is found in U. Duchrow and F. Hinkelammert, 2004, *Property for People, Not for Profit*, Geneva: World Council of Churches. See also the more recent R. Mshana and A. Peralta (eds), 2013, *Linking Poverty, Wealth and Ecology: The AGAPE Process from Porto Alegre to Busan*, Geneva: World Council of Churches.

2 L. Boff and C. Boff, 1987, *Introducing Liberation Theology*, Maryknoll, NY: Orbis Books, p. 4.

3 Boff and Boff, *Introducing*, p. 4.

4 G. Gutiérrez, 1969, 'The Meaning of Development', in *In Search of a Theology of Development*, Geneva: SODEPAX, p. 152.

5 T. Cooper, 2007, *Controversies in Political Theology: Development or Liberation?* London: SCM Press, p. 13.

6 Cooper, *Controversies*, p. 175.

7 From a secular point of view, this motif is exemplified in the post-development school of thought. For a classic statement of this position, see W. Sachs (ed.), 1992, *The Development Dictionary*, London: Zed Books. For more recent articulations, see many of the writings of Jason Hickel, including, for instance, J. Hickel, 2015, 'The Death of International Development'. Available at: www.redpepper.org.uk/essay-the-death-of-international-development/ (accessed 14 July 2016).

8 I. Petrella, 2006, *The Future of Liberation Theology: An Argument and Manifesto*, London: SCM Press.

9 J. N. K. Mugambi, 1995, *From Liberation to Reconstruction*, Nairobi: East African Educational Publishers.

10 Mugambi, *From Liberation*, p. xv. For more on the African theology of reconstruction, see E. Farisani, 2003, 'The Use of Ezra-Nehemiah in a Quest for an African Theology of Reconstruction', *Journal of Theology for Southern Africa* 116, July, pp. 27–50; J. Gathogo, 2007, 'A Survey on an African Theology of Reconstruction', *Swedish Missiological Themes* 95:2, pp. 123–48; J. Gathogo, 2008, 'The Tasks in African Theology of Reconstruction', *Swedish Missiological Themes* 96:2, pp. 161–83; I. Phiri and J. Gathogo, 2010, 'A Reconstructive Motif in South African Black Theology in the Twenty-First Century', *Studia Historiae Ecclesiasticae* 36, July, Supplement, pp. 185–206.

11 I. Swart, 2008, 'Meeting the Challenge of Poverty and Exclusion: The Emerging Field of Development Research in South African Practical Theology', *International Journal of Practical Theology* 12:1, January, pp. 104–49.

12 Swart, 'Meeting', pp. 135–6. The material in quote marks is Swart quoting himself from I. Swart, 2008, 'Market Economic Development, Local Economic Experience and the Christian Movement towards Alternatives in a South African City Region', in S. de Gruchy, N. Koopman and S. Strijbos (eds), *From Our Side: Emerging Perspectives on Development and Ethics*, Amsterdam: Rozenberg, p. 270.

13 'This explanation . . . sees poverty as a collective and also conflictive phenomenon, which can be overcome only by replacing the present social system with an *alternative* system. The way out of this situation is *revolution*, understood as the transformation of the bases of the economic and social system' (emphasis in original). Boff and Boff, *Introducing*, p. 27.

14 G. Guttiérez, 2001, *A Theology of Liberation*, London: SCM Press, p. 124.

15 J. M. Sung, 2007, *Reclaiming Liberation Theology: Desire, Market, Religion*, London: SCM Press, pp. 97–8.

16 C. Elliot, 1987, *Comfortable Compassion*, London: Hodder & Stoughton, p. 156.

17 See n. 64. T. S. Maluleke, 2016, 'Christian Mission in a World under the Grip of an Unholy Trinity: Inequality, Poverty and Unemployment', in M. Auvinen-Pöntinen and J. A. Jørgensen (eds), *Mission and Money: Christian Mission in the Context of Global Inequalities*, Boston: Brill, p. 72.

18 Elliot, *Comfortable Compassion*, p. 105.

19 See also Heslam who also argues for a reformed rather than overthrown capitalism. P. Heslam, 2002, *Globalization: Unravelling the New Capitalism*, Cambridge: Grove Books.

20 Boff and Boff, *Introducing*, p. 94.

21 M. Aguilar, 2013, 'The Hermeneutics of Bones: Liberation Theology for the Twenty-First Century', in T. Cooper (ed.), *The Reemergence of Liberation Theologies*, New York: Palgrave Macmillan, p. 35.

22 C. Rowland in conversation with T. Gorringe, 2016, 'Practical Theology and the Common Good – Why the Bible is Essential', *Practical Theology* 9:2, p. 109.

23 R. Das, 2016, *Compassion and the Mission of God*, Carlisle: Langham Global Partnership, p. 162.

24 T. Wigg-Stevenson, 2013, *The World Is Not Ours to Save*, Downers Grove, IL: InterVarsity Press, p. 55.

25 M. Taylor, 2015, *Christ and Capital: A Family Debate*, Geneva: World Council of Churches, pp. 157, 159.

26 W. Wink, 1992, *Engaging the Powers*, Minneapolis, MN: Fortress Press, p. 136. See also R. Nadella, 2016, 'The Two Banquets: Mark's Vision of Anti-Imperial Economics', *Interpretation: A Journal of Bible and Theology* 70:2, pp. 172–83. Nadella argues that Mark's anti-imperialistic rhetoric was not as simple as mere resistance or accommodation, but that at times one has to both engage with the empire while subverting from within.

27 M. Maggay, 2008, 'Justice and Approaches to Social Change', in J. Thacker and M. Hoek (eds), *Micah's Challenge: The Church's Responsibility to the Global Poor*, Milton Keynes: Paternoster, pp. 129–30. See also L. Newbigin, 1989, *The Gospel in a Pluralist Society*, London: SPCK, pp. 198–210.

28 M. Volf, 2011, *A Public Faith*, Grand Rapids, MI: Brazos Press, pp. 89–93.

29 D. Freeman, 2012, 'Development and the Rural Entrepreneur: Pentecostals, NGOs and the Market in the Gamo Highlands, Ethiopia' in D. Freeman (ed.), *Pentecostalism and Development*, New York: Palgrave Macmillan, pp. 159–80.

30 D. Freeman, 2012, 'The Pentecostal Ethic and the Spirit of Development', in Freeman (ed.), *Pentecostalism*, pp. 1–37.

31 M. Weber, 1958 [1904], *The Protestant Ethic and the Spirit of Capitalism*, New York: Charles Scribner's Sons, pp. 21–2.

32 In addition to Freeman's work, see Peter Berger who has also argued that Pentecostalism is reprising the Weberian Protestant work ethic, and that it too is mostly having a positive influence on economic prosperity and social mobility. P. Berger, 'Max Weber is Alive and Well, and Living in Guatemala: The Protestant Ethic Today', *The Review of Faith and International Affairs* (8:4, 2010) pp. 3–9.

33 Freeman, 'The Pentecostal Ethic', p. 20.

34 Freeman, 'The Pentecostal Ethic', p. 20.

35 Freeman, 'The Pentecostal Ethic', p. 21.

36 Freeman, 'The Pentecostal Ethic', p. 21.

37 Freeman, 'The Pentecostal Ethic', p. 21.

38 P. Gifford, 2015, *Christianity, Development and Modernity in Africa*, London: Hurst & Co., p. 48.

39 P. Hiebert, 1982, 'The Flaw of the Excluded Middle', *Missiology* 10:1, p. 43.

40 Gifford, *Christianity*, p. 57.

41 Gifford, *Christianity*, p. 57.

42 Weber, *The Protestant*, pp. 21–2. See also M. Weber, 1978, *Economy and Society*, Berkeley, CA: University of California Press, p. 379.

43 Weber, *Economy*, p. 378.

44 Weber, *Economy*, p. 376.

45 A. Banerjee and E. Duflo, 2011, *Poor Economics*, London: Penguin, p. 192. See also D. Wilson, 2015, 'Western Mission-Established Churches and Ministry in Mali's Collectivist Economy', in J. Cheong and E. Meneses (eds), *Christian Mission and Economic Systems*, Pasadena, CA: William Carey Library. For an alternative view of the economic benefits of sharing among extended family members, see M. Mtika, 2015, 'Subsistent and Substantive Communities Under Attack: The Case of Zowe in Northern Malawi', in Cheong and Meneses (eds), *Christian Mission*, pp. 179–210.

46 Gifford, *Christianity*, p. 60.

47 Gifford, *Christianity*, p. 61.

48 Gifford, *Christianity*, p. 67.

49 J. K. Asamoah-Gyadu, 2010, 'From "Calvary Road" to "Harvesters International": An African Perspective on the Cross and Gospel of Prosperity', advance paper for 2010 Lausanne Global Conversation Cape Town. Available at: www.lausanne.org/content/from-calvary-road-to-harvesters-international-an-african-perspective-on-the-cross-and-gospel-of-prosperity (accessed 12 May 2015).

50 One further critique that has so far not appeared in my analysis is that offered by Sharpe. He writes, 'Faced with collective social problems demanding a structural analysis and concerted political action, Prosperity is charged with promoting self-centred individualism, and diverting converts' attention away from the lasting causes of their social deprivation.' M. Sharpe, 2013, 'Name It and Claim It: Prosperity Gospel and the Global Pentecostal Reformation', in M. Clarke (ed.), *Handbook of Research on Development and Religion*, Cheltenham: Edward Elgar, p. 174. See also R. Woodberry, 2008, 'Pentecostalism and Economic Development', in J. Imber (ed.), *Markets, Morals and Religion*, New Brunswick, NJ: Transaction Publishers, pp. 157–77. Woodberry takes a more empirical approach to the question of whether Pentecostalism favours economic development and notes the huge absence of reliable data that speaks to this question. Nevertheless, on balance, he writes that 'Pentecostalism has a number of important economic consequences . . . and . . . most of these consequences are positive – particularly among poor people in developing countries.' Woodberry, 'Pentecostalism', p. 159.

51 I say to varying degrees because on some issues the papacy has been happy to issue specific policy guidance, for example around the use of contraception.

52 Paul VI, 1967, *Populorum Progressio*, n. 76.

53 Paul VI, *Populorum Progressio*, n. 76

54 Leo XIII, 1891, *Rerum Novarum*, n. 5.

55 Leo XIII, *Rerum Novarum*, n. 61.

56 Leo XIII, *Rerum Novarum*, n. 44.

57 Leo XIII, *Rerum Novarum*, n. 45.

58 Paul VI, *Populorum Progressio*, n. 59.

59 Paul VI, *Populorum Progressio*, n. 22.

60 Paul VI, *Populorum Progressio*, n. 14.

61 Benedict XVI, 2009, *Caritas in Veritate*, n. 29.

62 Benedict XVI, *Caritas in Veritate*, n. 29.

63 S. Deneulin, 'Christianity and International Development: An Overview', in Clarke (ed.), *Handbook*, p. 59.

64 *The Common Good and the Catholic Church's Social Teaching*, 1996, p. 19. Available at www.catholic-ew.org.uk/Catholic-News-Media-Library/Archive -Media-Assets/Files/CBCEW-Publications/The-Common-Good-and-the-Catholic -Church-s-Social-Teaching (accessed 10 July 2016).

65 John Paul II, 1987, *Sollicitudo Rei Socialis*, n. 38.

66 Francis, 2013, *Evangelii Gaudium*, nn. 84, 85.

67 E. H. Prodromou and N. Symeonides, 2016, 'Orthodox Christanity and Humanitarianism: An Introduction to Thought and Practice, Past and Present', *The Review of Faith and International Affairs* 14:1, pp. 1–17.

68 Particularly worthy of mention are B. Myers, 1999, *Walking with the Poor: Principles and Practices of Transformational Development*, Marynoll, NY: Orbis Books; C. Moe-Lobeda, 2013, *Resisting Structural Evil*, Minneapolis, MN: Fortress Press; R. Sider, 1997, *Rich Christians in an Age of Hunger*, London: Hodder & Stoughton; Elliott, *Comfortable Compassion*; P. Vallely, 1990, *Bad Samaritans*, London: Hodder & Stoughton; see also *Wholly Living: A New Perspective on International Development*, 2010, Theos; S. Corbett and B. Fikkert, 2009, *When Helping Hurts*, Chicago, IL: Moody Publishers; M. Clarke, 2012, *Mission and Development: God's Work or Good Works?* London: Continuum; *A Call to Commitment and Partnership: A World Evangelical Alliance Brief on the Evangelical Community and Humanitarian Development*, 2015; R. Mshana and A. Peralta (eds), 2013, *Linking Poverty, Wealth and Ecology: The AGAPE Process from Porto Alegre to Busan*, Geneva: World Council of Churches.

69 *Christian Aid Annual Report and Accounts 2014/15*. Available at: www .christianaid.org.uk/images/annual-report-14-15.pdf (accessed 14 June 2016).

70 www.christianaid.org.uk/resources/churches/what-we-believe.aspx.

71 P. Clifford, 2010, *Theology and International Development*, London: Christian Aid, p. 4.

72 Clifford, *Theology*, pp. 7–8.

73 Clifford, *Theology*, pp. 8–9.

74 Clifford, *Theology*, p. 10.

75 Clifford, *Theology*, p. 10.

76 *The Code of Conduct for the International Red Cross and Red Crescent Movement and NonGovernmental Organisations (NGOs) in Disaster Relief*, 1994, IFRC, clause 3. Available at: www.ifrc.org/en/publications-and-reports/code-of -conduct/ (accessed 10 June 2016).

77 P. Bickley, 2015, *The Problem of Proselytism*, Theos, p. 13.

78 Clifford, *Theology*, p. 14

79 Clifford, *Theology*, pp. 14–15.

80 Clifford, *Theology*, p. 20.

81 Clifford, *Theology*, p. 21.

82 Clifford, *Theology*, p. 20.

83 Clifford, *Theology*, p. 20.

84 Clifford, *Theology*, p. 20.

85 M. Tsele, 2001, 'The Role of the Christian Faith in Development', in D. Belshaw, R. Calderisi and C. Sugden (eds), *Faith in Development*, Oxford: Regnum Books, p. 208.

86 Clifford, *Theology*, p. 30.

87 T. Wright, 2007, *Surprised by Hope*, London: SPCK, p. 205.

88 Clifford, *Theology*, p. 18.

89 G. ter Haar, 2011, 'Religion and Development: Introducing a New Debate', in G. ter Haar (ed.), *Religion and Development: Ways of Transforming the World*, London: Hurst & Co., p. 16.

90 A. Evans and R. Gower, 2015, *The Restorative Economy*, London: Tearfund, p. 7 (emphasis mine). Available at: www.tearfund.org/en/about_you/campaign/report/ (accessed 16 June 2016).

91 Evans and Gower, *The Restorative Economy*, p. 23.

92 Evans and Gower, *The Restorative Economy*, p. 26.

93 Evans and Gower, *The Restorative Economy*, pp. 26–7.

94 S. Doherty, 2015, 'The Kingdom of God and the Economic System: An Economics of Hope', in J. Kidwell and S. Doherty, *Theology and Economics*, London: Palgrave Macmillan, p. 149.

95 It is interesting to note that in a parallel series of papers, the theme of hope is recurrent: *Theology: For a Just and Sustainable Economy*, 2014, London: Tearfund.

96 *Overcoming Poverty Together: Tearfund's Theory of Poverty*, 2012, London: Tearfund, p. 43. When going to press, this work was unavailable publicly, but is shortly to be made public on the Tearfund website. It is quoted with permission.

97 Evans and Gower, *The Restorative Economy*, p. 41.

98 See also their even more recent report, *Virtuous Circle*. R. Gower and P. Schröder, 2016, *Virtuous Circle: How the Circular Economy can Create Jobs and Save Lives in Low and Middle-Income Countries*, London: Tearfund. Incidentally, I think this approach to poverty alleviation is going to be far more effective than so-called 'effective altruism', which in some development circles has been garnering support, but which is really no more than a contemporary utilitarianism, and suffers from the same critiques to which historic utilitarianism is subject.

99 Christian Aid refer to campaigning, advocacy and education. Tearfund refer to envisioning the global Church and challenging unjust policies and practices. It is quite possible that in practice the advocacy work of both organizations represents largely the same proportion of their work.

100 Evans and Gower, *The Restorative Economy*, p. 6.

101 I have developed this argument in relation to soteriology. However, I think it would be perfectly possible to make the same case in respect of pneumatology. The reason I haven't is partly because neither Christian Aid nor Tearfund emphasize the work of the Spirit and partly because of reasons of space.

PART 5

Consummation

15

New heavens and new earth[1]

Among contemporary theologians, there is significant agreement that the nature of our eternal hope is not some disembodied, ethereal existence in which we float around as souls; rather, the hope to which we are called is an embodied existence in a new or renewed earth. Professor Edward Donnelly writes:

> Perhaps the great obstacle to a true appreciation of heaven is our inability to imagine our bodies there. Though we believe in the resurrection of the body, 'heaven' still brings to mind a realm which is immaterial, not physical in any real sense . . . Yet the Bible tells us that heaven is the ideal environment for them. At Christ's second coming this earth, which God created for our habitation and his glory, will be restored and renewed . . . heaven and earth will come together in a wonderful unity.[2]

This hope of an embodied existence in a new earth has not always been the case. John Colwell has noted that a description of the afterlife in terms of 'the immortality of the soul', rather than the 'resurrection of the body', has frequently been the more popular motif across the ages. However, he describes this as a departure from the early apostolic hope and goes on to refer to the 'widespread repudiation of this development, particularly amongst scholars of the New Testament'[3] in the last hundred years or so. Our ultimate hope then is for a renewed earth with a new body. Yet, the question remains as to what further can be said regarding its nature – what will it be like beyond this mere affirmation?

Revelation 21.1–5 is probably where we should begin to look in answer to this question.

> Then I saw a new heaven and a new earth; for the first heaven and the first earth had passed away, and the sea was no more. And I saw the holy city, the new Jerusalem, coming down out of heaven from God, prepared as a bride adorned for her husband. And I heard a loud voice from the throne saying, 'See, the home of God is among mortals. He will dwell with them; they will be his peoples, and God himself will be with them; he will wipe every tear from their eyes. Death will be no more; mourning and crying and pain will be no more, for the first things have passed away.' And the one who was seated on the throne said, 'See, I am making all things new.'

Here we have the clearest affirmation of what most of us look forward to in the new heavens and new earth: 'Death will be no more; mourning and crying and pain will be no more, for the first things have passed away.' It is this absence of physical suffering that becomes, for many of us, the defining feature of heaven. Whatever else heaven is, heaven is a place where pain no longer exists. It is perhaps for this reason that, far too often, heaven is pictured in a disembodied fashion. If, in this life, it is our bodies that experience pain, and if, in the life to come, the characteristic feature is the absence of pain, then it is a short step to imagine a disembodied life in the hereafter. For whatever else a disembodied life is, it must be a pain-free life.

Interestingly, one can raise the hypothesis that one of the reasons that we have rediscovered in the last hundred years the notion of an embodied eternal existence is the reality that our lives – at least in HICs – are to a large extent free from physical suffering and pain. We certainly do not experience, either first- or second-hand, the physical torment that would have been commonplace in earlier centuries. It may be the case, then, that we are more ready to accept an embodied eternity, because such embodiment does not fill us with the dread of physical pain that would have affected the ancients – or our contemporary brothers and sisters in LICs.

Yet, having said all that, perhaps we could have avoided at least some of these theological wanderings if we had paid closer attention to the biblical texts themselves in their description of the eternity to come. For I would suggest that the primary idea in the biblical descriptions of the life to come is not the *absence* of pain and suffering, but rather the *presence* of God. And importantly, a re-evaluation of heaven in terms of God's presence, rather than pain's absence, leads us to some significant conclusions regarding our present existence and mandate.

In the seminal passage from Revelation quoted earlier, our eyes rapidly skate over the first few verses until we get to those that address our real concern: pain. However, it is in those first few verses that the framework for the life to come is laid out.

> Then I saw a new heaven and a new earth, for the first heaven and the first earth had passed away, and the sea was no more. And I saw the holy city, the new Jerusalem, coming down out of heaven from God, prepared as a bride adorned for her husband. And I heard a loud voice from the throne saying, 'See, the home of God is with mortals. He will dwell with them; they will be his peoples, and God himself will be with them; he will wipe every tear from their eyes.'

There are three essential points in this passage, some of which we too frequently ignore in our consideration of heaven. First, something *new* is taking place here. We are told three times of that which is *new*: heaven, earth and Jerusalem. And, in case we did not get it, the point is hammered home by indicating that the old has gone; it has 'passed away'. Indeed, based on this language, some have suggested that what takes place at the eschaton, the end of times, is a complete destruction of the cosmos, followed by an entirely new act of creation. I am more persuaded by those accounts that posit a renewed rather than new creation, but the important point is that something distinctively different is occurring: things will not be the same.

Second – and perhaps most surprising – the direction of movement in relation to the new heavens and new earth is not of us leaving this physical world, ascending through the clouds and then joining God in some spiritual (as in non-material) realm. Rather, the trajectory that occurs is that heaven comes down and joins earth. The direction of travel is *downwards* not *upwards*.[4] 'I saw the holy city, the new Jerusalem, *coming down out of heaven from God,* prepared as a bride adorned for her husband' (my emphasis). The same point is made in Revelation 3.12, which describes the new Jerusalem that 'comes down from my God out of heaven' (see also Rev. 21.10). We must not overstate the significance of this trajectory, but the relevant point is that our ultimate future is wonderful not because we leave this earth, but because heaven joins us here.

That leads us to the third and most important motif in this passage: the presence of God. 'See, the home of God is among mortals. He will dwell with them; they will be his peoples, and God himself will be with them; he will wipe every tear from their eyes.' This idea of God being or living with his people is one that runs throughout the whole of the Scriptures, both Old and New Testaments (Ex. 29.45; Lev. 26.11–12; Ez. 37.27; Zech. 2.10–11; John 1.14; 2 Cor. 6.16). It is the concept of God's *shekinah*, the *presence* of God. For the Jews, this was exemplified by God's presence in the Temple in Jerusalem, which is why the author of Revelation, in describing the eternal presence of God with us, puts it in terms of 'The new Jerusalem, coming down out of heaven from God'. The author is not really trying to persuade us that an actual city, complete with utilities, will descend from the clouds, but rather is speaking metaphorically of God's *presence,* his *shekinah* joining us on earth. The point, though, of these biblical descriptions of God's active presence is not just geographical, but sociological or relational. Their emphasis is that we truly become the people of God, not when God is absent, but rather when God is present – in close proximity. 'I will live in them and walk among them, and I will be their God, and they shall be my people' (2 Cor. 6.16).

Of course, this is borne out by what happened in the Garden of Eden, and by the presence of Christ with us. In Genesis, we have this picture of the Lord God 'walking in the garden in the cool of the day', and yet, due to their sin, the first man and woman are hiding. Although God is there, it is his *presence* that their sin cannot bear. And so the result of the fall is banishment from the presence of God. In other words, at the point at which humanity lost its perfect relationship with God and the created order, that loss is expressed in terms of a separation from the *presence* of God. The corollary of this is the fact that when the Saviour that restores that relationship is described, he is named in terms of God's active presence with us. 'Look, the virgin shall conceive and bear a son, and they shall name him Emmanuel, which means, "God is with us"' (Matt. 1.23; cf. Isa. 7.14). The sense we are getting, then, is that the people of God are truly the people of God when God is with them. Moreover, it is by means of his presence that the blessings associated with being the people of God are realized (Jer. 32.38–41).

This is especially evident when we consider an evocative phrase from the passage in Revelation above: 'He will wipe every tear from their eyes.' Here we see that the *presence* of God is not merely spatial proximity, but also the presence of intimacy. In being near, God demonstrates his concern. Moreover, it forms the bridge to our usual conception of heaven in terms of the absence of pain. The point that seems to be made is that the reason that there is no more pain or suffering or death or mourning is not because, in the abstract, these things have been removed, but rather because God's *presence* banishes them, or prevents them from being realized. When God is absent, then fear, pain and suffering may flourish. But where God is present, these things simply cannot be. So, for instance, the struggles for Adam and Eve began not when they were still in the garden, but when they left. And in Revelation 7.16–17, where another description is given of the suffering-free existence that awaits, it is clear that the absence of such suffering is entirely down to the *presence* of God. 'They will hunger no more; and thirst no more; the sun will not strike them, nor any scorching heat; *for the Lamb at the centre of the throne will be their shepherd, and he will guide them to springs of the water of life,* and God will wipe away every tear from their eyes' (my emphasis; see also Rev. 21.22–23; 22.1–5). We have here a wonderful description of the eternity that awaits, but the author is clear that what makes our experience so different in this setting is not so much that hunger or thirst have been banished as such, but rather that the Christ will be with us to lead us – to direct us to that which meets our needs.

Hence, what makes heaven heaven is not so much the absence of pain and suffering – however welcome that may be – but rather the unhindered presence of God.[5] As I will go on to show, this has profound consequences for our responsibilities in the here and now, but we will approach those responsibilities by first exploring the difference that the *presence* of Jesus made to those in first-century Palestine.

Jesus and the kingdom

One of the toughest challenges to those of us who would support the notion of an interventionist God is simply this: if God can heal the blind man, why not cure blindness? If God can cure the lame, then why not cure all paralysis? If God has the power to intervene for some, then why does he not intervene for all? It was on precisely this question that Alister McGrath, then Professor of Historical Theology at Oxford University, and one of the most gifted British apologists, came unstuck – albeit temporarily – in a recent debate with Richard Dawkins.[6] It certainly is a difficult question.

However, the beginnings of a response to this challenge are evident as we examine Jesus' own declarations in relation to the kingdom of God.

When [Jesus] came to Nazareth, where he had been brought up, he went to the synagogue on the sabbath day, as was his custom. He stood up to read, and the scroll of the prophet Isaiah was given to him. He unrolled the scroll and found the place where it was written: 'The Spirit of the Lord is upon me, because he has anointed me to bring good news to the poor. He has sent me to proclaim release to the captives and recovery of sight to the blind, to let the oppressed go free, to proclaim the year of the Lord's favour.' And he rolled up the scroll, gave it back to the attendant, and sat down. The eyes of all in the synagogue were fixed on him. Then he began to say to them, 'Today this scripture has been fulfilled in your hearing.' (Luke 4.16–21)

All commentators on the life of Jesus acknowledge that this is a pivotal passage in understanding the nature of his ministry and identity. In the midst of the synagogue, Jesus draws attention to a passage in Isaiah, a passage that for hundreds of years had been understood as declaring the kingdom of God, heaven on earth if you will, and Jesus says, 'Today this scripture has been fulfilled in your hearing.' We must not lose sight of the sheer audacity evident here.

Jesus was not just saying that the kingdom was coming – many had said that. He was not just outlining the nature of the kingdom – the passage itself did that. Rather, he was declaring that now, in his person, by means of his presence, this Kingdom would be realized. As Tom Wright puts it:

The Kingdom of God, he said, is at hand. In other words, God was now unveiling his age-old plan, bringing his sovereignty to bear on Israel and the world as had always intended, bringing justice and mercy to Israel and the world. And he was doing so, apparently, through Jesus.[7]

Or, as Steve Chalke and Alan Mann summarized it, 'The Kingdom, the in-breaking *shalom* of God, is available now to everyone *through me*.'[8] This is huge.

The point of note is the personal manner in which Jesus draws this conclusion:

'The Spirit of the Lord is upon *me*, because he has anointed *me* to bring good news to the poor. He has sent *me* to proclaim release to the captives and recovery of sight to the blind, to let the oppressed go free, to proclaim the year of the Lord's favour.'

Jesus was not just saying, God's Spirit is now here for everyone, so that we all preach the good news, proclaim freedom, cure blindness and so on. No, this was a personal declaration. Even in Isaiah, from where the quotation is taken, the messianic subject does not merely announce the good news, but also brings it about. And consider Jesus' dramatic declaration on finishing his reading: 'Today this scripture has been fulfilled in *your* hearing.' Once again, it is not: 'Today this scripture has been fulfilled', but rather it has been fulfilled in '*your* hearing', that is, in the presence of those who were there – and this is so because Jesus was there, personally present.

What can we conclude from this? That God's in-breaking kingdom is present and available in the person of, and by means of, the actions and teaching of his anointed servant, Jesus Christ. In the same way that the absence of suffering that characterizes the new heaven and new earth is made possible by the *presence* of God, so the *shalom* of God that characterizes the kingdom is made possible by the presence and actions of Jesus Christ. In neither case is the absence of pain, or peace that is promised, available in general, or in the abstract. Rather, they are possible because Jesus makes it so.

A similar conclusion can be drawn from Jesus' use of parables. Tom Wright has drawn attention to the fact that, in the parable of the sower, Jesus is not so much making a general point regarding the propensity or otherwise of people to respond to God's message. Rather, his emphasis is 'what God was doing in Jesus' own ministry'. Similarly, in the parable of the prodigal son, it is not, once again, a universal principle regarding the love of God.

> The parable was not a general illustration of the timeless truth of God's forgiveness for the sinner . . . It was a sharp-edged, context-specific message about what was happening in Jesus' ministry. More specifically, it was about what was happening through Jesus' welcome of outcasts, his eating with sinners.[9]

The kingdom, then, does not come in the abstract. It comes in and through the person and work of Jesus Christ. Even when the disciples heal and forgive, it is not because they have some general ability to do so, rather it is because Jesus has specifically given them the authority to go and continue his kingdom work. It is for precisely this reason that we have Jesus' otherwise remarkable statement at the time the 72 were sent out. 'Whoever listens to you listens to me, and whoever rejects you rejects me, and whoever rejects me rejects the one who sent me' (Luke 10.16). The point Jesus is making is that any ability the 72 have to enact the kingdom is only realized because Jesus is there in power. Moreover, any ability Jesus has is only because God is at work in him. The kingdom never comes in the abstract, but only by means of God's active presence, whether in his Son or Spirit, or in us as we allow the Son and Spirit to work through us.

The answer, then, to the question of why God healed the blind man but not blindness is simply this. God does heal blindness, and lameness and so on, but only where he is fully present. It is his unhindered presence that brings *shalom*, not the casting of some universal magic spell. In the age to come, his *shekinah* – his full and unveiled presence – will be operative everywhere (consider Rev. 22.5), and hence there will be no more suffering or pain. However, in this age, in the time before he comes again, his presence is experienced in veiled form. In the first place, this was true of his Son, who though fully God had his glory hidden as he lived among us.[10] Such a veiled presence meant that shards of light could and did break through to bring healing, forgiveness and restoration – but this was not the unhindered presence that we will all experience in the age to come, when we will see him 'face to face'. In the second place, though, that task of bringing God's presence to the world – and so the all-encompassing *shalom* of God – is now ours. Our job is to continue in the glorious building project that God in Christ has begun.

Heaven on earth

> So then you are no longer strangers and aliens, but you are citizens with the saints and also members of the household of God, built upon the foundation of the apostles and prophets, with Christ Jesus himself as the cornerstone. In him the whole structure is joined together and grows into a holy temple in the Lord, in whom you also are built together spiritually into a dwelling-place for God. (Eph. 2.19–22)

> What Jesus was to Israel, the Church must now be for the world. Everything we discover about what Jesus did and said within the Judaism of his day must be thought through in terms of what it would look like for the Church to do and be this for the world. If we are to shape our world, and perhaps even to implement the redemption of our world, this is how it is to be done.[11]

In John 20.21, when he has risen from the dead, Jesus says this to the disciples: 'As the Father has sent me, so I send you.' The phrase has occurred before in John 17.18, and in both places the Greek uses a tense that refers to an ongoing state of being resulting from some past action. The sense, then, is not that at some point in the past Christ was sent and now it is our turn, but rather that Christ is in an ongoing state of *having been sent*. The significance of this is that it indicates the way in which what we are doing is merely the continuation of what Christ was doing. In fact, it is not so much that we do it for God, or on behalf of God, but rather that God continues his work through us as we are united to Christ and empowered by his Spirit. And what is that task? To be the presence of God in the world and so bring his *shalom* to bear. The importance here is that both these aspects go together: being the presence of God and bringing his *shalom* to bear.

I have suggested that the new heavens and new earth, the kingdom of God on earth, will be characterized by the absence of suffering primarily because its defining feature is the presence of God. I have, therefore, indicated that our task in this life, before that kingdom is fully realized, is to continue the work that Jesus inaugurated by being God's presence and bringing his reign of *shalom* to the world. In this sense, then, there is a direct continuity between what we do now and our experience in the age to come. To put it bluntly, our eternal life starts now – the moment we get on with it!

This is further highlighted by Revelation 22, where there is a curious phrase that occurs in the middle of the wonderful vision of heaven that is outlined. After talking of the river of life, the throne of God and the Lamb, the glorious fruit that is there, we find this: 'But the throne of God and of the Lamb will be in it; and his servants will serve him' (Rev. 22.3, KJV). It echoes a similar verse in Revelation 7.15, but what is their point? Well, it is possible to interpret them both in terms of the Elders and Angels singing and praising God as the relevant Greek verb, *latreuō*, can be translated worship as well as service. However, there are good reasons for thinking that the latter idea is the predominant one. In the Septuagint, the Greek translation of the Old Testament, *latreuō* is primarily used for the whole of the people's service towards God, everything they do in their lives for him.[12] In this sense, then, the continuity between our present existence and the one to come is that in both we seek to offer our full response to the God who brings us peace.

However, is it not also possible to see in this passage in Revelation 22.3 echoes of another vision in which the Lamb is on his throne, with all his angels in attendance, and the nations before him – Matthew 25.31–46? On that occasion, reference is also made to those who served the King:

'For I was hungry and you gave me food, I was thirsty and you gave me something to drink, I was a stranger and you welcomed me, I was naked and you gave me clothing, I was sick and you took care of me, I was in prison and you visited me.' (Matt. 25.35–36)[13]

And if we recall the point that the King makes on that occasion, that 'just as you did it to one of the least of these who are members of my family, you did it to me', then the theological point to be made here is that our practical service of the poor now and our ongoing service and worship of God in the age to come are both from the same stable: a heart responding fully to God.

Given this, the challenge before us is that we join with the angels in heaven and participate in heavenly worship not so much by singing songs, but by feeding the hungry and poor, speaking out on their behalf, challenging injustice and critically monitoring our lifestyle. In a strange paradox, then, heaven on earth is experienced most where we least expect it: among those in need.

Notes

1 Most of this chapter is largely reproduced, with permission, from J. Thacker, 2008, 'New Heavens and New Earth', J. Thacker and M. Hoek (eds), *Micah's Challenge: The Church's Responsibility to the Global Poor*, Milton Keynes: Paternoster.

2 E. Donnelly, 2001, *Heaven and Hell*, Glasgow: Banner of Truth Trust, p. 112.

3 J. Colwell (ed.), 2000, *Called to One Hope: Perspectives on Life to Come*, Carlisle: Paternoster, p. xi.

4 An important point to be considered by all those enamoured with the *Left Behind* series of novels.

5 Incidentally, this is not to deny the omnipresence of God, but it is to say that though God is present everywhere, he is not present everywhere in unveiled fashion. His presence is cloaked, as it were. The *presence* or *shekinah* that brings God's blessing is a presence without hindrance.

6 www.youtube.com/watch?v=Cl1QwJ54Poc.

7 N. T. Wright, 2000, *The Challenge of Jesus*, London: SPCK, p. 21.

8 S. Chalke and A. Mann, 2004, *The Lost Message of Jesus*, Grand Rapids, MI: Zondervan, pp. 28–9.

9 Wright, *Challenge*, pp. 23–4.

10 The transfiguration is the exception to this, and see also John 17.5.

11 Wright, *Challenge*, p. 34.

12 A. Konig, 1989, *The Eclipse of Christ in Eschatology*, Grand Rapids, MI: Eerdmans, p. 241.

13 NB the references in Revelation 7.16 to hunger, thirst and destitution may strengthen this point.

16

The poor always with you

While he was at Bethany in the house of Simon the leper, as he sat at the table, a woman came with an alabaster jar of very costly ointment of nard, and she broke open the jar and poured the ointment on his head. But some were there who said to one another in anger, 'Why was the ointment wasted in this way? For this ointment could have been sold for more than three hundred denarii, and the money given to the poor.' And they scolded her. But Jesus said, 'Let her alone; why do you trouble her? She has performed a good service for me. For you always have the poor with you, and you can show kindness to them whenever you wish; but you will not always have me. (Mark 14.3–7)

One of the challenges facing those of us who would seek to maintain a certain level of activism in regard to serving the world's poor is how to motivate that activism, in particular how to motivate it in a sustainable way. We exist in a culture of immediacy that applies just as much to global campaigns as to fast food, and if results are not readily forthcoming then it is very easy for the initial enthusiasm to similarly fall by the wayside. Social media are replete with short-lived campaigns for a range of issues encouraging us to tip buckets of iced water on our heads, do push-ups, wear safety pins and so on. All of this represents easy virtue, for social media allow one to demonstrate support for a cause with almost negligible effort. Wigg-Stevenson calls it 'sinner's prayer activism'; it 'is attractive because it is essentially cost-free, which is appealing to anyone who is working like crazy to live a decent life but who can't shut out those cries from the global Jericho road'.[1]

It is partly for this reason that global campaigners become especially exercised by Mark 14.7 (and Matt. 26.11; John 12.8) – 'the poor you will always have with you' – for the great danger for such social activism is a waning of interest, and if we always have the poor with us then what is the point of continuing our efforts? This fear is especially clear in the Christian Aid report that was examined in Chapter 14. In two significant places they address this pericope, arguing consistently that it cannot mean what it appears to mean – namely that poverty will always exist. For Christian Aid, it is very important that they are able to maintain a narrative that says poverty alleviation is indeed possible. They write:

It cannot be the case that an organisation whose ambition it is to tackle poverty should want to stop short of saying it wants to abolish it absolutely.

Quite obviously, one agency can never hope to eradicate this alone. However, working together with others – not just NGOs and their partner organisations worldwide, but with churches, governments, national and international bodies – it has to be possible to remodel the social and economic structures that keep people poor . . . It is, however, only relatively recently that the idea that poverty could be ended by undertaking specific measures within human control came to be seen as a real possibility. So it is not surprising that, in the past, theologians have no more ventured to challenge the assumption of a perpetual rich–poor divide than did the writers of the Pentateuch. Yet the more we learn about the causes of poverty, the more untenable becomes the concept of some kind of divine ordinance that divides rich and poor.[2]

Of course, the reason that Christian Aid maintain this stance is because, as we have already suggested, they are influenced by the pragmatist zeitgeist, and in particular the utilitarianism that pervades contemporary Western societies. We live in a results-driven culture and therefore the rhetoric that is required to generate ongoing compassion for the poor has to be a rhetoric that is steeped in the language of accomplishment, including promises that, in the words of one campaigning slogan, 'We can end poverty'.[3] The problem with Jesus' words, then, is that they appear to represent a stark challenge to that assumption: while the campaigners claim that poverty can be over, Jesus would appear to say no it cannot, at least in this age.

The exegetical arguments in support of the notion that Jesus' words do not mean what they appear to mean vary. The Christian Aid report seems to suggest that it is simply the fact that the ancient Near East was unaware that poverty could one day be ended. Others have pointed to the context of the passage, that Jesus was in the home of Simon the Leper (at least in the Matthew and Mark versions), and therefore the statement was intended to indicate not that the poor will always exist as such, but that Christians will always be found among the poor. 'The poor will always be with you' is taken to mean that the poor will always be found with the Christians, among the Christians – for that is the nature of those who follow Christ, to associate themselves with the poor. So Ched Myers writes: 'This passage – notoriously misunderstood and misused by preachers and politicians alike – is not about the inevitability of poverty but about the social location of the church – a place where the poor can find good news.'[4] And Jim Wallis states: 'Jesus is assuming the *social location* of his followers will always put them in close proximity to the poor and easily able to reach out to them.'[5] Of course, this interpretation requires there to exist poor people among whom the Christians can be present, and in this way it collapses into the simple affirmation that poverty will always exist. Nevertheless, the emphasis has at least changed so that it is no longer about the continual existence of poverty; it is more about the kind of mission and ministry that the followers of Christ will undertake.

The problem with such interpretations is that they fail to take sufficiently into account the context of the passage, for when Jesus made his statement in the home of Simon the Leper, he was quoting a Deuteronomic text: 'There will always be poor people in the land. Therefore I command you to be open-handed towards your fellow Israelites who are poor and needy in your land' (Deut. 15.11, NIV). At a stroke, this removes the relevance of the particular location when Jesus made his statement, for he wasn't talking about the precise locale where he was, but about a more general principle that had existed for at least 1,000 years. The fundamental problem here is that in the Deuteronomic text we have combined both an empirical statement – 'There will always be poor people' – and an ethical imperative – 'Therefore I command you to be generous'. In Deuteronomy, these two aspects are necessarily connected. Earlier on in the same chapter, we have already read 'there need be no poor people among you' (Deut. 15.4), which at face value might seem to contradict verse 11 – 'There will always be poor people'. For why will there always be poor people (verse 11) if there need not be (verse 4). The apparent tension in these empirical statements on whether the poor will always exist or not is resolved by recognizing that this state of affairs is dependent upon adherence to a particular ethical imperative, for verse 4 continues, 'there need be no poor people among you, for in the land the LORD your God is giving you to possess as your inheritance, he will richly bless you, if only you fully obey the LORD your God and are careful to follow all these commands I am giving you today' (Deut. 15.4–5, NIV). In other words, *if* we obey the commands that God is giving, in particular the commands concerning Sabbath release as outlined in this chapter, then there will be no poor. However, precisely *because* the nation of Israel will not always adhere to these commands (ethical), there will always be poor people (empirical), and so the nation is continually called to be generous and open-handed (ethical). Christopher Wright summarizes thus:

> On the one hand, [the Old Testament] holds up ideals and goals (there need be no poverty if people would live according to the principles and systems God has provided for human flourishing). But, on the other hand, [the Old Testament] is realistically aware of the endemic nature of human greed and violence and the perpetuation of poverty that results.[6]

This represents the background, then, to Jesus' words in Mark 14, Matthew 26 and John 12. The problem with some contemporary interpretations of this passage is that they have torn apart the ethical and the empirical, keeping the aspect they want but failing to recognize their necessary connection. So, some on the political Right have used Jesus' words to argue that *because* the poor are always with us there is no need to seek to alleviate their poverty – they will always be there. In response to this view, Patrick Miller stresses, 'That, of course, is exactly the opposite of what this text says.'[7] While I am in much sympathy with Miller's ethical motivation for this conclusion, I think he goes too far in describing this view as 'exactly the opposite'. For the exact opposite would be that 'we need not be generous to the poor because there are no poor among us'. That is the opposite of 'we need to be generous because there are poor among us'. Nevertheless, where Miller is correct is that the political Right's assumption that we need not be generous because the poor will always exist is certainly not what either the Deuteronomic author or Jesus was trying to communicate. The Right can only reach that conclusion by separating the empirical statement which they retain – 'the poor will always be with you' – from the imperative statement which they disregard – 'therefore be generous to the poor'.

At the same time, and in response to this argument from the Right, the Left are also guilty of separating the two halves of this clause, though they do it in a different way. For they are so nervous that the empirical statement can be used as a justification to ignore the ethical statement that they effectively deny the empirical statement and hold on merely to the ethical. So, they conclude that we must continue to be generous to the poor but not think this is because the poor will always exist. Indeed, they actually reverse the argument that is presented in Deuteronomy. For while Deuteronomy argues that we should be generous *because* the poor will always be among us, Wallis, Myers and Christian Aid seem to be arguing that we should be generous *because* we can end poverty. Similarly, their fear seems to be that if we acknowledge that the poor will always be with us, this work of poverty eradication will never end and then everyone will give up. So Christian Aid write:

> Rather than understand Jesus's words as a resigned statement of defeat, we should see them instead as an encouragement to eradicate poverty in his kingdom on earth. To see a permanent division between rich and poor as somehow being God's will is not a Christian option.[8]

The way this statement is phrased seems to suggest a fundamental misunderstanding about the nature of God's will and sin. Deuteronomy has made it abundantly clear that God's will is that there should be no poor people among the Israelites. Yet it is also clear that because of sin, the refusal of the nation to adhere to God's commands, there will always be poor people among them and so they must continually be open-handed and generous. The very fact that poor people will always exist no more means this is 'God's will' than to say that the permanence of sin is 'God's will'. Neither is God's will, and yet both will remain the case until the end of this age. As Wigg-Stevenson has commented:

> We should not confuse our ability to undertake fundamentally *tactical* efforts – that is, working on highly specific, discrete, comprehensible problems – with an ability to transform the existential condition that gives rise to injustice in the first place. We are in trouble if that is the goal that motivates our work.[9]

As I indicated in Chapter 14, the reason that Christian Aid get into this difficulty is because they have an inadequate doctrine of salvation. If you do not sufficiently emphasize the victory that Christ has won, then you have to end up believing that humans have won it, or can win it. But that leads inevitably to thinking that humanity has all of the solutions to all of the world's problems. In his fantastic book exploring the dangers of such Christian utopianism, Wigg-Stevenson points out that 'Our job is not to win the victory, but to *expose* through our lives that the victory has been won on our behalf. As a result, we will see shoots of God's kingdom erupt in our midst.'[10] One can only have confidence in this way if one has a strong doctrine of redemption.

Notes

1 T. Wigg-Stevenson, 2013, *The World is not Ours to Save*, Downers Grove, IL: InterVarsity Press, p. 56ff.

2 P. Clifford, 2010, *Theology and International Development*, London: Christian Aid, p. 28.

3 See also J. Sachs who, from a secular point of view, argues that we can end poverty. J. Sachs, 2006, *The End of Poverty: Economic Possibilities for Our Time*, London: Penguin.

4 C. Myers, 2002, 'Proclaiming Good News in Hard Times: Reflections on Evangelism and the Bible', in D. Neville (ed.), *Prophecy and Passion: Essays in Honor of Athol Gill*, Hindmarsh: Australian Theological Forum, p. 286. See also C. Myers, 2007, *The Biblical Vision of Sabbath Economics*, Oak View, CA: Bartimaeus Cooperative Ministries.

5 J. Wallis, 2005, *God's Politics: Why the American Right Get it Wrong and the Left Doesn't Get It*, Oxford: Lion Hudson, p. 211.

6 C. Wright, 2004, *Old Testament Ethics for the People of God*, Nottingham: InterVarsity Press, p. 179.

7 P. Miller, 1990, *Deuteronomy, Interpretation*, Louisville, KY: John Knox Press, p. 137. See also R. Wafawanaka, 2014, 'Is the Biblical Perspective on Poverty that "there shall be no poor among you" or "you will always have the poor with you"?', *Review and Expositor* 111:2, p. 112.

8 Clifford, *Theology*, p. 18.

9 Wigg-Stevenson, *The World*, p. 54.

10 Wigg-Stevenson, *The World*, p. 182.

17

The problem of aid utopianism

The previous chapter sought to indicate that the fundamental Christian confession is that Jesus Christ has won the definitive victory over sin and death, but that this victory has not yet been fully realized. The kingdom – in which all will flourish – has been inaugurated, but it is not yet complete. We live between the times. This fundamental framework should have a major impact on how we go about seeking to address the issue of global poverty in our time.

Motivation for the long haul

As we have already seen, for some there is apparently a great danger in arguing that poverty will never, in this life, be eradicated. Their great fear is that this will demotivate a wide range of poverty-alleviation efforts. Yet, as Wigg-Stevenson points out, it is also arguable that precisely the reverse is the case. His concern is that a generation of Christians has been brought up on a narrative that 'we can end poverty' and so when – assuming Jesus' words are correct – it turns out that we cannot, the motivational impact on these young Christians will be that they give up. There is certainly a well-worn narrative that in one's youth and early twenties, one is filled with all kinds of hopes and dreams about changing the world, and when in one's thirties and forties we realize that life is not that simple often the result is that people give up. So, Wigg-Stevenson comments, 'A generation of Christians that thinks it is called to save the world is a generation firing on the fuel of false hopes. It is signing up for exhaustion and disillusioned burnout.'[1] In contrast to this, one of the primary reasons why Wigg-Stevenson is keen to emphasize that we can never solve the problem of poverty is precisely because it engenders the steely resolve that will not give up when it becomes clear that easy solutions are not round the corner.

> Confronted with this tension, the only response is resolute commitment. We can realize that there is no solution and simultaneously refuse to be defeated or paralyzed by that fact. We can ensure that the solutionlessness of our condition does not harden our souls. We can labour against injustices so vast that their remedy is beyond our capacity to execute and in spite of the knowledge that we are unlikely to see their resolution.[2]

As he says elsewhere:

> We live on top of unmendable cracks, and the insoluble nature of the world means that the question posed to us is not 'how do we fix this?' but 'how can we live out the love of God [in] the midst of such brokenness?'[3]

What is interesting about this approach is the contrast that it represents with Christian Aid's approach. For Christian Aid – as we have seen – the great danger is that if we do not believe we can solve the world's problems then inevitably we will give up. For Wigg-Stevenson, it is precisely the opposite argument that is in play: if we falsely believe that we can change the world and then hit the buffers of reality, at that point we will give up. It seems to me that both empirically and ethically Wigg-Stevenson is correct here. If one's only motivation for poverty alleviation is the mistaken belief that one can be part of the generation that will finally solve this problem then one is empirically mistaken, for it represents hubris of the most atrocious kind to think that our generation is going to be the first to solve a problem that has existed since the dawn of humanity; it is also ethically shallow. One's motivation for poverty alleviation should be the lack of flourishing experienced by one's brothers and sisters in LICs, not the sense of self-worth that is derived from being part of the generation that finally fixed the problem. For Stephen Plant, the problem with this attitude is that it confuses our ultimate hope with our penultimate endeavours. He writes that 'Christians . . . have a proper *penultimate* interest in life before death, but their *ultimate* peace and fulfilment as human beings lies in the love of God.' His argument is that the Christian account of hope is not the same as secular belief in progress through development.[4]

> The gift exchanges, of nourishment, of forgiveness and so on, are not part of a totalizing programme of change, for example of making poverty history. Forgiveness, bread, the giving of a cup of water: these are perhaps best not thought of as steps on the way to some programme to transform unjust social structures (which may, nonetheless be a result of them). Rather, they are to be considered in the same way as the celebration of the Lord's Supper, or Eucharist is considered: as a first taste of a state of fulfilled or consummated created existence, a sign and instance in the present of something that is promised.[5]

Similarly, Longenecker writes: 'The corporate meals of urban Jesus followers were not intended as a means of simply filling stomachs: instead they were seen as incarnations of the kingdom or empire of God.'[6]

A temporary and shallow motivation, however, is not the only problem associated with development utopianism. It can also foster ethnocentrism. It is becoming increasing clear that, while the problem of poverty is ever more present on the screens of HIC household, attitudes towards poverty are hardening. 'Donor fatigue' has become a real issue in Western societies over the last ten to twenty years, with fewer and fewer people supporting foreign aid compared to previously. One of the primary reasons given for this reluctance concerns doubts about aid effectiveness. The public have simply become unconvinced that their hard-earned money is being spent well. Why would this be the case? Part of the issue has got to be the increasing numbers of stories about corruption in poor countries. But that is not the whole of the picture. For, in addition to increasing suspicion of corruption, it is arguable that the problem stems from the claims of the development community themselves.

Voluntourism

The second problem associated with aid utopianism springs from the first, and it is the phenomena of voluntourism – that is, voluntary work which is focused more on the needs and desires of the person doing the work than the requirements of the community which in theory is being served. One of the remarkable phenomena of recent years has been an explosion in short-term missioners. Fanning suggests that more than 1.5 million US Christians go on short-term mission trips each year, a rise of over 600 per cent since the early 1990s.[7] Clearly, part of the reason for this phenomenal growth is cheaper air travel, but it has also been fuelled by our exposure to global poverty via the internet. It is relatively easy to ignore the global poor when you only read about them, but when their faces are presented to you on a daily basis then the ethical incentive to go and do something becomes even more pressing. Robert Priest comments in relation to the US scene:

> What we have is a grassroots movement in which, for example, youth pastors as a normal and expected part of their job take their youth groups to Mexico, West Virginia, Guatemala or Haiti on mission trips. Many congregations now routinely organize mission trips for all ages scheduled to fit around school and work schedules.[8]

Typically, short-term missioners are defined as anyone going overseas to work cross-culturally, especially in a poor community, for anything from one week to a few months, and there are of course a range of potential benefits to such trips. In the first place, they can provide some kind of practical benefit to the recipient community – perhaps a school or home is built, or some English education is delivered. They can facilitate global church partnerships, and often relationships formed after short-term mission trips are longstanding and mutually beneficial. Indeed, this is the one aspect of short-term mission that Edwin Zhener highlights in his review of the benefits of short-term mission, stating that 'the relationships through which short-term missions flow may function as ministerial enhancement, strengthening the local churches rather than weakening them'.[9] He describes 'a metaphor of "friendship" between churches, and with individual pastors and team members, that seemed especially empowering to those who told the stories'.[10] Further, short-term mission by definition provides opportunities for cross-cultural exposure that may minimize cultural ethnocentrism and in turn foster global partnerships. It also provides an experience of global Christianity and global theologies that both broaden one's own understanding and experience, and enable one to recognize the relatively restrictive contours of one's own contextual faith. It is also often claimed that short-term mission increases one's compassion for the world Church, especially the global poor, and may lead to increased charitable giving to global causes specifically and increased giving in general. Finally, it is also argued that short-term mission can lead to significant spiritual growth and may even lead to individuals contemplating long-term overseas service. There is, potentially, a long list of benefits from short-term overseas experience.

However, the problem with this list is that most of these benefits are merely potential. The empirical evidence to date does not consistently support the idea that these benefits accrue, and there is a mounting corpus of evidence that suggests either that short-term mission simply does no good, or in fact that it can be potentially harmful. In saying this, I am not impugning the motives of specific individuals who engage in short-term mission, I am simply arguing that the good we often think we are doing may not always be realized. This truth is vividly illustrated by a particular short-term missioner – Pippa Biddle – who blogged about her experience on her return. She describes a trip she made as a high school student to Tanzania:

> Our mission while at the orphanage was to build a library. Turns out that we, a group of highly educated private boarding school students, were so bad at the most basic construction work that each night the men had to take down the structurally unsound bricks we had laid and rebuild the structure so that, when we woke up in the morning, we would be unaware of our failure. It is likely that this was a daily ritual. Us mixing cement and laying bricks for 6+ hours, them undoing our work after the sun set, re-laying the bricks, and then acting as if nothing had happened so that the cycle could continue.[11]

While this experience may not be typical, it illustrates a range of problems that can impact short-term mission escapades. The first of these is that unskilled people are sent to undertake tasks that really require skilled input. In this example, it was bricklaying, but the same rationale applies to education, healthcare, youth and children's work. There sometimes seems to be an assumption within HICs that if we are from a so-called developed country then we will automatically have the skills required to undertake a range of tasks that, under other conditions, would normally require several years' (or at least a week's) training. Of course, the counter-argument is to say that if we do not go with our unskilled labour then no one will undertake the task, but, as Ms Biddle's argument shows, that is not always the case. In addition, the impetus for the local authorities or national government to provide skilled labour to undertake the teaching, healthcare and so on will be diminished if it is always filled by unskilled and inappropriate, and certainly cheap, Westerners.

This leads to the second problem associated with short-term mission: it can reduce employment opportunities in the local labour market. In 2006, Kurt ver Beek undertook a case study of short-term mission exploring house construction in Honduras following hurricane Mitch. The study involved interviews with Hondurans who had benefited from the houses built by short-term missioners, as well as those who had not, and the employees of Honduran agencies who had facilitated the trips. One of those employees commented on the short-term missioners that 'They gather money to come here to do work. Work that we are capable of doing.'[12] In the same study, ver Beek also showed how, when you included all the costs of travel, accommodation and so on for the short-term missioners, then the houses they built cost an average of $30,000, while the same homes – if built by local labour – would have cost around $2,000.[13] As such, it is arguable that this short-term mission represents an inordinate waste of resources, resources that could have been much more efficiently spent locally. Considering the air travel involved, it also represents significant damage to the environment.

A further argument in support of short-term missioners is that it brings about a significant transformation in those who go, but again the empirical evidence for this is lacking. Indeed, worse than this, there is evidence that we fool ourselves into thinking such experiences have been more transformative than they have actually been. In ver Beek's study of house-building in Honduras he found this to be the case in regard to financial giving. This study included a survey of 162 short-term missioners who had been involved in the house-building programme. Perhaps unsurprisingly, many of these people self-reported that the trip had a significant impact on their life. More specifically, 10 per cent of them claimed that their financial giving had increased significantly as a result of the trip, and 49 per cent said it had increased somewhat. Ver Beek, however, was able to analyse actual increases in giving to the relevant charity and this showed that while the average donation before the trip was $31 per person per year, this had increased to a mere $33 per person per year after the trip.[14] In other words, short-term missioners would appear to consistently overestimate the transformative effect of the trip on their lives. Paul Blezien conducted a similar study which involved a pre- and post-trip survey of 159 students with controls which showed 'no statistically significant difference was found between the pre-test and post-test scores of the students who travelled overseas for summer short-term mission projects'.[15]

One of the problems with the literature on short-term missioners is that if one wants to find a positive impact of them then it is very easy to identify a particular case study or particular individual in which the recipient community or short-term missioner was genuinely transformed. However, when more rigorous statistical analysis is done at a wider level then the stated benefits of short-term mission often fall by the wayside. So LiEvin Probasco undertook such a rigorous statistical analysis of the impact of high school mission trips on long-term giving and volunteering. She found that 'high school participation in an international mission trip has no significant association with adult volunteering or giving when other factors . . . are taken into account'.[16] She concludes:

Taken together, these results indicate a need to rethink the assumption that trips are a mechanism for increased social participation . . . They also indicate that claims about mission trips' broad, positive impact on future civic participation should be tempered by more precise statements.[17]

Priest also surveyed the extant research regarding short-term missioners and found that despite much positive rhetoric regarding the benefit of short-term mission, a range of studies demonstrated that there was no actual increase in the number of long-term missionaries, that any increase in giving is only short-term, that there was no difference in the extent of materialism and attitudes to poverty among those who went and those who did not, and there were no reductions in ethnocentrism among those who went. Commenting on one study that explored the ethnocentrism of 169 high school students, they found that the previous number of overseas trips bore no relation to the degree of ethnocentrism exhibited by the student, 'That is, the sheer fact of encounter with cultural difference is as likely to increase ethnocentrism as decrease it.'[18]

These are not, however, the only potential problems associated with short-term mission. Others have argued extensively that it fosters a paternal attitude in those going and a dependency attitude in those receiving. Glenn Schwartz, in his book *When Charity Destroys Dignity*, tells the story of a group from North America who went to Guyana to build a church. Having successfully completed the project over three weeks, they returned home with a sense of pride in what they had achieved. Two years later, Schwarz notes, the group leader received a letter which read, 'The roof on *your* church building is leaking. Please come and fix it.'[19] Similarly, Ralph Hanger commenced his recent article exploring this issue with a quotation from a BMS worker, 'No visitor comes empty handed, so what have you brought for me?'[20] This is what was said to the worker by a church leader in Western Uganda as she arrived in the country. There was an assumption that any visitor from a high-income country would be providing material goods. The explosion in short-term missions has simply encouraged this, where indeed many of the short-term missioners are explicitly told to take something with them that they can give. The problems associated with such dependency are numerous, however, and all of these represent the flip side of the paternalism that was discussed in Chapter 2 of this book.

For all of these reasons, ver Beek concludes his systematic analysis of short-term missions (STM) by saying:

> The research outlined above demonstrates that STM as they are currently being practiced, are creating very little lasting positive change in the participants . . . While the STM trip is often a mountaintop experience for the participants, a few weeks or months later their good intentions to raise money for world missions, work for social justice or deepen their faith have not been translated into actions. If we hope to see those good intentions translated into accomplishments something needs to change.[21]

In conclusion, perhaps the biggest issue with short-term missions is simply the inordinate waste of resources they involve. It costs a huge amount to train, vaccinate, fly over and then accommodate someone from a HIC – money which could probably have been spent far more effectively in country. Of course, if these experiences did lead to lasting transformations in those who went then perhaps it would be justified, but the empirical evidence does not support that claim. None of this is to say that there should be no short-term missions. It is rather to say that they should be undertaken far more carefully so that only those which really are of lasting benefit and conducted in genuine partnership with the local community are run. We want to engage in cross-cultural learning, not just voluntourism.

The link between this issue and utopian dreams of ending poverty is that it's precisely because the claims to end poverty are so motivational that they inspire large numbers to go overseas on short-term trips. If what you are told is that there is some unimaginable evil in the world and the solution to that evil is within your grasp, and all you need to solve it is give a little more either in time or money, then of course many of us will jump at the chance. Whether or not we have the skills to help, whether in reality our well-meaning efforts do more harm than good – these are not factors we consider. After all, we are ending poverty – except we're not!

Messiah complex

The next problem to be discussed regarding aid utopianism is that it encourages a messiah complex in the more economically prosperous parts of the world. We start to believe that we are the solution to the world's problems, instead of recognizing that in fact we are the problem. South African Molefe Tsele has written:

> It is the inherent temptation of all human beings to make history, to solve big problems, to be remembered beyond our earthly lives, to seek immortality. In a sense there is a hidden struggle to be messiahs in our own way, be it small or large. The temptation is greater for those of us who have the power and can use it to change people's lives. We are tempted to become redeemers and thus commit the fundamental error of playing God. Development workers, like political liberators, tend to forget that they are human after all, and that there are some problems that simply are beyond our capacity to solve. We are not the Mr. Fix-It of societies' woes.[22]

Tsele describes the problems that occur when those in the development industry come to believe that they can solve all problems, including in particular a failure to take the time to understand the issue before them. LICs are littered with white elephants – equipment left by well-meaning supporters who thought they could solve a problem just by sending over a few crates of materials. Yet in the process we leave behind our detritus. Perhaps the best illustration of this messiah complex can be found in the Kenyan mockumentary *The Samaritans*, in which a fictional development agency works hard at doing nothing remotely useful. The fact that this programme originated in a LIC speaks volumes.

Theologically, the problem is to confuse our role with that of Christ. While we are indeed the body of Christ, and therefore the arms, legs, mouths, hands and so on that are co-builders with God of his kingdom, this does not mean that we have saved, or can save, the world, and it does not mean that the kingdom will ever be fully inaugurated in this age. As Wigg-Stevenson puts it:

> We get our *calling* wrong when we imagine that God needs us, to be the hero of our own story, rather than Christ . . . we routinely misdiagnose the *problem of our world*, underestimating the brokenness of sin and overestimating our ability to fix things.[23]

Similarly, Charles Elliot has written:

> If we are to be faithful to a New Testament understanding of power, it is Christ that redeems our structures. We need to grasp that, in order to be delivered from the conventional notion that it *we* who redeem them.[24]

The fundamental problem here is to fail to take seriously the victory that has been won by Christ. If one is operating with a system in which God has not won the ultimate victory over evil, then humanity is all that one is left with. In such a context, one either becomes resigned to a life that is 'short, brutal and nasty' or one works tirelessly to address issues of poverty. However, in order to do the latter, the only means at one's disposal is the belief that humans have all the answers to the world's problems and the only motivation available is the idea that this is achievable, that we can do it. A goal of simply improving someone's life a bit does not have sufficient motivational power, which is why it has to be replaced with the goal that we can end poverty. Another way of saying this is that an inadequate doctrine of the atonement leads ineluctably to an underestimation of sin, an exaggerated anthropology and an over-realized eschatology.[25]

Detracts from the real issue

Finally, and perhaps the biggest problem with aid utopianism in respect of global poverty, is that it detracts from the real change that is required. As I have already argued, if we are really going to solve the problem of global poverty, this will not be done by installing more water pumps, twinning with a few more latrines or cows, or even by vaccinating a few more children – it will only occur if we fundamentally change the way in which our global economic system works. This is not to say that those other activities are not useful. They are, and I support all of them in practice. But we must not think that by themselves they are going to solve the problem of global poverty. They will not.

What will get us nearer to a more just world is if we in the economically richer parts of the world stop robbing LICs of the monies that we owe them, money that we have taken as part of our colonial legacy and current exploitative practices. The challenge for us is that if this were to happen, our own HIC economies would shrink as a result. In short, we would become poorer. And this is, I think, fundamentally why we like the utopian messages. They enable us to avoid the stark reality that genuinely ending global poverty also means that those of us in the rich world would become poorer.

I previously quoted Gustavo Gutiérrez, the father of liberation theology, when he wrote of aid as a salve to our consciences, 'producing superficial social changes which in the long run will only help to prolong the situation of misery and of injustice'.[26] I think he's right. And Gutiérrez isn't alone. There are a long line of voices from LICs now arguing for a different approach that takes us beyond aid. It is time to listen to them, for while the message that, with a little help, we can be the saviours of the world is one that sounds nice, it isn't one that in reality will change the world. Elliot wrote the following in the 1980s, but it is still a message that needs to be heard today:

The rich Christians, the rich Churches, rich nations, were prepared to give charitably of their abundance: they were not prepared to look critically at the economic and political structures which kept poor people poor, and which ensured that the major beneficiaries of their charitable giving were the non-poor.[27]

Notes

1 T. Wigg-Stevenson, 2013, *The World is not Ours to Save*, Downers Grove, IL: InterVarsity Press, p. 60.

2 Wigg-Stevenson, *The World*, p. 60.

3 Wigg-Stevenson, *The World*, p. 41.

4 S. Plant, 2009, 'International Development and Belief in Progress', *Journal of International Development* 21:6, p. 853.

5 S. Plant, 2011, 'Christian Theology on Setting Goals for International Development', *Epworth Review*, January, p. 22. Incidentally, this emphasis on development as liturgy can also be found in Orthodox writings on humanitarianism. E. H. Prodromou and N. Symeonides, 2016, 'Orthodox Christanity and Humanitarianism: An Introduction to Thought and Practice, Past and Present', *The Review of Faith and International Affairs* 14:1, pp. 1–17.

6 B. Longenecker, 2009, 'Afterword', in B. Longenecker and K. Liebengood (eds), *Engaging Economics*, Grand Rapids, MI: Eerdmans, p. 311.

7 D. Fanning, 2009, 'Short Term Missions: A Trend that is Growing Exponentially', *Trends and Issues in Missions*, Paper 4, pp. 1–2.

8 R. Priest et al., 2006, 'Researching the Short-Term Mission Movement', *Missiology* 34:4, p. 433.

9 E. Zehner, 2013, 'Short-Term Missions: Some Perspectives from Thailand', *Missiology* 41:2, p. 140.

10 Zehner, 'Short-Term Missions', p. 141.

11 P. Biddle, 'The Problem with Little White Girls (and Boys): Why I Stopped Being a Voluntourist'. Available at: http://pippabiddle.com/2014/02/18/the-problem -with-little-white-girls-and-boys/ (accessed 4 July 2016).

12 K. ver Beek, 2006, 'The Impact of Short-Term Missions: A Case Study of House Construction in Honduras after Hurricane Mitch', *Missiology: An International Review* 34:4, p. 483.

13 Ver Beek, 'The Impact', p. 493.

14 Ver Beek, 'The Impact', p. 486.

15 P. Blezien, 2004, 'The Impact of Summer International Short-Term Missions Experiences on the Cross-Cultural Sensitivity of Undergraduate College Student Participants', dissertation, Azusa, CA: Azusa Pacific University, p. 110.

16 L. Probasco, 2013, 'Giving Time, Not Money: Long-Term Impacts of Short-Term Mission Trips', *Missiology* 41:2, p. 219.

17 Probasco, 'Giving Time', p. 220.

18 Priest *et al.*, 'Researching', p. 444.

19 G. Schwartz, 2007, *When Charity Destroys Dignity*, Bloomington, IN: AuthorHouse, p. 239.

20 R. Hanger, 2014, 'No Visitor Comes Empty Handed – Some Thoughts on Unhealthy Dependency', *Transformation* 31:1, p. 21.

21 K. ver Beek, 2008, 'Lessons from the Sapling: Review of Quantitative Research on Short-Term Missions', in R. J. Priest (ed.), *Effective Engagement in Short-Term Missions: Doing It Right!* Pasadena, CA: William Carey Library, p. 494.

22 M. Tsele, 2001, 'The Role of the Christian Faith in Development', in D. Belshaw, R. Calderisi and C. Sugden (eds), *Faith in Development*, Oxford: Regnum Books, p. 211–12.

23 Wigg-Stevenson, *The World*, p. 21.

24 C. Elliot, 1987, *Comfortable Compassion*, London: Hodder & Stoughton, p. 152. See also Doherty, who writes that the kingdom of God 'is not accomplished by human effort. We cannot make it happen, and thinking we can will not only bring failure but absolutism.' He then helpfully adds, 'But this does not mean human agency is irrelevant.' S. Doherty, 2015, 'The Kingdom of God and the Economic System: An Economics of Hope', in J. Kidwell and S. Doherty, *Theology and Economics*, London: Palgrave Macmillan, p. 152.

25 Rory Stewart provides an interesting secular example of what happens when the West's exaggerated sense of what it can achieve is let loose on the world stage. R. Stewart, 2006, *Occupational Hazard: My Time Governing in Iraq*, Basingstoke: Picador.

26 G. Gutiérrez, 1969, 'The Meaning of Development', in *In Search of a Theology of Development*, papers from a Consultation on Theology and Development held by SODEPAX in Cartigny, Switzerland, Geneva: SODEPAX, p. 152.

27 Elliot, *Comfortable Compassion*, p. 52.

18

So why should we bother?

In light of the foregoing discussion, it might be asked, what then should we do? If we cannot fix the world's problems, why then should we act? This is where an appropriate eschatological framework comes into its own. An under-realized eschatology, especially when coupled with a premillennial or amillenial framework, will make one think that nothing can be done, that all actions are futile. Excluding some brands of conservative evangelicalism, it is rare now to find that outlook. Much more common is the over-realized approach that we have been addressing in this part of the book.[1] Such an over-realized eschatology is manifest in a range of secular development theories when they believe that the problem of poverty can be solved; it is also manifest in a range of Christian development theologies to the extent that they downplay their theological moorings and embrace the secular development theorists.

In contrast to both these extremes, what is required is an appropriate eschatology that recognizes the victory has been won, but that the kingdom has only been inaugurated, not yet completed. Moe-Lobeda writes:

> Here appears a third paradox of hope central to Christian tradition. It is the strange dialectic between absolute trust in God's power to bring about the liberation and healing of the world on the one hand, and on the other hand the conviction that humans beings – while unable to bring about the reign of God through human effort alone – are called to dedicate our lives to that very endeavour. God, not humans, can and will save the world. Yet, we are to live our lives toward that end, devoting our gifts and resources to it.[2]

In *Christ and Capital*, Michael Taylor highlights the motivational aspect of such an eschatology. He points out that 'If we ask about the function of theology, in this case eschatology, and the role it is playing generally and in this debate, the most obvious answer is that it gives us grounds for hope.'[3] 'The Christian does not wish for something to happen, or even believe that it might: he has the assurance that it will, because God is God.'[4] Taylor is right to draw attention to the reality that Christian eschatology does provide hope. Our efforts in this life on behalf of the poor are not in vain and one day a community of complete human flourishing will be realized. However, the weakness of Taylor's analysis is that he doesn't go on to link eschatology to ethics. For Taylor, eschatology seems to have no function beyond motivating our work. He notes that although it may be useful in that regard, 'it did not prove to be especially relevant or useful in the later stages of the debate about capitalism'.[5] What Taylor is ignoring here is the function of Christian eschatology, not only in motivating action – about which he is correct – but in guiding our action as well.

In his very useful chapter on this theme, Sean Doherty takes to task those theologians who have interpreted the relevance of eschatology to economics in purely formal, rather concrete terms. His target are those who are guilty of an under-realized approach that views the chasm of sin as so great that while the kingdom of God is a future hope, it is not a present reality. So he criticizes Reinhold Niebuhr thus:

> 'Because Niebuhr believes that all human economic orders fall short, he cannot give sin any tangible, specific description. It is not something concrete, to be opposed and overcome. As with Barth, sin functions as the *unbridgeable* gulf between the relative and the absolute.[6]

By way of contrast, Doherty argues that 'history should be construed as an arena in which genuine improvement and change can take place. This transformation may be piecemeal and inadequate. The "breaking in" is neither complete nor permanent – but it is genuine.'[7] Doherty's point is that eschatology does guide economic ethics in real and concrete terms (*pace* Taylor). He is concerned that a failure to appreciate this point has left Christian theologians with a 'supine and bland' economic ethics.[8] In light of this, in the rest of this chapter I will explore a series of eschatological parables to see how they might inform the work that we undertake in the present era.

We begin with the parable of the rich man and Lazarus (Luke 16.19–31). We find in this story a well-known depiction of a reversal of eschatological fortunes. Lazarus spends this life sitting at the rich man's gate, but in the age to come the rich man is depicted as requesting comfort from the realm where Lazarus now resides. This reversal motif is one that has already been foreshadowed in Luke's version of the beatitudes:

> 'Blessed are you who are poor, for yours is the kingdom of God.
>   'Blessed are you who are hungry now, for you will be filled.
>   'Blessed are you who weep now, for you will laugh.'
>   . . .
> 'But woe to you who are rich, for you have received your consolation.
>   'Woe to you who are full now, for you will be hungry.
>   'Woe to you who are laughing now, for you will mourn and weep.'
> (Luke 6.20–21, 24–25)

Darrell Bock has pointed out that the parable had parallels in the Ancient Near East in both Egypt and in Judaism, in which a rich and poor man trade places in the afterlife.[9] Its purpose then is ethical – and certainly not meant as a literal description of life after death. It comes shortly after Jesus has chastised the Pharisees for their love of money and his proclamation to them that they cannot serve two masters (Luke 16.13). In this context, and in the whole

Lucan context, the parable is a story not about the life to come but about this life. It points forward to the eschaton, not to inform us about the reality that is to come but to guide us in our ethical action now. Specifically, the parable acts as a criticism of those who would store up wealth and fail to share it with the poor in our midst. The point of the rather gruesome depiction of hades – 'Father Abraham, have pity on me and send Lazarus to dip the tip of his finger in water and cool my tongue, because I am in agony in this fire' – is intended to motivate and guide our behaviour today. Its goal is to shock us into divesting of our wealth for the sake of the poor. It is, in short, a parabolic command that our goal should be equality. Read in this light, it is highly surprising that Taylor suggests eschatology has not proved useful in the 'debate about capitalism', because what this eschatological parable indicates is that even if we do not achieve it, the way in which we construct our capitalism should be in an egalitarian direction. In other words, this parable points in the direction of the reformed capitalism that we have been arguing for throughout this book. To say that eschatology is of no use in guiding practice is to fail to appreciate the ethical purpose of much eschatological writing.

The same point is evident in the parable of the grand eschatological banquet depicted in Luke 14. In this parable, Jesus tells the story of a man who invited many to his house for a great banquet. One by one they all make excuses and so the master of the house sends the servants out into the streets in order to invite 'the poor, the crippled, the blind, and the lame' (Luke 14.21). What is often missed in examining this story is its significant Jewish background. The story begins with one of Jesus' fellow diners stating, 'Blessed is anyone who will eat bread in the kingdom of God!' (Luke 14.15). In saying this, the diner – probably a Pharisee – was referring to the well-known Jewish expectations that the age to come would be characterized by a banquet. This is clear in a large section of inter-testamental literature,[10] but is indicated directly in the book of Isaiah:

> On this mountain the LORD of hosts will make for all peoples
>   a feast of rich food, a feast of well-matured wines,
>   of rich food filled with marrow, of well-matured wines strained clear.
> And he will destroy on this mountain
>   the shroud that is cast over all peoples,
>   the sheet that is spread over all nations;
> he will swallow up death for ever.
> Then the LORD GOD will wipe away the tears from all faces,
>   and the disgrace of his people he will take away from all the earth,
>   for the LORD has spoken.
> It will be said on that day,
>   Lo, this is our God; we have waited for him, so that he might save us.
>   This is the LORD for whom we have waited;
>   let us be glad and rejoice in his salvation. (Isa. 25.6–9)

This passage makes it abundantly clear that what is being depicted here is an *eschatological* banquet: the shroud over all people is destroyed; death is swallowed up; all tears are wiped away. But at the same time, what is indicated is a celebration characterized as a *banquet*: a feast of rich food; a feast of wines; food filled with marrow; wines made clear. This, then, is what the Pharisee is referring to when he says to Jesus that 'Blessed is anyone who will eat bread in the kingdom of God'. It is this eschatological bread that the Pharisee has in mind. But at the same time, it is almost certainly the case that the *people* the Pharisee envisages sitting round the table with him will at most be those who are also Jews, and minimally those who have resolutely stuck to the law in the way that he has. Certainly, this dinner guest would not have expected the unclean, the Gentiles and the law-breakers to be at this eschatological feast.

Yet this is the point of Jesus' parable: it is precisely those whom the Pharisee expects to see there who will not be there – because they have refused to come – and those the Pharisee not expect to be there are those who will be found at the table – the poor, the crippled, the blind and the lame. We have here the same kind of eschatological reversal motif that was evident in Luke's beatitudes and in the parable of the rich man and Lazarus. Those who have suffered during this life, those who have been marginalized, are those who will sit down with the Messiah and feast in the kingdom of God. Those who in this life have received their fill, those who expect that a place in the eschatological banquet is theirs by right are those who will be absent. But at the same time it is especially clear that the major point of Jesus' parable is not to inform us of the particular make-up of the age to come or even to describe the nature of that age. Rather, the major thrust of Jesus' parable – in parallel to the major thrust in Luke 16 – is to guide our ethical behaviour in this life. Immediately prior to the parable, indeed providing the co-text for the parable, Jesus is shown to be having dinner at the house of a Pharisee, and he says this:

'When you give a luncheon or a dinner, do not invite your friends or your brothers or your relatives or rich neighbours, in case they may invite you in return, and you would be repaid. But when you give a banquet, invite the poor, the crippled, the lame, and the blind'. (Luke 14.12–13)

In this way, Jesus is directly indicating the ethical purpose of the subsequent parable. He uses the parable to expand and explain the ethical imperative he has provided round the dinner table. His point is that just as the kingdom of God – when fully realized in the age to come – will be characterized by an equality in which all are welcome, in particular those are welcome who cannot hope to repay the favour, so in this life we bring that kingdom about, we *build for* the kingdom, when we also demonstrate eschatological values in our generosity to the poor, in our offer of hospitality, in our welcoming of strangers. Jesus seems to be saying, this is what it is going to be like when the Messiah comes in his kingdom, so this is what it should also be like now if you are to be members of that kingdom. The eschatological vision, then, not only motivates our action but also guides it – in this particular case our moral boundaries should know no limits, the doctrine of moral proximity is fundamentally flawed and does not reflect the kingdom of the risen Messiah.

One final parable will illustrate the ethical dimensions of eschatological reality:

> Someone in the crowd said to him, 'Teacher, tell my brother to divide the family inheritance with me.' But he said to him, 'Friend, who set me to be a judge or arbitrator over you?' And he said to them, 'Take care! Be on your guard against all kinds of greed; for one's life does not consist in the abundance of possessions.' Then he told them a parable: 'The land of a rich man produced abundantly. And he thought to himself, "What should I do, for I have no place to store my crops?" Then he said, "I will do this: I will pull down my barns and build larger ones, and there I will store all my grain and my goods. And I will say to my soul, Soul, you have ample goods laid up for many years; relax, eat, drink, be merry." But God said to him, "You fool! This very night your life is being demanded of you. And the things you have prepared, whose will they be?" So it is with those who store up treasures for themselves but are not rich towards God.' (Luke 12.13–21)

The context of the parable is a man asking Jesus to adjudicate regarding an inheritance issue. While the Old Testament provided a series of laws to govern this situation, Joel Green suggests that there was sufficient ambiguity for not every eventuality to be covered, and therefore a dispute over an inheritance was not an uncommon occurrence.[11] Given this, while at first glance it may have seemed as if the plaintiff was seeking redress in an issue of fairness or justice, Jesus correctly points out that at the heart of this matter is an issue of greed. Indeed, we do not know the details, but the plaintiff might have a good case. Perhaps his brother really was being unfair. Yet, Jesus' response appears to minimize that because of the bigger issue of greed that is at stake. As we shall see, a parallel can be drawn with how the rich farmer is depicted. For him, the issue is not so much one of fairness but one of sound economic practice. One can imagine him defending his actions as just good business sense. Yet, like the plaintiff, Jesus sidesteps that consideration to say the bigger issue here is greed. Even if it is sound economics, even if you are due a certain portion of the inheritance – Jesus would appear to be saying – do not let greed characterize your response. In 1 Corinthians 6, Paul criticizes church members for their lawsuits against one another and writes, 'Why not rather be wronged? Why not rather be defrauded?' (1 Cor. 6.7). In parallel, in this passage, we can imagine Jesus saying, 'Why not rather lose your inheritance? Why not rather make poor business decisions? If in the process you avoid greed and so save your soul.'

There are, then, three particular eschatological lessons that we can draw from the parable. The first is simply the danger of an over-realized eschatology. This seems to be the problem affecting the man in the parable. He finds himself in the fortunate position of one with more goods than he requires. In response, he constructs a way to hold on to that surplus, but then makes the fatal mistake of resting on that abundance: 'And I will say to my soul, Soul, you have ample goods laid up for many years; relax, eat, drink, be merry.' At this point, the moral failure of the man simply seems to be that he has an unrealistic view of

his position. He wrongly believes that because he has this abundance of possessions, there is nothing for him to fear – and into that context, God speaks,
'You fool! This very night your life is being demanded of you.'

One of the frequent misconceptions of the doctrine of last things is that we
limit its relevance to the future. We look forward with hope and anticipation
to that which will come, and view its contemporary relevance as being no
more than providing us with the motivation to keep going. The eschaton on
this understanding becomes the mountain top that we will eventually reach
as long as we persevere. What we too often fail to appreciate, however, and
what I have been trying to argue in this chapter, is that eschatology does not
just speak to our future, and does not just provide motivation to keep going in
the present, but it also guides how we walk in the present. It is about ethics as
much as it is about hope. And we see that in this parable, for the fundamental
lesson that the rich fool failed to appreciate is that, because God states the final
yes or final no, that puts a terminus on the significance of human efforts. In this
way, the eschaton represents the ultimate Sabbath – and indeed for that reason
is called in the book of Hebrews a Sabbath rest. For the permanency of the age
to come delimits both the extent and significance of what we achieve in this life.
We have already noted that in this life we work with God in building for his
kingdom, but the significant point is that we are building for God's kingdom,
not our own. Our efforts may in some sense last into eternity but only to the
extent that we are part of God's kingdom, not our own. This is what the rich
fool fails to realize. He is building an empire for himself, not a kingdom for
God. And precisely because it is for himself, that is why it will not last. That
is why God declares the final 'no' to his endeavours. In this way, the very fact
of the eschaton puts our work into perspective. It causes us to be humble, to
recognize that, when we are building for ourselves, such activity is mere hubris
and arrogance – it is not of the kingdom of God. As Wigg-Stevenson has put
it, 'The Christian calling is grounded in the peace that comes with accepting
our limitations and finitude – an acceptance that allows us to pour ourselves
out in divine service.'[12] The relevance for poverty alleviation is simply this – if
we are seeking to end poverty for our own glory or in order to point to what
we have achieved, then such efforts, though maybe worthwhile in some sense,
are not for eternity, and one day we will be called to account for them. The
purpose of poverty alleviation is the glory of God, which is revealed in the
mutual flourishing of our brothers and sisters across the world. Eschatology is
fundamentally humbling. There is an end of history, but it will not occur when
the aid agencies end poverty (for they won't), or when Africa is converted into
a consumer capitalist culture (which unfortunately it might), but it will end
when Jesus comes again.

The second challenge presented in the parable is that it critiques acquisitive
greed. As Green has pointed out, what this man does makes complete sense
from an agribusiness point of view, but fails to take into account a kingdom
perspective in which the welfare of all is of paramount concern.

What is 'good business practice' for this wealthy farmer-landlord has det-
rimental consequences for the peasants and tenants who are his neighbours

and who far outnumber him in the village economy. Not least because of his evidently vast landholdings and the magnitude of his surplus yield, his decision to hold back his produce will reflect harmfully on the regional economy. It will, at the same time, secure his economic power and position of status in the village as others are made more and more dependent on him.[13]

Green points out that from an individual, 'business' point of view it makes sense to store excess grain at a time of surplus rather than sell it, because to sell it in that context of abundance would generate a lower price than to wait until the price has risen once again. In short, the landowner is maximizing his potential yield by storing and then selling later.[14] What is noteworthy is the way in which these business practices are challenged. The man is implicitly criticized for putting his faith in his 'abundance of possessions' and for storing up treasures for himself. In the context of Luke as a whole, and in the specific context of this passage, at least part of the problem of this man is his lack of generosity to the poor. Just a few verses later, where very evidently the same topic is under discussion, Jesus states, 'Sell your possessions, and give alms. Make purses for yourselves that do not wear out, an unfailing treasure in heaven, where no thief comes near and no moth destroys' (Luke 12:33). The repetition of themes makes it evident that this is all one discourse concerning our attitudes to wealth and possessions vis-à-vis eternal wealth in the age to come, and Jesus' injunction is clear: 'Sell your possessions, and give alms.' This rich fool has done the complete opposite of all this. Not only has he not divested himself of his possessions, he has sought to gain more. Not only has he failed to give alms, he has in effect taken from the poor by withholding cheap grain from the subsistence farmers that would have surrounded him. He is then the apotheosis of acquisitive greed and Jesus' parable represents a stark rebuke to that stance.[15] As Bruce Longenecker points out, 'It is this acquisitive dimension of poverty and wealth that, when it appears on the scriptural radar, is denounced almost ubiquitously.'[16]

Finally, the parable is a stark reminder that what lies underneath both the exaggerated sense of what the man could achieve by himself and his acquisitive greed is his failure to recognize God. The term 'fool' in verse 20 is no accident, for it is used repeatedly in the Scriptures and the Septuagint to describe those who choose to ignore God. Classically, this is found in Psalm 14:1 'Fools say in their hearts, "There is no God."' Perhaps more obviously, the parable itself makes it clear that it is this ignoring of God that is the underlying issue here. In the final clause, the critique that is offered is that the man in storing up possessions for himself has not been rich towards God. This last phrase is particularly interesting, for what does it mean to be rich towards God? A number of contemporary commentaries state that the point is not so much about wealth per se, but rather in how one uses one's wealth. But ethically, it is hard to distinguish those two aspects. For if one has wealth, then by definition one is at least not using it by giving it away to the poor, one is storing it at least for a period of time. The distinction between having it and using it is questionable. Moreover, it is telling that ancient commentaries on the text, perhaps reflecting their greater familiarity with issues of poverty, are far keener to point out the problems of simply hoarding wealth. So Cyril of Alexandria writes:

> He who is rich toward God is very blessed and has glorious hope. Who is he? . . . It is one whose hand is open to the needs of the poor, comforting the sorrows of those in poverty . . . He gathers in the storehouses that are above and lays up treasures in heaven.[17]

Augustine draws a similar connection:

> The redemption of a man's soul is his richness. This silly fool of a man did not have that kind of riches. Obviously he was not redeeming his soul by giving relief to the poor. He was hoarding perishable crops . . . He was planning to fill his soul with excessive and unnecessary feasting, was proudly disregarding all those empty bellies of the poor. He did not realize that the bellies of the poor were much safer storerooms than his barns.[18]

These ancient commentators, then, seem to be drawing the connection between Luke 12.21, 'be rich towards God', and Luke 12.33, 'sell your possessions and give alms', much more readily than some current commentators. For Augustine and Cyril it is obvious that the way in which we are rich towards God is by building up treasures in heaven, striving for his kingdom, and the way we do that is by serving the poor. Proverbs 14.31 reminds us that 'Those who oppress the poor insult their Maker, but those who are kind to the needy honour him.' In other words, the thrust of this parable is certainly on how the rich man responded to God, but – and this is an important but – the way in which we demonstrate such richness towards God is precisely by prioritizing the needs of the poor above ourselves. This is why 1 John can so easily write, 'How does God's love abide in anyone who has the world's goods and sees a brother or sister in need and yet refuses help? Little children, let us love, not in word or speech, but in truth and action' (1 John 3.17–18).

All of this brings us back full circle. We began by noting that to be created in the image of God means to be created as a community of human flourishing, to be created as a people of shalom. We further saw that to image God means that as a corporate body we image that shalom that is enjoyed within the Godhead among ourselves and in our relations to both God and non-human creation. We conclude, then, by noting that what it means to love God is simply to work towards his kingdom, which in practice means seeking to restore that image which was our original purpose.

In the final summation, the picture of heaven with which we are presented is of a city. Oftentimes, it is thought that what the Scriptures present is a circular motif – we begin in a garden of paradise and that is where we will end. But that is categorically not what is presented. Instead, we begin in a garden and we end in a city. Both are places where we live in sinless community with all of our needs met, but there is a difference. That difference relates to human endeavour. The garden of Eden was not the fruit of our labour, but simply what God provided. A heavenly city represents what has been achieved when we rightly image

God as one body, when all are flourishing and so subduing and stewarding creation as we were meant to do. God has a grand eschatological project that will one day be fulfilled. In the present time, we can work towards it, recognizing Christ's definitive victory that assures it and so building for *his* kingdom.

Notes

1 In saying this, I would seem to be in disagreement with Sean Doherty who suggests that the prevailing eschatological framework in regard to economics is under-realized. This may reflect the fact that Doherty and I have different interlocutors, for of course both frameworks exist among Christian theologians and economists. Either way, Doherty and I are in agreement that some form of inaugurated eschatology that eschews both false idealism and inexpectant realism is appropriate. S. Doherty, 2015, 'The Kingdom of God and the Economic System: An Economics of Hope', in J. Kidwell and S. Doherty, *Theology and Economics*, London: Palgrave Macmillan, pp. 143–56.

2 C. Moe-Lobeda, 2013, *Resisting Structural Evil*, Minneapolis, MN: Fortress Press, p. 154.

3 M. Taylor, 2015, *Christ and Capital: A Family Debate*, Geneva: World Council of Churches, p. 102.

4 'The Christian Hope', 1952, *Ecumenical Review* 5:1, p. 77, cited in Taylor, *Christ and Capital*, p. 103.

5 Taylor, *Christ and Capital*, p. 108.

6 Doherty, 'The Kingdom', p. 148.

7 Doherty, 'The Kingdom', p. 152. I am not sure I would have used the word 'permanent' here, for while Doherty is correct that the transformation is not permanent in the sense that it is incomplete – further transformation is required – it is permanent in the sense that the kingdom that is inaugurated here is *the* kingdom of Christ, not some other one.

8 Doherty, 'The Kingdom', p. 143.

9 D. Bock, 1996, *Luke 9:51–25:53*, Grand Rapids, MI: Baker Books, p. 1362.

10 B. Pitre, 2009, 'Jesus, the Messianic Banquet and the Kingdom of God', *Letter & Spirit* 5, pp. 134–9.

11 J. Green, 1995, *The Theology of the Gospel of Luke*, Cambridge: Cambridge University Press, p. 488.

12 T. Wigg-Stevenson, 2013, *The World is not Ours to Save*, Downers Grove, IL: InterVarsity Press, p. 102.

13 Green, *The Gospel*, p. 491.

14 Green, *The Gospel*, p. 490.

15 For more on the relationship of greed to structural sin from a Latin American perspective, see E. Tamez, 2010, 'Greed and Structural Sin', *Trinity Seminary Review* 31:1, pp. 7–16.

16 B. Longenecker, 2010, *Remember the Poor: Paul, Poverty and the Greco-Roman World*, Grand Rapids, MI: Eerdmans, p. 29.

17 Cyril of Alexandria, 2003, 'Commentary on Luke, Homily 89', in T. Oden (ed.), *Luke: Ancient Christian Commentary on Scripture*, Downers Grove, IL: InterVarsity Press, p. 208.

18 Augustine, 'Sermon 36.9', in Oden, *Luke*, p. 207.

19

Conclusion: the question of equality

The scope of inequality

One of the more obvious facets of our contemporary world is that it is plagued by inequality. In 2013, if you were born in the West African country of Benin you had a life expectancy at birth of 59 years, a probability of dying by age 5 of 85 per 1,000 live births, and a likelihood of just 3 years of schooling ahead of you. By way of contrast, if you had been born in the USA in the same year, your life expectancy was 79, your probability of dying by age 5 just 7 per 1,000 live births, and you could reasonably expect to enjoy 13 years of schooling. It goes without saying that our world is a very unequal place.

Having said that, the statistics around equality, particularly as to whether they are improving or getting worse, are not quite so straightforward. One of the problems is that economic indicators really need to be converted into purchasing power parity (PPP) because what matters is what you can actually buy with your dollar in the local currency. Whether you adopt absolute or relative definitions of poverty and whether you change the absolute definition of poverty can also suddenly bring a whole load of people either in or out of the class 'poor', depending on what your political goal might be. But in addition, there seem to be different trajectories depending on whether you examine economic inequalities within a single country, between different countries or across the globe as a whole.

All of this means that competing claims can be made even when based on the same statistics. In 2012, *The Economist* championed the good news take on poverty when it declared, 'A fall to cheer: for the first time ever, the number of poor people is declining everywhere.'[1] A number of development charities have used these kinds of headlines to argue that what they are doing is effective, that aid works and that we simply need to continue with the current approach. At the same time, others with a different political objective can claim that 'Africans are far worse off today than they were a half century ago. Overall per-capita income is lower today than in the 1970s.'[2] All of this means that, when examining the problem of inequality, one needs to be cautious about what is actually being claimed and on what statistics the claim is based.

For the truth is that inequalities between countries are decreasing, but this is not – at least predominantly not – due to aid being given to the most impoverished countries, but rather due to the economic development of China and India in particular. This means that, globally, there are fewer poor people (defined as living on less than $1.25 dollars per day) than there were 10 or 20 years ago, but aid has not been the primary cause of this, an emergent capitalist economy has. Indeed, if one excludes China from the calculations then the absolute number of people who are poor (less than $1.25 per day) has remained essentially static.[3] At the same time as noting the relative improvement of inequality between countries, there is also mounting evidence of increasing inequality *within* countries. This is true not just of wealthier nations such as the USA, but also of emergent capitalist economies such as China and India.[4]

What this means is that if you want to justify the benefits of capitalism then it is very easy to point to the capitalist development in China and India, and on that basis argue that capitalism is the only effective tool to reduce both poverty and inequality at the global level. However, a more nuanced reading will show that such economic growth has come at the price of worsening inequality within those countries, and that in general economic growth is accompanied by increases in inequality. The only place in which growth does not generate inequality has been in the very specific measure of between-country inequality, although even this has recently been challenged.[5] All other aspects of inequality are worsened by economic growth. As Angus Deaton puts it, 'economic growth has been the engine of international income inequality'.[6] More troubling for those that would defend growth capitalism as the solution to inequality and poverty is the evidence that Foreign Direct Investment (FDI) is the precise mechanism that fosters the inequality by concentrating resources in the hands of a few.[7]

So, for instance, across a range of countries the share of national income taken by the wealthiest 1 per cent has increased significantly over the last 40 years. In Australia, this has gone from 5.6 per cent to 8.3 per cent; in South Korea from 7.5 per cent to 12.2 per cent and in the USA from 8.2 per cent to 18 per cent.[8] In other words, in all these countries, and this applies to a wide range of countries, incomes continue to concentrate at the top end of the distribution. If we examine not just the top 1 per cent of income, but the Gini coefficient for individual countries, a measure that takes account of income across the whole distribution, then the pattern remains the same, that for the vast majority of countries within-country inequality is on the rise, though with the notable exception of much of Latin America.[9] What makes this picture even worse is that, as Thomas Piketty and others have shown, rising inequality is not just about income but perhaps even more so about wealth (i.e. the total assets owned by individuals).[10]

One consequence of all this is that we need to pay far more attention to disaggregated rather than aggregated data. If you explore the issue of poverty at the global or national level, then it is relatively easy to generate, as Jason Hickel would put it, 'a good news narrative'. But if you look in more detail at what is actually happening within countries, then the startling picture is not just that inequality is increasing, but that the poverty headcount might be increasing too. Hickel argues that the standard measure of $1.25 per day is insufficient to achieve basic nutrition and that instead we should adopt what has been called 'the ethical poverty line', a figure that enables people to achieve an average life expectancy of 74 years. If poverty is defined towards the top end of this line at $5 per day then:

> The global poverty headcount is 4.3 billion. And the number has risen considerably over time (even without excluding China), with one billion

additional poor people since 1981, and about 500 million additional poor since the MDG baseline of 1990 . . . These poverty lines suggest that global poverty is much worse than the official narrative would have us believe. Most analysts recognise that the $1.25 line is too low, but it remains in favour at the World Bank and the UN because it is the only line that shows any progress against poverty – at least when you include China. Every other line tells the opposite story.[11]

I am not convinced that the $5 per day line is correct, not least because as I argued earlier in this book I think some kind of multi-dimensional definition of poverty is what is required. But my point is simply to illustrate the fact that a narrative of improving prosperity at national and global levels is not necessarily accurate or helpful. It would be perfectly possible for a nation to have a rising GDP, and yet have 95 per cent of its population in slavery. National GDP is not what matters. It is what is actually happening to our individual brothers and sisters across the globe that matters, and for many of them lives of poverty remain their daily reality, poverty that is compounded by the increasing inequality they see around them.

Does inequality matter?

The question then arises – does any of this matter? After all, maybe, as Grudem and Asmus argue, inequality is the natural result of people having different gifts, talents and luck, and any attempt to rectify this situation simply makes things worse. Yet inequality does matter. In the first place, it matters because it is highlighted as a major concern by a significant majority of people who are poor. A recent Pew Global Attitudes survey revealed that just over 70 per cent of the population in 5 sub-Saharan African countries considered the gap between rich and poor as 'a very big problem', and on average it was considered a 'major challenge' by 60 per cent in the 44 countries surveyed.[12] In addition, it seems as if humans are hard-wired to recognize inequality as unjust.

The ultimatum game is a well-described psychological experiment in which one player receives a sum of money and offers a portion of that money to another player. The second player can then either accept or reject the offer made by the first player. If they reject it, then neither of them gets any money; if they accept it, then they receive whatever is offered and the first player keeps whatever is left. Crucially, the second player is aware of how much money the first player has to distribute. Economic theory would suggest that if we act as rational, utility-maximizing individuals then the first player should always offer the minimum that is allowed under the rules of their particular game (e.g. just one penny if the money is allowed to be segmented to that degree), and the second player should accept any offer above zero, because to do so improves their economic position. In practice, however, when this game is played across a wide range of cultures individuals frequently offer far more generous terms than this, often as much as 50 per cent and responders frequently reject any offer that they perceive to be unfair (ie. less than a 50–50 split), especially if the offer is less than 20 per cent.[13] In other words, even if it will harm them economically, people prefer a situation of equality rather than one of inequality. Unsurprisingly, experimenters have also found that social distance has an impact on how the ultimatum game is played. In one particular experiment, responders decided either for themselves or for a close social contact or a stranger. The investigators found that people are far more likely to tolerate unfairness if it is being experienced by a stranger than if it is being experienced by themselves or a close social contact.[14] We seem not to mind if the world is unfair to others as long as it is not unfair to me or those I know. Of course, one could interpret this phenomenon as support for the moral proximity argument as previously discussed. Instead I would interpret it as an effect of the fall. The fact that we care less for strangers than for those we know is not something to be championed, but something to be wept over. My point, though, in discussing this aspect of economic psychology is that it does seem that there is something within us that cries out for equality, for even in respect of the stranger most participants still rejected very unfair offers. To reiterate, the conclusion to be drawn from the experiment is that we prefer equality even when this harms our own economic position. We are not, thank God, utility-maximizing autonomous individuals, the so-called *homo economicus*, we are in fact created in the image of God as and for community.

There have recently been a large series of national studies demonstrating the impact of inequality on a range of social measures. In their book *The Spirit Level*, Kate Pickett and Richard Wilkinson explore this in relation to psychological health, drug use, life expectancy, obesity levels, educational performance, teenage pregnancy rates, infant mortality, levels of trust and violent crime. They find that inequality impacts all of these measures negatively.[15] While Pickett and Wilkinson have pointed to the social consequences of inequality, Stiglitz, in his book *The Price of Inequality*, has highlighted the economic consequences, arguing that inequality stifles growth, hinders productivity and reduces social mobility. Perhaps most damaging, Stiglitz argues that inequality is not some random outcome of the market, as Grudem and Asmus would appear to suggest, but is rather the deliberate outcome of political policies that facilitate monopolistic behaviour by those who have already become wealthy. In other words, the problem of markets is that they are too easily controlled by those with power to generate even more wealth for themselves. As he says, 'politics have shaped the market, and shaped it in ways that advantage the top at the expense of the rest'.[16]

In addition to all this, and perhaps far more importantly, inequality matters biblically and theologically. In Chapter 12 I pointed out how, in relation to the gift to the Jerusalem church, Paul makes it clear that this is the intention of the gift:

Our desire is not that others might be relieved while you are hard pressed, but that there might be equality. At the present time your plenty will supply what they need, so that in turn their plenty will supply what you need. The goal is equality. (2 Cor. 8.13–14 NIV).

In terms of the Levitical economic codes, Chris Wright points out that the goal was not absolute equality, but simply sufficiency: 'This did not mean that everyone should have the *same*, but that every family should have *enough* – enough to be economically viable.'[17] Similarly, for the Old Testament prophets the intention that lay behind many of their economic precepts was that the society would be fairer, more just. The issue was not simply that the poor suffered a material deprivation – and so life was hard as they sought food, clothing, shelter and so on – but, in addition to this, as Chris Wright comments, 'It was the imbalance in a society that was supposed to be based on covenantal equality and mutual support that most angered the prophets.'[18] There are at least three ways in which inequality works counter to the purposes of God.

First, inequality denies the creation mandate that everyone is to subdue creation. We have already seen in Chapter 1 how this task was given to the whole of humanity. We were to be fruitful and multiply, to bring non-human creation not under dominion but under stewardship, so that we can enjoy a state of mutual flourishing. But in a situation of inequality, this is precisely what does not happen. In a number of capitals in LICs today, gated communities with barbed-wire protection can exist alongside those who are homeless and hungry. This is not the situation of mutual flourishing that is envisaged in the opening chapters of Genesis. It was intended in Genesis that as we mutually support one another we would all steward creation for the benefit of all. But rampant inequality not only points to the fact that some have become subjects rather than stewards of creation, but also that the mutual partnership that humans were meant to achieve is not being realized.

Second, a situation of gross inequality works to deny the relational anthropology that is ours in God. We have previously pointed to the astonishing democratizing effect of the *imago* language. In the ancient world, only the king bore the image of God. Yet, in the pages of Scripture, we have the clear affirmation that everyone – both men and women – bear the divine image. This speaks to an anthropological equality that is unique in the ancient world. Under God, there is no difference. We are all equal. That is what the image of God-language testifies to. And so, when one man has to beg another for a piece of bread, or when one has the power to cause sickness, homelessness, hunger and poverty in another, this is not the equality that the *imago Dei* indicates. If we recall the fact that our identity resides in our relationships, then vast imbalances of wealth and power necessarily damage our identity as being made in the image of God.

Finally, and perhaps most pernicious, inequality fosters sin. Specifically, huge differences in wealth engender pride in the rich and envy in the poor. I have spent much time in this book arguing that justice is evident when right relationships exist. But what is a 'right relationship'? It is a situation when, as a minimum, I seek your flourishing to the same extent as I seek my own. This has to be the implication of Jesus' command that we love others as we love ourselves. But in a situation of gross inequality, this is very hard to achieve, if not impossible. For in such a situation the poor person, perhaps understandably, often desires their own flourishing either at the expense of the rich (we have seen this enough times in the history of revolutionary overthrows) or is likely to desire the oppressive lifestyle that is exhibited by the rich (the incipient consumer capitalism in many LICs is evidence of this). At the same time, the rich person also is unlikely to seek the mutual flourishing of the poor person, for as Stiglitz has pointed out, much of the wealth of the rich has come precisely at the expense of the poor, and therefore to seek your wealth – by paying better wages to one's workers, for instance – directly eats into the wealth that might have accumulated to the rich person. Inequality fosters a zero-sum mentality that says if I win, you lose, and if I lose, you win. It doesn't enable the mutual flourishing that should flow from loving one's neighbour as oneself.

A genuine desire towards mutual flourishing is far easier in a situation of equality rather than inequality. To imagine what such mutual flourishing looks like consider any effective sports team. In such a situation, the individual players are less concerned with their own glory than with how they can bring the best out of one another. They know that they will play best as a team if they play for, rather than against, each other. Indeed, we have all seen sports teams fail – despite the individual talent they possessed – precisely because those individuals refused to play for the collective. The reason good teams work as teams is because they value the contributions that each member of the team provides. In a situation of gross inequality, this is what does not happen. When an oppressive manager considers his staff as merely tools to further his own career and wealth, when a transnational corporation considers its subcontracted workers as merely someone else's responsibility whom it can exploit, then we do not have a situation of mutual flourishing, we do not have one of equality. Gross inequalities prevent functioning teams, and so prevent genuine mutual love to occur. As Walter Wink has argued, 'The gospel of Jesus champions economic equality, because economic inequalities are the basis of domination. Ranking, domination hierarchies, and classism are built on accumulated power provided by excel wealth.'[19]

So what is the solution?

If inequality is extensive, if it matters socially, economically, biblically and theologically, the question that needs to be answered is 'What should we do about it?' In particular, what is the goal that should be pursued? As we have seen, Grudem and Asmus are very clear that the goal is continual economic growth, but not only will that increase inequality and so fail to bring any overall improvement in personal well-being, it will in the long run bring about much environmental destruction that leads to the deaths of millions in LICs. Continual economic growth is simply not a sustainable solution for the whole planet; it is only a solution for a rich minority.

Neither is the solution in some form of collectivist socialism, for that simply brings a different set of injustices. I reject the argument of Grudem and Asmus that our only options are neoliberal capitalism or state collectivism. There is a range of moderating positions that are effective, more just and more sustainable. In this way, my response to the deep-seated problems of inequality is not to argue for absolute equality of outcome. Practically this would be very difficult to achieve and quite possibly unjust in itself for other reasons. More to the point, it is inappropriate for the simple reason that people value different outcomes.

Instead, what most people want is simply the opportunity to flourish, to use their gifts and talents to live a rich and meaningful life. Now, what one person understands as rich and meaningful will be very different to another. And it is here where I think Amartya Sen's concept of capabilities is a very useful addition to development discourse. The freedoms that people have reason to value will vary from individual to individual. I can think of individuals who greatly value being given positions of responsibility. I can think of other individuals who find responsibility a fearful prospect. I know of individuals who want to prioritize being a homemaker and raising children; I can think of other individuals who want to prioritize building status through their careers. Everyone I know wants enough money to feed themselves, pay for shelter, educate their children and obtain good healthcare, but beyond such basic needs people do vary tremendously in how much wealth they even desire. For this reason, even if it were possible, I'm not sure that complete equality of outcome is anywhere near the goal.

At the same time, I'm not even convinced that equality of opportunity – at least as it is often talked about – is the goal. At its most basic, equality of opportunity is the idea that we remove any artificial barriers (such as race, gender, class, sexuality) in making appointments and offering rewards, so that someone's position, role, wages and so on are entirely based on their talents and efforts, not on what are considered extraneous features such as their familial relationships or which school they went to. The idea is increasingly being applied to a wide range of issues that go far beyond formal job offers or conditions, and would include, for instance, school and university admissions, healthcare access and voting rights. Formal or simple equality of opportunity is largely concerned with eliminating direct forms of discrimination. Substantive concepts of equality of opportunity take this further by also addressing indirect forms of discrimination and also seeking to eliminate unfair disadvantages that may impact a candidate's performance. So at the educational institution in which I work various forms of educational support are provided to those with specific educational needs, but at the point of marking assignments everyone is treated equally, for the theory is that the extra educational support has eliminated the disadvantages posed by their additional educational needs.

There are of course a range of practical problems with implementing full equality of opportunity, particularly in its substantive form, and there are even greater difficulties in demonstrating that one has achieved it – with measurement criteria often collapsing into equality of outcome measures. But there are also conceptual problems with equality of opportunity. The first of these is that once again it is very individualistic, for the unit of concern is the individual aspiring to some particular position. It also fails to adequately account (either conceptually or practically) for the impact on the rest of society, including community relations, of ensuring that all forms of direct and indirect discrimination are removed.

However, the broader problem with equality of opportunity discourse is that it assumes a hierarchy of socially desirable goods, whether these be more money or higher status. If we return to the example of the student with educational needs, we can see that this model assumes that higher marks are in some sense desirable. The whole system is predicated on the notion that we must enable this student to achieve as high marks as they can get. While empirically it might well be the case that most students want higher marks, we should not assume that is the case. I work in a UK Christian college where some of our students are of course motivated to study by higher grades; but some are motivated by other factors, such as the love of studying itself, or the value of the studies to their professional ministry.[20] Particularly for those students who are studying with us as a second degree, often the focus is far less on getting as high marks as they can, and instead is on getting as much as possible out of the course that will help them in their day-to-day work. And while our assessments dovetail to some extent with professional ministry, it is impossible for all assessments to be individually tailored to the professional ministry needs of each individual student. Therefore, some courses and some assessments will be less relevant professionally than others. In such a setting, which is more just, to provide a student with educational needs support that will enable them to get the highest marks that are possible, or to provide the student with the support that is required (if any) to get what they desire for their own professional development, or even – if this is their desire – to enjoy the course as much as possible for its own intrinsic interest? As I've indicated, in many courses these goals will overlap, but not in all. So what is justice or fairness in such a situation?

As I've suggested, equality of opportunity language assumes that some outcomes are more desirable than others. But what if, for some individuals in some circumstances, those outcomes are not the ones that are desired? And yet, for other reasons beyond the officially sanctioned purposes, the individual wants to participate in the process. The problem with equality of opportunity is not just that it assumes this hierarchy, but it also provides social and philosophical support for the hierarchy. The current way in which educational support is legislated propagates a system in which high marks and employability are desirable while intrinsic interest is not, for instance; similarly, the current way in which employment legislation requires avoidance of discrimination propagates a system in which high salaries and high status are desirable. But what if valuing status, money and achievement in this way is itself unjust? For there are of course some individuals with severe intellectual deficits who will never achieve high (or even pass) grades in educational assessments irrespective of how much support has been provided. For those individuals, equality of opportunity not only is of no value, but arguably it is also counter-productive, for it foments a system in which they can never play a meaningful part. The same argument can be made in respect of money and status. There are a number of men and women who view their life's calling to raise their family and be a homemaker. For them, this is the highest and greatest achievement that is possible. Yet, they are placed within a society that hardly values that contribution at all, assuming that all such men and women who make that choice are doing so out of necessity rather than choice. The problem here is that equality of opportunity both assumes and then encourages this kind of hierarchy of values – that money is better, that status is better, that educational attainment is better.

Perhaps closer to the mark in terms of the goal to which we should be aspiring is the concept of justice as participation. The key idea behind justice as participation is that everyone is encouraged and supported to play the part in community life that their desires, talents and attributes would indicate. It has been described in this way:

> Justice as participation would mean envisioning and working toward the creation of a global economy whose institutions, rules, and practices permit the healthy participation of persons and nations. This challenge would place strong priority on efforts that seek to eliminate all obstacles and barriers that prevent the marginalized, poor, and all those outside the 'mainstream' of society from having adequate access to those opportunities, institutions, practices, and goods that constitute social life.[21]

As a concept it has been particularly developed by David Hollenbach, and was described in the 1986 pastoral letter *Economic Justice for All*, written by the United States Conference of Catholic Bishops, which had been influenced greatly by Hollenbach.[22] The bishops had written that 'justice demands that social institutions be ordered in a way that guarantees all persons the ability to participate actively in the economic, political, and cultural life of society'.[23] Hollenbach has said:

> To be a person is to be a *member* of society, active within it in many ways, through diverse sets of relationships . . . When persons face hunger, home-lessness and the extremes of poverty and society fails to allocate its resources to meet their needs, in effect the poor are being treated as non-members.[24]

The emphasis, then, on justice as participation is in the way in which *all* members of society are to make a meaningful contribution to that society. It recognizes that the way in which the current economic order is structured at global, national and local levels prevents many people from participating as they would wish. And one of the crucial insights of Hollenbach, drawing on work by Michael Walzer, is that what participation looks like, and therefore what justice demands, is variegated depending on the particular type of community to which admission is sought.

> The criteria of membership, of course, are different for different kinds of communities, and therefore the criteria of justice will vary from one zone of life to another. Justice has a plurality of meanings because we have many kinds of relationships in our lives. In some of them, such as the political community, a standard of strict equality applies: One person, one vote. In others, the criterion of merit is relevant; the grading of exams is a case in point. In still other areas, need is the relevant measure. Parents do not do justice to their children if they treat one who is physically disabled in an identical way with one who is not.

> Respect for the richness of social life, therefore, calls for a nuanced and differentiated understanding of the meaning of justice. A single criterion, such as need or merit, administered by a single institution, such as the government or the market, betrays the rich and complex reality of social existence.[25]

There is much in the concept of justice as participation that is to be admired. In particular, while sharing much ideological space with the concept of equal opportunities and at times explicitly building on such language, its emphasis would appear to be on the positive participation of *everyone* rather than merely the removal of barriers for certain, predetermined values or goals. Perhaps it should be thought of as equality of opportunity at its best or most ideal. In addition, justice as participation would also seem to have this emphasis on the variegated nature of justice, that what it means for one person to participate may be entirely different to another person, and therefore the standard of justice that is applied also needs to be different. This is a useful and necessary insight.

But having said all this, there are still areas where I do not think justice as participation is quite articulating an adequate response to the problem of inequality. One of its problems is that the concept of justice as participation, at least as articulated by Hollenbach and the Catholic bishops, is that it still tends to view only one section of the population as being excluded and marginalized. The framework they are operating with would seem to be one in which there is a particular state of affairs, what Krueger termed the 'mainstream', and which is what rich, white, healthy people have reason to value and undertake. Justice as participation would seem do define 'participation' as being part of that particular society, albeit in varied forms. So the Catholic bishops write:

> The poor, the disabled, and the unemployed too often are simply left behind. This pattern is even more severe beyond our borders in the least-developed countries. Whole nations are prevented from fully participating in the international economic order because they lack the power to change their disadvantaged position.[26]

In saying this, the bishops would appear to be normalizing what the 'developed' countries do or what the rich, able-bodied, employed do, and set that as the standard to which all should aspire. But why should that be the case? One of the most interesting aspects of the disability literature is that some who are considered disabled do not consider themselves in that way at all. Rather, they simply view society as having been constructed to suit a particular view of ability. Alternative ways to structure society would be possible, and if society was structured that way their so-called 'disability' would not even be recognized.[27] Black theologians have done much to challenge the concept of white normativity, and it seems to me that a similar economic conscientization is required here. Why should wealth or consumer capitalism be considered the ideal to which everyone aspires? As we have previously argued earlier in this book, we need to allow other nations and other individuals to define their own path of progress.

In addition, justice as participation fails to appreciate that the rich, white, consumer capitalist is also trapped in a cycle of destruction, albeit a different one to the rest of the global population. In this book we have previously spoken about what Ignatius Swart calls a 'double movement' towards both the rich and the poor, Tissa Balasuriya 'the liberation of the affluent', and Rowan

Williams our 'toxic and unjust situation in which we, the prosperous, are less than human'.[28] And as Shane Claiborne rightly points out, the problem with the rich young ruler was not that he had everything, but rather that he lacked something.[29] What all these authors are getting at is that it is not just the poor and powerless who are failing to flourish, but also the rich and powerful. To reprise what I have previously articulated, we are guilty of ethnocentrism if we think that it is the poor who have a problem, and we – the rich world – have the solution, irrespective of whether we think that solution is more consumer capitalism, more aid or even a reformed, more benevolent capitalism. This paradigm insufficiently recognizes that we in the rich world have a problem too. It might well be a different problem to those in the economically poorer parts of the world, but it is still a problem from which we need deliverance. A true theological anthropology recognizes that we are being fully human, fully imaging the creator God, not merely when we have subdued creation, but perhaps especially when we exist in a network of right relationships in which all of us are mutually flourishing.

In this book, I have been trying to argue for a theological anthropology that says that none of us are fully imaging God until we are *all* imaging God. Indeed, we represent God as we are meant to only when collectively we are all mutually flourishing. In this sense, the call to participation should not be some more socially conscious version of the modernization thesis: come and join us at this place where we have arrived. Rather, the call to participation should we one in which everyone encourages everyone in mutual participation and mutual flourishing whatever the nature of that flourishing. Therefore, the current global poor have much to teach the consumer, capitalist world about Sabbath economics and living within the limits of what our planet can sustain; and in this way they can liberate us from the consumer dependency to which we are addicted. At the same time, there are many ways in which HICs can more effectively support LICs to enable them to more effectively subdue the creation around them so that they are not subject to creation in hunger, disease and death, but rather become stewards of that creation as they are meant to be.

Finally, my role as a citizen of this planet is not merely to pursue my own ends and desires while ensuring I don't get in the way of you pursuing yours. Rather, my role – theologically speaking – is to love you to the same extent that I love myself, which means that I am called to help and enable you to flourish as much as I seek my own flourishing, while at the same time you do the same for me. This, it seems to me, is the picture of mutual flourishing that the Scriptures hold out for us. Flourishing does not consist in a crass equality of outcomes (for we desire and are suited to different ends), but neither does in consist in a formal equality of opportunity (for who says that the rich world is the ideal), but rather consists in mutual flourishing as each one of us pursues and realizes the distinct ends to which each of us is called, while actively supporting and facilitating others to pursue their ends. In other words, the right goal is that each of us in the whole of this planet and for generations to come be the people that God is calling us to be in mutual and loving support of one another. Or, as Bruce Longenecker has put it in reflecting on the Pauline texts, 'Not communism, not charity, but community,'[30] for that is where the image of God is to be found.

Notes

1 'A Fall to Cheer', 2012, *The Economist*, 3 March. Available at: www.economist.com/node/21548963 (accessed 14 July 2016).

2 This claim is simply wrong, however you analyse the data. No source is provided in the book for it. R. Lupton, 2011, *Toxic Charity*, New York: HarperCollins, p. 3.

3 J. Hickel, 2016, 'The True Extent of Global Poverty and Hunger: Questioning the Good News Narrative of the Millennium Development Goals', *Third World Quarterly* 37:5, pp. 5–6. A. Deaton, 2013, *The Great Escape: Health, Wealth and the Origins of Inequality*, Princeton, NJ: Princeton University Press, pp. 44–6.

4 J. Verbeek, 2015, 'Increasingly, Inequality Within, Not Across, Countries is Rising'. Available at: http://blogs.worldbank.org/developmenttalk/increasingly-inequality-within-not-across-countries-rising (accessed 17 July 2016).

5 K. Bosmans, K. Decanq and A. Decoster, 2014, 'The Relativity of Decreasing Inequality between Countries', *Economica* 81:322, pp. 276–92.

6 Deaton, *The Great Escape*, p. 5.

7 J. Cypher, 2014, *The Process of Economic Development*, 4th edn, Oxford: Routledge, p. 552.

8 F. Alvaredo, T. Atkinson, T. Piketty, E. Saez and G. Zucman, *The World Wealth and Income Database*. Available at: www.wid.world/#Home (accessed 14 July 2016).

9 World Bank Data. Available at: http://data.worldbank.org/indicator/SI.POV.GINI (accessed 19 July 2016).

10 T. Piketty, 2013, *Capital in the Twenty-First Century*, Cambridge, MA: Harvard University Press.

11 Hickel, 'The True Extent', p. 7.

12 'Emerging and Developing Economies Much More Optimistic than Rich Countries about the Future', 2014, Pew Research Center. Available at: www.pewglobal.org/2014/10/09/emerging-and-developing-economies-much-more-optimistic-than-rich-countries-about-the-future/ (accessed 20 July 2016).

13 J. Henrich, 2000, 'Does Culture Matter in Economic Behaviour? Ultimatum Game Bargaining among the Machiguenga of the Peruvian Amazon', *The American Economic Review* 90:4, p. 974.

14 H. Kim, S. Schnall, D.-J. Yi and M. White, 2013, 'Social Distance Decreases Responders' Sensitivity to Fairness in the Ultimate Game', *Judgement and Decision Making* 8:5, pp. 632–8.

15 K. Pickett and R. Wilkinson, 2009, *The Spirit Level: Why More Equal Societies Almost Always Do Better*, London: Allen Lane.

16 J. Stiglitz, 2012, *The Price of Inequality: How Today's Divided Society Endangers Our Future*, New York: Norton & Co., pp. xix–xx.

17 C. Wright, 2004, *Old Testament Ethics for the People of God*, Nottingham: InterVarsity Press, p. 157.

18 Wright, *Old Testament Ethics*, p. 175.

19 W. Wink, 1992, *Engaging the Powers*, Minneapolis, MN: Fortress Press, p. 113.

20 J. Thacker, 2015, 'Motivation among UK Bible College Students', unpublished presentation delivered as part of the requirements for the Post-graduate Certificate in Learning and Teaching in Higher Education, Sheffield Hallam University.

21 D. Krueger, 1995, 'Can Christian Ethics Inform Business Practice? A Typological Road Map and Criteria of Adequacy for an Ethic of Capitalism', in S. Natale and B. Rothschild (eds), *Work Values: Education, Organization and Religious Concerns*, Amsterdan: Rodopi, p. 65.

22 D. Hollenbach, 1988, 'Justice as Participation: Public Moral Discourse and the U.S. Economy', in C. Reynolds and R. V. Norman (eds), *Community in America: The Challenge of Habits of the Heart*, Berkeley, CA: University of California Press, pp. 217–29; *Economic Justice for All*, 1986, Washington, DC: United States Conference of Catholic Bishops. Available at: www.usccb.org/upload/economic _justice_for_all.pdf (accessed 6 August 2016). See also K. Ahern, M. Clark, K. Heyer and L. Johnston (eds), 2016, *Public Theology and the Global Common Good: The Contribution of David Hollenbach*, Maryknoll, NY: Orbis Books.

23 *Economic Justice*, p. 19.

24 Hollenbach, 'Justice', p. 227.

25 Hollenbach, 'Justice', p. 226

26 *Economic Justice*, p. 18.

27 See, for instance, D. Creamer, 2009, *Disability and Christian Theology*, New York: Oxford University Press; A. Yong, 2011, *The Bible, Disability and the Church*, Grand Rapids, MI: Eerdmans.

28 I. Swart, 2008, 'Meeting the Challenge of Poverty and Exclusion: The Emerging Field of Development Research in South African Practical Theology', *International Journal of Practical Theology* 12:1, January, p. 134; T. Balasuriya, 2002, 'Liberation of the Affluent', *Black Theology: An International Journal* 1:1, p. 112; R. Williams, 'A Theology of Development', p. 5. Available at: http:// clients.squareeye.net.

29 S. Claiborne, 2006, *The Irresistible Revolution*, Grand Rapids, MI: Zondervan, p. 103.

30 B. Longenecker, 2010, *Remember the Poor: Paul, Poverty and the Greco-Roman World*, Grand Rapids, MI: Eerdmans, p. 287.

Epilogue

What does this mean in practice?

For those left wondering what all of this means in practice, I can do no better than reproduce in abbreviated form the recommendations of the Tearfund *Restorative Economy* report. For full details of these recommendations see their report.[1]

Individual recommendations

1 Live within our fair share of the world's resources and environmental limits

Food: Everything we eat has been produced using land, water and other inputs such as fertilizers and fuel (to transport it to our tables). Some types of food are more resource intensive than others, with *meat and dairy often the most intensive*, including in terms of their greenhouse gas emissions. Cutting down on these types of food – and, crucially, *wasting less* – will help leave more 'environmental space' for others around the world, and keep food prices within reach of poor consumers.

Travel: This relates to whether you drive a car, how far you drive and your car's engine size and fuel type; how much you use trains or buses, or whether you cycle or walk instead; and – above all – how many flights you take. A single return economy class flight from London to New York emits more than half of one person's annual sustainable carbon allowance, at the equivalent of 1.06 tonnes of CO_2 per passenger. *Flying less is one of the single biggest steps you can take towards reducing your carbon footprint*, and it's also one of the strongest ways of sending a message to friends, family and colleagues that you think climate change is real and urgent, and that you're willing to make sacrifices to help stop it.

Home: Here, the biggest variable is how much energy you use – and where that energy comes from. A huge part of tackling climate change is de-carbonizing our electricity system, so if you *switch to a renewable energy supplier*, especially one that promises to use your custom to invest in new renewable-generating capacity, then this transforms your electricity use from being part of the problem to being part of the solution. Of course, for many of us, electricity does not heat our homes or provide hot water: we rely on gas or heating oil instead.

This is why it is also important to think about *energy efficiency measures*, such as insulation, condensing boilers and double glazing. You can also consider *generating renewable energy yourself, from ground- or air-source heat pumps, a wood-fired boiler (or stoves), or solar water heating*: government grants are available in many cases, sometimes worth thousands of pounds.

Stuff: This word covers everything from purchases of goods (especially big ticket items such as furniture, white goods, electronics and clothes) through to recycling and composting. Reducing your footprint in this area requires a change of mindset: we need to distinguish ourselves from a culture that says 'we are what we buy' and instead consume less. For example, although turning off the tap while you brush your teeth might save a litre or two of water, choosing not to buy a t-shirt will save 2,500 litres, the amount needed to grow the cotton to create the shirt. [The website www.ethicalconsumer.org is a great place to help in making these decisions.]

2 Respond to poverty and inequality with radical generosity

While many people don't earn enough to make ends meet or to be able to support their families, many of us are fortunate enough to earn or own more than we really need for the essentials of life. Many people already tithe (i.e. give away one-tenth of their income), including many Christians, given tithing's clear biblical basis (e.g. Num. 18.30; Deut. 14.23; 26.12–14); the practice is also growing in popularity more broadly as a basis for charitable giving.

Ultimately, though, we think we should aspire to a higher standard than just tithing. Jesus commends the widow in Mark 12.41–44 not because of how much she gives in absolute terms, but because what she gives is such *a high proportion of her income*. In Matthew 23.23, he observes that while the Pharisees do tithe, they have 'neglected the more important matters of the law: justice and mercy and faith'. Throughout the Gospels, Jesus insists that 'life does not consist in an abundance of possessions' (Luke 12.15) and encourages radical generosity. So while we strongly support tithing, we would ultimately argue that each of us should work towards a higher standard, even giving away all income above the level that we actually need.

3 Speak out prophetically

Previous movements marched, sang and opted out of systems that they felt embodied the injustice they were fighting – from the bus boycotts in Montgomery, Alabama, in 1955 and 1956, to the refusal of Gandhi's followers to pay the stringent British salt tax. This is a tradition stretching right back to the furious denunciations of injustice by Old Testament prophets such as Ezekiel and Jeremiah. It's one that is alive and well in Jesus' ministry too, for example when he turns the money-changers out of the Temple (Matt. 21.12).

Christians have often been adept at harnessing the power of protest and political theatre in our own times. For example, Christians have helped force issues such as developing world debt relief onto the political agenda, have been at the forefront of 'shareholder activism' (including taking action against a payday lender), have used boycotts to protest against companies, and have used worship as a form of protest or silent witness against injustice.

4 Use our power as a voter, a citizen and a consumer

Previously, we said that one of the key determinants of a movement's success is clear and actionable demands that can be used to bring influence to bear on the ballot box. So we think that, if individuals are to bring about the transformational change that is the aspiration of this report, they need to work towards having a clear, succinct list of policy asks that they can use to gauge political parties and present to politicians as the price of their support at election time.

At the same time, there's much that we can achieve through the power we exert when we make decisions about what to buy and how to invest. Many companies are increasingly focused on reputational issues. Given their own power as purchasers, they themselves are increasingly able to drive change throughout supply chains – if they perceive that there is strong demand for it from their consumers. So buying ethically does matter – from Fairtrade-approved items such as coffee or chocolate, to environmentally certified goods such as Marine Stewardship Council-approved fish or Forest Stewardship Council-accredited wood and timber.

Socially responsible investment, meanwhile, is also becoming increasingly significant. In the United States, for example, total assets in 'socially screened' portfolios were worth $5.67 trillion at the start of 2014 – a 76 per cent increase since 2012. One in six dollars under professional management in the US is now involved in socially responsible investing. *We think that there's particular potential for Christians to build on this by leading the charge on pushing our pension fund managers to pull out of fossil fuel investments.* You can start by writing to your pension fund manager and asking how much of your pension is invested in coal, oil and other fossil fuels, and how much is invested in renewables, as this information is not always publicly available.

5 Live restoratively and prioritize relationships

Finally, and perhaps most importantly of all, we must each do all we can to restore the broken relationships we see around us. This form of poverty is not limited to poor countries: it is also found right on our doorsteps. But the reality is that many of our day-to-day interactions with those who need help do more to reinforce broken identities than restore them. Instead, we need to see these interactions as opportunities to affirm the dignity of someone who is made in the image of God, and is thus worthy of the same level of respect, dignity and love.

Truly transformational development should restore the identities of both giver and receiver. As Jean Vanier, founder of L'Arche Communities – a global federation of homes, programmes and support networks involving people who have learning disabilities – asserts, 'The strong need the weak,' as much as vice versa. For example, many of the so-called 'weak' have much to teach the 'strong' about vulnerability, love and 'finding strength in weakness'.

Some of us have spare time, and we can use this to huge restorative effect by volunteering – as foster parents, as mentors for young people, as friends for lonely older people, as advisers at Citizens' Advice Bureaux, as helpers for newly arrived refugees, or in thousands of other ways in which we can become the 'living sacrifices' (Rom. 12.1) that God wants us to be.

Policy recommendations[2]

1 **Create a circular economy** through powerful incentives for resource efficiency and ensuring that nothing goes to landfill, and that instead everything is reused over and over again, in keeping with God's design principles in nature.

2 **Double food production and halve resource intensity with a twenty-first-century Green Revolution,** above all in Africa, where crop yields are far lower than the rest of the world – by making the sustainable increase of agricultural productivity a top priority in Britain's international aid programme.

3 **Accelerate the shift to a 'zero-carbon' economy,** in particular by banning coal-fired power generation by the early 2020s, ending fossil fuel subsidies including the reduced rate of VAT for electricity and gas, and introducing mandatory carbon stress-testing for pension funds and institutional investors.

4 **Agree a carbon jubilee** by defining a safe global emissions budget that keeps the world to 1.5°C of warming. This budget should be shared between countries in proportion to their populations, on a per capita basis – recognizing that the sky belongs to God, not us, and that this would create a major new source of development finance – from trade, not aid.

5 **Allow poor people everywhere to meet their basic needs by introducing a global social protection floor,** including healthcare, education, nutrition and basic income security. In the case of the poorest or most fragile countries, the funding for this will need to be raised internationally.

6 **Make the UK a world leader in ensuring markets work for poor people around the world.** While retaining the UK's commitment to spending 0.7 per cent of national income on aid, buttress this with a stronger focus on helping developing countries create environments in which the private sector can flourish.

7 Go much further in tackling international tax avoidance, increasing developing countries' capacity to finance their own development from their own tax revenue, and doing much more to help them recover stolen assets from abroad.

8 Adopt a jubilee stance on inequality by implementing measures that give modern-day expression to the principles behind the jubilee reset of land ownership. For example, this could be through stronger and fairer taxation of property (via a land value tax) and of wealth transfers (via replacing traditional inheritance tax with a wealth receipts tax).

9 Ensure that the financial sector contributes to shared prosperity – and doesn't jeopardize it. In particular, we need to reduce the capacity for unsustainable levels of debt (or leverage) to build up, for example by radically raising reserve requirements for banks, or creating a new maximum leverage target for the financial system as a whole.

10 Rebalance the tax system in line with jubilee principles by shifting more of the burden of taxation onto activities we want to *discourage* (such as carbon emissions, pollution, waste or the excessive concentration of wealth), and away from those activities we want to encourage (such as work).

Notes

1 A. Evans and R. Gower, 2015, *The Restorative Economy*, London: Tearfund, p. 7. Available at: www.tearfund.org/en/about_you/campaign/report/ (accessed 16 June 2016). See also the recommendations in Tearfund's more recent circular economy report, R. Gower and P. Schröder, 2016, *Virtuous Circle: How the Circular Economy Can Create Jobs and Save Lives in Low and Middle-Income Countries*, London: Tearfund.

2 These are specifically targeted to the UK, but are illustrative of changes that could be made worldwide.

Bibliography

Books, papers and articles

D. Agbiboa, 2014, 'Under-Development in Practice: Nigeria and the Enduring Problem of Corruption', *Development in Practice* 24:3.

M. Aguilar, 2013, 'The Hermeneutics of Bones: Liberation Theology for the Twenty-First Century', in T. Cooper (ed.), *The Reemergence of Liberation Theologies*, New York: Palgrave Macmillan.

K. Ahern, M. Clark, K. Heyer and L. Johnston (eds), 2016, *Public Theology and the Global Common Good: The Contribution of David Hollenbach*, Maryknoll, NY: Orbis Books.

M. S. Alam, 2000, *Poverty from the Wealth of Nations*, London: Macmillan.

F. Alvaredo, T. Atkinson, T. Piketty, E. Saez and G. Zucman, *The World Wealth and Income Database*. Available at: www.wid.world/#Home.

K. Anatolios, 2011, *Retrieving Nicaea: The Development and Meaning of Trinitarian Doctrine*, Grand Rapids, MI : Baker.

G. O. Anie, 2004, 'Christian Theology of Work: Its Implications for Nation-Building in Nigeria', *Ogbomoso Journal of Theology*, 1 December.

J. K. Asamoah-Gyadu, 2010, 'From "Calvary Road" to "Harvesters International": An African Perspective on the Cross and Gospel of Prosperity', advance paper for 2010 Lausanne Global Conversation, Cape Town. Available at: www.lausanne. org.

T. Balasuriya, 2002, 'Liberation of the Affluent', *Black Theology: An International Journal* 1:1, pp. 83–113.

D. Balia, 2009, *Make Corruption History*, London: SPCK.

A. Banerjee and E. Duflo, 2011, *Poor Economics*, London: Penguin.

A. Barrera, 2013, *Biblical Economic Ethics*, Plymouth: Lexington Books.

K. Bediako, 1996, 'Theological Refle ctions', in T. Yamamori, B. Myers, K. Bediako and L. Reed (eds), *Serving with the Poor in Africa*, Monrovia, CA: MARC Publications.

B. Beltran, 1998, 'Towards a Theology of Holistic Ministry', in T. Yamamori, B. Myers and K. Luscombe (eds), *Serving with the Urban Poor*, Monrovia, CA: MARC Publications.

Benedict XVI, 2009, *Caritas in Veritate*.

P. Berger, 2010, 'Max Weber is Alive and Well, and Living in Guatemala: The Protestant Ethic Today', *The Review of Faith and International Affairs* 8:4, pp. 3–9.

P. Bickley, 2015, *The Problem of Proselytism*, London: Theos.

P. Biddle, 'The Problem with Little White Girls (and Boys): Why I Stopped Being a Voluntourist'. Available at: http://pippabiddle.com.

J. Bimson, 2006, 'Reconsidering a 'Cosmic Fall'', *Science and Christian Belief*, 18:1.

P. Blezien, 2004, 'The Impact of Summer International Short-Term Missions Experiences on the Cross-Cultural Sensitivity of Undergraduate College Student Participants', dissertation, Azusa, CA: Azusa Pacific University.

H. Blocher, 1984, *In the Beginning*, Leicester: InterVarsity Press.

H. Blocher, 2000, *Original Sin*, Westmont, IL: InterVarsity Press Academic.

C. Blomberg, 1999, *Neither Poverty Nor Riches*, Leicester: Apollos.

D. Bock, 1996, *Luke 9:51–25:53*, Grand Rapids, MI: Baker Books.

A. Boesak, 2015, *Kairos, Crisis, and Global Apartheid: The Challenge to Prophetic Resistance*, New York: Palgrave Macmillan.

L. Boff and C. Boff, 1987, *Introducing Liberation Theology*, Maryknoll, NY: Orbis Books.

J. Bonk, 2006, *Missions and Money*, Maryknoll, NY: Orbis Books.

D. Bosch, 2011, *Transforming Mission: Paradigm Shifts in Theology of Mission*, Marynoll, NY: Orbis Books.

K. Bosmans, K. Decanq and A. Decoster, 2014, 'The Relativity of Decreasing Inequality between Countries', *Economica* 81:322.

A. Bradley and A. Lindsley (eds), 2014, *For the Least of These: A Biblical Answer to Poverty*, Grand Rapids, MI: Zondervan.

L. Bretherton, 2015, 'Poverty, Politics, and Faithful Witness in the Age of Humanitarianism', *Interpretation: A Journal of Bible and Theology* 69:4.

B. Brock, 2015, 'Globalisation, Eden and the Myth of Original Markets', *Studies in Christian Ethics* 28:4.

W. Brueggemann, 1997, *Theology of the Old Testament: Testimony, Dispute, Advocacy*, Minneapolis, MN: Fortress Press.

A Call to Commitment and Partnership: A World Evangelical Alliance Brief on the Evangelical Community and Humanitarian Development, 31 July 2015.

A Call to Prophetic Action: Zimbabwean Kairos Document, 1998, Harare: Ecumenical Support Services.

W. T. Cavanaugh, 2008, *Being Consumed*, Grand Rapids, MI: Eerdmans.

S. Chalke and A. Mann, 2004, *The Lost Message of Jesus*, Grand Rapids, MI: Zondervan.

M. Chaney, 2014, 'The Political Economy of Peasant Poverty: What the Eighth-Century Prophets Presumed but Did Not State', *Journal of Religion and Society* 10, pp. 34–60.

S. Claiborne, 2006, *The Irresistible Revolution*, Grand Rapids, MI: Zondervan.

M. Clarke, 2012, *Mission and Development: God's Work or Good Works?* London: Continuum.

P. Clifford, 2010, *Theology and International Development*, London: Christian Aid.

D. Clough, 2012, *On Animals: Volume 1, Systematic Theology*, London: T & T Clark.

The Code of Conduct for the International Red Cross and Red Crescent Movement and Non-Governmental Organisations (NGOs) in Disaster Relief, 1994, Geneva: IFRC, clause 3. Available at: www.ifrc.org.

J. Colwell (ed.), 2000, *Called to One Hope: Perspectives on Life to Come*, Carlisle: Paternoster.

A. Constanzo (ed.), 2001 [1745], *The Interesting Narrative of the Life of Olaudah Equiano*, Ontario: Broadview Literary Texts.

T. Cooper, 2007, *Controversies in Political Theology: Development or Liberation?* London: SCM Press.

S. Corbett and B. Fikkert, 2009, *When Helping Hurts*, Chicago, IL: Moody Publishers.

C. Cosgrove, 2002, *Appealing to Scripture in Moral Debate: Five Hermeneutical Rules*, Grand Rapids, MI: Eerdmanns.

A. Costello *et al.*, 2009, 'Managing the Health Effects of Climate Change', *Lancet* 373.

D. Creamer, 2009, *Disability and Christian Theology*, New York: Oxford University Press.

R. Culpeper and N. Kappagoda, 2016, 'The new face of developing country debt', *Third World Quarterly* 37:6.

J. Cypher, 2014, *The Process of Economic Development*, 4th edn, Oxford: Routledge.

S. Dailey, 2008, *Myths from Mesopotamia*, rev. edn, Oxford: Oxford University Press.

R. Das, 2016, *Compassion and the Mission of God*, Carlisle: Langham Global Partnership.

R. Davis, 2009, 'What about Justice? Toward an Evangelical Perspective on Advocacy in Development', *Transformation: An International Journal of Holistic Mission Studies* 26:2.

A. Deaton, 2013, *The Great Escape: Health, Wealth and the Origins of Inequality*, Princeton, NJ: Princeton University Press.

S. de Gruchy, 2008, 'Christian Leadership in "Another Country": Contributing to an Ethical Development Agenda in South Africa Today', in S. de Gruchy, N. Koopman and S. Strijbos (eds), *From Our Side: Emerging Perspectives on Development and Ethics*, Amsterdam: Rozenberg Publishers, pp. 9–20.

A. de Janvry and E. Sadoulet, 2016, *Development Economics: Theory and Practice*, London: Routledge.

S. Deneulin and L. Shahani (eds), 2009, *An Introduction to the Human Development and Capability Approach: Freedom and Agency*, London: Earthscan.

S. Deneulin, 2013, 'Christianity and International Development: An Overview', in M. Clarke, *Handbook of Research on Development and Religion*, Cheltenham: Edward Elgar.

V. Desai and R. Potter, 2014, *The Companion to Development Studies*, 3rd edn, Oxford: Routledge.

S. Doherty, 2015, 'The Kingdom of God and the Economic System: An Economics of Hope', in J. Kidwell and S. Doherty, *Theology and Economics*, London: Palgrave Macmillan, pp. 143–56.

J. Donahue, 2004, *Seek Justice that You May Live*, Mahwah, NJ: Paulist Press.

E. Donnelly, 2001, *Heaven and Hell*, Glasgow: Banner of Truth Trust.

H. Doucouliagos and T. D. Stanley, 2009, 'Publication Selection Bias in Minimum-Wage Research? A Meta-Regression Analysis', *British Journal of Industrial Relations* 47:2.

U. Duchrow and F. Hinkelammert, 2004, *Property for People, Not for Profit*, Geneva: World Council of Churches.

S. Durber, 2016, *Putting God to Rights: A Theological Reflection on Human Rights*, London: Christian Aid.

E. Dussel, 2003, 'Exodus as a Paradigm in Liberation Theology', in E. Mendieta (ed.), *Beyond Philosophy: Ethics, History, Marxism, and Liberation Theology*, New York: Rowman and Littlefield.

W. Easterly, 2006, *The White Man's Burden*, Oxford: Oxford University Press.

D. Edwards, 1988, *Evangelical Essentials*, Downers Grove, IL: InterVarsity Press.

J. Elkington, 1997, *Cannibals with Forks: The Triple Bottom Line of 21st Century Business*, Oxford: Capstone.

C. Elliot, 1987, *Comfortable Compassion*, London: Hodder & Stoughton.

'Emerging and Developing Economies Much More Optimistic than Rich Countries about the Future', Washington, DC: Pew Research Center. Available at: www.pewglobal.org.

G. Esteva, 1992, 'Development', in W. Sachs (ed.), *The Development Dictionary*, London: Zed Books.

A. Evans and R. Gower, 2015, *The Restorative Economy*, London: Tearfund. Available at: www.tearfund.org/en/about_you/campaign/report/.

D. Fanning, 2009, 'Short Term Missions: A Trend that is Growing Exponentially', *Trends and Issues in Missions*, Paper 4.

E. Farisani, 2003, 'The Use of Ezra-Nehemiah in a Quest for an African Theology of Reconstruction', *Journal of Theology for Southern Africa* 116, July.

D. Fergusson, 2014, *Creation*, Grand Rapids, MI: Eerdmans.

Francis, 2013, *Evangelii Gaudium*.

D. Freeman, 2012, 'The Pentecostal Ethic and the Spirit of Development', in D. Freeman (ed.), *Pentecostalism and Development*, New York: Palgrave Macmillan, pp. 1–37.

D. Freeman, 2012, 'Development and the Rural Entrepreneur: Pentecostals, NGOs and the Market in the Gamo Highlands, Ethiopia', in D. Freeman (ed.), *Pentecostalism and Development*, New York: Palgrave Macmillan, pp. 159–80.

D. Freeman (ed.), 2012, *Pentecostalism and Development*, New York: Palgrave Macmillan.

T. Friedman, 2005, *The World is Flat: A Brief History of the Twenty-First Century*, New York: Farrar, Straus and Giroux.

S. Friesen, 2004, 'Poverty in Pauline Studies', *Journal for the Study of the New Testament* 26:3.

F. Fukuyama, 2011, *The Origins of Political Order: From Prehuman Times to the French Revolution*, New York: Farrar, Straus and Giroux.

R. Gaffin, 2012, 'The Redemptive-Historical View', in S. E. Porter and B. M. Stovell (eds), *Biblical Hermeneutics: Five Views*, Downers Grove, IL: InterVarsity Press Academic.

J. Gathogo, 2007, 'A Survey on an African Theology of Reconstruction', *Swedish Missiological Themes* 5:2.

J. Gathogo, 2008, 'The Tasks in African Theology of Reconstruction', *Swedish Missiological Themes* 96:2.

D. George, 2001, 'Changing the Face of Poverty: Representations of Poverty in Nonprofit Appeals', in J. Trimbur (ed.), *Popular Literacy*, Pittsburgh, PA: Pittsburgh University Press.

P. Gifford, 2015, *Christianity, Development and Modernity in Africa*, London: Hurst & Co.

J. Glas, 2015, 'The Gospel, Human Flourishing and the Foundation of Social Order', *The Southern Baptist Journal of Theology* 19:2.

P. Gooder, 2014, *Thirty Pieces of Silver: An Exploration of Corruption, Bribery, Transparency and Justice in the Christian Scriptures*, London: Bible Society.

D. Gowan, 1987, 'Wealth and Poverty in the Old Testament: The Case of the Widow, the Orphan, and the Sojourner', *Interpretation* 41:4, October.

R. Gower and P. Schröder, 2016, *Virtuous Circle: How the Circular Economy can Create Jobs and Save Lives in Low and Middle-Income Countries*, London: Tearfund.

G. Green, 2002, *The Letters to the Thessalonians*, Grand Rapids, MI: Eerdmans, 2002.

J. Green, 1994, 'Good News to Whom?', in J. Green and M. Turner, *Jesus of Nazareth Lord and Christ*, Grand Rapids, MI: Eerdmans.

J. Green, 1995, *The Theology of the Gospel of Luke*, Cambridge: Cambridge University Press.

W. Grudem and B. Asmus, 2013, *The Poverty of Nations: A Sustainable Solution*, Wheaton, IL: Crossway Books.

G. Gutiérrez, 1969, 'The Meaning of Development', in *In Search of a Theology of Development*, papers from a Consultation on Theology and Development held by SODEPAX in Cartigny, Switzerland, Geneva: SODEPAX.

G. Gutiérrez, 1990, *The Truth Shall Make You Free*, Marynoll, NY: Orbis Books.

G. Gutiérrez, 2001, *A Theology of Liberation*, London: SCM Press.

D. A. Hagner, 1995, *Word Biblical Commentary: Matthew 1–13*, Dallas: Word Books.

R. Hanger, 2014, 'No Visitor Comes Empty Handed: Some Thoughts on Unhealthy Dependency', *Transformation* 31:1.

K. C. Hanson and D. Oakman, 1998, *Palestine in the Time of Jesus: Social Structures and Social Conflicts*, Minneapolis, MN: Fortress Press.

G. Hasel, 1974, 'The Polemic Nature of the Genesis Cosmology', *Evangelical Quarterly* 46, April–June.

S. Hauerwas, 1991, *After Christendom*, Oxford: Abingdon Press.

G. Haugen, 2002, 'Integral Mission and Advocacy', in T. Chester (ed.), *Justice, Mercy and Humility*, Carlisle: Paternoster.

G. Haugen, 2014, *The Locus Effect: Why the End of Poverty Requires the End of Violence*, Oxford: Oxford University Press.

J. Daniel Hays, 2001, 'Applying the Old Testament Law Today', *Bibliotheca Sacra* 158:629.

P. Hebblethwaite, 1993, 'Let My People Go: the Exodus and Liberation Theology', *Religion, State and Society* 21:1.

J. Henrich, 2000, 'Does Culture Matter in Economic Behaviour? Ultimatum Game Bargaining among the Machiguenga of the Peruvian Amazon', *The American Economic Review* 90:4.

P. Heslam, 2002, *Globalization: Unravelling the New Capitalism*, Cambridge: Grove Books.

J. Hickel, 2015, 'The Death of International Development'. Available at: www.redpepper.org.uk.

J. Hickel, 2016, 'The True Extent of Global Poverty and Hunger: Questioning the Good News Narrative of the Millennium Development Goals', *Third World Quarterly* 37:5.

P. Hiebert, 1982, 'The Flaw of the Excluded Middle', *Missiology* 10:1.

K. Himes, 1986, 'Social Sin and the Role of the Individual', *Annual of the Society of Christian Ethics 6*.

M. Hoek, J. Ingleby, A. Kingston-Smith and C. Kingston-Smith (eds), 2013, *Carnival Kingdom: Biblical Justice for Global Communities*, Gloucester: Wide Margin.

D. Hollenbach, 1988, 'Justice as Participation: Public Moral Discourse and the U.S. Economy', in C. Reynolds and R. V. Norman (eds), *Community in America: The Challenge of Habits of the Heart*, Berkeley, CA: University of California Press, pp. 217–29.

S. Holmes, 2012, *The Quest for the Trinity: The Doctrine of God in Scripture, History and Modernity*, Downers Grove, IL: InterVarsity Press Academic.

R. Horsley, 2015, 'You Shall Not Bow Down and Serve Them: Economic Justice in the Bible', *Interpretation: A Journal of Bible and Theology* 69:4.

W. Howard-Brook and A. Gwyther, 1999, *Unveiling Empire: Reading Revelation Then and Now*, Marynoll, NY: Orbis Books.

D. Hughes, 2008, *Power and Poverty: Divine and Human Rule in a World of Need*, Downers Grove, IL: InterVarsity Press.

S. Ilo, 2014, *The Church and Development in Africa*, Eugene, OR: Pickwick Publications.

'IPCC, 2014: Summary for Policymakers', 2014, in C. B. Field *et al.* (eds), *Climate Change 2014: Impacts, Adaptation, and Vulnerability. Part A: Global and Sectoral Aspects. Contribution of Working Group II to the Fifth Assessment Report of the Intergovernmental Panel on Climate Change*, Cambridge: Cambridge University Press.

R. M. Isaac, 2014, 'Markets and Justice', in A. Bradley and A. Lindsley (eds), *For the Least of These: A Biblical Answer to Poverty*, Grand Rapids, MI: Zondervan.

S. Jeffery, M. Ovey and A. Sach, 2007, *Pierced for Our Transgressions*, Nottingham: InterVarsity Press.

John Paul II, 1981, *Laborem Exercens*.

John Paul II, 1984, *Reconciliatio et Paenitentia*.

John Paul II, 1987, *Sollicitudo Rei Socialis*.

M. Jones, 2014, *Investigating our Investments*, Methodist Tax Justice Network.

E. Kang, 2015, 'Human Immunodeficiency Virus (HIV) Stigma: Spoiled Social Identity and Jürgen Moltmann's Trinitarian Model of the *imago Dei*', *International Journal of Public Theology* 9.

T. Kelsall, 2008, 'Going with the Grain in African Development?', *Development Policy Review* 29:s1.

H. Kim, S. Schnall, D.-J. Yi and M. White, 2013, 'Social Distance Decreases Responders' Sensitivity to Fairness in the Ultimate Game', *Judgement and Decision Making* 8:53.

B. Kingsolver, 1998, *The Poisonwood Bible*, London: Faber and Faber.

J. Klaasen, 2013, 'The Interplay between Theology and Development: How Theology can be Related to Development in Post-Modern Society', *Missionalia* 41:2, August.

N. Klein, 2000, *No Logo: Taking Aim at the Brand Bullies*, Toronto: Village Canada.

A. Konig, 1989, *The Eclipse of Christ in Eschatology*, Grand Rapids, MI: Eerdmans.

D. Kotter, 2015, 'Greed vs. Self-Interest: A Case Study of How Economists can Help Theologians Serve the Church', *The Southern Baptist Journal of Theology* 19:2, Summer.

D. Krueger, 1995, 'Can Christian Ethics Inform Business Practice? A Typological Road Map and Criteria of Adequacy for an Ethic of Capitalism', in S. Natale and B. Rothschild (eds), *Work Values: Education, Organization and Religious Concerns*, Amsterdan: Rodopi.

S. R. Kumalo, 2008, 'Paying the Price for Democracy: The Contribution of the Church in the Development of Good Governance in South Africa', in S. de Gruchy, N. Koopman and S. Strijbos (eds), *From Our Side: Emerging Perspectives on Development and Ethics*, Amsterdam: Rozenberg Publishers, pp. 171–87.

D. Landes, 1969, *The Unbound Prometheus*, Cambridge: Cambridge University Press.

M. Lang, 2014, 'The Patterns of Corruption in Christian Churches of Cameroon: The Case of the Presbyterian Church in Cameroon', *Transformation: an International Journal of Holistic Mission Studies* 31:2.

M. Large, 2010, *Common Wealth: For a Free, Equal Mutual and Sustainable Society*, Stroud: Hawthorn.

Leo XIII, 1891, *Rerum Novarum*.

B. Levy, 2014, *Working with the Grain: Integrating Governance and Growth in Development Strategies*, Oxford: Oxford University Press.

N. F. Lohfink SJ, 1987, *Option for the Poor: The Basic Principle of Liberation Theology in the Light of the Bible*, Berkeley, CA: BIBAL Press.

D. S. Long, 2000, *Divine Economy: Theology and the Market*, London: Routledge.

B. Longenecker, 2009, 'Afterword', in B. Longenecker and K. Liebengood (eds), *Engaging Economics*, Grand Rapids, MI: Eerdmans.

B. Longenecker, 2010, *Remember the Poor: Paul, Poverty and the Greco-Roman World*, Grand Rapids, MI: Eerdmans.

B. Longenecker and K. Liebengood (eds), 2009, *Engaging Economics*, Grand Rapids, MI: Eerdmans.

T. Lorenzen, 2000, 'Towards a Theology of Human Rights', *Review and Expositor* 97.

R. Lupton, 2011, *Toxic Charity*, New York: HarperCollins.

G. Macaskill, 2009, 'Critiquing Rome's Economy', in B. Longenecker and K. Liebengood (eds), *Engaging Economics*, Grand Rapids, MI: Eerdmans, pp. 243–59.

A. MacIntyre, 1981, *After Virtue: A Study in Moral Theory*, Notre Dame, IN: University of Notre Dame Press.

M. Maggay, 2008, 'Justice and Approaches to Social Change', in J. Thacker and M. Hoek (eds), *Micah's Challenge: The Church's Responsibility to the Global Poor*, Milton Keynes: Paternoster.

M. Maggay, 2013, 'The Influence of Religion and Culture in Development in the Philippines', in M. Hoek, J. Ingleby, A. Kingston-Smith and C. Kingston-Smith (eds), *Carnival Kingdom: Biblical Justice for Global Communities*, Gloucester: Wide Margin.

T. S. Maluleke, 2016, 'Christian Mission in a World under the Grip of an Unholy Trinity: Inequality, Poverty and Unemployment', in M. Auvinen-Pöntinen and J. A. Jørgensen (eds), *Mission and Money: Christian Mission in the Context of Global Inequalities*, Boston, MA: Brill, pp. 63–84.

S. Marzagora, 2016, 'The Humanism of Reconstruction: African Intellectuals, Decolonial Critical Theory and the Opposition to the "Posts" (Postmodernism, Poststructuralism, Postcolonialism)', *Journal of African Cultural Studies* 28:2.

J. Matunhu, 2011, 'A Critique of Modernization and Dependency Theories in Africa: Critical Assessment', *African Journal of History and Culture* 3:5.

J. R. Middleton, 1994, 'The Liberating Image? Interpreting the Imago Dei in Context', *Christian Scholar's Review* 24:1.

J. R. Middleton, 2005, *The Liberating Image: The Imago Dei in Genesis 1*, Grand Rapids, MI: Brazos Press.

J. Milbank, 2012, 'Against Human Rights', *Oxford Journal of Law and Religion* 1:2.

P. Miller, 1990, *Deuteronomy, Interpretation*, Louisville, KY: John Knox Press.

C. Moe-Lobeda, 2013, *Resisting Structural Evil*, Minneapolis, MN: Fortress Press.

R. Albert Mohler Jr, 2015, 'Economics and the Christian Worldview: 12 Theses', *The Southern Baptist Journal of Theology* 19:2.

J. Moltmann, 1985, *God in Creation*, London: SCM Press.

J. Moltmann, 1993, *The Trinity and the Kingdom*, Minneapolis, MN: Fortress Press.

J. Moltmann, 1999, *God for a Secular Society: The Public Relevance of Theology*, London: SCM Press.

D. Moyo, 2009, *Dead Aid: Why Aid is Not Working and How there is Another Way for Africa*, London: Penguin.

R. Mshana, 2013, *The European Union, the United States and China in Africa: The Development Dialogue*, Geneva: World Council of Churches.

R. Mshana and A. Peralta (eds), 2013, *Linking Poverty, Wealth and Ecology: The AGAPE Process from Porto Alegre to Busan*, Geneva: World Council of Churches.

M. Mtika, 2015, 'Subsistent and Substantive Communities Under Attack: The Case of Zowe in Northern Malawi', in J. Cheong and E. Meneses (eds), *Christian Mission and Economic Systems*, Pasadena, CA: William Carey Library, pp. 179–210.

O. Muchena, 1996, 'Sociological and Anthropological Reflections', in T. Yamamori, B. Myers, K. Bediako and L. Reed (eds), *Serving with the Poor in Africa*, Monrovia, CA: MARC Publications.

J. N. K. Mugambi, 1995, *From Liberation to Reconstruction*, Nairobi: East African Educational Publishers.

M. F. Murove, 2008, 'Neo-Liberal Capitalism, African Elites and ICT: Challenges and Prospects for a Development Ethic Based on *Ukama* and *Ubuntu*', in S. de Gruchy, N. Koopman and S. Strijbos (eds), *From Our Side: Emerging Perspectives on Development and Ethics*, Amsterdam: Rozenberg Publishers, pp. 135–50.

R. Musasiwa, 1996, 'Missiological Reflections', in T. Yamamori, B. Myers, K. Bediako and L. Reed (eds), *Serving with the Poor in Africa*, Monrovia, CA: MARC Publications.

B. Myers, 1999, *Walking with the Poor: Principles and Practices of Transformational Development*, Marynoll, NY: Orbis Books.

B. Myers, 2016, 'How did Britain Develop? Adaptive Social Systems and the Development of Nations', *Transformation* 33:2.

C. Myers, 2002, 'Proclaiming Good News in Hard Times: Reflections on Evangelism and the Bible', in D. Neville (ed.), *Prophecy and Passion: Essays in Honor of Athol Gill*, Hindmarsh: Australian Theological Forum.

C. Myers, 2007, *The Biblical Vision of Sabbath Economics*, Oak View, CA: Bartimaeus Cooperative Ministries.

R. Nadella, 2016, 'The Two Banquets: Mark's Vision of Anti-Imperial Economics', *Interpretation: A Journal of Bible and Theology* 70:2.

D. Narayan *et al.*, 1999, *Voices of the Poor Volume 1: Can Anyone Hear Us?*, Washington, DC: World Bank.

D. Narayan *et al.*, 2000, *Voices of the Poor Volume 2: Crying Out for Change*, Washington, DC: World Bank.

C. Nederman, 2008, 'Men at work: Poesis, Politics and Labor in Aristotle and Some Aristotelians', *Analyse & Kritik* 30.

D. Nelson, 2011, *Sin: A Guide for the Perplexed*, London: T & T Clark.

L. Newbigin, 1989, *The Gospel in a Pluralist Society*, London: SPCK.

L. Newbigin, 1995, *Foolishness to the Greeks*, London: SPCK.

Ngugi wa Thiong'o, 1983, *Devil on the Cross*, London: Heinemann.

M. Novak, 1982, *The Spirit of Democratic Capitalism*, New York: Simon & Schuster.

R. Nozick, 1974, *Anarchy, State and Utopia*, New York: Basic Books.

N. Nunn, 2008, 'The Long-Term Effects of Africa's Slave Trades', *Quarterly Journal of Economics* 123:1.

M. Nussbaum, 2011, *Creating Capabilities: The Human Development Approach*, London: Harvard University Press.

P. Oakes, 2004, 'Constructing Poverty Scales for Graeco-Roman Society: A Response to Steven Friesen's "Poverty in Pauline Studies"' *Journal for the Study of the New Testament* 26:3.

T. Oden (ed.), 2003, *Luke: Ancient Christian Commentary on Scripture*, Downers Grove, IL: InterVarsity Press.

J. Oswalt, 1998, *The Book of Isaiah Chapter 40–66*, Grand Rapids, MI: Eerdmans.

C. R. Padilla, 2014, 'The Globalization of Greed', *Journal of Latin American Theology* 9:2.

R. Patterson, 1973, 'The Widow, the Orphan, and the Poor in the Old Testament and the Extra-Biblical Literature', *Bibliotheca Sacra*, July.

Paul VI, 1967, *Populorum Progressio*.

I. Petrella, 2006, *The Future of Liberation Theology: An Argument and Manifesto*, London: SCM Press.

M. Perry, 2000, *The Idea of Human Rights*, Oxford: Oxford University Press.

I. Phiri and J. Gathogo, 2010, 'A Reconstructive Motif in South African Black Theology in the Twenty-First Century', *Studia Historiae Ecclesiasticae* 36, July, Supplement, pp. 185–206.

K. Pickett and R. Wilkinson, 2009, *The Spirit Level: Why More Equal Societies Almost Always Do Better*, London: Allen Lane.

T. Piketty, 2013, *Capital in the Twenty-First Century*, Cambridge, MA: Harvard University Press.

B. Pitre, 2009, 'Jesus, the Messianic Banquet and the Kingdom of God', *Letter & Spirit* 5.

S. Plant, 2009, 'International Development and Belief in Progress', *Journal of International Development* 21:6.

S. Plant, 2011, 'Christian Theology on Setting Goals for International Development', *Epworth Review*, January.

C. Plantinga, 2010, 'Sin: Not the Way It's Supposed to Be', Christ on Campus Initiative.

L. Polman, 2010, *War Games*, London: Penguin.

M. Prasad and A. Nickow, 2016, 'Mechanisms of the "Aid Curse": Lessons from South Korea and Pakistan', *The Journal of Development Studies*, May.

R. Priest *et al.*, 2006, 'Researching the Short-Term Mission Movement', *Missiology* 34:4.

L. Probasco, 2013, 'Giving Time, Not Money: Long-Term Impacts of Short-Term Mission Trips', *Missiology* 41:2.

E. H. Prodromou and N. Symeonides, 2016, 'Orthodox Christanity and Humanitarianism: An Introduction to Thought and Practice, Past and Present', *The Review of Faith and International Affairs* 14:1, pp. 1–17.

V. Ramachandra, 2008, *Subverting Global Myths*, Downers Grove, IL: InterVarsity Press.

J. Rawls, 1999, *A Theory of Justice*, Cambridge, MA: Harvard University Press.

E. Reed, 2014, 'Tax and International Justice', in *Tax for the Common Good: A Study of Tax and Morality*, London: Christian Aid.

L. Reed, 2014, 'A Poverty Program that Worked', in A. Bradley and A. Lindsley (eds), *For the Least of These: A Biblical Answer to Poverty*, Grand Rapids, MI: Zondervan.

A. Ritchie, 2014, 'Tax and Government', in *Tax for the Common Good: A Study of Tax and Morality*, London: Christian Aid.

R. Riddell, 2007, *Does Foreign Aid Really Work?* Oxford: Oxford University Press.

W. Rostow, 1960, *The Stages of Economic Growth: A Non-Communist Manifesto*, Cambridge: Cambridge University Press.

M. Rothbard, 1998, *The Ethics of Liberty*, New York: New York University Press.

C. Rowland in conversation with T. Gorringe, 2016, 'Practical Theology and the Common Good – Why the Bible is Essential', *Practical Theology* 9:2.

W. Sachs (ed.), 1992, *The Development Dictionary*, London: Zed Books.

J. Sachs, 2006, *The End of Poverty: Economic Possibilities for Our Time*, London: Penguin.

J. Schneider, 2002, *The Good of Affluence*, Grand Rapids, MI: Eerdmans.

G. Schwartz, 2007, *When Charity Destroys Dignity*, Bloomington, IN: AuthorHouse.

T. Sedlacek, 2011, *Economics of Good and Evil*, Oxford: Oxford University Press.

A. Sen, 1973, *On Economic Inequality*, Oxford: Oxford University Press.

A. Sen, 1992, *Inequality Reexamined*, Cambridge, MA: Harvard University Press.

A. Sen, 1999, *Development as Freedom*, Oxford: Oxford University Press.

J. Shao, 2001, 'Alleviating Poverty in Africa', in D. Belshaw, R. Calderisi and C. Sugden (eds), *Faith in Development*, Oxford: Regnum Books.

M. Sharpe, 2013, 'Name It and Claim It: Prosperity Gospel and the Global Pentecostal Reformation', in M. Clarke (ed.), 2013, *Handbook of Research on Development and Religion*, Cheltenham: Edward Elgar.

R. Sider, 1997, *Rich Christians in an Age of Hunger*, London: Hodder & Stoughton.

D. A. Small, G. Loewenstein and P. Slovic, 2006, 'Sympathy and Callousness: The Impact of Deliberative Thought on Donations to Identifiable and Statistical Victims', *Organizational Behavior and Human Decision Processes* 102:2.

K. Smith, 2008, 'Symposium Introduction. Mitigating, Adapting, and Suffering: How Much of Each?', *Annual Review of Public Health* 29, pp. 11–25.

W. Smith, 2012, 'Triage in Mass Casualty Situations', *Continuing Medical Education* 30:11.

R. Stark, 2011, *The Triumph of Christianity*, New York: Harper Collins.

R. Stewart, 2006, *Occupational Hazard: My Time Governing in Iraq*, Basingstoke: Picador.

J. Stiglitz, 2002, *Globalization and Its Discontents*, New York: W. W. Norton.

J. Stiglitz, 2012, *The Price of Inequality: How Today's Divided Society Endangers Our Future*, New York: Norton & Co.

J. Stiglitz and A. Charlton, 2007, *Fair Trade for All*, Oxford: Oxford University Press.

J. M. Sung, 2007, *Reclaiming Liberation Theology: Desire, Market, Religion*, London: SCM Press.

G. Sunshine, 2014, 'Who are the Poor?', in A. Bradley and A. Lindsley (eds), *For the Least of These: A Biblical Answer to Poverty*, Grand Rapids, MI: Zondervan.

I. Swart, 2008, 'Market Economic Development, Local Economic Experience and the Christian Movement Towards Alternatives in a South African City Region', in S. de Gruchy, N. Koopman and S. Strijbos (eds), *From Our Side: Emerging Perspectives on Development and Ethics*, Amsterdam: Rozenberg.

I. Swart, 2008, 'Meeting the Challenge of Poverty and Exclusion: The Emerging Field of Development Research in South African Practical Theology', *International Journal of Practical Theology* 12:1, January.

E. Tamez, 2010, 'Greed and Structural Sin', *Trinity Seminary Review* 1:1.

J. R. Tan, 2015, 'Christian Mission Amidst the Cultural and Socioeconomic Dynamics of Bribery and Extortion Practices in the Philippines', in J. Cheong and E. Meneses (eds), *Christian Mission and Economic Systems*, Pasadena, CA: William Carey Library.

M. Tapper, 2013, 'Social Sin and Needed Corporate Reform in the Wesleyan Tradition', *Wesleyan Theological Journal* 48:2, September.

A. Tausch, 2011, 'Globalisation and Development: The Relevance of Classical "Dependency" Theory for the World Today', *International Social Science Journal* 61:202.

M. Taylor, 2003, *Christianity, Poverty and Wealth*, London: SPCK.

M. Taylor, 2015, *Christ and Capital: A Family Debate*, Geneva: World Council of Churches.

G. ter Haar, 2011, 'Religion and Human Rights', in G. ter Haar (ed.), *Religion and Development: Ways of Transforming the World*, London: Hurst & Co.

G. ter Haar, 2011, 'Religion and Development: Introducing a New Debate', in G. ter Haar (ed.), *Religion and Development: Ways of Transforming the World*, London: Hurst & Co.

J. Thacker, 2007, *Postmodernism and the Ethics of Theological Knowledge*, Aldershot: Ashgate.

J. Thacker, 2008, 'New Heavens and New Earth', J. Thacker and M. Hoek (eds), *Micah's Challenge: The Church's Responsibility to the Global Poor*, Milton Keynes: Paternoster.

J. Thacker, 2009, 'A Holistic Gospel: Some Biblical, Historical and Ethical Considerations', *Evangelical Review of Theology* 33:3, July.

J. Thacker, 2015, 'From Charity to Justice: Revisited', *Transformation* 35:2.

J. Thacker, 2015, 'Motivation among UK Bible College Students', unpublished presentation delivered as part of the requirements for the Post-graduate Certificate in Learning and Teaching in Higher Education, Sheffield Hallam University.

N. Townsend, 2014, 'Surveillance and Seeing: A New Way of Reading Mark 12:17, "Give Back to Caesar ..."', *Studies in Christian Ethics* 27:1.

M. Tsele, 2001, 'The Role of the Christian Faith in Development', in D. Belshaw, R. Calderisi and C. Sugden (eds), *Faith in Development*, Oxford: Regnum Books.

R. Valerio, 2016, *Just Living: Faith and Community in an Age of Consumerism*, London: Hodder & Stoughton.

P. Vallely, 1990, *Bad Samaritans*, London: Hodder & Stoughton.

W. van Eekelen, 2013, 'Revisiting Child Sponsorship Programmes', *Development in Practice* 23:4.

K. ver Beek, 2006, 'The Impact of Short-Term Missions: A Case Study of House Construction in Honduras after Hurricane Mitch', *Missiology: An International Review* 34:4.

K. ver Beek, 2008, 'Lessons from the Sapling: Review of Quantitative Research on Short-Term Missions', in R. J. Priest, *Effective Engagement in Short-Term Missions: Doing It Right!* Pasadena, CA: William Carey Library.

J. Verbeek, 2015, 'Increasingly, Inequality Within, Not Across, Countries is Rising'. Available at: http://blogs.worldbank.org/developmenttalk/increasingly-inequality-within-not-across-countries-rising.

C. Villa-Vincencio, 1992, *A Theology of Reconstruction: Nation Building and Human Rights*, Cambridge: Cambridge University Press.

M. Volf, 1998, *After Our Likeness: The Church as the Image of the Trinity*, Grand Rapids, MI: Eerdmans.

M. Volf, 2011, *A Public Faith*, Grand Rapids, MI: Brazos Press.

R. Wafawanaka, 2014, 'Is the Biblical Perspective on Poverty that "there shall be no poor among you" or "you will always have the poor with you"?', *Review and Expositor* 111:2.

J. Wallis, 2005, *God's Politics: Why the American Right Get It Wrong and the Left Doesn't Get It*, Oxford: Lion Hudson.

B. Walsh and S. Keesmat, 2004, *Colossians Remixed: Subverting the Empire*, Downers Grove, IL: InterVarsity Press.

B. Waltke, 2005, *The Book of Proverbs: Chapters 15–21*, Grand Rapids, MI: Eerdmans.

M. Weber, 1958 [1905] *The Protestant Ethic and the Spirit of Capitalism*, New York: Charles Scribner's Son.

M. Weber, 1978, *Economy and Society*, Berkeley, CA: University of California Press.

J. Webster, 2007, 'Introduction: Systematic Theology', in K. Tanner, J. Webster and I. Torrance (eds), *The Oxford Handbook of Systematic Theology*, Oxford: Oxford University Press.

C. G. Weeramantry, 1998, *The Lord's Prayer: Bridge to a Better World*, Liguori, MO: Liguori/Triumph.

S. Wells, 2015, *A Nazareth Manifesto*, Chichester: John Wiley & Sons.

G. Wenham, 1987, *Genesis 1–15*, Dallas, TX: Thomas Nelson.

L. White, 1967, 'The Historical Roots of Our Ecological Crisis', *Science* 155, 10 March.

J. Whitlark, 2014, *Resisting Empire: Rethinking the Purpose of the Letter to "the Hebrews"*, London: T & T Clark.

Wholly Living: A New Perspective on International Development, 2010, London: Theos.

T. Wigg-Stevenson, 2013, *The World is Not Ours to Save*, Downers Grove, IL: InterVarsity Press.

R. Williams, 'A Theology of Development'. Available at: http://clients.squareeye .net.

D. Wilson, 2015, 'Western Mission-Established Churches and Ministry in Mali's Collectivist Economy', in J. Cheong and E. Meneses (eds), *Christian Mission and Economic Systems*, Pasadena, CA: William Carey Library.

J. Wind, 2015, 'Not Always Right: Critiquing Christopher Wright's Paradigmatic Application of the Old Testament to the Socio-Economic Realm', *The Southern Baptist Journal of Theology* 19:2.

W. Wink, 1992, *Engaging the Powers*, Minneapolis, MN: Fortress Press.

B. Witherington III, 1995, *Conflict and Community in Corinth*, Grand Rapids, MI: Eerdmans.

N. Wolterstorff, 2006, 'Justice, Not Charity: Social Work through the Eyes of Faith', *Social Work & Christianity* 3:2.

N. Wolterstorff, 2008, *Justice: Rights and Wrong*, Princeton, NJ: Princeton University Press.

R. Woodberry, 2008, 'Pentecostalism and Economic Development', in J. Imber (ed.), *Markets, Morals and Religion*, New Brunswick, NJ: Transaction Publishers, pp. 157–77.

C. Wright, 2004, *Old Testament Ethics for the People of God*, Nottingham: InterVarsity Press.

C. Wright, 2006, *The Mission of God: Unlocking the Bible's Grand Narrative*, Nottingham: InterVarsity Press.

N. T. Wright, 2000, *The Challenge of Jesus*, London: SPCK, 2000.

N. T. Wright, 2003, *The Resurrection of the Son of God*, Minneapolis, MN: Fortress Press.

T. Wright, 2007, *Surprised by Hope*, London: SPCK.

B. Wydick, P. Glewwe and L. Rutledge, 2013, 'Does International Child Sponsorship Work? A Six-Country Study of Impacts on Adult Life Outcomes', *Journal of Political Economy* 121:2, April.

W. Wyman, 2005, 'Sin and Redemption', in J. Mariña (ed.), *The Cambridge Companion to Friedrich Schleiermacher*, Cambridge: Cambridge University Press.

A. Yong, 2011, *The Bible, Disability and the Church*, Grand Rapids, MI: Eerdmans.

E. Zehner, 2013, 'Short-Term Missions: Some Perspectives from Thailand', *Missiology* 41:2.

J. Zizioulas, 1985, *Being as Communion*, Crestwood, NY: St Vladimir's Seminary Press.

Websites and online

www.alliancesud.ch
www.amnesty.org
www.catholic-ew.org.uk
www.christianaid.org.uk
www.concordeurope.org
www.economist.com
www.financialsecrecyindex.com
www.theguardian.com
http://.jubileedebt.org.uk
http://methodisttaxjusticenetwork.nationbuilder.com
https://newint.org
www.oxfam.org
https://ophi.org.uk
www.redpepper.org.uk/
http://richarddawkins.net
http://steverholmes.org.uk
https://sustainabledevelopment.un.org
www.tearfund.org
www.transparency.org
www.un.org/
www.unfpa.org
http://data.worldbank.org

Index of Bible References

Index of Names and Subjects